Letter
Law Student

Letters to a Law Student

Third edition

Nick McBride
with Jason Varuhas

Harlow, England • London • New York • Boston • San Francisco • Toronto • Sydney
Auckland • Singapore • Hong Kong • Tokyo • Seoul • Taipei • New Delhi
Cape Town • São Paulo • Mexico City • Madrid • Amsterdam • Munich • Paris • Milan

PEARSON EDUCATION LIMITED
Edinburgh Gate
Harlow CM20 2JE
United Kingdom
Tel: +44 (0)1279 623623
Web: www.pearson.com/uk

First Published 2007
Second edition published 2010
This edition published 2014 (print and electronic)

ISBN: 978-1-447-92265-0 (print)
        978-1-4479-2266-7 (eText)

British Library Cataloguing-in-Publication Data
A catalogue record for the print edition is available from the British Library

Library of Congress Cataloging-in-Publication Data
A catalog record for the print edition is available from the Library of Congress

10 9 8 7 6
17 16

Print edition typeset in Minion Pro Regular 10/13 by 75
Print edition printed and bound in the UK by Ashford Colour Press Ltd, Gosport, Hants

NOTE THAT ANY PAGE CROSS REFERENCES REFER TO THE PRINT EDITION

To the magical
Isabel, Ines and Luca
I miss you very much, dear friends;
you are my joy and my crown
(Phil. 4:1)

Table of Contents

Preface

This book has been written for anyone who is doing, or thinking about doing, a law degree at university. The book comprises a series of letters to a law student, Alex. The first letter is sent to Alex while Alex is doing A-Levels and thinking about doing a law degree at university. The final letter finds Alex just about to graduate from university, having done a law degree. The thirty letters in between track Alex's progress from school to university, giving advice to Alex on various issues such as how to study law, how to write legal essays, and how to revise for exams.

Alex does not exist, and no one who is thinking about studying law or actually studying law will share all of the concerns that prompt the letters to Alex set out in this book. Some letters will be of more relevance to you than others. If you are considering studying law at university then you should read chapters 1–6, 10, and 24 to get a feel for what law is about and what sort of skills studying law will require you to have and develop; and chapters 11–12, and 14 to get more of a sense of what studying law is like. If you have made up your mind to study law at university, and are in the process of making applications to study law, then chapters 1–6 would still be useful as reinforcing and deepening your choice to study law, and chapters 7–10 will be highly relevant to you. If you have been accepted to study law at university, then you should still read chapters 1–2 and 4–6 to help you get ready for the experience of studying law; you should also read chapters 10–23 before you go to university, chapters 24–25 and 27–28 in your first few days at university; and chapters 26, 29–32 as required.

One of the themes of this book is that to remember information, it is not enough to read it; you have to use it as well. Anyone who reads letters 12–30 just the once is likely to forget quite quickly what they have to say about how to study law and how to write well as a lawyer, and as a result their studies and their legal writing will not benefit at all from the advice contained in those letters. Aim instead to re-read constantly letters 14–16, 19, 23, 25 and 27 in the early stages of your legal studies, to ensure that you are putting the lessons of those letters into practice. If you do this, you'll soon find that you'll never have to read those letters again to remember what they say; the habits of study and writing that they seek to inculcate will have become completely natural to you.

Because Alex doesn't exist, it was necessary to give Alex an identity – to make certain assumptions about Alex. I've assumed that Alex is doing a normal three-year law degree. So Alex is not doing a mixed law degree, such as a degree in Law & Politics or Law & Criminology; and Alex is not doing a degree that involves going somewhere on the Continent for one or two years to find out what the law says over there. I've also assumed that Alex is studying law at an English or Welsh university, and not a university in Northern Ireland or Scotland.

The third edition of this book was written against the background of an admissions round at Cambridge where a number of colleges – including mine – that had plenty of applicants for law found themselves unable to fill the number of places they had to offer those applicants. The problem, it seems to me, is that we live in a society that does very little to help students leave school with the sort of skills that would make them naturally suited to studying law at university. It seems to me that there are nowadays fewer and fewer students who leave school equipped with the abilities to argue properly, to think rigorously, and express themselves persuasively – precisely the sort of skills that law students need to have in order to perform well as law students. For anyone who is concerned for the future health of our country, this is profoundly worrying. I am, of course, not arguing that what the country needs is more law students, or more lawyers – that is certainly not the case. But we will face a very bleak future if we do not equip many more people with the kinds of skills that studying law encourages students to develop and which we look for, and too often fail to discover even in rudimentary form, in those applying to study law at university.

I hope the third edition of *Letters to a Law Student* will help make some small contribution to reversing this decline in our country's intellectual capital – at least among students who are thinking of studying law, and those who are actually studying law.

There are only a handful of books in this world that are incapable of being improved and this book is definitely not one of them. Students or teachers who have read this book and have constructive suggestions as to how it might be changed for the better shouldn't hesitate to get in touch with me at njm33@ cam.ac.uk. I would very much welcome hearing from you.

Nick McBride
Pembroke College, Cambridge
18 March 2013

Acknowledgements

This book would not exist without the help and support of a huge number of people and institutions:

My family – my mother and my brothers Chris, Ben and Damian.

My best friend Isabel; her adorable son Luca; and her amazing daughter Ines – the little master from whom I have learned so very much.

Pearson Education, who publish this book and my textbook on tort law (co-authored with Roderick Bagshaw); Owen Knight, the commissioning editor who worked on this book; Priyadharshini Dhanagopal who oversaw production of this book; Anne Henwood who efficiently copy-edited the book; and Kelly Miller who produced the book's cover.

The Fellows of Pembroke College, Cambridge, whose support and loyalty towards me have been unstinting.

The Law Faculty at Hong Kong University, which employs me to teach an introductory course on studying law and helped stimulate a number of the new chapters in this edition.

Jason Varuhas, who kindly wrote Chapter 26 of this book, on writing a dissertation.

Helena Roy, who invited me to her school to deliver the speech reproduced in Appendix D of this book.

My academic colleagues, who provide me with a huge amount of support, encouragement and advice. In particular: Trevor Allan, Rod Bagshaw, John Bell, Paul Davies, Lusina Ho, Lee Mason, Jason Neyers, Jane Stapleton, Sandy Steel, Rob Stevens, Bill Swadling, Jason Varuhas, Fred Wilmot-Smith, and Po Jen Yap.

My teachers, to whom I'll always be indebted: Peter Birks, Hugh Collins, John Davies, and John Gardner.

My students, who have always taught me more than I teach them. In particular: Hannah Bill, Charlie Brearley, Leigh Edgar, Tom Fletcher, Sam Kahan, Clare Kissin, Ashish Kumar, Kyle Lawson, Liz Lowe, Helen Mackey, Anna Midgley, Alex Robson, Gabi Rutherford, Julia Schulman, Emily Smith, Siobhan Sparkes McNamara, Peter Sugden, Natalie Wilkins, Matteo Yoon, and Megan Young.

My little girl, and my wonderful father.

PART 1

Thinking About Studying Law

PART

Thinking About
Studying Law

What Is Law?

- From: Nicholas J. McBride [dearnick@pearson.com]
- To: Brown, Alex
- Subject: What Is Law?

Dear Alex,

Thanks for your email. Your question – Why should I study law at university? – is a pretty big one, and deserves a letter rather than just a quick emailed response. For what it's worth, my quick answer would be: People should do a law degree because studying law is interesting, important, and educational. That doesn't necessarily mean that *you* should do a law degree. Law isn't for everyone. But as a subject for study, I think it's tough to find another that is as fascinating, as significant, and as transformative as law is. So – that's the quick answer, but it's going to take me two letters to give you the long version. To understand what is so great about studying law, you first need to understand a bit about what law *is*. That's what I will talk about in this letter. I'll then send you a follow-up letter explaining why studying law at university is something you should give serious consideration to.

Law as a conversation

The question of 'What is law?' is one that continues to vex philosophers. But we might be able to make the concept of law more understandable through the following analogy. Suppose that you and I and a whole bunch of other people decide that we are going to go on holiday together. We all like each other, and we like spending time with each other, and a holiday is a great opportunity to do more of that. So – we're going on holiday, but we still have to decide where to go, when to go, where to stay, what to do, how we are going to get there, how much everyone is going to contribute to the cost of the holiday, who is going to be in charge of what. Loads of things. To work out the answers to these questions, *we need to talk to each other.* There are some issues that all of us may have to talk about together, such as where we are going to go and when. There are other issues (such as transportation and accommodation) that we might be able to delegate to a few members of our party – and they will work those issues out together and report back to us. But however the various issues arising out of our plan to go on holiday are resolved, resolving them will require lots and lots of *conversations.*

What I want to suggest is that we can draw an analogy between the notion of law and the process of talking to each other in order to decide on the details of the holiday we are all going to go on. Instead of talking to each other to determine what sort of holiday we should go on, our law-makers talk to each other to determine *what sort of society we should live in.* So when we say 'What does the law say on such and such an issue?', we are really asking, 'Where are our law-makers at the moment in their conversation about what sort of society we should live in? Have they decided this issue already? If they have, what did they decide and is there any possibility of this issue being re-opened? If they haven't, then what does the state of conversation indicate at the moment about how our law-makers might resolve this issue?' The conversation is ongoing and intergenerational. The fact that a previous generation of law-makers may have taken a particular position on what sort of society we should live in does not mean that future generations cannot take a different position, thereby bringing about a change in the law. However, the views of previous generations of law-makers do not die with the law-makers; the record of those views lives on and has the potential to influence the views of the current generation. So great law-makers of the past such as Sir Edward Coke (1552–1634), Lord Mansfield (1705–1793), Lord Shaftesbury (1801–1885), and Lord Denning (1899–1999) continue to have a voice in the conversations that go on today among our law-makers as to what sort of society we should live in.

Those conversations are conducted among and between two classes of law-maker: *judges* and *legislators.* Judges decide concrete *cases,* telling the parties to each case what the law says in that particular case. Legislators lay down general rules in the form of *statutory provisions,* both for people's guidance as to how they should behave and in order to empower people to act in socially productive ways. Both judges and legislators are engaged in determining what sort of society we should live in, and in performing their functions each give effect to visions of what sort of society we should live in. Law that emerges from the way judges decide concrete cases is known as *common law*. Law that is laid down by legislators is known as *statute law*.

The ultimate power to decide what sort of society we should live in rests with the legislators: in deciding cases, the judges must give effect to any relevant legislative provisions that have been validly laid down by the legislators. Judges are subject to a further constraint that legislators are not. In deciding a case, a judge is required to give effect, not to his or her own *personal* vision of what sort of society we should live in, but to the vision that seems to be supported by the way the conversation among law-makers on this issue has evolved so far. For example, in *R (on the application of Nicklinson)* v *Ministry of Justice* (2012), a man who was completely paralysed and wished no longer to live sought a declaration from the courts that it would be lawful for a doctor to kill him. The judges who decided the case may have *personally* thought that we should live in a society where this sort of thing is allowed to be done. However, there was absolutely no support for the idea that we should live in a society that practises euthanasia either in statutory provisions created by legislators or cases previously decided by the judges. So the idea that euthanasia is acceptable is not one that had so far found any support in the evolving conversation between law-makers as to what sort of society we should live in. Given this, the court in *Nicklinson* had no option but to turn down the application, ruling that it could not hold that euthanasia was lawful until legislation had been passed making it lawful.

The requirement that judges not give effect to their own personal views as to what sort of society we should live in, but rather the emerging consensus among law-makers on this issue is a salutary one – however frustrating a particular judge (for example, one who believes strongly in the acceptability of euthanasia) might find it. The question of what sort of society we should live in is a very large and difficult one, and no one judge (or, indeed, any human being) can claim a monopoly of wisdom on this subject. Given this, a wise judge will listen with respect to the views of other law-makers – both past and present – on the issue of what sort of society we should live in, and will give greater weight to those views than his own, possibly mistaken, convictions on this issue. Of course, there are some judges (I could name a few . . .) who are determined to give effect to their own convictions, come what may – but there exist procedures for marginalising them: their judgments can be overturned on appeal, and they tend not to get promoted to the higher courts where they can have more influence on the direction of the conversation among law-makers as to what sort of society we should live in.

● A concrete example

Let me now give you an example to make clearer the idea I am advancing here of seeing law as an ongoing conversation that is aimed at determining what sort of society we should live in. In the *Belmarsh* case, *A* v *Secretary of State for Home Department* (2004), the issue was whether the government was entitled to detain indefinitely non-nationals whom it suspected of being involved in terrorism. (The non-nationals were detained in Belmarsh Prison; so that's why the case is referred to as the *Belmarsh* case, for short.) Part of what makes the *Belmarsh* case fascinating is that so many different (though not necessarily incompatible) views as to what sort of society we should live in were relevant to deciding the case. All of these views have found their place in the ongoing conversation among our law-makers as to what sort of society we should live in. In deciding the *Belmarsh* case, the House of Lords had to determine which view should take precedence.

(1) The rule of law

There is, first, the view that we should live in a society that places strict controls on how government power is exercised, so as to ensure that it is not exercised tyrannically or arbitrarily. This view – expressed by the ideal that we should be governed 'by law, and not by men'; in other words, that we should live under the *rule of law,* and not be ruled by arbitrary government fiat – is wonderfully expressed in both the arguments and judgment in the case of *Entick* v *Carrington,* which was decided way back in 1765. In that case, Entick sued Carrington and three others for trespassing on his land: they had gone into his house and searched it for papers, in pursuance of a warrant issued by a Secretary of State that purported to authorise them to make searches to find out who was publishing 'very seditious papers intitled *The Monitor,* or *British Freeholder'*. Entick's barrister argued:

> A power to issue such a warrant as this, is contrary to the genius of the law of England, and even if they had found what they searched for, they could not have justified under it . . . the verdict says such warrants have been granted by Secretaries of State ever since the Revolution; if they have, it is high time to put an end to them, for if they are held to be legal the liberty of this country is at an end; it is the publishing of a libel which is the crime,

and not the having it locked up in a private drawer in a man's study; but if having it in one's custody was the crime, no power can lawfully break into a man's house and study to search for evidence against him; this would be worse than the Spanish Inquisition; for ransacking a man's secret drawers and boxes to come at evidence against him, is like racking his body to come at his secret thoughts. The warrant is to seize all the plaintiff's books and papers without exception, and carry them before Lord Halifax; what? has a Secretary of State a right to see all a man's private letters of correspondence, family concerns, trade and business? this would be monstrous indeed; and if it were lawful, no man could endure to live in this country.

The Lord Chief Justice, Lord Camden, found in favour of Entick:

The great end, for which men entered into society, was to secure their property. That right is preserved sacred and incommunicable in all instances, where it has not been taken away or abridged by some public law for the good of the whole . . . By the laws of England, every invasion of private property, be it ever so minute, is a trespass. No man can set his foot upon my ground without my license, but he is liable to an action . . . If he admits the fact, he is bound to show by way of justification, that some positive law has empowered or excused him. The justification is submitted to the judges, who are to look into the books; and if such a justification can be maintained by the text of the statute law, or by the principles of common law. If no excuse can be found or produced, the silence of the books is an authority against the defendant, and the plaintiff must have judgment. According to this reasoning, it is now incumbent upon the defendants to show the law by which this seizure is warranted. If that cannot be done, it is a trespass. Papers are the owner's goods and chattels: they are his dearest property; and are so far from enduring a seizure, that they will hardly bear an inspection . . . Where is the written law that gives any magistrate such a power? I can safely answer, there is none; and therefore it is too much for us without such authority to pronounce a practice legal, which would be subversive of all the comforts of society.

On this view, any government power to detain people indefinitely on suspicion of being involved in terrorist plots is legally suspect as it places too much power in the hands of the government to act oppressively and arbitrarily.

(2) Necessity

On the other hand, there is a view that we should live in a society where the government is empowered to do what is necessary to ensure the safety and security of the populace. This view – expressed by the Latin tag *salus populi suprema lex est* ('the safety of the people is the supreme law') – actually finds some support at the end of Lord Camden's judgment in *Entick* v *Carrington*:

> One word more for ourselves; we are no advocates for libels, all Governments must set their faces against them, and whenever they come before us and a jury we shall set our faces against them; and if juries do not prevent them they may prove fatal to liberty, destroy Government and introduce anarchy; but tyranny is better than anarchy, and the worst Government better than none at all.

The view that in an emergency, the government should be empowered to act in ways that would ordinarily be regarded as oppressive and tyrannical in order to secure public safety underlies the Civil Contingencies Act 2004, which purports to allow the government in an 'emergency' (defined as an event or situation 'which threatens serious damage' either to 'human welfare in', or to 'the environment of', 'a place in the United Kingdom') to make emergency regulations 'to make provision for the purpose of preventing, controlling or mitigating an aspect or effect of the emergency' when there is an urgent need to do so. This view also underlay the decision of the House of Lords in *Liversidge* v *Anderson* (1944), holding that where someone was detained under wartime regulations allowing the Home Secretary to order the internment of someone whom he had 'reasonable cause to believe [was] of hostile origin or associations', the courts would not inquire into whether there *was* reasonable cause to believe the detainee was 'hostile'; it would be enough that the Home Secretary *said* there was reasonable cause to believe this:

> The appellant's counsel truly say that the liberty of the subject is involved. They refer in emphatic terms to Magna Carta and the Bill of Rights, and they contend that legislation dealing with the liberty of the subject must be construed, if possible, in favour of the subject and against the Crown . . . I hold that the suggested rule has no relevance in dealing with an executive measure by way of preventing a public danger.

So, on this view, the ordinary requirements of the rule of law – which suggest that the exercise of government powers should be strictly controlled – should be relaxed where the public safety is at stake. On this view, then, giving the government power to detain people indefinitely when they are suspected of involvement in terrorism might not be so objectionable.

(3) Democracy

A third view that was of crucial importance to the outcome of the *Belmarsh* case was the view that in our society difficult questions of how to balance the need for security against the need to respect people's liberties should be decided through democratic institutions that can fairly reflect the desires of the majority as to where that balance should be struck. This view underlies the doctrine of Parliamentary sovereignty, according to which the courts are not allowed to set aside or refuse to give effect to an Act of Parliament. (Note that – consistently with the theme of this letter – 'Parliament' literally means 'talking shop'.) The doctrine of *Parliamentary sovereignty* is felt to be so important that when Parliament passed the Human Rights Act 1998 and committed the UK to being a society in which the State observes people's human rights, as set out in the European Convention on Human Rights – even then, Parliament took care to provide in section 4 of the Act that the courts would still have to give effect to an Act of Parliament which the courts thought was inconsistent with the European Convention on Human Rights; all they could do in such a case was issue a 'declaration of incompatibility' and leave it up to Parliament to decide whether or not to amend the offending legislation and, if so, how.

The relevance of this third view to the outcome of the *Belmarsh* case is that Parliament had legislated to authorise the detention of the non-nationals whose detention had given rise to the litigation in *Belmarsh*. Under the Immigration Act 1971, the Home Secretary had a power to detain a non-national in custody while he was awaiting deportation. So a non-national who was suspected of being involved in terrorism could be deported from the UK and detained in custody under the 1971 Act while awaiting deportation. But many non-nationals who were suspected of being involved in terrorism could not be deported from the UK as there was a real fear that they would be tortured in the countries to which they would be deported. Such non-nationals could not be detained while awaiting deportation under the 1971 Act because deportation was not a prospect for them. Section 23 of the Anti-terrorism, Crime and Security Act 2001 dealt with this problem by providing that a non-deportable non-national who was a 'suspected international terrorist' could still be detained in custody 'while awaiting deportation' under the Immigration Act 1971 even though in practice he or she could never be deported.

The effective result of this provision was to allow the government to detain indefinitely in custody a non-national who was a 'suspected international terrorist' but who could not be deported from the UK. In creating this power, Parliament made it clear that it thought the need to ensure the security of the British people by detaining in custody non-nationals who were suspected of being involved terrorism outweighed any concerns about depriving such non-nationals of their liberty. Given this, how could the courts justify taking a different view?

(4) Discrimination

But there is, fourthly, a view that we should live in a society where the government and other important institutions are not allowed to discriminate against people for morally arbitrary reasons. This view has only comparatively recently found its way into the conversation among our law-makers about what sort of society we should live in. It finds expression in Lord Denning MR's great judgment in *Nagle* v *Feilden* (1966), where the Court of Appeal held that a horse owner could sue the Jockey Club for denying her a licence to act as a trainer merely because she was a woman:

> The common law of England has for centuries recognised that a man has a right to work at his trade or profession without being unjustly excluded from it. He is not to be shut out from it at the whim of those having the governance of it. If they make a rule which enables them to reject his application arbitrarily or capriciously, not reasonably, that rule is bad. It is against public policy. The courts will not give effect to it. Such was held in the seventeenth century in the celebrated case of the *Tailors of Ipswich* [1614] where they had a rule that no person was to be allowed to exercise the trade of a tailor in Ipswich unless he was admitted by them to be a sufficient workman. Lord Coke CJ held that the rule was bad, because it was "against the liberty and freedom of the subject" . . . I have said before, and I repeat it now, that a man's right to work at his trade or profession is just as important to him as, perhaps more important than, his rights of property. Just as the courts will intervene to protect his rights of property, they will also intervene to protect his right to work . . . When an association, who have the governance of a trade, take it upon themselves to license persons to take part in it, then it is at least arguable that they are not at liberty to withdraw a man's licence – and thus put him out of business – without hearing him. Nor can they refuse a man a licence – and thus prevent him from carrying on his business – in their uncontrolled discretion. If they reject him arbitrarily or capriciously, there is ground for thinking that the courts can intervene.

(Note how Lord Coke can be seen here as talking to Lord Denning across a 300-year interval to shape Lord Denning's vision of what sort of society we should live in.) Lord Denning's theme was taken up by Parliament in passing the Equal Pay Act 1970 (requiring employers to pay their employees the same amount for work of equal value, regardless of their sex), the Sex Discrimination Act 1975 (requiring employers, education providers, shops and landlords not to discriminate unjustifiably between people on grounds of their sex), and the Race Relations Act 1976 (banning discrimination on grounds of race by employers, education providers, shops, and landlords). The view that we should live in a society where the government and other important social institutions do not discriminate against people on morally arbitrary grounds has most recently been given expression in the Equality Act 2010, which brings together many earlier anti-discrimination provisions. It also underlies Article 14 of the European Convention on Human Rights, which provides that:

> The enjoyment of the rights and freedoms set forth in this Convention shall be secured without discrimination on any ground such as sex, race, colour, language, religion, political or other opinion, national or social origin, association with a national minority, property, birth or other status.

The relevance of this view to the *Belmarsh* case was that the power to detain suspected international terrorists that was under scrutiny in *Belmarsh* only applied to non-nationals: that is, people who were not UK citizens. So a UK citizen could not be detained indefinitely under s. 23 of the Anti-terrorism, Crime and Security Act 2001 even if he was also a 'suspected international terrorist'. One can understand why Parliament ended up in this position. On one view, Parliament may have thought that it was simply plugging a loophole in the original Immigration Act 1971, under which the government could only detain suspected terrorists who it wanted to deport if deportation was a practical option. As the power to deport only applied to non-nationals, Parliament's 'fix' of the Immigration Act 1971 also only applied to non-nationals. On another – more cynical – view, it may be that Parliament intended that s. 23 of the 2003 Act should operate in a discriminatory fashion. Parliament may have thought that the people in the UK would not put up with the indefinite detention of a UK citizen on mere suspicion of being a terrorist, but might be relatively indifferent to someone who was not a UK citizen suffering a similar fate. Either way, the effect of s. 23 was that the power to detain suspected terrorists indefinitely in custody applied in an unacceptably discriminatory fashion – it worked against non-nationals but not against UK citizens when there might have been no morally significant difference between them.

The outcome of the case

The doctrine of Parliamentary sovereignty made it inevitable that the House of Lords would have to rule that the indefinite detention of non-nationals who were suspected international terrorists was lawful under s. 23 of the 2001 Act. However, the House of Lords also made it very clear that the existence of such a power was repugnant to *their* vision of what sort of society we should live in, and declared that the power to detain indefinitely non-nationals who were suspected of involvement in terrorism was incompatible with the European Convention on Human Rights. Lord Hoffmann gave the most outspoken judgment:

> This is one of the most important cases which the House has had to decide in recent years. It calls into question the very existence of an ancient liberty of which this country has until now been very proud: freedom from arbitrary arrest and detention. The power which the Home Secretary seeks to uphold is a power to detain people indefinitely without charge or trial. Nothing could be more antithetical to the instincts and traditions of the people of the United Kingdom . . .

> Freedom from arbitrary arrest and detention is a quintessentially British liberty, enjoyed by inhabitants of this country when most of the population of Europe could be thrown into prison at the whim of their rulers. It was incorporated into the European Convention in order to entrench the same liberty in countries which had recently been under Nazi occupation. The United Kingdom subscribed to the Convention because it set out rights which British subjects enjoyed under the common law . . . This country, more than any other in the world, has an unbroken history of living for centuries under institutions and in accordance with values which show a recognisable continuity . . .

> [A] power [to detain on suspicion of being involved in terrorism] is not compatible with our constitution. The real threat to the life of the nation, in the sense of a people living in accordance with its traditional laws and political values, comes not from terrorism but from laws such as these.

Though it was under no obligation to do so, Parliament listened to the House of Lords' views and repealed s 23 of the 2001 Act, replacing it with a power under the Prevention of Terrorism Act 2005 to impose 'control orders' on an individual in order to prevent or restrict 'involvement by that individual in terrorism-related activity.'

Where we are now

The *Belmarsh* case was just one episode in the great, centuries-long conversation between our law-makers about what sort of society we should live in. Stepping back a bit, it might be worth giving you an overview of where we are at the moment in this conversation. Our law-makers seem to agree at the moment that we should live in a society where . . .

Persons

(1) ... people are required to observe certain minimum standards of decent conduct in the way they treat other people, and will be able to obtain effective remedies from the courts when those minimum standards are not observed. These requirements and remedies are set out in the *law of tort*.

(2) ... people who deliberately fail to observe these minimum standards may be punished by the State. The conditions under which such a person may be so punished are laid out in the *criminal law*.

(3) ... people have the power to make binding promises, and enter into binding agreements, with other people, and effective remedies will be available from the courts when such binding promises or agreements are broken. These powers and remedies exist under the *law of contract*.

(4) ... people are able to recover the value of money or other benefits that they have conferred on other people by mistake or under unacceptable pressure or in the confident expectation of getting something in return which never came. This power to recover a benefit one has conferred on someone else exists under the *law of restitution* or the *law of unjust enrichment* (different people prefer different titles for this area of law).

(5) ... the sort of education people get, or where they work, or where they live, or what goods and services they can buy, or the way they are treated by the government will not be affected by their gender, or their race, or their sexual orientation, or any other morally irrelevant characteristic. Provisions ensuring that this is the case make up *anti-discrimination law*.

Property

(6) ... people are able to acquire and dispose of property, and will have effective powers to control, retain and recover such property after they have acquired it and before they have disposed of it. The powers to acquire and dispose of property, and to control, retain, and recover it are the subject matter of the *law of property* (which area of law is usually split up into *land law*, the *law of personal property* (or *commercial law*), and *intellectual property law*).

Markets

(7) ... people are able to trade goods and services with each other, and are left free to determine for themselves the terms of trade – at least where they are of equal bargaining power. These powers to trade with each other and determine the terms of trade (and the limits on these powers) are also dealt with by the *law of contract*.

(8) . . . people are free to combine together to form companies, through which they can trade goods and services, sharing in the profits made by the company, while limiting their liabilities if the company is unsuccessful. These powers are dealt with by *company law*.

(9) . . . traders in the marketplace are required not to conspire together to rig their prices, or to abuse a dominant position that they have acquired in the marketplace to drive out any remaining competitors. These limits are dealt with by *competition law*.

Families

(10) . . . people are empowered to enter into lifelong commitments of care and support to each other by marrying each other; on dissolution of the marriage, the courts will enforce those commitments by fairly redistributing the assets and future incomes of the parties to the marriage. The power to marry and the conditions for, and consequences of, a dissolution of a marriage are dealt with by *family law*.

(11) . . . parents have special responsibilities to look after their children, and powers to control what happens to their children; and non-parents are empowered to take on parental responsibilities towards children who are no longer cared for by their natural parents. Again, these aspects of social life are dealt with by *family law*.

The State

(12) . . . the State is empowered to define certain forms of anti-social conduct as punishable, and to punish those who engage in such forms of conduct. These forms of conduct and the punishments applicable to those engage in them are laid out in the *criminal law*.

(13) . . . the State operates under the rule of law, which means that exercises of government power (other than the power to pass Acts of Parliament) are subject to strict controls to ensure that such powers are exercised rationally and in a way that is consistent: (i) with the reasons why those powers were created in the first place, (ii) with people's legitimate expectations as to how those powers will be exercised; (iii) with certain fundamentally important values such as the need to respect people's liberties and the importance of observing due process before making decisions that have a major impact on an individual's life. These limits on the exercise of government power are dealt with by *administrative law* or *public law* (different people use different titles for this area of law).

(14) . . . foreigners who have a well-founded fear of persecution in their own countries will be able to seek asylum here. The power to seek asylum in the UK is dealt with by *immigration law*.

(15) . . . Parliament is free to change any aspect of (1) – (14) above. As we have seen, this is known as the *doctrine of Parliamentary sovereignty*, and forms part of what is known as *constitutional law*.

Two points need to be made about this overview.

First, being an overview, it is necessarily extremely superficial. The study of law involves getting a much more detailed understanding of all of these different areas of law – finding out, for example, *what* we are required to do for each other under the law of tort, *what* sort of things are capable of amounting to property and what are not, *what* will happen when a marriage is dissolved, and so on. Studying law also involves getting an understanding of how tensions between these different areas of law are resolved. For example, what happens when you and I enter into a contract under which you agree that I can treat you in a way that would normally be forbidden by the law of tort? And what happens when Parliament legislates to relax the controls that the courts would normally place on the exercise of government power?

Secondly, if this overview seems very familiar – and, dare I say it, a little bit boring (don't worry, the law gets a lot more interesting the more you know about it) – that is because it's basically describing the society you live in. Our law-makers made it that way, making a reality of their visions of what sort of society we should live in. Things could have been different. There were plenty of alternative visions of what sort of society we should live in available to our law-makers which they might have gone for, with the result that we would live today in a very different kind of society. And it may be that things will be very different in future: the conversation between our law-makers as to what sort of society we should live in may evolve in surprising directions in the next fifty years or so, with the result that our society will become unrecognisably different from the sort of society we live in at the moment.

To be continued . . .

That's enough from me for the time being. I hope you've got a good idea from this letter of what we are talking about when we talk about 'law' and obtained a few insights into the current state of the law in this country. If you have, you'll be in a much better position to understand my next letter – in which I'll explain why Law is such a great subject to study at university. Until then,

All best wishes,

Nick

Four Reasons for Studying Law

● From: Nicholas J. McBride [dearnick@pearson.com]
● To: Brown, Alex
● Subject: Four Reasons for Studying Law

Dear Alex,

As promised, here's my follow-up letter setting out the various reasons why I think people should be interested in studying law at university. I've got four of them. Let's get straight into them.

● Brain training

The first reason for studying law at university is that doing a law degree is great at helping you learn how to think *carefully, imaginatively* and *sensibly*. I am not sure how much schools do nowadays in helping their students to *think* – students I meet say that much more emphasis is placed on rote learning and regurgitating information. Certainly, when I ask them to discuss a situation raising some issue of law, their responses seem to be much more guided by their instincts and emotions, rather than by carefully and imaginatively reasoning their way to a sensible conclusion. I find this really sad. In these benighted times, we need more than ever people who can think properly – and if you haven't acquired that ability at school, then doing a law degree is a great way to catch up.

So how does studying law help you to think properly? Well, consider the following situation which I sometimes ask students to think about. You are told that:

> Someone commits murder if his or her actions cause another to die and he or she performed those actions intending to kill someone or to cause someone to suffer serious bodily harm and he or she had no lawful justification or excuse for acting as he or she did.

In light of this information, consider whether D has committed murder in the following situation:

> T, a notorious terrorist, kidnaps D's wife and two children and threatens to kill them unless D delivers a package containing a bomb to V, the ambassador at an embassy to which D has access. D delivers the package. When V opens the package, it explodes and V dies.

So – what do you *think*? If you are thinking carefully, you will note that the definition of murder with which you have been supplied has three elements – and *all* of them need to be present for murder to be committed. So we need to establish that: (1) D's actions caused V to die; and (2) D acted as he did with an intent to kill or an intent to cause serious bodily harm; and (3) D had no lawful justification or excuse for acting as he did.

Taking each element in turn, it is clear that D's actions did cause V to die – had he not done what he did, V would not have been killed. But did D have an intent to kill when he acted as he did? This is where a lot of students trip up – they say that if D knew that the package contained a bomb, then he intended to kill V when he delivered the bomb. In that situation, D will certainly have *foreseen* that V would very probably die if he delivered the package – but if we are thinking *carefully* we will wonder whether we can always be said to intend what we foresee will happen as a result of our actions. After all, why would we have two different words for what we intend and what we foresee if they were the same thing? In order to test out whether we can always be said to intend something that we foresee will happen as a result of our actions, we have to use our *imagination* to come up with a *hypothetical example* to test this out. For example, I foresee that writing this letter to you will result in my getting quite tired. (Thinking *is* hard work!) But does that mean that I intend to get tired when I write to you? That sounds pretty implausible. Intending something to happen seems to be different from foreseeing that something will happen. If you intend something to happen, you *try* to make it happen – and when D delivers the package, he isn't trying to kill V. He is just trying to deliver the package. So if we are careful in the way we think about the situation presented above, we will conclude that D is not guilty of murder.

But what about this situation?

> T, a notorious terrorist, kidnaps D's wife and two children and threatens to kill them unless D kills his best friend, V, who is an important politician. D kills V.

Here D's actions have caused V to die, and D acted as he did with an intention to kill – he was trying to kill V when he killed V. So D will have committed murder in this situation *unless* he had a lawful justification or excuse for acting as he did. At this point instincts or emotions will lead a lot of students to say that he did have a justification or excuse for acting as he did. After all, if he hadn't done what he did, three people would have died, and surely three people surviving and one person dying is better than three people dying and one person surviving?

Well, let's *think* about it. If we were thinking carefully, we would note that the definition of murder refers to someone having no lawful *justification* or *excuse* for acting as they did. The fact that two different words are used here might indicate that they are referring to two different things. When we say that X's actions are justified, we seem to be saying that X did the *right thing*, in the circumstances. But when we say that X's actions are excused, we seem to be saying something different. Doing the right thing needs no excuse. It's only when you do the wrong thing, that you might seek to be excused for what you did. And when people ask to be excused, they almost always do so on the basis that their conduct, while wrong and regrettable, was so *understandable* that it would be *wrong to blame them* for acting as they did.

So this indicates that D has two ways of arguing that the final element in the definition of murder was not present in his case. He could argue that: (1) he did the right thing in acting as he did; or (2) he did the wrong thing in acting as he did, but his actions were so understandable that it would be wrong to blame him for acting as he did. So let's think about whether he can make either of these claims.

First of all, did D do the right thing in doing what he did? As we have just seen, a lot of students instinctively think that he did – three people living and one person dying is better than three people dying and one person surviving. But let's *think* about that for a second, with the help of another hypothetical example. Suppose that you suffer from some medical condition which means that you only have one year to live. But you are told that your condition can be completely cured by a full-body blood transfusion, which would involve replacing your entire blood supply with blood extracted from X's body. The transfusion would have the effect of killing X – who would, as a result, have to be forced into donating his blood – but will save your life. Would you want to go ahead with the blood transfusion? I think most people would say 'no'. They would not want their continued existence to be paid for with the killing of an innocent person like X. If this is right, then D's wife and two children might each prefer that D not preserve their lives by killing V. And if that is right, then it becomes much harder to argue that D did the right thing in killing V – if the very people for whose sake he was killing V would have preferred him not to do so, then it's hard to find a basis for arguing that he did the right thing in killing V.

D might find it easier to argue that he should be excused for doing what he did. He would claim that while he might have done the wrong thing in killing V, it was understandable that he found it difficult, if not impossible, to stand up to T's threats and allow T to kill his wife and children. Different people might have different views on this. This is what Lord Hailsham thought, in rejecting the idea that an ordinary person could not be expected to stand up to T's threats and that it would have required D to exhibit an extraordinary degree of heroism to do so:

> I must say that I do not at all accept in relation to the defence of murder it is either good morals, good policy or good law to suggest . . . that the ordinary man of reasonable fortitude is not to be supposed to be capable of heroism if he is asked to take an innocent life rather than sacrifice his own. Doubtless in actual practice many will succumb to temptation . . . But many will not, and I do not believe that as a "concession to human frailty" the former should be exempt from liability to criminal sanctions if they do. I have known in my own lifetime of too many acts of heroism by ordinary human beings of no more than ordinary fortitude to regard a law as either "just or humane" which withdraws the protection of the criminal law from the innocent victim and casts the cloak of its protection upon the coward and the poltroon in the name of a "concession to human frailty".

What do *you* think? Note that Lord Hailsham is only talking there of a situation where someone kills an innocent person in order to save his *own* life.

Might things be different where you kill in order to save the lives of other people whom you love?

This is just one example of how studying law encourages you to think straight. If you want some other examples, my college – Pembroke College, in Cambridge – has set up a 'virtual classroom' in law on its website. You can access it most easily through *my* website – www.mcbridesguides.com. Hover the cursor over the 'Legal skills' section of the website and click on the 'Virtual classroom' part of the drop-down menu. All of the exercises under the 'Legal skills' section of the classroom test out various different reasoning skills that become second nature to those who study law.

◉ Rhetoric

So the first reason for studying law at university is that it helps sharpen your mind. The second reason for studying law is that it helps sharpen your tongue and pen as well. Studying law is the closest you can come to getting a course in what the ancient Greeks and Romans would have called *rhetoric*: the art of persuading someone to adopt a particular point of view by speaking and writing effectively.

Rhetoric is not something that is taught any more in schools, and it shows when my students come to university. As a general rule, they don't know how to write effective essays: essays that argue effectively for a particular point of view. Their essays are full of 'On the one hand . . . on the other hand'; 'It is necessary to bear the following points in mind . . .'; 'It might be argued that . . .' They are very painful to read, and must be pretty boring to write. There is no sense of any spark of life or inspiration behind them; no sense that the essay is animated by a positive desire to change the way the reader thinks about things. It is all just lifeless going through the motions.

Studying law at university helps change all that. Because law is, at base, all about a conversation about what sort of society we should live in, the one immutable rule for lawyers is: *Express yourself clearly or die*. Let's call this the *iron rule of lawyering*: If you cannot express yourself clearly, there is no room for you in the law. So, for example, if you are a law-maker, obscurity will doom to failure all your efforts at making law. Lon Fuller makes this point vividly in a parable about a would-be law-maker, Rex:

> Rex . . . announced to his subjects that henceforth he would act as a judge in any disputes that might arise among them. In this way . . . he hoped that [by]

> proceeding case by case, he would gradually work out a system of rules that could be incorporated in a code.
>
> Unfortunately ... [t]he venture failed completely. After he had handed down literally hundreds of decisions neither he nor his subjects could detect in those decisions any pattern whatsoever. Such tentatives toward generalization as were to be found in his opinions only compounded the confusion, for they gave false leads to his subjects and threw his own meagre powers of judgment off balance in the decision of later cases ...
>
> Rex now realized that there was no escape from a published code declaring the rules to be applied in future disputes. ... Rex worked diligently on a revised code, and finally announced that it would shortly be published. This announcement was received with universal gratification. The dismay of Rex's subjects was all the more intense, therefore, when his code became available and it was discovered that it was truly a masterpiece of obscurity. Legal experts who studied it declared that there was not a single sentence in it that could be understood either by an ordinary citizen or by a trained lawyer. Indignation became general and soon a picket appeared before the royal palace carrying a sign that read, "How can anybody follow a rule that nobody can understand?"

I don't know of any judge whose voice is still listened to in the ongoing conversation among law makers about what sort of society we should live in who is not a master at expressing himself (or herself) clearly. (Have a look at any of the judgments quoted in my last letter to see some examples of judges expressing themselves extremely clearly.) Obscure and unclear judgments have a very short shelf-life. The same is true of statutory provisions. Any statutory provision that is not expressed clearly enough to be understood is soon withdrawn or revised, or attracts such a wealth of case law trying to make it clear what the statutory provision says that you might as well just retain the case law and throw away the underlying provision.

The *iron rule of lawyering* also applies to legal academics writing about the law. A legal academic who cannot make him- or herself understood by his or her peers will have no future as an academic. I can count on the fingers of one hand the number of legal academics who have achieved some kind of world renown without being able to write really clearly – but as soon as they retire, their renown will quickly fade as people become less and less willing to make the effort to try to understand what they were trying to say. Law has seemed immune from the modern fad for identifying obscurity with profundity that has invaded other disciplines such as English, or Theology, or Philosophy or any of the social sciences other than law. Students in those disciplines have to weary their minds trying to make sense of rubbish like this:

> Both Pound's "Portrait [d'une Femme]" and Eliot's ["Portrait of a Lady"] constitute a kind of *epyllion* which, as we shall see, is a pattern they used a great deal – the parallel actions function as a plot and counterplot which enrich each other by their interplay. Poe's "Descent into the Maelstrom" has structurally much in common with the vortices of the Cantos. Similarly, the "Sargasso Sea" is a vortex that attracts multitudinous objects but which also tosses things up again in recognizable patterns which serve for survival.

Law students, in contrast, get to feast on gems like this:

> A search warrant has to be specifically justified or it gives no authority to enter premises or take away goods. So held Lord Camden. A Good Thing. The policeman may, however, seize any suspicious goods he finds. So holds our Court of Appeal. A Bad Thing. Lord Denning MR explains that there are more wicked people about now; more innocent people, consequently, must suffer without redress. Diplock LJ refuses to follow the liberal reasoning of *Entick* v *Carrington* on the ground that our police forces are better today; might they not become better still if they had to pay for their mistakes? Salmon LJ said that the warrant could have been drawn so as to protect the police; his decision means that they needn't bother: *Chic Fashions (West Wales) Ltd* v *Jones* [1968] 2 WLR 201.

> Can it be said on occasion . . . judges give effect in court to political views which might fairly be described as right-of-centre-upper-middle-class? I think it is possible to argue that they do, and that, on occasion, when free to do otherwise they either go out of their way to protect the well-to-do, or make decisions within the framework of tolerated debate which is congenial to that group only. Some litigation is conducted with little overt sensitivity to the political context in which it takes place. It is not that two views are debated and one rejected but rather, as in a one-party state, only two variants of one view. Some judges like to say that the most important person in court is the party who is going to lose. Every effort must be made to persuade him that his views have been listened to. They are also often aware that there are parties not before the court for whom the matter is at least as important. What has to be said is that there are sometimes political non-party losers whose views are wholly unrepresented in the debate. We are all of us in favour of protecting the rights of the individual, but it is possible to disagree as to what those rights are when they meet with the novel demands of a welfare state. Collectivism will not hold the same terror for the down-and-out as it holds for the up-and-in.

Practising lawyers such as solicitors (who represent clients in legal matters outside court) and barristers (who represent clients in legal matters inside court) are also bound by the *iron rule*. Solicitors who cannot advise their clients clearly as to their legal rights will lose those clients very quickly. A barrister who cannot argue a case effectively in court will soon find him- or herself running short of briefs.

Finally, law students are not exempt from the *iron rule*. Law students are expected to write essays that make effective arguments in favour of a particular view of what the law says, or what it should say. In exams, these essays tend to have to be written in as little as 40 minutes to an hour. So law students who want to be successful as law students need to learn how to say a lot, and to say it clearly, in two or three pages. This is very difficult: brevity is always much harder to achieve than loquaciousness. (Blaise Pascal, the French mathematician and philosopher, once joked: 'I have made this letter longer than usual, because I lack the time to make it short.') But you cannot do well as a law student without learning how to get to the point quickly and make every word count.

It is no accident, I think, that so many of the greatest orators of all time – such as Demosthenes, Cicero, Daniel Webster, Henry Clay, Abraham Lincoln, William Jennings Bryan (and even Barack Obama, in our own time) – were all lawyers before going on to achieve fame as great speech-makers. It's no accident either that the speech for which Abraham Lincoln is most famous – the Gettysburg Address – is only 272 words long. (In contrast, the Professor of Greek Literature who spoke before Lincoln at the Dedication Ceremony at Gettysburg spoke for two hours.)

○ Politics

The third reason for studying law is that it helps you to form your own views as to what sort of society we should live in, and puts you in a good position to provide an informed contribution to the future shaping of our society – whether simply by voting in elections, or by working within politics yourself. Of course, it might be argued that studying philosophy at university would serve just as well to prepare you for a career in politics. However, there is a crucial difference. When you study philosophy, you are looking at a set of thinkers' *abstract* ideas as to how society should be ordered. But law exists at the cutting edge of shaping society. As a result, law-makers have a special responsibility that philosophers are not subject to – the ideas for arranging society that law-makers give effect to *have to work in practice*. They have to do more good than harm. If they don't, then the law-makers' efforts will eventually be overturned. Once the law-maker is off the scene (either fired or retired), his or her contributions to the law will be reversed and the law will be put on a more beneficent path. Dr Martin Luther King Jr liked to say that 'the arc of the moral universe is long, but it bends towards justice'. Whether that is true or not of the 'moral universe', it is certainly true of legal systems. In Lord Mansfield's striking phrase, the law eventually 'works itself pure' of its past failures. So when you study law, you develop a practical sense of what works and what doesn't work in ordering society. That, I think, is a very important thing to know if you are going to get involved in politics – and that is not something that studying abstract political theories on a philosophy course can give you. Indeed, it is striking how many philosophical ideas, once put into practice, have proven to have terrible consequences.

Moreover, studying law – and, in particular, English law – introduces you to a particular *method* of effecting social change. This is perhaps English law's greatest contribution to the world – the *common law method* of making law. All law-makers are faced with the problem of their lack of omniscience – the fact that they cannot anticipate all the consequences of their law-making activity, and can end up doing much more harm than good through that activity. The common law method of making law was the English lawyers' solution to this problem. Until the twentieth century, the English law was primarily *common law*; that is, law that had been developed as a result of the decisions of the courts in concrete cases. And in developing the law, the courts would decide on a *case by case basis* what the law said. This method of making law – the *common law method* – allowed the English courts a lot of leeway to experiment with the law.

In a particular case, one judge might suggest that the law said *x*. In later cases, other judges would have a look at this suggestion and ignore it, modify it, apply it, or expand on it. And then other judges in further cases would see what they made of that development, and adjust it accordingly. In this way, the common law – the law as developed in the courts – emerged out of a process of trial and error, where only rules and doctrines that generally satisfied the judges as being reasonable would survive to become part of the established common law. In this way the law-maker's problem of lack of omniscience was avoided. If new situations came up that had not been anticipated before, the rules and doctrines of the common law could be adjusted to take account of them, and a new but necessarily temporary understanding of what those rules and doctrines were would come into existence.

As I said, up until the twentieth century, this was *the* way in which law was developed in England. One consequence of this was that it was difficult to say with any certainty *what* the law said on a particular question – for that, you would have to look at all the previous cases that had some bearing on that question, and make educated guesses as to what the courts would say on that question, given those previous decisions. But this method of law-making was the humble tribute that English lawyers paid to their own fallibility and inability to predict the future – they adopted a method of law-making that was flexible enough to make their incapacity irrelevant. And this recognition that law-makers could not completely anticipate the future, and the consequent desire for lots of flexibility in administering the law, had a huge political effect. It may be the most important reason why the UK managed to get through the nineteenth and twentieth centuries without any kind of revolution, unlike virtually every country on the Continent. The preference that English lawyers had for changing the law through a cautious, step-by-step, process made English society as a whole resistant to, and suspicious of, revolutionaries who claimed that with one 'big leap forward' society could be transformed into a utopian ideal.

Of course, in the twentieth century, things changed. *Legislation* – laying down general rules and provisions for people to abide by and take advantage of – became a much more dominant source of law; and this reflected a utopian turn in political thinking, whereby it became much more acceptable to think that a more perfect society could be magicked into existence through legislative *fiat*. But it is precisely because this utopian turn still remains very dominant in our politics – and philosophical discussions of politics – that those entering politics should be exposed to the alternative, more organic and incremental, approaches to changing society that were once second nature to our law-makers. But you can only be exposed to this alternative approach by studying it in action, in the development of the common law.

● Legal training

I've left until last the reason you might have expected me to start with – that doing a law degree is the best preparation you can have for becoming a practising lawyer. This is for three reasons. First, I didn't want you to get the impression that you should only consider studying law if you want to become a practising lawyer. The skills and knowledge that you acquire as a law student are invaluable for a range of different careers. Secondly, I'm not sure that people should choose to study a subject at university based purely on careers-based considerations: you should use your time at university to study a subject you would love to explore in depth. Thirdly, there are people who endorse what we can call the *astonishing hypothesis* that studying law at university is *not* the best preparation for becoming a practising lawyer. (I call this the '*astonishing hypothesis*' because I think people would be astonished to be told that doing a degree in medicine is *not* the best preparation for becoming a doctor, or that doing an engineering degree is *not* the best preparation for becoming an engineer; so it would be similarly astonishing if studying law at university were not the best preparation for becoming a lawyer.) And I didn't want you to think that, if the *astonishing hypothesis* turned out – astonishingly – to be correct, there was no reason to study law at university.

For the purposes of this letter, I'll just take the commonsensical position that the *astonishing hypothesis* isn't true. If you want me to deal with it, I'll address that in another letter. But for the time being, let's assume that doing a law degree *is* the best preparation for becoming a practising lawyer. But this only gives you a reason to study law if you want (or think you might want) to become a practising lawyer. And you may have your doubts about that. Many people think that you have to sell your soul to become a lawyer. I understand why people might think that way. Anyone who has the power to argue convincingly on either side of a case will always attract suspicion. (One of the first philosophers in history, Socrates, was executed in Athens in 399 BC. One of the charges in the indictment against him was that he had the power to make the weaker case seem stronger.) The lawyer's ability to take either side of a case seems to indicate an unprincipled indifference to right and wrong. Lawyers – it is suspected – sell out their consciences and simply seek to represent whichever side in a dispute is willing to pay them the most for their services.

Let me act like a typical lawyer and put the other side of the case. Deciding to become a lawyer is just as morally worthwhile as choosing to become a doctor, or a teacher. This is because you can't have a functioning legal system without lawyers, and a society's legal system is as vitally important to the flourishing of the people living in that society as are that society's health or education systems. We tend to forget this in Western societies because we take our legal systems – and the benefits we obtain from living under our legal systems – for granted. To appreciate how important our legal systems are, I want you to do two things.

First of all, imagine what it would be like to live in a society where everything is permitted. We don't have to try too hard to do this: we just have to watch or read the news from other parts of the world to see examples of societies that have no legal systems worth speaking of – where there are no effective limits on what the State may do to its citizens, or what its citizens may do to each other. Life in such societies is 'solitary, poor, nasty, brutish, and short', in the words of the philosopher Thomas Hobbes, who lived through the breakdown of social order triggered by the English Civil War. People who live in such societies are condemned to live in chaos and disorder and to experience all the evils that flourish in conditions of chaos and disorder: murder, rape, arson, theft, starvation, despair, suicide. The fact that we don't live in such a society is due to the fact that we live under the rule of law. That is, we live under a legal system that sets strict limits on what the State may do to us and what we may do to each other, and those limits are – by and large – observed.

Secondly, imagine what it would be like to live in a society where there is no trade. In other words, imagine a society where each of us has to grow, or make, everything we need for ourselves and our families. Again, it's not too hard to do this – thinking about what life is like in the poorest areas of the world should give you some idea of what this sort of existence would be like. There would be no shops, no buildings bigger than those that could be built by a few pairs of hands, no guaranteed water supply, no food other than what you and your family could grow on land that you are lucky enough to have inherited, no tools to grow food other than those a single person could make for him- or herself, no books, and no retirement in old age. Life in such a society would not necessarily be marked by chaos and disorder, but it would still involve a desperate and continuous struggle to stay alive. Again, the fact that we don't live in such a society is due to the fact that we live under a legal system that helps people to trade with each other. Our legal system helps people to trade with each other by doing two things in particular. First of all, it gives people something to trade by granting them legally enforceable rights over such things as their bodies, land, things, and ideas. Secondly, our legal system allows people to enter into binding contracts with each other, under which contracts their legal rights can be transferred to other people. Almost everything around you owes its existence to the fact that our legal system helps people trade with each other. Just think, for example, of the immense network of transactions that was required simply to produce the computer on which I am typing this letter.

So we in the West owe everything to the legal systems under which we live. Without them, our lives would be unimaginably different, and unbelievably difficult. And as you can't have a legal system without lawyers to run it, it follows that we should regard the lawyers who help to keep our legal system running as public heroes, in the same way that we regard doctors and nurses and teachers as heroic for the work they do. That, then, is my positive argument for thinking that becoming a lawyer is a morally worthwhile thing to do. But like any good lawyer, I won't close my argument without first considering, and dismissing, three arguments that might be made on the other side.

(1) Defending evil

A question criminal lawyers are often asked is, 'How can you defend someone you know is guilty?' And a question corporate lawyers are often asked is, 'How can you work for a company that pollutes the environment/pays its workers so little/does as much as it can to avoid paying taxes?' The implication of both questions is that the work that the lawyer does is, at least on occasions, morally disreputable. The implication is unjustified. The short answer to both questions is that our legal system simply won't work properly if people are denied access to its benefits by lawyers who stand in judgment on them and refuse to work for them on the ground that they are not entitled to those benefits, or don't deserve them. The rule of law would be fatally undermined if the mere fact that you looked guilty ensured that you were found guilty without a proper trial. Freedom to trade under the law would be similarly undermined if the mere fact that people disapproved of the way you ran your business meant that you could not find adequate representation. If our legal system is going to work properly, and provide us with the benefits set out above, then lawyers have to be willing to represent unpopular or unpleasant clients, and do their best for them.

(2) Irrelevance

It might be argued that the UK is no longer a country that lives under the rule of law. Whatever limits UK law does place on what the State can do to us, and what we may do to each other, these limits are largely theoretical. In practice, these limits are regularly transgressed without any sanction or redress. As a serving police officer has observed,

> Crime doesn't get investigated properly and it hasn't done for a long time now . . . Just about every single reported theft of a mobile phone is recorded as lost property. You will find very, very few recorded attempted burglaries

because they all get recorded as criminal damage ... Crimes only get detected if they're easily solvable . . . There just [aren't] enough people to investigate crimes properly. If, say, there is a queue of 20 jobs and you have five officers to deal with them, it's impossible to fully investigate a crime properly.

And there are some crimes that the police, seemingly, simply will not investigate: the last successful prosecution of police officers for their involvement in a death in police custody was in 1969; over 44 years ago. This is despite the fact that over 1,000 people have died in police custody in the last 12 years.

So it might be argued, then, that the games lawyers play are largely irrelevant to the vast majority of society and make little or no contribution to ensuring that we don't slide into living in a society where everything is permitted. To borrow the legal philosopher Roberto Mangabeira Unger's striking language, lawyers are 'like a priesthood that [has] lost [its] faith and kept [its] jobs . . . [standing] in tedious embarrassment before cold altars'. But even if this were true (which I don't think it is), then you have even more of a reason to want to become a lawyer. If it is true that the UK cannot be said at the moment to live under the rule of law, and it's only morality or custom that currently stands between us and our living in a society where everything is permitted, then your generation can turn things around and start rebuilding the rule of law in the UK. If the rule of law is as important as I say it is – and it is – then no enterprise could be more valuable, or more urgent, or make more of a contribution to people's welfare. But to get involved in this great enterprise, you have to become a lawyer.

(3) Corruption

The third argument against the view that becoming a lawyer is a morally worthwhile thing to do goes as follows:

Becoming a lawyer is morally dangerous. In theory, you could do a lot of good as a lawyer in exactly the ways Nick McBride describes – you could help to uphold (or rebuild) the rule of law in the UK by becoming a criminal lawyer or a tort lawyer, or you could help foster commerce within the UK by becoming a commercial lawyer, or a corporate lawyer, or a land lawyer. But lawyers also have the potential to do great evil. They can use their position to help destroy the rule of law in the UK, for example, by telling lies to the courts to ensure that guilty clients go free. And they can use their position to damage commerce, for example, by threatening their clients' competitors with expensive and potentially ruinous legal actions if they attempt to market a new invention that would transform the lives of millions. Unfortunately, the likelihood is that someone who becomes a lawyer will end up doing evil, rather than good. The power of money is too great to resist – a client who offers a lot of money to a lawyer in return for their doing something wrong or unethical will usually not be turned away. So whatever good you could do as a lawyer, it's better to do something else where you could do an equivalent amount of good (if not more), and not be exposed to the temptations to do evil that lawyers are routinely exposed to, and to which many lawyers succumb.

This argument fails, at two levels. First of all, it's simply not true that lawyers are more likely than not to end up acting immorally. If that were true, decent lawyers would be extremely hard to come by. That is not my experience: most lawyers I come across are decent people, who haven't been corrupted by money, but instead seek to fulfil their professional responsibilities as best they can. Secondly, even if the factual basis of this argument were correct, and if this argument were accepted, it would mean that no one should become a lawyer, which – as we have seen – would be ruinous for our society. A society without lawyers is one without any kind of future. If it is true that lawyers are very susceptible to being tempted to do the wrong thing, the proper response to that fact is not for people to stop becoming lawyers, but for us to strengthen the sanctions against lawyers who do the wrong thing, so as to encourage them to resist temptation.

So far as morality is concerned, then, there is absolutely nothing wrong with becoming a lawyer. Quite the opposite: lawyers are just as important to the functioning of society as teachers or doctors. However, I should sound a warning note here. Precisely because the idea of becoming a lawyer is so attractive to a lot of people, the market for jobs as lawyers – particularly to become a solicitor in a top city law firm, or a barrister in a good set of chambers – is becoming increasingly competitive. So if you think you might want to become a lawyer, you have to be realistic about what the chances are of your achieving that ambition after you leave university. A useful website to look at for this purpose is www.unistats.com. This will give you some information about what percentage of law graduates from a particular university obtain jobs once leaving university, and general levels of student satisfaction with the courses they receive. Look at the universities you are likely to be applying to and see how they rate for law. (Also ask the universities themselves for any statistics that they might have on this.)

If they don't rate so highly, don't despair! Just be careful – think about what other careers you might be interested in, and what sort of skills and qualifications they would require, and think about whether a law degree would put you in a good position to pursue those other careers, if a career as a lawyer doesn't happen to work out for you. If the other careers you are interested in (I am thinking in particular here of teaching) require you to have done a degree other than a law degree at university, remember it is always open to you to do a non-law degree at university and then qualify to practise as a lawyer by doing a one-year Graduate Diploma in Law (GDL) – essentially a crash course in the core legal subjects – at a College of Law before then going on to do a one-year course to qualify to practise as a solicitor or a barrister. (Someone who does a law degree is exempt from the need to do a GDL and can go straight on to the one-year course to qualify to practise as a solicitor or a barrister.) So if you are not confident of your chances of making it as a lawyer once you leave university, given the universities you are likely to be applying to, and there are other careers you might be interested in and doing a non-law degree at university would be a better preparation for those careers, it might be an idea to hedge your bets by doing a non-law degree at university and then spend a year after that doing a GDL, and then see whether you can get a job as a lawyer on the basis of that, and the degree you obtained at university.

● Summary

You don't have to want to become a lawyer to do a law degree. The analytical and rhetorical skills you will acquire in doing a law degree means that doing a law degree can provide excellent training for working in politics, journalism, business, or public service. But you shouldn't let all the lawyer jokes we both know and the caricatures of lawyers projected in the media put you off the idea of becoming a lawyer after you leave university. Lawyers perform an extremely important role in society. If you do want to become a lawyer, then doing a law degree would obviously provide you with everything you needed to become a very good and successful lawyer. However, you should be aware of how competitive it is now to become a lawyer, and you should think carefully about how likely it is that your law degree will provide you with a reliable launchpad for entering the legal profession, and how useful a law degree would be to you for other careers you might be interested in pursuing if it turned out that you weren't able to pursue a career in law.

If you haven't made up your mind whether or not you want to become a lawyer, you should read a book by a journalist called Jonathan Harr. The book is called *A Civil Action*. It may well inspire you to become a lawyer. The book was made into a film – but try to read the book: it's much better than the film. If you want to watch some really great films about the law, get hold of *To Kill A Mockingbird*, *The Verdict*, *True Believer*, *Indictment: The McMartin Trial*, *The Rainmaker*, *Erin Brockovich*, and *Flash of Genius*. If those films don't make you want to become a lawyer, then nothing will.

If you want to get a bit of a taste of what it is like to study law, and get a better idea of how important law is to our daily lives, then I recommend that you have a look at *What About Law?*, a book edited by three of my colleagues here in Cambridge: Catherine Barnard, Janet O'Sullivan, and Graham Virgo. Each chapter introduces you to a different area of law by focusing in great detail on a particular case that is relevant to that area of law.

Please don't hesitate to get in touch if you have any more questions.

All best wishes,

Nick

Why Not Just Do a Conversion Course?

- From: Nicholas J. McBride [dearnick@pearson.com]
- To: Brown, Alex
- Subject: Why Not Just Do a Conversion Course?

Dear Alex,

Thanks for your email. So, if I've got it right, you've been encouraged by my last letter to think you might want to become a lawyer, but now your history teacher is telling you that the *astonishing hypothesis* is, astonishingly, true – that doing a law degree is not necessarily the best preparation for becoming a practising lawyer. And he's been telling you that Lord Sumption, one of the latest recruits to the Supreme Court of the United Kingdom, agrees with him. Well, remember that even if the *astonishing hypothesis* is correct, there are still plenty of other reasons, which I identified in my last letter, for studying law at university. However, I'll use this letter to address the *astonishing hypothesis* and explain why I think it's wrong. But first I have to clarify something. The *astonishing hypothesis* comes in two forms: a strong form and a weak form.

The *strong* form of the *astonishing hypothesis* says that if you want to be a practising lawyer, it would be positively *better* to do some degree other than law at university, and then do a one-year conversion course (otherwise known as a 'GDL', for 'Graduate Diploma in Law') that will ground you in the basics of law and allow you to go on to the professional training one-year courses run by a Bar School (if you want to be a barrister) or a Law School (if you want to be a solicitor). The *weak* form of the *astonishing hypothesis* says that if you want to be a practising lawyer, you have no reason to want to do law as opposed to any other degree at university. In other words, doing a law degree provides *no better* preparation for becoming a lawyer than doing any other degree does. So in this letter, I'll be explaining why I think both the strong and weak forms of the *astonishing hypothesis* are incorrect. Let's start with the strong form.

● The strong form of the *astonishing hypothesis*

Lord Sumption seems to be a supporter of the strong form of the *astonishing hypothesis*: if you want to practise law, it would be positively better if you did some degree other than law at university. Your history teacher probably came across a report of Lord Sumption's views that was carried in the *Daily Telegraph* on July 8, 2012, and which you can easily look up online. But the *Telegraph* was reporting on an interview which Lord Sumption gave to the barristers' magazine *Counsel,* and which was published in July 2012. That interview is not available online, but *Counsel* magazine have kindly agreed to allow me to reproduce the relevant portion of the interview here:

> **Would you recommend people coming to the Bar to do a law degree or would you say there is as much value in doing an arts subject as an undergraduate?**
>
> I've made a lot of enemies, though I have to say very kindly enemies, by saying publicly on a number of occasions that I think it is best not to read law as an undergraduate. I've sometimes been misinterpreted when I say this as suggesting that law is not well taught to undergraduates in British universities. That is not my view: I think it's superbly well taught to undergraduates in British universities. The problem is that we have a generation of lawyers, and this applies to solicitors as well as barristers, who are coming into the profession with much less in the way of general culture than their predecessors. It is very unfortunate, for example, that many of them cannot speak or read a single language other than their own. I think the difficult thing about practising law is not the law but the facts. Most arguments which pretend to be about the law are actually arguments about the correct analysis and categorisation of the facts. Once you've understood them it's pretty obvious what the answer is. The difficulty then becomes to reason your way in a respectable way towards it. Of course sometimes you just can't, in which case you change your mind.
>
> This is why the study of something involving the analysis of evidence, like history or classics, or the study of a subject which comes close to pure logic, like mathematics, is at least as valuable a preparation for legal practice as the study of law. Appreciating how to fit legal principles to particular facts is a real skill. Understanding the social or business background to legal

problems is essential. I'm not sure that current law degree courses train you for that, nor really are they designed to. That is not a criticism of the course. It's simply a recognition of the fact that a command of reasoning skills, an ability to understand and use evidence, and a broad literary culture are all tremendously valuable to any advocate. If you don't have them, you are going to find it more difficult to practise. If you don't know any law that is not a problem: you can find it out.

Notice how the interviewer is simply asking about the weak version of the *astonishing hypothesis*: Is it true that there is just 'as much value' in doing a degree such as history if you want to become a barrister? But Lord Sumption goes much further and says that if you want to be a barrister 'it is *best not to read law* as an undergraduate' (emphasis added). There he is endorsing the strong version of the *astonishing hypothesis* – that if you want to become a practising lawyer, you should positively *not* study law at university, but should do something else.

In order to explain why I reject the strong version of the *astonishing hypothesis,* I want to pick up on two things Lord Sumption says in the passage above.

(1) A generation of lawyers . . . with much less in the way of general culture than their predecessors

At the moment, law firms and sets of chambers tend to recruit from students who have done a law degree and students who have done a degree other than law on a 50:50 basis – that is, about half of the people to whom they offer a training contract (if they are a law firm) or a pupillage (if they are a set of barristers' chambers) will have done a law degree, and the other half will have done some law degree other than law. So if Lord Sumption is right (and I'm in no position to say that he is wrong) that there is a *whole* generation of lawyers 'coming into the profession with much less in the way of general culture than their predecessors', that would seem to suggest doing a degree other than law is not the solution to this problem. Those who are coming into the law profession with non-law degrees suffer from the *same* lack 'of general culture' as those who have done law degrees. If this is right, then it seems that the source of the problem that Lord Sumption is worried about has nothing much to do with what *degree* the new generation of lawyers did at university and is more rooted in our *culture*, which tends not to encourage people to use their spare time to read Tolstoy, or learn a foreign language, or attend a set of evening lectures on astrophysics. If Lord Sumption wants to do something about this problem, then he would do better to address this general feature of our culture rather than offer the completely inadequate solution of urging would-be lawyers to do a degree other than law at university.

So Lord Sumption's only argument in favour of doing a degree other than law at university doesn't get off the ground. And in fact, it could be argued that one part of the solution to the problem Lord Sumption identifies is to encourage prospective lawyers to study *law* at university. Law is so multi-faceted – involved as it is with every different aspect of our society – that studying law at university *requires* you to make much more of an effort to acquire more 'in the way of general culture' than you would have to if you were studying, say, mathematics or classics. Studying criminal law or criminology requires you to know something about economics, philosophy, psychology, and sociology. You can't study contract law or tort law without knowing something about economics and philosophy. Studying constitutional law or jurisprudence requires you to know something about political theory. The same is true of international law; and students of international law would also be well advised to take an interest in game theory. Game theory is also relevant to family law (particularly in the way family law handles breakdowns of relationships), as are sociology and psychology. Intellectual property law can only be done well by students with a combined interest in science, economics, art and literature. Comparative law encourages you to take an interest in the legal systems of countries on the Continent. Many universities offer their law students the option of spending a year in a foreign country, studying law, which helps to expand their horizons, and develop their foreign language skills. And history is relevant to all of these subjects because when we study law we are looking at how past decisions – and the influences that were brought to bear on those decisions – have influenced where we are now as a society. So if a would-be lawyer wants to enter the legal profession with much *more* 'in the way of general culture' than his or her contemporaries, then studying law at university would be an ideal way of doing that.

(2) If you don't know any law that is not a problem, you can find it out

I want to make two points about this statement.

First, Lord Sumption has just been promoted to the UK Supreme Court. I wonder, when he and his colleagues are faced with a difficult legal question (which is the only sort of question that gets to the UK Supreme Court), whether he tells them, 'I don't know what the problem is: we can just find out what the law says on this issue!' Of course he doesn't. That's because there is nothing to find out: when faced with a difficult legal question, the UK Supreme Court has to *decide* what the law says on that question. But they aren't free to adopt any method they like of deciding this question. They can't, for example, toss a coin to decide what the law says. They have to decide the case in a way that best guarantees that they will make a *reasonable* decision. That requires them to show some humility and take account of any views that have been expressed by other law-makers in the past that might be relevant to the decision that they have to make. It also requires them to think hard about what implications their decision might have: Will it have undesirable effects on people's civil liberties, or be harmful to the public interest in some other way? Will it make it harder for people to understand what the law says? Will it encourage future judges to develop the law in undesirable directions? Will it undermine Parliament's intentions as to what the law should say in this area? Learning to reason in this way takes time and discipline. Doing a law degree helps you to do this; and doing some other degree does not come even close to helping you to apply your mind to legal questions in this kind of way. Of course, you could argue: But only judges need to learn how to reason in this way. But barristers who want to get a judge to decide a difficult legal question in favour of their client also need to know how the judge is likely to approach that decision. And solicitors who need to advise their clients on difficult legal questions need exactly the same skill. And that skill – of knowing how to think like a lawyer – is best acquired by doing a law degree.

Second, consider the following situation:

> An explosion occurs at a huge petrol refinery. The explosion damages the fabric of a number of houses nearby. The owners of the houses want compensation for the damage done to their houses. Someone who was renting a room in one of the houses has had to move out and is finding it difficult to find equivalent accommodation at the same rent elsewhere. She also wants to sue for compensation.

You don't know anything about what the law says in this area, but Lord Sumption says that isn't a problem – you can just find it out. So – go on: find it out. How would you go about finding out whether or not the people involved in this situation are entitled to compensation? You would obviously need access to a law library, so let's assume you've got that. But where do you go then? There is no book on 'explosions at petrol refineries'. And there is no book on 'the law of compensation'. You might, in wandering through the library, find some books on land law which tell you about the rights of owners of houses, and tenants who lease property, but they don't deal with this situation. At this stage, you might get a bit desperate and ask someone who actually knows something about the law where on earth you should be looking, and he or she might point you in the direction of the books on tort law. But when you get to those, you will be dismayed to find that they are all over 1,000 pages long – so short of reading all 1,000+ pages of the book, how do you find out which part of the book you should be looking at? In fact, you should be looking first of all at the section of the book on the 'rule in *Rylands* v *Fletcher*'. But if you haven't done a law degree but done some other degree instead and then a conversion course, you probably won't know about the rule in *Rylands* v *Fletcher* because it is very likely that your conversion course provider decided – in an attempt to teach its students seven legal subjects in just one year – that the rule in *Rylands* v *Fletcher* could be dropped from the syllabus. So how would you know to find out what the law says on the rule in *Rylands* v *Fletcher* when you don't even know that the rule exists? The truth is that the best way of putting yourself in a position to find out what the law says on any given legal issue is to do a law degree. Anyone who doesn't do a law degree and wants to find out what the law says on a particular question will almost inevitably find themselves depending at some point on other people who *have* done law degrees to give them a helping hand. I think if I wanted to be a practising lawyer, I would rather be the kind of lawyer who has, through doing a law degree, acquired a good overview of the different areas of law and knows how legal knowledge is arranged in a law library so that I can work on my own to research a legal issue and reach a reliable conclusion on that issue. And I wouldn't want to be the kind of lawyer whose state of knowledge depends on the vagaries of what I was taught on my conversion course and any titbits of knowledge that I had been able to pick up from other people after entering the profession.

● The weak form of the *astonishing hypothesis*

I think I've said enough by now to show that Lord Sumption's arguments in favour of the strong form of the *astonishing hypothesis* simply don't stand up.

(1) Doing a law degree is at least as good as any other degree in helping a would-be lawyer acquire the sort of 'general culture' that Lord Sumption thinks it is so important that a practising lawyer have; and there is good reason to think that, in these benighted times, doing a law degree does

a much better job than most other degrees of encouraging a would-be lawyer to develop the kind of hinterland that Lord Sumption would like to see practising lawyers have.

(2) Doing a law degree is a far better way of helping a practising lawyer acquire the knowledge and skills that he or she will need to find out what the law says on any given issue; or in cases where the law is uncertain, to make an educated guess as to what the courts are likely to decide the law says.

If points (1) and (2) are correct, then we should also reject the weak form of the *astonishing hypothesis*. It is not the case that a would-be lawyer has no reason to prefer studying law at university as opposed to doing some other kind of degree. There are a number of reasons why someone who has made up their mind that they want to be a practising lawyer should positively want to do a law degree at university. Not just the reasons I've already mentioned, but also:

(3) Law students at university get lots of opportunities, through things like law societies and law events, to make valuable connections with law firms and sets of chambers that can help them pursue a legal career later on. They are also given far more opportunities than non-law students to develop the sort of skills that will make them attractive to law firms and sets of chambers. So for example, a decent university law society will regularly organise moots – that is, opportunities to argue a legal point in front of a judge – which provide good preparation for life as a barrister. Whenever a law firm contacts me to ask if it can put on an event for my law students, I always ask them to do some sessions on commercial awareness and negotiating skills, as those abilities are particularly prized by law firms: but it's my law students who profit from those sessions, not students who have opted to do some other degree.

(4) It is increasingly the case that students are expected to have done a post-graduate degree in law if they want to pursue a career as a barrister. It is obviously much, much easier for a student to do such a degree if they have already studied law as an undergraduate. I am not saying that it is impossible for a student who has done something other than law, and has then done a conversion course, to do a post-graduate degree in law, but it is obviously much tougher.

(5) The conversion course is also tough – someone who does the conversion course has to master seven different subjects in one year that students who have done a normal law degree get to spread out over three years.

This doesn't stop people doing the conversion course, and doing it well, but it is not a pleasant experience and one that could have been avoided by simply doing a law degree.

(6) And someone who does a conversion course only gets to study seven legal subjects. In contrast, a student doing a three-year law degree could expect to study at least twelve different areas of law during the course of his or her degree. This gives a law student a much broader understanding of the law, and a much greater opportunity to discover what sort of areas of law really excite him or her and that he or she would like to specialise in after leaving university.

(7) Law students get a one-year head start over their non-law contemporaries in pursuing a legal career. They are exempt from having to do the first year of law school or bar school – which is the conversion course – and can go straight on to the second year, which is concerned with professional training. At a time when education is becoming increasingly expensive, it is not clear why someone who knew that they wanted to be a practising lawyer would incur a whole extra year's worth of fees and expenses doing a conversion course, and put off by a year the date when they can actually start earning some money, so that they could study some other subject at university.

(8) As I said above, law firms and sets of chambers tend to recruit law and non-law graduates on a 50:50 basis. That might indicate that they endorse the weak form of the *astonishing hypothesis*: they don't care what degree you have done at university, so why should you? But if that 50:50 ratio is maintained in future, then that has an important implication for people's abilities to get jobs in the legal profession while the current economic crisis continues. Ever since the crisis began, jobs in the public sector and the financial sector have dried up. This has resulted in a big increase in non-law graduates applying for law jobs. So in the current crisis, the amount of competition for a law job that you might face as a non-law graduate will be far higher than you would face as a law graduate. One way of appreciating this point is to imagine that all jobs with law firms are stored in a building with two equally sized doors – one marked 'law graduates' and one marked 'non-law graduates'. The more people who are attempting at any one time to get through the door marked 'non-law graduates' the harder it will be for everyone entering through that door to get into the building. But two things make it even harder for non-law graduates to get law jobs. First, in an effort to cut their costs, the big

city law firms are reducing the total number of training contracts (initial offers of employment) that they are willing to award graduates coming out of university – so the doors into the building of 'law firm jobs' are shrinking at a time when ever more non-law graduates are trying to get into the building through the non-law graduate door. Secondly, every big city law firm I have talked to is tilting towards recruiting more law graduates than they do non-law graduates on the basis that law graduates are less of a risk. So in future the non-law graduate door into the building of jobs with law firms may get much smaller and the law graduate door proportionately bigger. If this happens, the odds of getting a decent job with a city law firm will be far better if you have done a law degree than if you have done a non-law degree.

● Summary

I'm afraid to say that your history teacher is wrong. The *astonishing hypothesis* that there is no particular reason why someone who wants to be a practising lawyer should study law at university turns out, not so astonishingly, to be incorrect. That is why there is no other country in the world that allows someone to practise law without having done a law degree first, just as we here in the UK would never dream of allowing someone to practise medicine without having first done a degree in medicine. The continuing cachet that the *astonishing hypothesis* enjoys among some people in the UK has a lot to do, I think, with the very English cult of the amateur – the belief that it is possible to achieve great things without really trying, and without engaging in any specialised preparation or training. Wherever it rears its head, this cult of the amateur always has baleful effects. It explains why English football was for so long (and in some ways continues to be) a backwater in terms of skills and concrete achievement. It accounts for the UK's long industrial decline compared with other countries that take more seriously the need to ensure that a proportion of their population develops technical skills in engineering and the sciences. The UK needs to be immunised against this cult. Rejecting the *astonishing hypothesis* would be a very good start.

All best wishes,

Nick

But Is Law the Right Subject for Me?

● From: Nicholas J. McBride [dearnick@pearson.com]
● To: Brown, Alex
● Subject: But Is Law the Right Subject for Me?

Dear Alex,

You're quite right: I *did* say in my first letter to you that law isn't for everyone. Doing well as a law student requires a specific set of skills, and not everyone has those skills. In fact, I think the number of 17 or 18 year olds who have a natural aptitude for studying law is gradually getting smaller and smaller. I think that's down to a combination of two things. (1) I think the sort of society we live in doesn't really encourage children to develop the kind of skills that they need to have if they are to do well as law students. (2) People of your age don't really know what sort of skills successful law students need to have, and so have no idea that they need to work on themselves to develop those skills. But the good news is that most of the skills I'll be talking about in this letter *can* be acquired, if you want to develop them. So doing well in studying law shouldn't be beyond anyone; whether someone does well or not depends on whether they *want* to become the sort of person who can do well at law. Not everyone does; and it follows that law isn't for them.

So what I'll do in this letter is set out 12 qualities that I think are important for a law student to have, if they are going to do well in their studies. I'll also give you some tips as to how you can develop these qualities if you don't have them already. And then you can think about how many of these qualities you have already, and whether you are prepared to do what it takes to acquire the others. Here we go –

● (1) Self-belief

Henry Ford had a saying: 'Whether you think you can, or think you can't, you're probably right.' In other words, you won't be able to do anything that you don't believe you can do. This applies in spades to studying law. Law is very different from any other subject you will have studied so far (including law A-Level if that's one of your A-Levels). There are going to be times when you are going to feel that law is so strange and unfamiliar that it is never going to make sense. It will, eventually – but to get to the other side where the law becomes much more comprehensible you will need to believe that you have what it takes to get to the other side.

So – how do you develop a belief in yourself or your abilities if you don't have it already? In his closing address to the jury in the film *The Verdict,* Paul Newman's character says, 'In my religion, they say, act as if ye had faith. Faith will be given to you.' Aaron Sorkin later borrowed this line for *The West Wing.* Jed Bartlet is running for President and confesses to his campaign manager, Leo McGarry, that he isn't sure that he's the right man to become President. Leo replies: 'Ah, act as if ye have faith and faith shall be given to you. Put it another way, fake it til you make it.' If you lack faith in yourself, it doesn't really matter. Just act as though you did – do whatever you would do if you believed in yourself. And when things eventually come right, you'll see that you should have believed in yourself all along, and that will stand you in good stead the next time the chips are down.

● (2) *Sang froid*

Sang froid literally means 'cold blood'. Someone with *sang froid* is able to stay cool and composed under pressure. I think *sang froid* is a very important quality for a law student, particularly at the start of one's studies. When you are starting out as a law student, you come under a seemingly relentless barrage of information that you have to master, and you are expected to be able to do so many new things such as read a case or write an essay about the law in such a short period of time. In order to come through this 'blooding' relatively unscathed, you need to be able to keep cool, focus on what needs to be done, and get on with doing it.

Acquiring *sang froid* is just a matter of deliberately not looking at the bigger picture: of breaking everything you need to do down into much smaller steps and then focusing relentlessly on the little steps you need to make and not thinking about how far you have to go or how much more you have to do.

I write a very big textbook on a particular area of law, and the textbook is about 1,000 pages long. When I started out writing the textbook, if I had ever thought about how long it was going to be, I would never have been able to write it – I would have been overwhelmed by the sheer size of the task. But by focusing on writing one page, or one chapter, and always just focusing on that, it was eventually finished – and pretty quickly, too.

● (3) Organisation

The last point takes me on to the next quality required to be successful as a law student: the need to be organised. Look at this letter or my three previous letters. Look at how they are laid out, with headings and sub-headings and with some kind of order between the various different headings. Look at how, whenever I set out a list of points, I number each point. The way I write is a reflection of my personality, which is very organised and methodical in its approach to everything. I think that this is an important quality that anyone who wants to be successful as a law student needs to have. I'm *definitely* not saying that spontaneity and a bit of messiness in your thinking won't be valuable to you as a law student. People who only think in straight lines aren't capable of seeing the indirect connections that exist between different ideas and subjects. But in the end, you won't be able to express yourself clearly as a law student (remember the *iron rule of lawyering*: express yourself clearly or die) if you can't organise your thoughts; and you won't be able to cope with all the demands that studying law makes on you if you can't organise your time.

If you are a pretty disorganised person (and most teenagers are), the secret to changing that is again to act *as though* you are an organised person; if you do that for long enough, being organised will become the norm for you, and you will gradually become intolerant of disorganisation. So tidy up your room, and make an effort to keep it tidy. Start making lists of things you have to do and check them off as you do them – and make sure you do everything on your list. Take pride in any work you do for school and make it look classy. Take on jobs that require a lot of planning and organisation to be done properly (such as helping out backstage in a school drama production) and make sure no one has reason to criticise your performance.

● (4) Focus

The great French philosopher and mathematician, Blaise Pascal, once remarked that 'the sole cause of man's unhappiness is that he does not know how to stay quietly in his room.' Whether that's true or not of mankind generally (I tend to think it is), it's definitely true of law students. Any student who is restless and easily distracted will tend not to do very well in studying law. Focus is vital for a law student – the ability to work for sustained periods of time, concentrating on difficult legal issues that require sustained attention before they will yield and become comprehensible. Unfortunately, focus is something in small supply nowadays among students your age. There are so many distractions available to you – particularly from your computer and your mobile phone – that it is hard just to *stay still* for a long period of time and give your full attention to just one thing.

Your capacity to focus is like a muscle – the more exercise it gets, the stronger it gets. It follows that if you suffer from a weak attention span, the way to deal with that is to isolate yourself from possible sources of distraction so that the only thing you can focus on is whatever you are supposed to be paying attention to. So if you can't focus on your work because Facebook or YouTube are constantly calling to you, you need to work somewhere that you don't have access to those things. Gradually, the more you allow yourself to operate without distractions, the power of those distractions will become weaker and your capacity to focus will become correspondingly stronger.

● (5) Self-control

Of course, there's a reason why Facebook and YouTube are distracting – it's because they are fun and interesting. I can lose myself for hours surfing on YouTube, following one link to another and then another. So an essential quality that a law student needs is the capacity to say 'no' to things that any reasonable person would normally want to say 'yes' to. In other words, to be successful, a law student has to be able to defer gratification – to put off what is attractive now in order to achieve the sort of success that will allow him or her to obtain even more attractive things in the future.

It isn't totally clear whether there is a way to improve your capacity to defer gratification. In 1972, a study known as the 'marshmallow experiment' was conducted at Stanford University. A child would be left in a room with a marshmallow (or some other comparable treat) and told that if he or she waited 15 minutes without eating the marshmallow, then he or she would get another marshmallow. The children who ate the marshmallow as soon as they were left alone tended to do significantly less well later on in life than the children who were able to put off eating the marshmallow for 15 minutes. This may tend to indicate that the children's capacities for self-control remained unchanged as they grew up. However, the good news is that a very recent study indicates that children's capacity to defer gratification increases the more certain they can be that deferring gratification will result in their obtaining a reward later. If this is right, then the more often law students see that their long hours of study have resulted in their achieving some concrete reward, the more willing they will be to continue to put the hours in for future rewards. So it may be that a law student can build up his or her capacity for deferred gratification by setting up a programme of rewards for him- or herself – 'If I put the hours in this week, I'll reward myself with . . .' But someone who lacks even the capacity to follow through such a programme of rewards is unlikely to be able to do well as a law student.

● (6) Curiosity

Deferring gratification becomes much easier the more motivated you are to study law. Unfortunately, law is such an unfamiliar subject, any motivation you might have to study it is necessarily weak – you may like the idea of studying law in theory, but a theoretical attraction is hard to sustain when faced with the messy reality of what studying law involves. Most law students discover their motivation for studying law *after* they have started studying it – they fall in love with the subject and become fascinated with it. But this only happens if they really get stuck into studying law and start grappling with the details of the law instead of remaining content with a more broad brush overview of the subject. As I said in my first letter to you, the law tends to be pretty boring when you view it from a great distance – it's only when you get close up to the law and see it in all its glory that you can give yourself a chance of getting really interested in it. So to do well as a law student you need to feel driven not to approach the subject superficially, but to try to achieve a very detailed understanding of the law. In other words, you need to feel *curious* about the law. It is fundamentally curiosity which provides a law student with the initial push that they need to get on the road to success in studying law: if they feel curious about the law, then they will try to understand it in detail; and if they understand it in detail, they will want to know more and more about it. In contrast, someone who just wants to find out enough about the law to 'get by' will never get anywhere in their studies.

I assume that being curious about the law isn't really a problem for you – if you weren't interested in finding out more about law, you would hardly be reading this letter. So I don't need to give you any tips on how to overcome a basic lack of curiosity about the law. However, one thing I would advise is that you be careful not to *kill* your curiosity about law. If you are reading a book about law that bores you, then put it aside – you won't get anything out of it, and it could be very harmful. Some of the books I was told to read before starting to study law as an undergraduate at Oxford were shockingly tedious, but I must have been so excited about the prospect of studying law that that didn't put me off. However, you may not be so lucky. So avoid boring books and seek out interesting ones instead.

● (7) Love of reading

If you study law, you are going to be reading *a lot* of material. So you have to have a basic love of reading if you are going to be successful as a law student. If reading is, for you, a bore and a drag then law is not for you and you should do something that doesn't involve spending so much time with your head stuck in a book, such as science or engineering. Unfortunately, if reading *is*, for you, a bore and a drag then there isn't much I can suggest to engender a love of reading for you. Maybe starting to read *a lot* might help – but it's probably likely to do more harm than good. So I think this is one quality where, if you don't have it, it might be best to think about doing something other than law.

● (8) Foxiness

In an observation that is now so clichéd, you won't be able to believe how much I hate myself for repeating it, the ancient Greek poet Archilochus distinguished between the fox, who 'knows many things', and the hedgehog, who 'knows one big thing'. (The philosopher Isaiah Berlin borrowed the distinction to distinguish between writers ('hedgehogs') who attempt to explain the world in terms of one big idea, and writers ('foxes') who refuse to view the world in such simplistic terms.) Successful law students need to be foxy – they need to know about lots of different things. This is because the law has been, and will always be, influenced by lots of ideas coming from disciplines outside the law – such as philosophy, economics, psychology, political theory, history, even anthropology – that are taken into account by law-makers in their ongoing conversations about what sort of society we should live in. So if you truly want to understand why the law is the way it is, and to help shape the law in future by contributing to those ongoing conversations – you need to know something about those extra-legal disciplines.

Let me give you a couple of examples. First, you can't understand why competition law exists or why the law has been reformed since 1925 to make land more marketable without understanding something about economics, and how a society's economic health is affected by the existence of monopolies and by rules and regulations which make it hard to trade goods and services in the marketplace. Secondly, recent research in the field of what is called 'hedonic psychology' (basically, the study of human happiness) shows that human beings' levels of happiness are resilient. In other words, a human being who suffers an adverse event such as an injury soon recovers to the level of happiness that he or she was at before the adverse event. This research may have important implications for the law. For example, if our aim in imprisoning criminals is to reduce their levels of happiness, this research may show that we are imprisoning them for no good reason as their levels of happiness will, in the long run, be unaffected by their being imprisoned. Again: when the courts order that a defendant compensate a claimant for an injury that the claimant has suffered as a result of the defendant's actions, their aim is to give the claimant enough money to make up for the diminution in their quality of life that the claimant is supposed to have suffered as a result of being injured. However, it may be that there is no good reason for making the defendant pay compensation to the claimant as the claimant's level of well-being will eventually rebound back to his or her pre-injury levels whether or not he or she is compensated for that injury.

So someone who wants to be a successful law student needs to maintain an active interest in other disciplines, such as economics or political theory or psychology. How can you do this? Well, you are living at a very privileged time in human history where you can get a good grounding in the current state-of-the-art thinking in these disciplines very quickly and very cheaply. You only have to walk into a good bookshop and go to its social sciences section to find lots of very well-written and interesting books about all sorts of topics in politics, psychology, and economics. To give you a guide as to what sort of books you might like to look out for, go to my website: www. mcbridesguides.com. Click on 'Reading lists' and then click on 'Pre-U'. You'll then be supplied with a list of interesting books that you can buy on Amazon and that deal with issues in politics, philosophy, psychology, economics and thinking skills that are relevant to studying law. (You might also be able to get hold of any books that interest you very cheaply on the second-hand books site www.abebooks.com – but Amazon also gives you the option to buy second-hand copies of the books you want.) Or alternatively, just wander into a good bookstore and just flick through the books in the social sciences section and see what seems interesting to you. But the important thing is only to read books that interest you – anything that is boring is simply not going in, and you might as well chuck it and move on to something else.

● (9) Expressiveness

As I said in my first letter, law is fundamentally a conversation between different law-makers about what sort of society we should live in; and the study of law is a study of that conversation – where it has got to at the moment and where it might go in the future. So law is a talking game, and you have to be willing to express yourself if you are going to be able to get anywhere in that game. You have to be willing to express yourself in your written work, in discussing the law with your teachers and fellow students, and in confessing any difficulties you may be having with the work. If you find it hard to open up to other people about what you think then you are going to find it hard to succeed as a law student.

If you *are* someone who finds it hard to express yourself, then it's probably fear of what will happen if you do tell people what you think or what is going on with you that is holding you back. The only way to overcome any fear is to do the thing you are scared of, and see what happens. Almost always, nothing bad will happen and you'll see that you had nothing to be afraid of. And even if something bad does happen, you'll usually see that what happened wasn't *so* bad, and not bad enough to hold you back in future from doing the thing you were scared of doing. So if you do find it hard to express yourself, take a leap of faith, say what you want to say and see what happens. In almost every case, that's all you'll need to do to become more confident about expressing yourself in future.

● (10) Accuracy

Accuracy is vital to success as a law student. You cannot do well as a law student if you misstate the law where it is clear, or if you apply the law wrongly to a concrete situation, or if your arguments don't stand up to logical scrutiny. Being close to being right is nowhere near good enough in this game. For example, suppose that you are asked to determine whether someone is guilty of murder in the following situation:

> D sent his enemy, A, a parcel bomb, which was designed to explode and kill A when A opened it. Shortly after he posted the bomb, D repented of his plans and phoned the police to warn them of what he had done. He gave the police detailed instructions as to how to disarm the bomb. B, a member of the Bomb Squad, was given the job of defusing the bomb but in doing so he accidentally cut the wrong wire. As a result, the bomb blew up and B was killed.

You are told that a defendant will commit the crime of murder if his or her actions cause another to die and he or she performed those actions intending to kill someone or to cause someone to suffer serious bodily harm and he or she had no lawful justification or excuse for acting as he or she did.

You would be amazed (or I hope you would be amazed) at how many students your age are incapable of applying this definition accurately to the above situation. Either they say that D is not guilty of murder because at the time B was killed, he did not intend that anyone should die; when the definition makes it clear that it was his intentions at the time he did the thing which caused someone else to die which count. Or they say that D is not guilty of murder because when D sent the parcel bomb he intended to kill A, not B; when the definition makes it clear that all D has to have intended when he sent the parcel bomb was that *someone* should be killed or caused serious bodily harm. A student who applied the definition accurately to the above situation would realise that the only real issue here is whether D's sending of the parcel bomb *caused* B's death; if it did, then all the other elements in the definition are in place (D intended to kill someone when he sent the parcel bomb, and he had no lawful justification or excuse for doing so) for D to be found guilty of murder.

I think there must be something in the culture in which we live in nowadays that does not encourage the kind of accurate thinking that would allow *all* students your age to answer the above question correctly. Maybe schoolchildren are now led to think that getting close to being right *is* good enough, or are led to think that what is important is the way *they* react to a piece of writing rather than what the piece of writing *actually says*. Whatever the reason, it is very important that if you are going to be successful as a law student that you get rid of any bad habits that you have fallen into which mean that you fail to be clear, logical and rigorous in understanding the law or in discussing and applying the law. For example, it may be that you are very good at debating, and that has encouraged you to think that you would do very well as a law student. But in fact, debating encourages precisely the sort of inaccuracy that can be fatal to your prospects for success as a law student. This is because debating encourages you to dismiss other people's arguments with flip one-liners that put the other side down. But in law, you have to be much more careful in analysing other people's arguments and exposing precisely where they have gone wrong. Dismissing someone's arguments in a legal essay with a flip one-liner will result in your being dismissed yourself as a know-nothing dilettante. This isn't to say that if you are good at debating, you won't be a good law student – it just means you have to be careful to be on your guard against bad habits that your success in debating might have led you to acquire.

So how do you improve your abilities to be logical and rigorous? Doing logic puzzles – in particular Sudoku puzzles (easily available for free on the Internet: just Google 'Sudoku puzzles') – is very helpful. Also reading books on thinking skills (of the types you will find on the book list that I have posted for you on www.mcbridesguides.com) will give you some pointers as to common sorts of mental errors that you and other people might tend to fall into. Also reading beautifully reasoned books will help you think clearly and logically yourself. One book in particular I would recommend is Derek Parfit's *Reasons and Persons* (Oxford University Press, 1986) – a model of clear writing that everyone should seek to imitate. Other writers whose crystal clear prose should encourage you to think clearly and logically yourself are: (among law academics) Peter Birks, H.L.A Hart, Philip K. Howard, and Tony Weir; (among thinkers generally) Daniel Kahneman, Peter Kreeft, C.S. Lewis, Peter Singer, and David Stove; (among journalists) Nick Cohen, Theodore Dalrymple, Nick Davies, Ben Goldacre, Clive James, and Bernard Levin.

● (11) Flexibility

A successful law student will be *flexible* – he or she will be able to see both sides of an argument. Which is not to say that a successful law student will be incapable of coming to a conclusion as to which side of an argument is stronger – but he or she won't fall into the trap of thinking that only one side of the argument has any merit at all. Consider, for example, the following situation:

Peter and Mary are told that their newborn son Adam has a medical condition which may mean that he needs a bone marrow transplant a few years from now to save his life. Peter and Mary are both tested but unfortunately their bone marrow would not be suitable for Adam if the need arose for him to have a transplant. So they decide to have another child, in the hope that that child's bone marrow will match Adam's needs. After three years of trying, Mary gives birth to a daughter, Eve, whose bone marrow – it turns out – is a match for Adam's. Adam is now 12 and will die without a bone marrow transplant. But Eve is unwilling to undergo the operation, which is painful and difficult and will require a period of hospitalisation for her. There is no other suitable donor available. Should Peter and Mary be allowed to force Eve to have the operation to save Adam's life?

If your instinctive reaction is to say 'No – Eve has a right not to be made to undergo a medical operation', then think again. The question is *whether* Eve has such a right – and you cannot answer that question satisfactorily with the mere assertion that she *does* have such a right. Merely saying that Eve has a right not to be forced into giving up some of her bone marrow is a way of inflexibly closing one's mind down to the possibility that she might *not* have such a right.

So let's not close our minds – but instead consider the possibility that her parents should be allowed to force Eve to have this operation. A good starting point would be to consider whether there are any situations where it seems obvious that Eve's parents should be allowed to force her to have a medical operation. For example, what if Eve has a diseased tooth which needs to be extracted before it causes serious medical problems, but Eve is so scared of dentists she is refusing to visit one? It seems obvious in this situation that Eve's parents should be allowed to compel her to visit the dentist. But why? Well, in this situation it seems obvious that the operation would be in Eve's best interests.

This gives us some kind of intelligible basis for judging whether forcing Eve to have the bone marrow operation would be justifiable. We can ask whether the operation would be in Eve's best interests. A good law student with the ability to think flexibly will realise that things can be said on both sides of this issue. On the one hand, it would presumably not be in Eve's interests to lose her older brother, and all the benefits of his help and companionship. Moreover, it could prove psychologically damaging to Eve to have to live with the knowledge that she could have saved his life but chose not to. At the same time, it might not be in Eve's interests to be left with the feeling that her parents had no respect for her interests, and that they regarded her as simply a resource to be exploited when the time came that Adam needed what Eve had got. Moreover, the fact that Eve would have to go through the trauma of being physically forced to have the operation might count against our finding that it was in Eve's best interests to go through the operation. The question is finely balanced – but a good law student would realise that, and would not seek the refuge of the false certainty that a bold assertion about Eve's rights affords.

If you are someone who finds it hard to see both sides of an issue, you can easily expand this capacity by exposing yourself to alternative points of view. So if you tend to read *the Guardian*, try to read the *Daily Telegraph* as well. And if you don't read either, then start making a habit of reading the comments pages in both. Similarly, if you read *The Economist* or the *New Statesman,* also read the

Spectator or *Standpoint*. If you are reading a book which advances a particular point of view on some political or social or economic issue, take a note of whose views the book is opposing, and try to read something by the people whose views are being criticised and see what they have to say for themselves.

● (12) Judgment

It's not enough for a law student to be able to see both sides of a particular issue: a law student also has to be able to *judge* which side is stronger so as to form a view on that issue. The need for a law student to have good judgment crops up all over the place. For example, if you are taking notes – whether in a lecture or on materials you have been told to read – you have to be able to *discriminate* between what is important and what is not. In order to test your skills at doing this, consider the following passage, which is taken from Frederic Bastiat's pamphlet, *The Law* (published in 1850):

What is Law?

What, then, is law? It is the collective organization of the individual right to lawful defence.

Each of us has a natural right—from God—to defend his person, his liberty, and his property. These are the three basic requirements of life, and the preservation of any one of them is completely dependent upon the preservation of the other two. For what are our faculties but the extension of our individuality? And what is property but an extension of our faculties? If every person has the right to defend even by force—his person, his liberty, and his property, then it follows that a group of men have the right to organize and support a common force to protect these rights constantly. Thus the principle of collective right—its reason for existing, its lawfulness—is based on individual right. And the common force that protects this collective right cannot logically have any other purpose or any other mission than that for which it acts as a substitute. Thus, since an individual cannot lawfully use force against the person, liberty, or property of another individual, then the common force—for the same reason—cannot lawfully be used to destroy the person, liberty, or property of individuals or groups.

Such a perversion of force would be, in both cases, contrary to our premise. Force has been given to us to defend our own individual rights. Who will dare to say that force has been given to us to destroy the equal rights of our brothers? Since no individual acting separately can lawfully use force to destroy the rights of others, does it not logically follow that the same principle also applies to the common force that is nothing more than the organized combination of the individual forces?

If this is true, then nothing can be more evident than this: The law is the organization of the natural right of lawful defence. It is the substitution of a common force for individual forces. And this common force is to do only what the individual forces have a natural and lawful right to do: to protect persons, liberties, and properties; to maintain the right of each, and to cause justice to reign over us all.

A Just and Enduring Government

If a nation were founded on this basis, it seems to me that order would prevail among the people, in thought as well as in deed. It seems to me that such a nation would have the most simple, easy to accept, economical, limited, non-oppressive, just, and enduring government imaginable—whatever its political form might be.

Under such an administration, everyone would understand that he possessed all the privileges as well as all the responsibilities of his existence. No one would have any argument with government, provided that his person was respected, his labor was free, and the fruits of his labor were protected against all unjust attack. When successful, we would not have to thank the state for our success. And, conversely, when unsuccessful, we would no more think of blaming the state for our misfortune than would the farmers blame the state because of hail or frost. The state would be felt only by the invaluable blessings of safety provided by this concept of government.

It can be further stated that, thanks to the non-intervention of the state in private affairs, our wants and their satisfactions would develop themselves in a logical manner. We would not see poor families seeking literary instruction before they have bread. We would not see cities populated at the expense of rural districts, nor rural districts at the expense of cities. We would not see the great displacements of capital, labour, and population that are caused by legislative decisions.

The sources of our existence are made uncertain and precarious by these state-created displacements. And, furthermore, these acts burden the government with increased responsibilities.

>

The Complete Perversion of the Law

But, unfortunately, law by no means confines itself to its proper functions. And when it has exceeded its proper functions, it has not done so merely in some inconsequential and debatable matters. The law has gone further than this; it has acted in direct opposition to its own purpose. The law has been used to destroy its own objective: It has been applied to annihilating the justice that it was supposed to maintain; to limiting and destroying rights which its real purpose was to respect. The law has placed the collective force at the disposal of the unscrupulous who wish, without risk, to exploit the person, liberty, and property of others. It has converted plunder into a right, in order to protect plunder. And it has converted lawful defence into a crime, in order to punish lawful defence.

How has this perversion of the law been accomplished? And what have been the results?

The law has been perverted by the influence of two entirely different causes: stupid greed and false philanthropy. Let us speak of the first.

A Fatal Tendency of Mankind

Self-preservation and self-development are common aspirations among all people. And if everyone enjoyed the unrestricted use of his faculties and the free disposition of the fruits of his labor, social progress would be ceaseless, uninterrupted, and unfailing.

But there is also another tendency that is common among people. When they can, they wish to live and prosper at the expense of others. This is no rash accusation. Nor does it come from a gloomy and uncharitable spirit. The annals of history bear witness to the truth of it: the incessant wars, mass migrations, religious persecutions, universal slavery, dishonesty in commerce, and monopolies. This fatal desire has its origin in the very nature of man—in that primitive, universal, and insuppressible instinct that impels him to satisfy his desires with the least possible pain.

Property and Plunder

Man can live and satisfy his wants only by ceaseless labor; by the ceaseless application of his faculties to natural resources. This process is the origin of property.

But it is also true that a man may live and satisfy his wants by seizing and consuming the products of the labour of others. This process is the origin of plunder.

Now since man is naturally inclined to avoid pain—and since labor is pain in itself—it follows that men will resort to plunder whenever plunder is easier than work. History shows this quite clearly. And under these conditions, neither religion nor morality can stop it.

When, then, does plunder stop? It stops when it becomes more painful and more dangerous than labor.

It is evident, then, that the proper purpose of law is to use the power of its collective force to stop this fatal tendency to plunder instead of to work. All the measures of the law should protect property and punish plunder.

But, generally, the law is made by one man or one class of men. And since law cannot operate without the sanction and support of a dominating force, this force must be entrusted to those who make the laws.

This fact, combined with the fatal tendency that exists in the heart of man to satisfy his wants with the least possible effort, explains the almost universal perversion of the law. Thus it is easy to understand how law, instead of checking injustice, becomes the invincible weapon of injustice. It is easy to understand why the law is used by the legislator to destroy in varying degrees among the rest of the people, their personal independence by slavery, their liberty by oppression, and their property by plunder. This is done for the benefit of the person who makes the law, and in proportion to the power that he holds.

This passage is about 1,300 words long. Try to summarise it in about 100 words – and then compare your summary with mine, at the end of this letter. If you find this exercise difficult, or end up producing a summary that is very different from mine, don't worry about it. Schools seem to have given up on the idea of helping students your age acquire the skill of summarising long passages. But this is an essential skill that law students need to have, and one you can acquire through practice. Just take any article from a serious newspaper or magazine and try to reduce it to 10 per cent of its length. With enough practice, you will soon acquire a facility for discriminating between what is important and what is not important.

This facility is only one side of the general quality of good judgment that law students need to be successful. Another dimension of having good judgment is being blessed with practical wisdom – the ability to know what is the right thing to do when faced with a variety of options. For example, suppose that you are given an essay to do that asks you to suggest some reforms to the law on murder. You have 96 lines – what you could expect to write in the time available – to play with. What would it be best to do: (1) write an essay suggesting 16 reforms, devoting 6 lines to each; (2) write an essay suggesting 8 reforms, devoting 12 lines to each; (3) write an essay suggesting 3 reforms, devoting 32 lines to each?

Other things being equal, which essay is likely to impress the examiner the most? The answer is (3). There is no way that you will be able to make out a convincing case for reforming an aspect of the law on murder in 6 or 12 lines – so essays (1) and (2) are going to strike the examiner as being lightweight. Only essay (3) has any chance of getting a high mark from the examiner. A law student who is blessed with practical wisdom will realise this and confine him or herself to suggesting three reforms and spend quite a lot of time on each one. A law student who is not so blessed may well decide to adopt a 'scattergun' approach, suggesting lots of reforms, hoping that the examiner will be amazed by his thoroughgoing critique of the law of murder. Sadly, the examiner will probably *not* be impressed.

● Summary

So – those are the 12 qualities I think a law student needs to be successful. You can see why really good law students are so special: they have a combination of skills which doesn't naturally present in most people. However, most of these skills can be worked on and developed. Hence my point at the start of this letter that a major reason why it is getting harder to find students who will do very well studying law is that students your age simply don't know what sort of skills they will need if they want to study law and so don't do enough to help develop those skills. Now that you do know what sort of skills are required, if you do want to study law at university, then work on developing any of the skills that you currently think you are weak on.

One last thing – I'm sending you something called a 'Proust Questionnaire'.[1] It's a set of questions about you, and who you are. (The questionnaire is known as a 'Proust Questionnaire' because the writer Marcel Proust liked to fill

---

[1] See Appendix A.

such questionnaires out. Every issue of *Vanity Fair* now carries a version of a Proust Questionnaire with a celebrity.) I *absolutely, definitely* don't want to know what your answers to these questions are – they are just for you, no one else. I'm enclosing it so as to help you because I think a lot of young people nowadays (maybe a lot of old people as well!) don't have much clue about what's important to them, and what they are good at, and what they want to do. It's important that you do get in touch with what sort of person you are, so that you'll be in a better position to assess whether or not you have the skills needed to be a good law student, and more importantly whether you have the inclination to do what you need to do to develop the skills required to be a good law student. Doing the enclosed questionnaire is one way of finding out a bit more about yourself, thereby allowing you to get a better idea of whether law is the right subject for you.

All best wishes,

Nick

P.S. Here is my summary of the passage from Bastiat's *The Law*:

> The law exists to protect people's rights to life, liberty and the enjoyment of their property. If the law simply concerned itself with protecting people's rights, then no one would have any cause to blame the state for his misfortunes, and people would be free to satisfy their needs without any interference from the government. Unfortunately, the law has to be made and enforced by men, and because men are naturally greedy, those who are in charge of the law abuse it to deprive other people of their rights. (89 words)

PART 2

Preparing to Study Law

Arguing Effectively (1): Logical Arguments

○ From: Nicholas J. McBride [dearnick@pearson.com]
○ To: Brown, Alex
○ Subject: Arguing Effectively (1): Logical Arguments

Hi Alex,

As I've said before, probably the most important – and valuable – thing you'll have to do as a law student is learn how to argue effectively. Given that you've now decided you want to study law at university, I thought you might appreciate a few pointers on how to make good, effective, arguments of your own – and in so doing show you how to make up your mind whether an argument that is being made to you is any good or not. This won't just come in useful for your legal studies – it's also essential that you be able to argue effectively if you are applying to a university that interviews applicants before deciding whether to offer them a place.

There are two basic kinds of argument that you'll come across in doing your law degree, and in life generally. We can call them *logical arguments* (otherwise known as arguments by *deduction*) and *speculative arguments* (otherwise known as arguments by *induction*). I'll talk about speculative arguments in another letter, but in this letter I'll just concentrate on logical arguments. These take the following kind of form:

(1) All children like chocolate.

(2) Max is a child.

Therefore,

(3) Max likes chocolate.

Steps (1) and (2) in the argument are called the *premises* of the argument. Step (3) is called the *conclusion*. If (1) and (2) are correct, and (3) logically follows from (1) and (2), then we *have* to accept that (3) is correct – if we don't, we're just plain stupid, or crazy. An example of a logical argument that a lawyer might make goes as follows:

(1) The law says that A's promise to B is legally binding if B gives A something in return for that promise.

(2) Helen promised to mow Peter's lawn if Peter bought her a drink, and he did so.

Therefore,

(3) Helen is legally required to mow Peter's lawn.

I'll now make five points about logical arguments that you should always bear in mind either in making a logical argument of your own, or in making up your mind whether a logical argument that someone else has made to you is any good or not.

● Five points about logical arguments

(1) Circularity

The very first point about making a logical argument is that you have to ensure that it is not *circular*. A circular argument assumes in one or more of its premises the truth of its conclusion. A circular argument fails because it doesn't go anywhere: it just asserts that the conclusion is true without having done anything to establish that it is true. So a circular argument never even gets off the launch pad. Here's an argument against capital punishment that is very obviously circular:

> (1)   The State should not execute criminals.
>
>   Therefore,
>
> (2)   We should not have capital punishment.

(1) and (2) are basically identical statements, dressed up in different words. So (1) does not establish that (2) is true – it just assumes that (2) is true. Here's a more subtle form of circular argument:

> (1)   Killing is always wrong.
>
>   Therefore,
>
> (2)   We should not have capital punishment.

(1) and (2) are not identical – but the argument is still circular because (1) assumes that (2) is true. If capital punishment were morally justified, then killing would not always be wrong. So by saying 'Killing is always wrong' the person making the above argument is already assuming that 'We should not have capital punishment'. So he is really just asserting, rather than arguing, that 'We should not have capital punishment'.

This second form of circularity sometimes creeps into lawyers' arguments. Consider, for example, the case where someone pays Norman £1,000 to beat up Emily. It is uncontroversial that after Norman beats up Emily, he will be held liable to compensate Emily for her injuries. But can Emily sue Norman for the gain he has made from beating her up – the £1,000? Those in favour of what is called 'restitution for wrongs' often argue that Emily should be able to sue Norman for this gain by saying:

> (1)   No man should be allowed to profit from his wrong.
>
>   Therefore,
>
> (2)   Emily should be allowed to sue Norman for the gain that he has made by beating her up.

But this is circular. (1) assumes the truth of (2). If it would be wrong to allow Emily to sue Norman for the gain he has made, then it is not true that

'No man should be allowed to profit from his wrong' – Norman should be allowed to profit from his wrong. So by saying (1), the person making the above argument is simply assuming that (2) is true rather than making a serious argument in favour of (2) being true.

You'll notice that the above three circular arguments all just have one premise and then leap straight to a conclusion. This is a sure sign that something has gone wrong. A logical argument that works has at least *two* premises which *work together* to reach a conclusion. If a logical argument that you are making or looking at has only one premise then there is something wrong with it – and the problem will almost always be that the argument is circular.

(2) You can't derive an 'ought' from an 'is'

Consider this argument in favour of capital punishment:

> (1) Reintroducing the death penalty for murder would reduce the number of murders in this country.
>
> Therefore,
>
> (2) We should reintroduce the death penalty for murder.

Again, this argument only has one premise before leaping straight to a conclusion, so there is something wrong with it. But this time the problem is not circularity – premise (1) does not assume the truth of conclusion (2). The problem is that the person making this argument is trying to derive an 'ought' ('We *should* reintroduce the death penalty for murder') from an 'is' ('Reintroducing the death penalty for murder *would* reduce the number of killings in this country'). This is impossible: you cannot make a value judgment about what should or should not happen based purely on a bare statement of fact about what is or is not or would be or would not be or was or was not the case. What has gone wrong with the above argument is that it is too compressed. We need to introduce a value statement into the premises of the argument to make it work.

> (1) Reintroducing the death penalty for murder would reduce the murder rate in this country.
>
> (2) We should do everything possible to reduce the murder rate.

Therefore,

(3) We should reintroduce the death penalty for murder.

Because there is now a 'should' in the premises of the argument, it is now legitimate to have a 'should' in the argument's conclusion.

This basic principle – that you cannot derive an 'ought' from an 'is' – is not always observed as well as it should be by lawyers. For example, let's go back to the case of Norman and Emily. Should Emily be allowed to sue Norman for what are called 'exemplary damages' – damages designed to punish Norman for what he did to Emily? Those who say 'no' often argue:

(1) The function of an award of damages to the victim of a wrong is to compensate the victim for the losses she has suffered as a result of that wrong.

(2) Exemplary damages are punitive rather than compensatory in nature.

Therefore,

(3) Emily should not be allowed to sue Norman for exemplary damages.

Here, we are deriving an 'ought' ('Emily *should not* be allowed to sue . . .') from two 'is's ('The function of an award of damages . . . is . . .'; 'Exemplary damages *are* . . .') – not allowed! The above argument is a particularly bad one because it is impossible to save it. If we reformulate it to introduce a 'should' statement into the premises, as follows . . .

(1) The function of an award of damages to the victim of a wrong should be to compensate the victim for the losses she has suffered as a result of that wrong.

(2) Exemplary damages are punitive rather than compensatory in nature.

Therefore,

(3) Emily should not be allowed to sue Norman for exemplary damages.

. . . can you see what problem the argument now suffers from? Yes – it's now circular. The argument's first premise assumes that the argument's conclusion is true. If Emily should be allowed to sue for exemplary damages, then it can't be true that the function of an award of damages to someone like Emily should just be to compensate her for the losses that she has suffered. So by saying (1), the person making this argument is assuming that (3) is true rather than arguing that (3) is true.

(3) In a logical argument, the conclusion must follow logically from its premises

Consider the following argument for capital punishment:

> (1) We should reintroduce the death penalty for murder if doing so would reduce the number of murders in this country.
>
> (2) Studies have shown that reintroducing the death penalty would have no effect on the murder rate in this country.
>
> Therefore,
>
> (3) We should reintroduce the death penalty for murder.

It is pretty obvious what is wrong with this argument: its premises do not support its conclusion. If you are being logical, you simply cannot conclude on the basis of premises (1) and (2) that we should reintroduce the death penalty for murder. You should, instead, conclude that there is no case (so far as you know) for reintroducing the death penalty for murder.

So – when you are making a logical argument, make sure that your conclusion follows logically from its premises. If you don't do this, your argument isn't logical at all – it's illogical, and doesn't give anyone any reason to accept your conclusion.

One form of illogical argument that you have to be particularly on your guard against making is one which suffers from the *post hoc ergo propter hoc* ('after this, therefore because of this') fallacy – that is, the fallacy of thinking that because B happened *after* A, that B happened *because* of A. This argument – which, I repeat, you should be on your guard *against* making – takes the form:

(1) A happened.

(2) After A happened, B happened.

Therefore,

(3) B happened because A happened.

Even though B happened after A happened, it does not follow logically that B happened because A happened – B could have happened for any number of reasons, other than A's happening. A concrete example of an argument that suffers from the *post hoc ergo propter hoc* fallacy goes as follows:

(1) The death penalty for murder was abolished in 1965.

(2) After 1965, the murder rate rocketed, with more than double the murders per 100,000 of the population being committed in 2004 as compared with the rate in 1965.

Therefore,

(3) The murder rate more than doubled between 1965 and 2004 because the death penalty for murder was abolished in 1965.

Well, maybe (3) is true – but it certainly does not follow logically from (1) and (2). There could be an *alternative explanation* of why (2) happened: maybe the social trends that resulted in the death penalty being abolished in 1965 also resulted in the murder rate doubling between 1965 and 2004.

Another very common type of illogical argument is an argument that suffers from *tunnel vision*. A very good example of this kind of argument is provided by Henry Hazlitt's excellent book, *Economics in One Lesson,* which I recommend to anyone who wants an education in how to argue effectively. The book begins with a story: a baker's window has been broken by a teenager who has hurled a brick through it. A crowd gathers and concludes that actually the breaking of the window is a good thing. The baker will now have to pay a glazier to install a new window, thus keeping the glazier in business, and the glazier will in turn spend the money he has earned from the baker, thus keeping a variety of people in business, and they in turn will spend the money they have earned from the glazier, thus keeping yet more people in business etc., etc. So, the argument goes:

(1) It is good for people to be employed.

(2) The economic activity sparked by the breaking of the window will keep a number of different people in business.

Therefore,

(3) It was a good thing the window was broken.

This argument is illogical because it suffers from tunnel vision. What it leaves out of the picture is what the baker would have done with the money that he is now going to pay the glazier to replace his window. In Hazlitt's example, the baker would have used that money to pay the tailor to make a suit for him. Using the money to pay the tailor to make a suit would have sparked an *equal* amount of economic activity as that which will be sparked by paying the glazier to mend the window, thus keeping as many people in business as will be kept in business when the glazier is paid to mend the window. So had the window not been broken, the community as a whole would have had an intact window *plus* a new suit *plus* a certain amount of economic activity sparked by the buying of the new suit. But as it is – now that the window has been broken – the community as a whole will still have an intact window (once it has been mended by the glazier) *plus* a certain amount of economic activity sparked by the baker's paying to have the window mended *but it will have no new suit*. It follows that the breaking of the window has made the community worse off as a whole – so (3) is not true: it was *not* a good thing the window was broken. The crowd cannot see that because it suffers from tunnel vision. All it can see is the broken window and the economic activity that will be sparked by its replacement. It does not have the vision or imagination to see the new suit that would have been made had the window never been broken and the economic activity that would have been sparked by that new suit's being made.

Here is an argument *against* capital punishment that is illogical because it suffers from tunnel vision:

(1) It is a bad thing for innocent people to die.

(2) If we reintroduce the death penalty for murder, there is a danger that innocent people will be convicted of murder and be executed as a result.

Therefore,

(3) We should not reintroduce the death penalty for murder.

This is illogical: even though (1) and (2) are perfectly true, (3) does not follow from (1) and (2). The problem is that the person making this argument is simply focusing on the innocent people who might be killed by the *State* if the death penalty is reintroduced. What he is overlooking is that reintroducing the death penalty for murder might cut the murder rate and as a result save a lot of innocent people's lives. In order to restore some logic to the above argument against capital punishment, we need to get rid of the blinkers and take into account the possibility that innocent people's lives might be saved by reintroducing the death penalty for murder. There are two ways of doing this. We could argue . . .

(1) It is a bad thing for innocent people to die.

(2) If we reintroduce the death penalty for murder, there is a danger that innocent people will be convicted of murder and be executed as a result.

(3) There is also a possibility that reintroducing the death penalty for murder will reduce the murder rate and save innocent people's lives.

(4) The number of people who are likely to be wrongfully executed if we reintroduce the death penalty for murder exceeds the number of people who are likely to escape being murdered if we reintroduce the death penalty for murder.

Therefore,

(5) We should not reintroduce the death penalty for murder.

. . . or we could argue, more boldly:

(1) It is better that an unlimited number of innocent people be murdered than that one innocent person be executed by the State.

(2) If we reintroduce the death penalty for murder, there is a danger that an innocent person will be convicted of murder and executed by the State.

Therefore,

(3) We should not reintroduce the death penalty for murder, and this is so no matter how many innocent people's lives might be saved by doing so.

(4) A logical argument that is based on a false premise is worthless

Both of the arguments that have just been made against reintroducing capital punishment are perfectly logical. But the fact that an argument is logical does not mean we should accept it. If a logical argument is based on a false premise, it must be rejected. A logical argument that is based on a false premise doesn't give us any reason to accept its conclusion. In contrast, if the premises of a logical argument are correct (and, of course, the argument's conclusion logically follows from those premises) then that argument must be accepted – we would be crazy or stupid not to accept it. Consider, for example, the logical argument set out at the beginning of this letter:

(1) All children like chocolate.

(2) Max is a child.

Therefore,

(3) Max likes chocolate.

If (1) and (2) are true, then, we have to accept that (3) is true (because (3) follows logically from (1) and (2)) – otherwise we're just stupid or crazy. But if either (1) or (2) is not true, then this argument gives us no reason at all to think that Max likes chocolate. If it's the case that not all children like chocolate, or it's the case that Max is 45 years old, then the argument completely collapses and should be rejected. Of course, it may still be the case that (3) is true – Max may actually like chocolate. But the point is that if either (1) or (2) is not true, the above argument gives us no reason to think that Max likes chocolate.

Let's look again at one of the arguments made above against capital punishment:

(1) It is a bad thing for innocent people to die.

(2) If we reintroduce the death penalty for murder, there is a danger that innocent people will be convicted of murder and be executed as a result.

(3) There is also a possibility that reintroducing the death penalty for murder will reduce the murder rate and save innocent people's lives.

(4) The number of people who are likely to be wrongfully executed if we reintroduce the death penalty for murder exceeds the number of people who are likely to escape being murdered if we reintroduce the death penalty for murder.

Therefore,

(5) We should not reintroduce the death penalty for murder.

This argument is perfectly logical, so whether we accept its conclusion depends on whether its premises are correct. Premises (1) – (3) seem perfectly reasonable. So whether we should accept this argument or not all depends on whether premise (4) is correct. Unfortunately, premise (4) does not seem to be correct. In the UK, 636 people were murdered in 2010–11. It's not hard to imagine that, say, 30 of those 636 people would not have been killed if we still had the death penalty for murder. But it is hard to imagine that if we still had the death penalty for murder, in 2010–11 there would have been more than 30 wrongful convictions for murder resulting in the convicted being executed. So the above argument against capital punishment should be rejected – it rests on a false premise, and therefore doesn't give us any reason to think that we should not reintroduce the death penalty for murder.

Two common sources of false premises that you should always be on the lookout for when making your own logical arguments, or examining other people's, are wishful thinking and – again – tunnel vision. Consider the following argument that is often made for saying that animals do not have rights:

(1) You can only have rights if you have responsibilities at the same time.

(2) Animals do not have any responsibilities (for example, a responsibility not to kick their owner).

Therefore,

(3) Animals do not have rights.

(1) is obviously incorrect. If (1) were correct then babies or patients in a coma would not have rights either, and obviously they do. So why do people keep on saying (1)? Either they say it because they do not wish to admit that animals have rights, and so they wish (1) were true – the idea being that if (1) were true, then that would make it easy for them to deny that animals have rights. Or they say (1) because they suffer from tunnel vision – they don't have the vision or imagination to realise that (1) cannot be true because if it were, then babies or patients in a coma would not have rights either.

Here's another example of tunnel vision producing a false premise. This time the argument is meant to establish that it is okay sometimes to lie to someone else. The argument begins by supposing that we are in Nazi Germany. A woman runs into your house and says, 'I'm a Jew on the run – some Nazi soldiers are a couple of minutes behind me: if they catch me, they will kill me. Please hide me.' You usher the woman into your cellar. The soldiers bang on your door two minutes later and ask you, 'We are looking for an escaped prisoner who would have come by here – do you know where she is?' The argument goes as follows:

(1) Either you can tell the soldiers the truth that the woman is hiding in your cellar with the result that they will kill her or you can save the woman's life by lying to the soldiers, telling them that you saw someone running away down the road a couple of minutes earlier.

(2) It would be unacceptable to take the first option, given the consequences of doing so.

Therefore,

(3) You should lie to the soldiers.

But (1) is not true. Anyone not suffering from tunnel vision would realise that there are other options available to you in this situation. You could refuse to answer. Or you could give an answer which is literally true, 'Yes – a woman did come by here two minutes ago looking for help. She can't be that far away now.' Or you could remonstrate with the soldiers, thereby changing the subject and possibly doing some positive good at the same time, 'Yes – I saw a woman come by here a couple of minutes ago. You should be ashamed of yourselves, hunting down a poor girl like that – what would your mothers think if they knew?' So this particular argument in favour of establishing that it is acceptable under certain circumstances to lie to someone else simply does not work.

(5) Logical arguments that culminate in an 'ought' are often inconclusive

Consider another one of the arguments against capital punishment that was made above:

(1) It is better that an unlimited number of innocent people be murdered than that one innocent person be executed by the State.

(2) If we reintroduce the death penalty for murder, there is a danger that an innocent person will be convicted of murder and executed by the State.

Therefore,

(3) We should not reintroduce the death penalty for murder, and this is so no matter how many innocent people's lives might be saved by doing so.

Again, this argument is perfectly logical, so whether we accept its conclusion or not depends on whether its premises are correct. (2) is obviously true, so the crucial premise is (1). If (1) is true, then we should not reintroduce the death penalty for murder. So is (1) true?

Unfortunately, it's difficult to tell for certain. One school of thought holds that it is better to allow other people's rights to be violated than it is to violate someone else's rights oneself. On this view, (1) is true: even if thousands of lives could be saved by reintroducing the death penalty for murder it would still be wrong to reintroduce it if doing so would result in the State violating someone's rights sometime in the future. (On the same view, it would be wrong to torture an innocent person to discover where terrorists are planning to explode a nuclear bomb, even though doing so would prevent millions of people being murdered.)

However, there is another school of thought that says we should judge what to do by weighing up the costs and benefits of the consequences of our actions. On this view, (1) is obviously not true: if reintroducing the death penalty for murder would do more good than harm then it is obviously better to reintroduce the death penalty. Unfortunately, there is no rational way to determine which view is correct. No logical argument can be made that would show us that the deontological view is correct and the consequentialist view wrong, or that the opposite is true. So we have no way of determining for certain whether (1) is true. It follows that this particular argument against capital punishment must be labelled 'inconclusive'. It might be wrong or it might be right: we just don't know for certain.

This will often be the case with logical arguments that culminate in an 'ought' statement (here, 'We should not reintroduce the death penalty for murder . . .'). Because you can't derive an 'ought' from an 'is', logical arguments that conclude by saying that we should or should not do something will always have, as part of their premises, some kind of value judgment or 'should' statement. And – as we just saw– it's often very difficult to tell for certain whether that value judgment or 'should' statement is correct. So logical arguments that conclude by saying that we should or should not do something will often be inconclusive: we just won't know for certain whether we should accept them or not. But you shouldn't conclude from this that making logical arguments that culminate in an 'ought' statement is a waste of time.

First, there are some value judgments or 'should' statements that we know for certain are correct and can provide the basis for making conclusive logical arguments in favour of a particular 'ought' statement. It is wrong to stub out cigarettes on little babies. It is wrong to kill people for kicks or because of their political views. It is good to feed someone who is starving. We should be kind as often as possible. We know these things for certain and can sometimes use this knowledge to build conclusive arguments about what we should and should not do.

Secondly, making an inconclusive logical argument in favour of a particular 'ought' statement can be useful because doing so can help people make up their mind whether or not they accept that that 'ought' statement is true, and that in turn can influence their decisions about what to do or who to vote for in an election. So, for example, suppose you establish that the only logical argument that can be made against the reintroduction of the death penalty for murder is one which rests on the premise 'It is better that an unlimited number of innocent people be murdered than that one innocent person be executed by the State'. If this is the case, then most people will probably conclude – rightly or wrongly (we really can't tell) – that there is no good reason why we should not reintroduce the death penalty for murder and give their support to a political party that campaigns for the reinstatement of capital punishment.

● Types of logical argument

I've now said enough to allow you to ensure that any logical arguments you make in future will stand up to scrutiny, and to help you detect any flaws in a logical argument that is being made to you. But before I sign off, I'll just point out four very common types of logical argument that you may want to use in the future when trying to establish a particular point.

(1) 'Kill all the alternatives' arguments

This sort of argument goes as follows:

> (1) Either A or B or C is true.
>
> (2) Neither A nor B is true.
>
> Therefore,
>
> (3) C must be true.

This sort of argument underlay Sherlock Holmes' principle (as expressed in Arthur Conan Doyle's novel *The Sign of Four*) that 'Once you have eliminated the impossible, whatever remains, however improbable, must be the truth.' The Professor in C.S. Lewis' *The Lion, The Witch and the Wardrobe* used a 'kill all the alternatives' argument to establish that Lucy was telling the truth when she said that she had entered a magical world through the back of a wardrobe in the Professor's house:

> (1) Either Lucy is telling the truth, or she is lying, or she is mad.
>
> (2) We know that Lucy isn't a liar, and that she is not mad.
>
> Therefore,
>
> (3) Lucy must be telling the truth.

When you are examining whether a 'kill all the alternatives' argument stands up, be particularly on the lookout to see whether the first premise (which will be along the lines of 'Either A or B or C is true') suffers from tunnel vision – is there some other possibility that may *also* be true in this situation so as to make it possible that A and B and C may *all* be untrue? Is it possible that Lucy is not lying, and that she is not mad – but that she is not telling the truth either? Maybe the fur coats stored in the wardrobe give off fumes that overcame Lucy and caused her to go into a trance where she dreamed that she was in a magical world. The fact that this is perfectly possible destroys the Professor's argument. It has to be adjusted so that it goes as follows:

> (1) Either Lucy is telling the truth, or she is lying, or she is mad, or something happened to Lucy in the wardrobe to make her think (incorrectly) that she was in a magical world.
>
> (2) We know that Lucy isn't a liar, and that she is not mad.
>
> Therefore,
>
> (3) Either Lucy is telling the truth, or something happened to Lucy in the wardrobe to make her think (incorrectly) that she was in a magical world.

The Professor's argument no longer goes all the way to establish that Lucy must be telling the truth. For it to go that far, the only remaining alternative – that something happened to Lucy in the wardrobe to make her think (incorrectly) that she was in a magical world – has to be killed off.

(2) Arguments from contradiction

The Professor could have killed off this remaining alternative through another common kind of logical argument, which is an argument from contradiction. This argument goes as follows:

(1) For A to be true, B would also have to be true.

(2) But we know B is not true.

Therefore,

(3) A is not true.

So had anyone countered the Professor's first argument for thinking Lucy must have been telling the truth with the objection, 'But it's possible that when she went into the wardrobe she was overcome by fumes which caused her to hallucinate and think she was in a magical land', the Professor could have argued back:

(1) For that to be true, it would also have to be the case that she stayed long enough in the wardrobe to hallucinate all the experiences she said she had after she entered into the wardrobe.

(2) But we know she did not stay long enough in the wardrobe for that to happen – she came out of the wardrobe a few seconds after she entered into it.

Therefore,

(3) We cannot put what happened to Lucy down to a chemically induced trance.

When someone makes an argument from contradiction to you, again be particularly on the lookout to check that the first premise ('For A to be true, B would also have to be true') is correct: Is it really the case that B has also to be true for A to be true?

(3) Cost-benefit arguments

An extremely common form of logical argument is a cost-benefit argument. An example is:

(1)   We should do *x* if the benefits of doing *x* outweigh the costs.

(2)   The benefits of doing *x* outweigh the costs.

   Therefore,

(3)   We should do *x*.

In examining this argument, test whether its premises are correct. If doing *x* would violate someone's rights, then it would still be wrong to do *x* even if the benefits of doing *x* outweighed the costs: it cannot be right to sacrifice people for the greater good. So if doing *x* would violate someone's rights then (1) will not be correct.

In examining whether (2) is correct, watch out for two things. First of all, watch out for *sentimentalism*. An example of sentimentalism is when someone argues in favour of some security measure (such as ID cards) by saying 'If it just saves one life, it's worth it.' No, it's not. If life were that infinitely precious, then we would ban cars – doing so would save thousands of lives each year, and this saving of life would more than offset the colossal sacrifice in wealth and happiness that banning cars would involve.

The second thing you need to look out for is the problem of *incommensurability*. Two things are incommensurable if there is no common standard of measurement that we can use to compare the two. For example, suppose that it is proposed that we should raise taxes to fund a nationwide programme of home care for the mentally ill. The cost of doing this would be to retard economic growth by 0.5% a year. The benefit of doing this would be that the healthcare system in this country would treat the mentally ill with a greater level of respect and dignity than is currently possible. These two things cannot be weighed against each other: they are so completely different that there is no common standard of measurement that would allow us to say that the costs of raising taxes to fund this healthcare programme outweigh the benefits, or vice versa. So it's not possible to resolve the question of whether taxes should be raised to fund this programme through a cost-benefit argument. We simply have to *choose* which of these things – economic growth, and treating the mentally ill with dignity and showing them some respect – we value more.

(4) Arguments from analogy

Finally, a big favourite with lawyers are arguments from analogy. These kinds of arguments go as follows:

(1) In situation A, B is true.

(2) Situation C is identical to situation A in all material respects.
Therefore,

(3) In situation C, B is true.

So, for example, one of the most basic arguments that lawyers learn to make is the following argument from analogy:

(1) In case A, a previous court awarded damages to the claimant.

(2) The case here is identical to case A in all material respects.

(3) Like cases should be decided alike.
Therefore,

(4) In this situation, the court should award damages to the claimant in this case, my client.

In making up your mind whether an argument from analogy is correct or not, the thing to look at is whether the second premise ('This situation is identical to the first situation in all material respects') is true – is it really true that there is no material difference between the situation at hand and the situation we initially considered? For example, here is a very famous argument in favour of the view that pregnant women have a right to have an abortion, based on the philosopher Judith Jarvis Thomson's article 'A defense of abortion', published in 1971, in the first volume of the journal *Philosophy and Public Affairs*.

Consider the situation where Samantha has got extremely drunk one night, and has ended up in hospital. The doctors treating Samantha realise that she has the same blood type as Frederick, a world-famous violinist who is in the same hospital because he is in dire need of a kidney transplant. The doctors realise they have a way of saving Frederick's life. They insert a tube into the main artery leading away from Frederick's heart, and insert the other end of the tube into the renal artery leading into one of Samantha's kidneys. They then insert a tube into the renal vein leading away from the same kidney and pump the blood coming through that tube into Frederick's body. As a result, Frederick's blood is 'cleaned' by Samantha's kidney, thus removing the need for him to have an immediate kidney transplant. When Samantha wakes up, she asks why she is hooked up to the patient in the next bed in this way, and her doctors tell her, 'We've done this so he can survive until we get him a new kidney.' When Samantha protests, the doctors say, 'Look – if we disconnect you, he'll die, and he doesn't deserve that. Everyone has a right to live. Anyway, you can't complain – if you hadn't got so drunk last night, you wouldn't be in this position.' When Samantha asks how long she has to wait for Frederick to have a kidney transplant, the doctors say, 'Given his position on the waiting list, we think you'll have to stay like this for nine months.'

Now let's assume that in this situation, Samantha has a right to tell the doctors to get lost and disconnect her from Frederick, whatever the consequences for Frederick. If we accept that, then what about the case where Mandy gets extremely drunk one night, has unprotected sex, and discovers a few days later that she is pregnant? Does she have a right to have an abortion? The argument from analogy in favour of saying that she does goes as follows:

(1) Samantha has a right to be disconnected from Frederick, even though Frederick will die as a result.

(2) Mandy's case is identical to Samantha's in all material respects – after one drunken night, Mandy has discovered that someone else's life (the life of the foetus inside her) is dependent on her not disconnecting herself from that someone else (the foetus inside her), and that if she does not disconnect herself from that someone else, she will have to remain connected to that someone else for nine months.

Therefore,

(3) Mandy has a right to disconnect herself from the foetus inside her – that is, Mandy has a right to have an abortion.

Does this argument work? The crucial step in the argument is premise (2) – is Mandy's case really identical to Samantha's in all material respects? I'll leave you to think about that and tell you what I think in my next letter.

Be in touch soon,

Nick

Arguing Effectively (2): Speculative Arguments

- From: Nicholas J. McBride [dearnick@pearson.com]
- To: Brown, Alex
- Subject: Arguing Effectively (2): Speculative Arguments

Hey Alex,

As promised, here's another letter on arguing effectively. Just to finish up the point I left the last letter on, I don't think the argument from analogy presented at the end of that letter works to establish that Mandy has a right to an abortion. There is one big difference between Samantha's case and Mandy's case. In Samantha's case, the doctors violated her rights in hooking her up to Frederick. So requiring her to remain hooked up to Frederick would perpetuate the injustice that she initially suffered when the doctors started meddling with her body. In Mandy's case no one violated her rights in getting her pregnant. So there would be no injustice in requiring her to remain pregnant for the nine months necessary to give birth to the foetus inside her. It would be different if Mandy had been raped when she was drunk and that is why she is now pregnant – in that case, her situation would be very similar to Samantha's and if Samantha does indeed have a right to disconnect herself from Frederick then that would seem to establish by analogy that Mandy should have a right to have an abortion in the case where she was raped and that is why she is now pregnant.

I want to talk now about the other very common form of argument that you will make, and come across, as a lawyer and in life generally. That is – a speculative argument. This kind of argument takes the following kind of form:

(1) Every swan I have ever seen has been white.

Given this, it is sensible to suppose that

(2) All swans are white.

Again step (1) in the argument is called the premise of the argument; step (2) is the conclusion.

There are two important differences between logical arguments and speculative arguments. First, a logical argument starts from a generality and then moves from that generality to reach a conclusion about a specific thing. In contrast, a speculative argument goes in the opposite direction: it moves from a statement about a specific thing to reach a general conclusion about that kind of thing.

Secondly, you'll note that – unlike with a logical argument – a speculative argument can have only one premise for its conclusion. (You'll recall that any logical argument must have at least two premises to support its conclusion – if it has only one, it doesn't work.) This is because the conclusion in a speculative argument does not follow logically from its premise or premises. It does not necessarily follow that all swans are white just because every swan I have ever seen has been white. It may be that not all swans are white and I just happen never to have seen a non-white swan. In fact, not all swans are white – black swans exist in Australia. So, as it happens, we should reject the conclusion 'All swans are white'. But, as a general rule, if the premises of a speculative argument are correct, and the conclusion of that argument seems the most sensible one to draw from those premises, we should accept that conclusion until we are given good reason to think that it is not true. So up until the time Australia was discovered by Europeans, it was rational for Europeans to think that all swans were white because no European had seen anything but a white swan. But as soon as black swans were observed in Australia, Europeans no longer had good reason to think that all swans were white.

Just in case you are tempted by the non-logical nature of speculative arguments to think that there is something dodgy about them, I should point out that scientists make speculative arguments all the time, and that all scientific progress depends on such arguments being made:

(1)   Every time we throw an object into the air, it falls back down towards the earth.

Given this, it is sensible to suppose that

(2)   There exists a force (call it gravity) which pulls an object thrown into the air back down towards the earth.

Lawyers often reason like scientists. They will take a case or a line of cases and try to extrapolate from the results of those cases a rule or a principle which explains the results in that case or those cases – having done this, they then argue that that case or those cases establish that that particular rule or principle is part of English law. When a lawyer makes an argument like this, the argument will always be speculative in nature.

So, for example, in the 1995 case of *Spring* v *Guardian Assurance plc*, the defendant gave the claimant, an ex-employee of his, a bad reference. The House of Lords held that if the claimant did not deserve a bad reference and the defendant had been careless in preparing the reference, then the claimant could sue the defendant. The defendant, the House of Lords held, had owed the claimant a 'duty of care' in preparing the reference, and if he breached that duty, then the claimant could sue him. Now what legal rule or principle was the House of Lords relying on – and therefore introducing into English law – in deciding this case?

One lawyer might argue that the House of Lords thought that: 'Whenever one person gives another a reference, the referee will owe the subject of the reference a duty to prepare the reference with a reasonable degree of care and skill.' Another lawyer might argue that the rule the House of Lords was actually relying on in deciding *Spring* was: 'Whenever an employer gives an ex-employee a reference, the employer will owe his ex-employee a duty to prepare the reference with a reasonable degree of care and skill.'

It makes a big difference who is right. If the first lawyer is right, then if I undeservedly and carelessly give an ex-student a bad reference, then *Spring* v *Guardian Assurance plc* establishes that my ex-student can sue me: I owed him or her a duty of care in preparing the reference. If the second lawyer is right, then *Spring* v *Guardian Assurance plc* does not establish any such thing: my ex-student was not a former employee of mine, so *Spring* v *Guardian Assurance plc* has nothing to do with my case.

Whichever argument as to what the *Spring* case establishes is correct, both arguments are speculative in nature. They both take the basic form:

(1) In *Spring* v *Guardian Assurance* plc, the House of Lords decided that . . .

Given this, it is sensible to suppose that

(2) The House of Lords thought that an employer/referee will owe an ex-employee/the subject of the reference a duty of care in writing a reference for him or her . . .

This is not a logical argument because (2) does not follow logically from (1). Whatever you think was basis of the decision of the House of Lords in the *Spring* case, there will always be other possible explanations of the House of Lords' decision in that case. So we can only determine what was the basis of the House of Lords' decision in the *Spring* case by asking ourselves: What is the most sensible explanation of the House of Lords' decision in *Spring*?

Lawyers don't just make speculative arguments when they are trying to clarify what rule or principle underlay a particular case or line of cases. They also make speculative arguments when they are called upon to clarify what a particular legal word (or concept) means so that they can apply a particular legal rule which contains that word. So, for example, the law says that you will violate my rights (in legal parlance, commit a tort) if you directly interfere with goods that are in my possession when you have no legal justification or excuse for doing so. But when can we say that goods are in my 'possession'? What if I own a flat in Glasgow – are the things inside that flat in my possession while I am typing this letter in Cambridge? What if I drop my wallet in the street – is the wallet still in my possession while it is lying in the street? If a friend of mine sees the wallet fall out of my coat and picks it up, intending to give it back, is it in my possession at that point? To answer these questions, we look at all the cases which have something to say about when goods were and were not in someone else's possession, and construct from them a definition of when we can say that goods are in someone's possession. But coming up with a definition will involve making a speculative argument. It will involve making an argument along the following lines:

> (1) Case A said that goods were in X's possession when . . .; case B said that Y lost possession of goods when . . .; case C said that Z obtained possession of goods when . . .
>
> Given this, it is sensible to suppose that
>
> (2) Goods will be in someone's possession if and only if . . .

Having clarified why lawyers make speculative arguments at all, I'll now give you a bit of guidance as to what you should and shouldn't do in making speculative arguments of your own. As usual, my hope is that this guidance will help you make good, effective speculative arguments, as well as helping you spot any flaws in speculative arguments that you come across in your reading.

● A speculative argument based on a false premise is worthless

One thing that speculative arguments have in common with logical arguments is that a false premise will undermine a speculative argument just as effectively as it will a logical argument. If I argue that . . .

> (1) In *Spring* v *Guardian Assurance plc,* the House of Lords ruled that the defendant did *not* owe the claimant a duty of care in writing a reference for him.
>
> Given this, it is sensible to suppose that
>
> (2) . . . .

. . . whatever conclusion I draw from premise (1) will certainly not be worth the paper it's written on.

● 'Most' cannot mean 'all'

Suppose that Charles is a well-travelled man who has been to Australia. He gets into an argument one day down the pub about whether all swans are white. He argues:

(1) Most of the swans I have seen in my life have been white.

   Given this, it is sensible to suppose that

(2) All swans are white.

There is something wrong with this argument. If (1) is true, then (2) cannot be true. If most of the swans Charles has seen in his life have been white, then it follows that some of the swans Charles has seen have not been white. And if some of the swans Charles has seen have not been white, then it cannot be true that 'All swans are white'.

So, in making a speculative argument, you cannot infer that X is true of all Ns based on the premise that X is only true of most Ns. In fact, the only thing you can infer from this premise is that X is not true of all Ns. This elementary point is quite often overlooked by academics writing about the law.

For example, as a law student, you will come across statements such as 'The first requisite of a contract is that the parties have reached agreement' or 'The function of tort law is to determine when one person may justly be required to compensate another for a loss that that other has suffered' or 'Under English law, Parliament is sovereign, which means that a law created by Parliament must be given effect to by the courts until it is repealed by Parliament'. But if you read on (and look hard at what you are reading), you'll see that the only evidence given in support of these statements is that: 'Most contracts are based on agreement' (and it is acknowledged at the same time that some contracts can be made without the parties having reached any kind of agreement at all); 'Most tort cases involve one person suing another for compensation' (and it is acknowledged at the same time that there are some tort cases where the person suing isn't looking for compensation at all, but for some other remedy such as an injunction); 'Most laws created by Parliament are binding on the courts' (and it is acknowledged at the same time that laws purporting to bind what future Parliaments may do are of no effect). So in fact, what the textbooks should be telling you is that: 'You can make a contract with someone else without having reached an agreement with them'; 'Whatever the function of tort law might be, it is not just to determine when one person may justly be required to pay compensation to someone else'; 'Under English law, Parliament is not completely sovereign: there are limits on what sort of laws created by Parliament will be binding on the courts'.

Notice that the last three statements are more 'interesting' than the first three because they contradict the bog-standard accounts of English law that are routinely trotted out in the textbooks. 'Interesting' statements about the law are much more likely to be get high marks from your examiners than statements that have been lifted straight out of a textbook. (So long, that is, as you have backed up your 'interesting' statement with a good argument.) So remembering that what is acknowledged to be only true of 'most' cannot possibly be true of 'all' will not only help ensure that you get a much accurate understanding of the current state of English law than some of your textbooks may give you – it may also help you do well in your exams!

● Don't oversimplify

A bad habit that you should avoid in advancing a speculative argument is that of oversimplification. Your explanations should take account of the complexities of what you are trying to explain.

So, for example, suppose there is a line of cases A–F. In cases A–D, it could be argued that the courts relied on rule R to reach their decision. So cases A–D seem to indicate that rule R is part of English law. But if rule R were part of English law, we would have expected cases E and F not to have been decided the way they were. Let's suppose that *Academic* analyses these cases in the course of an article. Let's suppose further that *Academic* suffers – as academics sometimes do – from the bad habit of oversimplification. *Academic* will probably argue that:

> (1) Case A says . . .; case B says . . .; case C says . . .; case D says . . ..
>
>   Given this, it is sensible to suppose that
>
> (2) Rule R is part of English law.

Cases E and F are simply ignored. If one (forcibly) brings cases E and F to *Academic*'s attention, he will almost always simply dismiss cases E and F as 'wrongly decided'. But they're only wrongly decided if rule R is part of English law, which is what we are trying to establish in the first place. It would be more honest and straightforward to argue as follows:

(1) Case A says . . .; case B says . . .; case C says . . .; case D says . . ..

Given this, it is sensible to suppose that

(2) In these cases, the courts took the view that rule R is part of English law.

But

(3) Case E says . . .; and case F says . . ..

Given this, it is sensible to suppose that

(4) In these cases, the courts did not take the view that rule R is part of English law.

Given (2) and (4), it is sensible to suppose that

(5) It is uncertain whether rule R is part of English law or not; a majority of cases seem to take the view that it is, but a minority seem to take the view that it is not.

This conclusion fits more of the cases than *Academic*'s does and therefore gives us a better account of the current state of English law than *Academic* gives us. Moreover, this conclusion is more nuanced and therefore more 'interesting' than *Academic*'s conclusion. So someone who argues in favour of this conclusion in an exam is likely to do better than someone who adopts *Academic*'s line.

Academics are particularly prone to falling into the vice of oversimplification whenever they try to define a particular legal term (or concept). This is because academics tend to assume that there is a one-to-one relation between legal terms and definitions. As a result, they tend to think that a particular legal term is always used in the same way, to mean the same thing. So, for example, academics have endless debates over what it means to have a 'legal right'. Some argue that when we say Len has a 'legal right' we are saying that Len has an 'interest' which is protected by the law's imposing duties on other people not to violate that interest. Others argue that we are saying that Len has a power to do something that is either given to him by the law or is protected by the law. The possibility that when we say that Len has a 'legal right' we could mean either of those things, depending on the context, doesn't get a look-in.

A similar point can be made about the term 'trust'. Academics tend to assume that when we talk about a 'trust' (as in 'A holds this property on trust . . .') we are always talking about the same thing. And so they ask, 'What are the characteristics of a trust?', 'How is a trust created?', and 'Who has an interest in property that is the subject of a trust?' They hardly ever consider the possibility that in fact the term 'trust' does not refer to one thing, but in fact refers to a variety of different legal arrangements which bear a family resemblance to each other, but have nothing more in common than that. If this is the case, it simply makes no sense to ask, 'What are the characteristics of a trust?', 'How is a trust created?', and 'Who has an interest in property that is the subject of a trust?' The proper response to these questions can only be another question: 'What sort of trust are you talking about?'

You should aim higher. Always be on the lookout for definitional oversimplification, and avoid it like the plague wherever you come across it. Definitional oversimplification always involves a false economy: it just stores up trouble in the long run.

● Don't overcomplicate

Just as you shouldn't oversimplify in making a speculative argument, you also shouldn't overcomplicate. The most sensible explanation is usually the most simple. (This principle of argumentation is known as 'Occam's razor'.) So, for example, consider the following argument:

> (1) Case A says . . .; case B says; . . .. case Y says; case Z says . . ..
>
> Given this, it is sensible to suppose that
>
> (2) All judges belong to a secret society, the leaders of which dictate to them how they should decide their cases.

No – this is not sensible at all. The reason why this is not sensible is that for (2) to be true, all of these things would also have to be true: (i) there exists a society which has some means of contacting any judge who is appointed to the Bench; (ii) membership of this society is so attractive that every judge who is approached agrees to become a member of it; (iii) the leaders of this society are so charismatic that every judge who becomes a member of this society is happy to do whatever they say; and (iv) this society has some way of ensuring no word of its existence ever escapes into the media. So, in fact, (2) provides us with an incredibly complex explanation of how the cases in (1) were decided. And incredibly complex explanations are very unlikely to be correct.

For the same reason it is highly unlikely that judges decide cases the way they do in order to maximise the wealth of society. (Many academics, particularly in the United States, believe this. Academics who take this view belong to what is called the 'law and economics' school of legal thought.) For this to be true, it would also have to be true that: (i) all judges, in making their decisions, are interested in promoting wealth-maximisation to the exclusion of all other considerations (such as promoting equality of opportunity, or helping the needy, or maximising everyone's liberty); (ii) all judges are equipped with the economic knowledge that would enable them to determine what rules they should give effect to so as to maximise the wealth of society; (iii) all judges have agreed that they should keep the fact that their only concern in deciding cases is to maximise the wealth of society completely secret and not allow a word of this to enter into their judgments; (iv) barristers – who argue cases before judges – must be taken to be unaware of this agenda of the judges because they too fail to mention wealth-maximisation in their arguments, but as soon as a barrister becomes a judge he or she suddenly becomes interested in promoting wealth-maximisation to the exclusion of all other considerations, while at the same time acknowledging the need to keep quiet about this desire. All this is just so complicated that it makes 'wealth maximisation' completely implausible as an explanation of why judges decide cases the way they do.

● Don't be dogmatic

The final point I want to make about making speculative arguments is that you should always remember that they are speculative. As the facts on the ground that you are trying to explain change, you must be ready to change your explanations with them.

For example, the decisions in cases A, B, C and D may have led you to conclude that rule R is part of English law. If case E comes along and seems to deny that rule R is part of English law, you can't let yourself be carried away by a sentimental attachment to rule R into denouncing case E as 'wrongly decided'. You have to be ready to concede that the decision in case E has made the law uncertain and made it difficult to tell whether rule R is part of English law or not.

A great example of this willingness to change is provided by the late academic Professor Peter Birks. A lot of his work focused on the legal rule that if A has been unjustly enriched at B's expense, then B will be entitled to bring a claim for restitution against A and recover the value of that enrichment from A, so long – of course – as A cannot raise a defence to B's claim. But what does it mean to say that A has been *unjustly enriched* at B's expense? For about 20 years Peter Birks argued – on the basis of a close analysis of the relevant cases – that A will be unjustly enriched at B's expense if A obtains wealth from B without B's consent or under circumstances which meant B's consent to A's having that wealth was flawed in some way (because it was given because of a mistake, or under duress, or in expectation of something being given in return that never came). But in 1994 a case was decided – *Westdeutsche Landesbank* v *Islington LBC* – that did not fit Peter Birks' theory of unjust enrichment. In that case B was allowed to recover money that A had obtained from B even though B had consented to A's having that money and there were no facts in the case that allowed us to say that B's consent to A's having that money was flawed in some way. Instead, B's claim to recover the money he had paid A was allowed simply because – unknown to both A and B at the time – the contract under which B had paid A the money happened to be invalid.

So how did Peter Birks react? Well, he didn't reach for his gun and attempt to shoot down the decision in *Westdeutsche Landesbank* by denouncing it as 'wrongly decided'. Instead, he did something amazing. He junked the definition of when A will be unjustly enriched at B's expense that he had been advancing for the previous 20 years, and for the last few years of his life he argued that A will be unjustly enriched at B's expense if A obtains wealth from B and there is no valid legal basis for the transfer of wealth. This new definition was, he argued, superior to the old, because it accounted both for the old cases – on which his old definition was based – and it also accounted for the decision in the *Westdeutsche Landesbank* case.

● Summary

I'll now briefly attempt a summary of what I've said in the last two letters:

When making a logical argument, make sure that it isn't circular (that is, that it doesn't assume what it's trying to prove), check that the conclusion follows logically from the premises (and that you haven't done something silly like try to derive an 'ought' from an 'is'), and ensure that your argument isn't based on a false premise. The last point also applies when making a speculative argument, but when you make a speculative argument, check to see that your conclusion is the most sensible one to draw from the argument's premise or premises, remembering that the simplest explanation is probably the most sensible as well.

If you are interested in exploring the subject of arguing effectively any further, the best book I've yet to read on arguing effectively is Julian Baggini's *The Duck That Won The Lottery, and 99 Other Bad Arguments.*

Best wishes,

Nick

Choosing a University

- From: Nicholas J. McBride [dearnick@pearson.com]
- To: Brown, Alex
- Subject: Choosing a University

Hey Alex,

Thanks for your e-mail, asking me for advice on applying to university. Before I say anything about this, I want to emphasise that there is plenty of really helpful advice out there for you on choosing which universities to apply to.

(1) There is the Unistats website (www.unistats.co.uk) that I told you about in my second letter to you.

(2) The UCAS website (www.ucas.com) provides a lot of information about all the universities that you might be interested in applying to (go to http://www.ucas.com/students/choosingcourses/choosinguni/map/). UCAS also publishes a guide to applying to university.

(3) The websites for *The Times, Telegraph, Guardian* and *Independent* all have lots of information for prospective university students, with *The Times* and the *Guardian* each publishing their own guides to universities.

(4) The Student Room (www.thestudentroom.co.uk) might also contain useful inside information about universities that you are thinking of applying to – though I find it a bit hit and miss whether I'm able to get the information I want from the Student Room.

(5) The websites of the universities you are thinking of applying to will also be well worth looking at, especially for the dates of open days which would allow you to get a real flavour of what those universities are like.

So these should be your first ports of call in seeking advice on what universities you should apply to. But maybe I can say a few things that you might not learn from these other sources of information. Let's start with some economics.

● How universities make their money

There are basically five ways for universities to make the money they need in order to pay for the staff and facilities they need to function:

(1) Student fees

Cuts in government funding of universities were partly offset by allowing the universities to charge UK/EU undergraduates up to £9,000 a year in tuition fees. Most universities have taken advantage of this option to charge their UK/EU undergraduates the full £9,000 a year. (Though it should be emphasised that the initial cost of paying the fees will usually fall on the government, which will lend UK/EU students the money to pay these fees. The loans will then be gradually repaid after the student starts earning more than £21,000 a year. It should also be emphasised that students from poorer backgrounds may well be able to take advantage of university bursaries and other forms of assistance to reduce the amount of tuition fees that they have to pay.) Students coming from outside the EU may provide a very useful source of income for universities as they can be charged much higher fees than UK/EU students pay. Further income can be made by running short summer school courses for students.

(2) Government funding

For English universities, this is administered by the Higher Education Funding Council for England (HEFCE). Universities receive a range of different types of awards from HEFCE; but the principal forms of funding are for (i) teaching; and (ii) research. How much money a university receives from HEFCE to help fund its teaching activities depends on the numbers of students it admits and how much it costs the university to teach its courses. How much money a university receives from HEFCE in respect of its research work depends on HEFCE's assessment of the quality of the university's research 'outputs' in the form of books and articles. The latest assessment exercise will be run in 2014 under what is known as the 'Research Excellence Framework' (REF). Universities that are competing for REF money – and it is a competition – will be submitting the 'outputs' produced by their various faculties for assessment by REF panels, which will be awarding a number of stars for those outputs – four stars for world-leading research, three stars for work that is internationally excellent, two stars for work that is internationally recognised, and one star for work that has not made an impact outside the UK. Whoever gets the most stars wins the most funding.

(3) Investment income

Universities that have existed for a number of years will usually have built up some investment capital – known as the university's 'endowment' – that provides it with a yearly, though variable, source of income.

(4) Donations

A university can add to its endowment, or help cover its yearly running costs, through donations. Usually, donations come from a university's old members; though they can also come from companies or multi-millionaires who wish to be associated with a university in some way. A notable example of this was the donation of £20m to the School of Law at King's College London (KCL) by Dickson Poon, the Hong Kong businessman and philanthropist. This has helped endow a number of scholarships for law students at KCL, and the School of Law at KCL was renamed the 'Dickson Poon School of Law' in recognition of Poon's generosity.

(5) Renting out facilities

A university can also earn money through renting out its facilities – for example, by charging its students for their accommodation and access to computer facilities, and renting out its halls for conferences and weddings.

Once you understand how universities make their money, you can understand what a huge advantage Oxford and Cambridge have over other universities – because they (and their constituent colleges) can rely on all five sources of income to keep themselves running. High student numbers mean that they receive about £55m a year towards their teaching costs, and their academic reputation results in their being paid about £120m for their research. Their academic reputation also means that they can run the sort of postgraduate courses that are very likely to attract high-fee-paying students from across the world. Huge endowments (about £4bn in each case) bring in a lot of investment income; and the strong feelings of loyalty that ex-students feel towards their university – and especially their former colleges – mean that many ex-students are happy to donate money to support their university or their college. (For example, I owe my job to the money that was donated by former students of James Campbell, who taught Law at Pembroke College, Cambridge for almost 40 years, to provide Pembroke with enough money to fund the James Campbell Fellowship in Law.) The cachet of the Oxford and Cambridge name attracts corporate sponsors and support, and the beauty of both cities means that there is no lack of people wanting to rent out the universities' facilities for their events. As we'll see, the fact that other universities have to rely on more limited sources of funding has a big effect on how they operate – and it's useful to bear that in mind in choosing what university to apply to.

● Three types of law faculty

In light of what's just been said, let's compare three different law faculties. I'll assume in each case that the faculty is based in a university that doesn't have much of an endowment, and doesn't have much income coming in from donations or from renting out its facilities. So each of the faculties below is faced with the problem – how do you make enough money to sustain yourself given that sources of income (3), (4) and (5) aren't really available to you?

For *Faculty A* the answer is obvious: you maximise sources of income (1) and (2). But there's a problem. Accepting a lot of law students will help boost the faculty's income from student fees, and – to a limited extent – bring in some grants from HEFCE to contribute towards the cost of teaching those students. However, students need teaching; and teaching makes it harder to do the kind of research and produce the kind of work that will score highly on the REF and bring in lots of funding from HEFCE in recognition of the Faculty's research excellence. *Faculty A* solves that problem by recruiting a lot of academics whose job is *principally* to write books and articles. Of course, these books and articles have to be *good*. So the academics *Faculty A* recruits will be stars – the sort of academics who can be expected to produce really interesting work on a regular basis. These star academics will be expected to do some lecturing – particularly on postgraduate courses where the academic's star status will help to attract high-fee-paying non-EU students. But they won't be expected to mark essays or see students on a one-to-one basis or give them some feedback on their work or progress. *That* will be left to other people – usually graduates fresh out of university who are just starting out in their careers, don't have any kind of 'star' reputation, and are just looking to get on the first rung of the academic ladder.

Faculty B might like to do what *Faculty A* is doing but for some reason or another it can't. One reason might be that there are only so many star academics in the world, and it only takes a few *Faculty A*s (not to mention the law faculties at Oxford and Cambridge) to gobble them all up. Another reason might be that *Faculty B* just doesn't have the academic reputation or the kind of location that would help it attract the sort of star academics who would boost its research profile. So *Faculty B* can't hope to get that much money by way of funding for its research. Instead, *Faculty B* has to rely primarily on student fees to keep itself going. But again there's a problem. By definition, not that many law faculties will be in a position to pursue the sort of strategy that *Faculty A* is pursuing – as I've just said, there aren't that many star academics in the world, and there are only enough to boost the research profile of a few *Faculty A*s. So most law faculties will be in the position of *Faculty B* – of having to rely primarily on student fees to keep themselves going. And that fact means *Faculty B* will face *a lot* of competition from other law faculties for the law students that it needs to come through its doors every year to keep *Faculty B* afloat. *Faculty B* reacts to this competition by aiming to distinguish itself from its competitors by getting a reputation for providing its law students with a really first-class education. So while *Faculty A* is looking to recruit star researchers, *Faculty B* looks to recruit star teachers who can be relied upon to provide its students with inspirational lectures and guidance.

Faculty C is in the same position as *Faculty B* – it has to rely primarily on student fees to survive. But unlike *Faculty B,* it doesn't feel the need to distinguish itself for the quality of its teaching. Maybe it's based in a big city and it thinks that a lot of students from the city will apply to it to study law, attracted by the idea of economising on the costs of their education by living at home while studying at university. Maybe it's relying on the fact that it has the sort of name and historic reputation that could be expected to attract applicants, come what may. Or maybe it just can't be bothered – what *Faculty B* is doing is just too much like hard work. Whatever the reason, *Faculty C* is on the slide. As Abraham Lincoln said, 'You can fool all of the people some of the time, and some of the people all of the time, but you can't fool all of the people all of the time.' Eventually, students will realise that they are receiving a second-class education from *Faculty C* – and if they don't, law firms and other employers will – and that will cause a gradual decline in the number of applications to study Law at *Faculty C*. That in turn will kick off a vicious circle where *Faculty C* is forced to react to that decline by cutting costs, which in turn hurts its educational standards even more, thus causing even fewer people to apply to *Faculty C*. The only way *Faculty C* will be able to save itself in the long run is to wise up and turn itself into an example of *Faculty B* and start competing for students on the basis of the quality of its teaching.

So I'm very optimistic about the future for law faculties. I think it won't be long – particularly with students paying £9,000 a year tuition fees and demanding to see some value for that kind of money – where all the law faculties that aren't based in Oxford or Cambridge, and aren't able to pursue *Faculty A*'s strategy for making money, will have to operate in the way *Faculty B* does and attract law students through the quality of their teaching. Of course, this will mean some law faculties will go to the wall. Just as there cannot be more than a few *Faculty A*s, there simply aren't enough good law teachers to allow a very large number of law faculties to provide their students with an amazing legal education. But the future is bright for law students – the competition for law students among law faculties should result in educational standards among law faculties being driven ever upwards.

⬤ Factors to look out for in deciding where to apply

Now we're in a better position to talk about what factors you should take into account in deciding where to apply.

(1) Entry requirements

This is fundamental. Pitch your choice of university according to what sort of results you can expect to get at A-Level. You can find out what sort of entry requirements you would have to satisfy to study law at a particular university by going to the UCAS website at www.ucas.com and then clicking on 'Course Search' – you should be able to find your way to the information you want from there. If you are expecting to get at least 3As at A-Level, then you should be thinking about applying to Oxford or Cambridge as one of your choices. But I'll talk more about that in a separate section.

(2) Type of faculty

When considering what non-Oxbridge universities to apply to, think about what sort of law faculty you would like to study in. The advantage of studying at a Faculty A type law faculty is that you get lectured by a lot of high-quality academics who do interesting work; the trouble is, you don't get the benefit of being taught up-close by them – though there may be opportunities later on in your time at university to work with them as a research assistant.

The advantage of studying at a Faculty B type law faculty is the quality of the teaching and guidance you receive; but the courses might lack the sort of stimulation and cutting-edge excitement that a Faculty A can provide. I can't see much reason to study at a Faculty C – but if a law degree from a Faculty C has a good reputation among employers, and the faculty provides its students with good resources and facilities, there is no reason why you shouldn't be able to do well so as long you are willing to work hard and push yourself to do your absolute best in your studies. You can find out what a particular university's law faculty is like by attending an open day and asking some pointed questions: How much contact do the students have with their teachers? How much help does the university give students who are struggling with their studies? How many lectures do the students get each week, and in how many subjects? How many small group teaching sessions do the students have each fortnight, and in how many subjects? How much written work are students required to do? (You are NOT looking for the answer, 'Not much' – the more written work you can do, the better; though, obviously, there are limits.) Do students get good feedback on their written work? How much assistance do the students get in preparing them for the exams?

(3) Prospects after leaving university

What do law students who graduate from the university tend to do after they leave? Do those who are predicted to get Firsts or 2.1s in law from that university find it easy to land a training contract (a two-year stint at a law firm, after which you will qualify as a fully-fledged solicitor) or pupillage (a one-year stint at a barrister's chambers, after which – if they like you – you'll be offered a tenancy and allowed to practise out of that chambers)? You can find out some information on this from the unistats website – but you can also ask the university admissions office for this kind of information.

(4) Legal facilities

Law is one of the most self-taught courses you can do at university. You do need some help and guidance – but ultimately, it is down to you how well you do at the end of your time studying law. But you can't study law without access to proper facilities. So – How good is the university's law library? Are the textbooks up to date? How many areas of law are covered and in what kind of depth? Are there good computer facilities? If you have a laptop, is it easy to hook up to the Internet at the law library? What are the law library's opening hours? Is it easy to get something to eat and drink if you're working there? Is it easy to get to from where you would be living? What sort of online legal resources does the university give you access to? In particular, are you given free access to Westlaw (for cases, case commentaries and academic journals) and HeinOnline (a wonderful database of legal journals from all over the world)? Can you use these resources from your room in the university, or are they limited to the law library only?

(5) Opportunities to polish your CV

How much scope would you have to engage in law-related activities that would enhance your legal skills and your attractiveness to potential employers? For example, would you get the opportunity to work in a free legal advice clinic? Does the university regularly hold mooting competitions, where law students get to act like barristers and argue legal points before a judge (usually an academic)? Is there a university student law review that is run by the university's law students, and to which the university law students can contribute articles? Is there any scope to work as a (paid or unpaid) research assistant to one of the university's law academics during the holidays?

(6) General university-related factors, such as location, accommodation, facilities and security

Do you want to study at a university that is near home, or further away? Do you want to study at a university that is near the centre of town, or you happy with one which is some distance away from the nearest town centre? How easy is it to travel from your home to the university? How close is the nearest supermarket/bookstore to the university? What's the town or city that is closest to the university like? Would you be happy spending time there? Does the university promise to accommodate you throughout your time there? If not, how easy/cheap is it to secure good, alternative accommodation? What is the accommodation like? What are the kitchens, toilets and washing facilities (both bathrooms and laundry) that come with the accommodation like? What are the facilities that the university lays on for its students like generally? What are the bars/common rooms like? How active is the Student Union? What is the library like? What are the facilities for accessing the Internet like? Is there much to do in the evenings? How safe is the university campus? Is it well lit, and well populated? What measures does the university take to ensure the security of its students? If something goes wrong, what sort of support does the university provide?

(7) Support

Being at university, and being away from home for long periods of time, can be difficult for a lot of students. How much support does the university provide its students to help them adjust to living at university, and to help those who are having problems with coping either with their studies or other problems arising out of spending time at university?

● Two or three years?

One question that I think won't really be an issue for you, but which may become more important in the future, is whether you should do a law degree in two years or three years. The vast majority of universities require students studying law as a first degree to do it in three years. But both the College of Law – which has now renamed itself, oxymoronically, as 'The University of Law' (a university doesn't just teach one subject: it teaches a huge range of different subjects, reflecting the *universe* of human knowledge) – and the BPP Law School now offer undergraduates the option of doing an accelerated two-year law degree. The option of getting a law degree in just two years may prove quite attractive to students wanting to save money and get on with their lives; and it may be that other universities – in an attempt to remain competitive with institutions like the College of Law and BPP – may be tempted to offer first-time students the option of doing a two-year law degree. But at the moment, other universities will only allow a student to do a law degree in two years if they have done some other degree first.

My own view – for what it's worth – is that it is a really bad idea to do a law degree in two years. You simply won't get as much out of your law degree – in terms of all the benefits from studying law that I listed in my second letter to you – if you do a law degree in two years rather than three. Any money you might save by doing a two-year law degree simply won't be enough to compensate for the loss of those benefits. (Though this point applies more weakly to students from outside the EU who face having to pay a lot more money to study law at a UK university; in their case it's more understandable why they might seek to get a law degree in just two years rather than three, though if they could afford it I would always urge that they do the full three years.) Institutions like the College of Law and BPP might counter by arguing that their two-year law degrees offer students a different *kind* of legal education – one much more oriented towards preparing students to become practising lawyers – and that that can be done effectively over the course of a two-year law degree. Fair enough: but I don't think that's what legal education *should* be about. Legal education should be about *expanding* students' potentialities by helping them to think more rigorously, express themselves more effectively, understand their society more deeply – while picking up a lot of legal knowledge along the way which will be of some practical use to those students who go on to become practising lawyers. Someone who has studied law at university should not graduate with the ability to do just *one thing* well, but should instead leave university equipped with a range of skills and abilities that will allow him or her to accomplish *lots* of different things. And an 18- year old who might not have a clear idea what they want to do in life would be well advised to do a law degree that leaves them free to do lots of things in the future rather than one which puts them on a conveyor belt heading towards a particular profession. But doing such a law degree takes three years (and some would say that even three years is not enough), not two.

● Oxford or Cambridge?

Okay – let's talk about Oxford and Cambridge. I teach in Cambridge, but did my law degree (and a postgraduate Bachelor of Civil Law degree) in Oxford and taught in Oxford for five years before moving to Cambridge, so I'm well qualified to talk about both. However, it's a difficult time to talk about the law courses at Oxford and Cambridge as both institutions are currently reviewing their courses with a view to making them more flexible and enhancing their value to the students who take them. So what I have to say should be checked against both institutions' websites, to check that what I'm saying to you is still current.

Everybody runs Oxford and Cambridge together in their minds, but in fact the two law schools could not be more different, and in choosing between the two universities you should be aware of these differences. At the moment, there are five key differences – though, as I have said, this may change in the future.

(1) Entry requirements

The standard Oxford A-Level offer is still three As at A-Level. The standard Cambridge offer is A*AA. That may make a difference to your choice of whether to apply to Oxford or Cambridge. However, there is another point about entry requirements that you have to bear in mind. The system of admissions to study law at Oxford is a lot more centralised than the system at Cambridge. Students applying to study law at an Oxford college are subject to an initial sifting process, which is based purely on the students' paper records. If a particular college has had a lot of applicants – say 40 applicants – then the students who rank in (say) the top 20 after this initial sift will be summoned for interview at that college, and the others will either be reallocated for interview at another college or will not be interviewed at all. So to get through that initial sift, it's important that your paper record (which will include your score on the legal aptitude test – the LNAT – which applicants to study law at Oxford have to sit) be as strong as possible. If there is some aspect of your paper record which is not that strong – for example, you might have underperformed at GCSE before knuckling down to work hard at your A-Levels – then it might be worth thinking about applying to Cambridge rather than Oxford to study Law. In Cambridge there is no centralised initial sift of the candidates applying to study law. Instead, it is up to each individual college to decide which of the students applying to study there it will summon for interview. The Cambridge colleges still have a strong prejudice in favour of interviewing people who have applied to them, rather than turning them down flat without interview, so one weakness in your paper file will not necessarily prove fatal to your being interviewed at your preferred college, especially if that weakness is addressed and explained in your personal statement or your school's reference for you.

(2) Format of exams

An Oxford law student does exams ('Moderations') in three subjects at the end of his first two terms, and then he will have no exams at all until the end of his third year, when he sits 'Finals' – that is, exams in nine different subjects. A Cambridge law student will sit exams ('Tripos exams') at the end of each of the three years she studies law at Cambridge, with the result that she'll end up taking exams in about fourteen different subjects. So studying law at Oxford tends to be a less stressful affair – at least until the time to sit Finals comes around – and affords greater opportunities to think about the law and develop some interesting views about it than is the case with studying law at Cambridge. But at the same time, a Cambridge law student will study more subjects than an Oxford law student. As a result, a Cambridge law student will have greater scope to choose what subjects she is going to study than her Oxford counterpart. Moreover, she'll leave university with a wider (though not deeper) knowledge of the law than someone with a law degree from Oxford.

(3) Format of teaching

Law students in both Oxford and Cambridge are taught through a mixture of lectures and small-group teaching sessions (called 'tutorials' in Oxford; 'supervisions' in Cambridge) with an academic. However, in Oxford the main way you are taught law is through tutorials – lectures are an optional add-on, meant to supplement the teaching that you get in tutorials, and there's no real pressure to attend them. Lectures are also optional in Cambridge, but they are regarded as the main vehicle for teaching students law, and it's the supervisions that are regarded as supplementary (though they are most definitely compulsory): supervisions in Cambridge are designed to make sure that students are doing okay and not falling behind, and give students the opportunity to get help with resolving any problems that they are having with their studies.

(4) Emphasis in teaching

I think it's fair to say that the Cambridge law degree places a lot of emphasis on ensuring that the students develop a detailed knowledge of the law, while the Oxford law degree is a lot more interested in ensuring that students understand the principles and ideas that underlie different areas of the law, and are able to talk intelligently about how the law should be developed, rather than worrying about whether the students are completely up to date with the most recent developments and cases. This is reflected by the fact that Cambridge law exams are very heavy on problem questions, which usually test your knowledge of the details of the law. In contrast, Oxford law exams contain plenty of essays, which invite the students to show how much they understand about why the law says what it does, and talk about what the law should say on various issues.

(5) Environment

Finally, just in case it does make a difference, I think Cambridge is a much nicer place to live in than Oxford. Having said that, Oxford is a lot more vibrant. But visit both places and make your own mind up about that.

I hope that provides you with a few more things to think about in deciding which universities to apply to – but, as I said, there's no substitute for researching all the information on this topic which is available to you on the web and in hard copy. Good luck!

All best wishes,

Nick

The LNAT and Other Law Tests

- From: Nicholas J. McBride [dearnick@pearson.com]
- To: Brown, Alex
- Subject: The LNAT and Other Law Tests

Dear Alex,

As a follow-up to my last letter, I thought I'd send you one about the various legal aptitude tests that you might have to sit if and when you apply to do law at university. The principal such test is the LNAT (the 'National Admissions Test for Law'), which you will have to take if you are applying to any of the following universities: Birmingham, Bristol, Durham, Glasgow, King's College London, Nottingham, Oxford, and University College London. (Though check on the LNAT site – www.lnat.ac.uk - what the current position is: the list of universities that require and do not require you to have done the LNAT changes over time.) Applicants to Cambridge aren't required to do the LNAT, but will – on coming up to interview – instead have to sit the 'Cambridge Law Test'. I'll talk about both tests in this letter.

● The LNAT

If you're going to be taking the LNAT, you should definitely have a look at the LNAT website at www.lnat.ac.uk. The website provides a lot of helpful information, as well as a couple of practice papers.

As you'll see from the website, the point of the LNAT is to test students' aptitude to study law. Now – this doesn't mean that if you do badly on the LNAT, no one will accept you for a place to study law. Your performance on the LNAT is only one of the things that admissions tutors at the above universities will take into account in deciding whether or not to offer you a place. By the same token, if you do really well on the LNAT, that does not necessarily mean you are guaranteed a place to study law at whatever universities you are applying to.

Having said that, a poor performance on the LNAT won't help your case for admission to a place at university to study law; and a good performance could catch the selectors' eye and win you a place that you might not have obtained otherwise. So if you are applying to a university that requires you to take the LNAT, it is important that you do as well as you can on it – and to do well, you have to prepare for it.

The LNAT is made up of two parts. There is a multiple-choice section where you are given a passage to read and asked two or three multiple-choice questions about that passage. For example:

What point has not been made so far in Nick's letter to Alex about the LNAT?

(a) The LNAT test is very difficult.

(b) Some universities require law applicants to take the LNAT.

(c) Admissions tutors take the LNAT results into account in making admissions decisions.

(d) The official website about the LNAT is very helpful.

(e) It is important to prepare for the LNAT if you are applying to do law at one of the universities that require their applicants to have done the LNAT.

The answer is, of course, (a) – I haven't said anything so far about how difficult the LNAT is.

You will be asked questions on 12 different passages. The total number of multiple-choice questions you will be asked to answer is 36, and you will have 95 minutes to answer them. This doesn't sound like very much time. However, it should in fact be ample.

The second part of the LNAT is an essay section. You will be required to write one essay in 40 minutes. You will be given the choice of three different topics or quotes to write about. For example:

1 Many people argue that admissions tests to gain places at university discriminate against students who are educationally disadvantaged. Others argue that such tests help such students by detecting in them abilities that would otherwise go unnoticed. Which side do you agree with?

2 'Efforts to protect the environment are misplaced. Why should we care about preserving the world for generations that are as yet unborn?' Discuss.

3 'Driving different countries into a political union is simply a recipe for trouble.' Do you agree?

The LNAT website says that your essay should be about 500–600 words and not more than 750 words. Unlike the multiple choice section of the LNAT, your essay will not be marked centrally by the people who run the LNAT. Instead, it will be forwarded to the admissions tutors at any universities to which you are applying that require their applicants to do the LNAT. It will then be up to those admissions tutors to assess the quality of your essay.

If you are going to do the LNAT, you should have a look at the 'Preparation' section of the LNAT website, which contains a 'hints and tips' section. The multiple-choice section of the LNAT has a great deal in common with 'critical thinking' tests, so in theory it might be worth having a look at some books on critical thinking as preparation for the LNAT. However, in practice I'm not that impressed by the books on critical thinking that I've seen – so I can't recommend a specific book for you to read. But have a look in the bookshops yourself, and if there is a book on critical thinking that appeals to you, then use that. There are some books that have been specifically written to advise people on how to do well on the LNAT: *Passing the National Admissions Test for Law (LNAT)* by Rosalie Hutton, Glenn Hutton and Fraser Sampson (published by Learning Matters) and *Practise & Pass: LNAT* by Georgina Petrova and Christopher Reid (published by Trotman). You can also download a 'Preparation Guide' from the LNAT website for free.

I'll now get on with giving you some advice on doing the LNAT. (Very strong disclaimer at this point: my publisher owns the company (Pearson VUE) that currently runs the LNAT test. However, what follows definitely does not at all represent any 'inside knowledge' on my part on how to do well on the LNAT. These are my views, not anyone else's.)

The multiple choice section

(1) *Be careful.* That's my main piece of advice to you – be careful in reading and answering the questions. For example, suppose you are asked:

> Which of the following is an unstated assumption that the writer makes in the passage?

When you are going through the possible answers supplied, remember that you are not just looking for an answer that identifies an assumption that the writer has made in making out his argument in the passage supplied. You are looking for an answer that identifies an assumption that the writer has made in making out his argument in the passage supplied that is also not stated in the passage supplied. So don't mark as correct an answer that identifies an assumption that the writer has expressly said that he is making in the passage supplied. That statement may represent an assumption that the writer made in making out his argument – but it's hardly unstated, is it?

(2) *If you don't know the answer, you might as well guess.* In its present form, wrong answers in the multiple-choice section of the LNAT are not given a negative mark. So if you do not know the answer to a given question, you might as well guess the answer. You won't be punished if your answer is wrong, and you might well be lucky and guess the right answer. The admissions tutors at the universities you are applying to will not see your answers to the multiple-choice questions – all they will see is your total mark. So if your guess is wildly wrong, you won't be punished for that. No one will see your answers and think, 'Well – this candidate can't be very good if he or she thought that that was the right answer.' Now – if you come across a question in the LNAT that completely stumps you, don't spend too long agonising over it. You can always go back to it if you finish the rest of the multiple-choice section before the allotted 95 minutes are up. It's more important you move on to the other questions which you will probably have a better chance of knowing the answer to. So make your best guess as to what the answer is, and then swiftly move on. Once you have finished going through the whole of the multiple-choice section, then you can go back to the questions that you had real problems with and agonise over what the answers to those questions are.

(3) *Getting through the test in time.* You will have to decide for yourself – by doing practice tests such as the ones on the LNAT website or in the available books about the LNAT – what sort of approach to the multiple-choice questions will best allow you to get through the multiple-choice section of the LNAT in the time allowed. Most people seem to adopt the following approach

to answering multiple-choice questions on a given passage in the LNAT. They first of all read the passage carefully; they then look at the questions; and they then refer back to the passage to help them select the correct answers to those questions. You might want to think about adopting a different approach. This is to look at the questions first, and then search the passage for the answers. This seems to me a great timesaver if you get a question like:

> What is the main point that the writer is making in the last paragraph?

To answer that question, you don't have to have read the whole of the passage supplied. You simply have to look at the last paragraph of the passage. Similarly, if you get a question like:

> Which of the following is not a reason why the writer refers to the 1990s as the "golden age of television"?

Again, you don't have to have read the whole of the passage to answer that question – just look in the passage for the phrase 'the golden age of television' and then look around that phrase for the reasons why the writer thinks that the 1990s were the 'golden age of television'. And if you get a question asking

> Which of the following is not a statement of opinion?

or

> Which of the following is a statement of opinion?

– well, you don't need to have read the passage at all to answer that one.

I think this approach to doing the multiple-choice section of the LNAT is a lot faster, and allows you to spend much more time on the really tricky questions. But you will have to find out for yourself whether this approach works for you – or whether you are more comfortable adopting the more conventional approach to going through the multiple-choice section.

(4) *The importance of practice.* It is important – to give yourself the best possible chance of doing well in the multiple-choice section of the LNAT – to do the practice tests on the LNAT website. This will get you used to the sort of questions that you might be asked in this section of the LNAT, and also the kind of tricks the question-setters get up to in an attempt to find out how good your legal abilities really are.

The essay section

(1) *Selecting your essay title.* Be careful in choosing what essay to do in the essay section of the LNAT. Make sure that the essay title you pick allows you to write an interesting and effective essay that will impress an admissions

tutor reading it. So pick an essay title that allows you to make some strong arguments – or, even better, an essay title that allows you to make an unexpected or surprising point. For example, in the year the LNAT was introduced, students were required to write an essay on one of the following five topics:

1 'Sporting achievement should not be limited by the prohibition on the use of certain performance-enhancing drugs.' Do you agree?

2 What is your response to the view that the purpose of education is to prepare young people for the world of work?

3 'Women now have the chance to achieve anything they want.' How do you respond to this statement?

4 Modern society is too dependent on debt: we should all pay our way.' Do you agree?

5 Would you agree that travel and tourism exploit poorer nations and benefit only the richer ones?

(Nowadays, each student is given a choice of three essay questions that have been selected from a bank of possible essay questions. So different students will be given a different set of three essays to choose from.) Now – which of these essays would a good student do? Well, a good student would rule out doing (4) straightaway. Why? Well, the statement is so silly that there's no possibility of agreeing with it. And any arguments that one might make against the statement are just so obvious (without incurring debts, people couldn't afford to buy homes and cars; companies could not survive through lean times; the government would collapse) that an essay arguing that the statement is wrong wouldn't make for particularly interesting reading.

A good student would also rule out doing (5). This is partly because, again, the basis of the essay question is a statement ('travel and tourism exploit poorer nations and benefit only the richer ones') that is so silly that one cannot do anything but disagree with it. So the scope for saying anything interesting in response to the essay title is virtually nil. In addition, to write an effective essay on this title would seem to require a good grasp of the economic data on tourism; and not many students will have that sort of information to hand.

For similar reasons, a good student would also rule out doing essay (3). The statement seems obviously wrong. A woman with a baby might want to be paid £50,000 a year for working one day a week in a law firm, thus allowing her to spend most of her time raising her baby. But it can hardly be supposed that any woman (or man) would be allowed to do that. However, an essay that made that point would not be particularly interesting. It might be possible to narrow the statement in some way so as to make it more plausible – one could interpret it as saying that 'Women now have the chance to do any kind of work they want.' But, again, it's hard to see how one could write an interesting essay on that topic. Either the available information indicates that women have that chance or it indicates that they do not – there does not seem to be much room for interesting debate or discussion, either way.

Our good student is running out of options! What about (2)? Well, there is no way any student applying to study at a university will want to be caught agreeing with the idea that education is simply about preparing young people to do a job. So a student who did essay (2) would have to argue that the purpose of education is more wide-ranging. Could a student write an interesting essay that took that kind of line? It depends on whether he or she could come up with an interesting and convincing line as to what the 'purpose' of education is if it's not to prepare young people for work. Merely saying that the purpose of education is to 'cultivate one's mind' or to 'expand one's horizons' or make one 'question everything' wouldn't be enough – saying that is just not very interesting.

One interesting line which would link in quite well with the statement in the essay title would be to argue that the purpose of education is not to prepare young people for work but to prepare them for *leisure*. You could argue that the purpose of education is to prepare young people for what they should be doing in their leisure time. And one could move from there to say that it's noticeable that as education has become more work-oriented, the way young people spend their leisure time has increasingly become a social problem (examples: binge drinking, bored youths hanging around estates, joyriding). You could then say that this makes it all the more necessary that we move back towards a notion of education as preparing young people for how they spend their leisure.

That would make for quite an interesting essay on (2) that would impress any admissions tutor who read it. And note that while an essay that took this kind of line might refer to some features of contemporary life to make its points, doing this essay would not require the sort of in-depth knowledge of the real world that one would have to have if one attempted essays (3) or (5).

Finally, what about (1)? Again, there seems to be some scope for writing an interesting and effective essay on this topic. It's not so obvious that using performance-enhancing drugs in sport should be banned that it's impossible to think of interesting arguments on either side of the issue. For example, one could observe – if one wanted to argue in favour of allowing the use of performance-enhancing drugs – that athletes already use dietary supplements to help them train. So why not allow them to use steroids to build up their stamina and help them train longer? Against this, one could argue that steroids are bad for you, and athletes who do not want to endanger their health by using steroids should not be disadvantaged when competing against other athletes. There is scope here for getting an interesting debate going – which is simply not possible with essay (4). And there is no need to have access to very specialised knowledge to engage in that debate – something which, as we've seen, is not possible with essays (3) or (5). The debate is at the level of general principle, rather than hard fact.

So of these five essays, a good student would do essays (1) or (2). He or she would definitely not do essays (3), (4) or (5). So if you do the LNAT, be careful about your choice of essay – make sure you go through the same kind of process that I've gone through above. Discard the essay titles which – however do-able they might seem – offer little prospect of allowing you to write an interesting and effective essay.

(2) *Essay structure.* Suppose you have been told to write an essay on 'Is X true?' You have probably been taught to write an essay on this topic using the following structure:

1 Introduction.
2 Arguments for thinking that X is true.
3 Arguments for thinking that X is not true.
4 Your opinion on whether X is true, given the balance of the arguments.
5 Conclusion.

Please don't adopt this kind of structure in writing your LNAT essay. I'll say it again, just in case the message hasn't got through – *please, please, please don't adopt this kind of structure in writing your LNAT essay.* (In fact, once you leave school, please don't ever write an essay along these lines ever again.) Nothing is more guaranteed to send an admissions tutor to sleep than an essay that goes, 'On the one hand, it could be argued that . . . On the other hand, it could be argued that . . . On balance, I think that . . . So we can conclude that . . .'. If you want to impress an admissions tutor who is reading your essay – and remember he or she will probably have a large pile of these essays to wade through so you will want to do something to catch his or her eye – you will have to adopt a quite different approach. I'd like to encourage you to adopt this structure in writing your LNAT essay:

1 Conclusion.

2 Arguments in favour of your conclusion.

3 Arguments against your conclusion, and an explanation as to why they do not work.

4 Restatement of your conclusion.

This is a much more direct way of writing your essay. There are three big advantages to writing your essay in this way. First, your essay will be very easy to follow and understand – by stating at the start where you stand, you make it obvious where you are 'coming from'. Secondly, your essay will be much more interesting than an essay written in the more careful, plodding style you have probably been brought up to use. Thirdly, your essay will be a lot less wordy – a big advantage when you only have 500–600 words to play with. Of course, you can only employ this kind of essay structure if you know before you begin what your conclusion is going to be. So take some time before you start writing the essay to think it out and think about what sort of line you are going to take in the essay.

(3) *Preparation.* It might be an idea to try a few practice essay questions to get used to this different style of writing essays that I'm encouraging you to adopt. There are also some 'model' essays on the LNAT website which it might be an idea to look at – but they are so ridiculously good I think reading them might intimidate the hell out of you. Read them anyway – but in the knowledge that they are absurdly good and no student would be expected to write anything that elegant. (Incidentally, those model essays adopt a different structure from the one I recommend above. Their structure goes: 1. Clarification or rephrasing of the issues raised by the question. 2. Discussion of those issues. 3. Conclusions.) Another thing you should do by way of preparation for the essay section of the LNAT is to start reading – in full – a serious daily newspaper such as *The Times,* the *Daily Telegraph,* the *Independent* or the *Guardian.* Pay particular attention to the opinion/comment sections of the newspapers. It might be an idea to try to read the opinion/comment sections of both the *Daily Telegraph* and the *Guardian* each day, so that you are exposed to a variety of points of view. Also try, if you can, to read the *Spectator* or the *New*

Statesman or *The Economist* every week. Doing this will be of huge benefit to you in doing the essay section of the LNAT. First, reading serious newspapers and magazines will boost your knowledge of current affairs and therefore your ability to handle an essay question on current affairs. Secondly, doing this kind of reading will expose you to political ideas and discussions that you can then draw on in writing your essay. Thirdly, reading these kinds of newspapers and magazines will expose you to some good, serious debates on difficult issues, thus helping you see the sort of thing that you'll be expected to do in your essay.

● The Cambridge Law Test

That's all I want to say about the LNAT. I'll briefly say a few things about the Cambridge Law Test (CLT). This is an aptitude test for legal ability that students applying to study law at Cambridge have to do. So if you are applying to Cambridge and one or more universities that make their applicants do the LNAT, you'll end up doing both legal aptitude tests! Full details about the CLT can be found on the Cambridge Law Faculty's website at http://www.law.cam.ac.uk/admissions/cambridge-law-test.php. The test – which is sat when applicants come up to Cambridge for interview – will consist of an essay question *or* a comprehension question *or* a problem question. The colleges are given varieties of each type of question to pick from and it is up to them to determine which particular question their applicants will be asked to sit. So the CLT that law applicants to (say) Trinity College sit might be very different from the version of the CLT that applicants to my college would be made to sit.

If an applicant is required, under the version of the CLT that he or she has been supplied with, to do an essay question, he or she will be given a choice of three essay questions to do, and asked to do one essay – just like on the LNAT. And the guidance supplied above on writing essays for the LNAT equally applies to writing an essay for the CLT.

If an applicant is set a comprehension question for the CLT, that will usually take the form of a legal judgment or a couple of judgments, and the applicant will usually be asked to summarise the judgment(s) in his or her own words, and comment on the judgment(s). I have to say that students nowadays are pretty bad at writing summaries. Either they find it impossible to focus on the key ideas set out in the judgments, or they introduce irrelevant material speculating on what the judge 'really' thought or why the judge decided the case the way he or she did. The only way to improve your abilities at doing this kind of question is practice. Take any fairly lengthy story or comment piece from a newspaper or magazine and try to sum it up in not more than 100 words. (This is known as a *précis* exercise – the sort of thing that used to be standard in schools but is never done any more.) If you have a friend who's interested in doing the same thing, both of you should independently try to summarise the same story or article – then exchange your summaries and see whether you have both focused on the same key points. If you haven't, discuss whose summary was more precise. If you are asked to comment on a particular judgment, or asked what sort of judgment you would have given, take a clear line and come up with some clear arguments in favour of your position. If you have three arguments in favour of your position then number them or give each of them a name to make the distinctions between them clear. Obscurity is the enemy and you will be punished severely for fraternising with it – you must make what you are saying as clear as possible.

A CLT problem question will usually take the form of a set of rules drawn from a statute, and you will be asked to discuss how those rules apply to some concrete situations. The key to success in doing these sorts of questions is: *be precise* in applying the rules. Every term in the rule might be relevant to how that rule applies in a situation that you are considering – so pay attention to *every* term and what implications it might have for the situation you are considering. You have to be *accurate*: close is nowhere. Again, if you have a friend and both of you are applying to study law at Cambridge, you could both try the practice question on the Cambridge Faculty website and compare your answers and discuss any differences between them.

That's enough guidance from me. Good luck with all your applications and any tests you might have to do. Let me know how you get on.

Best wishes,

Nick

Tips for Interview

● From: Nicholas J. McBride [dearnick@pearson.com]
● To: Brown, Alex
● Subject: Tips for Interview

Hey Alex,

Good luck for your admissions interview! I'm sure you'll do very well. It's inevitable that you're going to be nervous – but I hope you'll be able to give a good account of yourself. To help you with that, here are some tips:

● The interviewer is on your side

I guarantee that your interviewers will be eager to see you do well. Don't think for a second that they will be out to trip you up, or trap you into making a fool of yourself. All your interviewers will be desperate to find some really good students among all the candidates they are interviewing – so they will want to do as much as possible to help you do justice to yourself in the interview.

● Smile!

The interviewers would not only like to find some really good students among all the candidates they are interviewing – they would also like to find some really good students who they actually like the idea of spending the next three years with. So – don't be grouchy, or standoffish in the interview: be as positive, enthusiastic, and as cheerful as the circumstances allow you to be.

● Be straightforward

Common sense is another thing your interviewers will be looking for in the people they interview. So, if you are given a legal rule and asked to apply it to a given situation, be straightforward in applying the rule. Think about what the common sense meaning of the rule is, apply it to the situation and see what the outcome is. Don't try to prejudge what the outcome 'should' be, and don't try to detect any hidden traps, or meanings, or exceptions in the rule you've been asked to apply. If there are any, they will soon be pointed out to you – until that happens, just apply the plain, commonsense meaning of the rule to determine how it applies in the situation you have been given.

● Think!

The ability to think for yourself is another thing your interviewers will be looking out for. To test for this, your interviewers may well give you a situation, ask what you think the legal outcome should be in that situation, then give you a slightly altered situation, and ask you again what the legal outcome should be. If they do this, they are testing to see whether you can identify the distinctions between the two situations, and see whether you are capable of thinking for yourself whether those distinctions make a difference. For example, you might be asked to consider the following situation:

(1) Two severely premature babies, Baby A, and Baby B, are born at the same time. Neither of them can survive without being put in an incubator, but there is only one free incubator in the hospital. Who should be placed in the incubator?

Your answer will almost certainly be: whoever has the better chance of survival if they are placed in the incubator unit. Okay – consider now this next situation:

(2) Two severely premature babies, Baby A, and Baby B, are born within a few hours of each other. Neither of them can survive without being put in an incubator. Baby B is born first, and placed in the one remaining free incubator in the hospital. Baby A was born a few hours later, but there is no free incubator for him to be placed in. The chances of Baby B surviving in

> the incubator have been assessed at 25%. It is clear that if Baby A were placed in Baby B's incubator, instead of Baby B, Baby A's chances of survival would be 75%. Should the doctors take Baby B out of her incubator, and replace her with Baby A?

Your response to situation (1) might suggest that you would favour Baby B being taken out of the incubator, and being replaced by Baby A. But your interviewers have not asked you to consider situation (2) just so that you can repeat – whoever has the higher chance of survival in the incubator should be placed in the incubator. They want to see if you can think for yourself: what are the distinctions between situations (1) and (2), and do those distinctions make a difference?

Well, let's consider the distinctions first. The key distinction is that in situation (2), Baby B is already in the incubator. So if you are going to put Baby A in the incubator, you have to do something positive to Baby B (take Baby B out of the incubator) that will have the effect of making Baby B worse off than she is at the moment. This is very different from situation (1), where if you put Baby A in the incubator, you are not doing anything positive to Baby B – you are merely failing to do something that would have the effect of saving Baby B's life. So: that's the distinction identified. The next issue is – does that distinction make a difference? Is doing something positive to Baby B, as a result of which act Baby B will die, worse than failing to do something for Baby B, as a result of which failure Baby B will die? Let's assume that you do think that it makes a difference. So you say that in situation (2), Baby B should not be taken out of the incubator. You might be asked to then consider this situation:

> (3) The same situation as situation (2), except Baby B was born five minutes before Baby A, and had only just been put in the incubator when Baby A was carried into the ward for severely premature babies. Should Baby B be taken out of the incubator, and replaced with Baby B?

In this situation, Baby B has only just been put in the incubator. Does this make a difference? Given that you thought Baby B should not be taken out of the incubator in (2), do you also think that Baby B should not be taken out of the incubator in (3)? Or does the fact that Baby B has not been in the incubator for very long make it more acceptable to take Baby B out of the incubator and replace her with Baby A?

○ Argue!

Once you have taken a position, you will be expected to argue in favour of it. And by argue, I mean genuinely argue – present reasons for thinking that your position is correct. Don't just say 'Well, that's my opinion': that's not an argument, that's an assertion.

So – suppose you've said that Baby B should not be taken out of the incubator in (2), but that she should be in (3). You will be asked to account for this apparent inconsistency in your views. What you will need to do is show how you are not being inconsistent at all, but identify why there is a material difference between the two situations. One way might be to argue that in some sense, the incubator becomes part of Baby B the longer she stays in it – it becomes part of her life system, and it would be just as wrong to deprive her of that, as it would be for me to rip out your heart to give it to someone else who may, with your heart, enjoy a better chance of long-term survival than you do. So in (3), the incubator and Baby B are not yet – at the relevant level – 'attached' to each other, so it would not be wrong to take the incubator away from Baby B in the same way that it would be wrong to take the incubator away from Baby B in (2). Okay – this argument seems a bit mysterious and metaphysical, but at least it's an argument. And you are going to have to draw on some argument like that to establish that there is a significant difference between (2) and (3) – if you can't do that, you'll just be reduced to incoherent babbling.

Alternatively, let's suppose that you think that Baby B should not be taken out of the incubator in either situation (2) or situation (3). In that case an objection will be made to your view – and you will be expected to argue that that objection does not work. The objection would go like this: 'If you think that Baby B should not be taken out of the incubator in situation (3), then you are letting the morally arbitrary fact that Baby B was born a mere five minutes before Baby A determine who gets the incubator – surely this is unsatisfactory?' How do you overcome this objection? You have to establish that you are basing your position that Baby B should not be taken out of the incubator in situation (3) on something more than just the fact that Baby B was born first. Well, one way of establishing this would be to observe that in situation (3), the people running the ward for severely premature babies have taken on the job – in lawyers' language, 'assumed the responsibility' – of looking after Baby B, and have not (yet) taken on the job of looking after Baby A. So the people running the unit are 'attached' to Baby B in a way that they are not to Baby A. This is not a morally arbitrary fact. Attachments matter. Once an attachment has been formed, it counts for something, and this is so even if the attachment would never have been formed but for an initial, arbitrary twist of fate. Again, the argument is a bit mysterious and metaphysical – but, again, at least it's an argument that helps you demolish the objection being made to your position.

● Don't stick to a hopeless position

But what if you are uninspired? What if you can't see an argument that will save your position? What if you've said that Baby B should not be taken out of the incubator in situation (2), but she should be in situation (3) – but you can't come up with a good argument to explain why there is a material difference between these two situations? If that's the case, then please, please don't 'stick to your guns'. Don't just blindly assert that there is a difference between (2) and (3), and that's your opinion and you are sticking to it. This will go down really badly – it will show a basic failure to think on your part. If you can't present a decent argument for thinking that there is a material difference between situations (2) and (3), you don't have a choice: you have to concede that there is no material difference between situations (2) and (3). And having made that concession, there are two ways you can go. You can stick with saying that in situation (2), Baby B should not be taken out of the incubator, and shift to saying that in situation (3), Baby B should also not be taken out of the incubator. Or you can shift your position on situation (2) and say that in that situation, Baby B should be taken out of the incubator, and say that, given this, it's obvious that in situation (3) as well, Baby B should be taken out of the incubator. Don't think for a second that doing that will get you out of trouble – you will be expected to argue in favour of the new position that you have adopted. But it will at least show the interviewers that you are not a nutcase who sticks rigidly to a position even though you cannot come up with a single good reason for doing so.

● Don't avoid the issue

A lot of students – perhaps because they intelligently perceive the dangers of taking a position which they will then be asked to defend – try to avoid taking a position on an issue that they have been asked to address. They evade the issue, rather than tackling it head on. So, for example, let's go back to situation (2), where Baby B is in the incubator, and Baby A comes along, with a much better chance of survival if he is put in the incubator, in place of Baby B. The issue is whether Baby B should be taken out of the incubator and Baby A put in her place. Many students will avoid addressing that issue by saying something like, 'Well, I think in this situation the hospital authorities should try to find another incubator for Baby A to go in.' It's just a waste of time saying that – the interviewers will simply say, 'Let's assume that there isn't another incubator: what should happen then?', thus forcing the interviewee to address the issue. So don't avoid the issue. If you want to show the interviewers that you are aware there might be alternative solutions to the problem they are making you consider, then say something like, 'Assuming that there isn't another hospital nearby that would be able to care for Baby A, I think . . .'

● Don't assume that there is a clear right answer

I don't want to say that there is *no* right answer to the issue of what should be done in the incubator cases we have been considering – I believe in right answers, especially in the field of morality. However, I do want to say that there is no *clear* right answer to these issues. Whatever answer you come up with, objections and counter-arguments can be made to your position. So don't think that there is a clear right answer to the questions you are being asked to consider and that you are being expected to come up with that answer and that if someone comes up with an objection to something you've said, that shows you answered the question wrongly. That involves a complete misunderstanding of why your interviewers might ask you to consider a series of situations such as the incubator cases set out above. They are not so much interested in your answers, as they are in probing your answers to gauge how intelligent you are. Can you come up with an argument to support a position you are taking? Can you deal with an objection to that argument? Can you recognise when your position is hopeless, and shift your position accordingly? These are the questions that your interviewers will really be interested in getting some answers to – not what your views are on whether Baby B or Baby A should get the last incubator on the ward for severely premature babies.

● Current affairs

Of course, you might not be asked at all about some hypothetical case and what should happen in that case. You might be asked about some recent incident or development that has made the news, and asked for your opinion about it. The interviewer's aim in asking you about this incident/development will be exactly the same – to probe your answers with a view to getting some idea as to how intelligent you are. But if you are asked about some recent incident/development in the news, you will be left hanging in the wind if you don't actually know much about it. So at least a couple of months before you attend your interview, make sure that you regularly read at least one of the *Spectator, The Economist,* and the *New Statesman* each week, and that you read the news and opinion sections of a decent daily newspaper – that is the *Times,* the *Guardian,* the *Daily Telegraph,* the *Independent* or the *Financial Times* – each day. Doing this will not only keep you up to date with the news, it will also give you ideas for intelligent things to say in the interview if you are asked about something that has happened in the news.

● Be prepared for the obvious questions

Your interview will probably open with a couple of questions about your personal statement on your UCAS form. These are meant to be 'soft' questions, designed to relax you and get you talking. But they can turn into a nightmare if you aren't prepared for them.

So if you have expressed an interest in reading fiction, be ready to say what you have read recently, and what you thought of it. If you say that you spent your summer holidays last year backpacking around Eastern Europe, be prepared to say something a little bit more enlightening about your experiences than just 'Yeah – it was great.' If you have said that you are deeply fascinated by the work of the International Criminal Court and you want to study law because you would like to work there one day, be prepared – be very prepared – to talk about the International Criminal Court, what it does, why it's important, and what sort of cases it might handle in the future. That last example shows that you should be very careful in writing your personal statement not to make any claims that you cannot back up. So, for example, I have seen more than one personal statement in the past that has said something along the lines of, 'I spent a week working in my local solicitors and my experience there has given me a great insight into the workings of our justice system.' Yeah, right. If you say something like that in your personal statement, you had better be ready to back it up with some examples of some 'insights' that you gained on your week's work experience – because you will definitely be asked for them.

There are other pretty obvious questions that you should have prepared to answer before your interview. Why do you want to do law? How easy do you find it to balance your work with all your extra-curricular commitments? (Dangerous one, that: the interviewers don't want to admit someone who will be too busy with all sorts of extra-curricular activities to put in the effort required to do well in their legal studies.) Why do you want to take a gap year? (If you do.) Why are your AS marks in History not as good as your other AS marks? (That's a very important question as the interviewers do pay a lot of attention to things like GCSE marks and AS marks in gauging how well someone is likely to do as a law student. So if you have had a couple of disappointing marks at GCSE, or at AS-Level, then be prepared to explain them.)

Having said that you should prepare for these questions to come up, don't overprepare for them. Don't try to memorise an answer that you'd give for each of these questions – you'll just come across all unnatural in the interview. Just come up with a rough idea of what you would say, and then don't worry about again.

● It's a conversation, not an interrogation

The best interviews are conversational in nature – there's a back-and-forth quality to them, where the interviewers say something, the interviewee says something that actually addresses what the interviewers have said, the interviewers then reply to the point that has been made to them, the interviewee responds, and so on, and so on. So try your best to go into the interview with the mentality that you are there to have a chat with the interviewers about some subjects that they are interested in talking about. Don't think that you are there to show off how clever you are, or to be pummelled into submission, or to be tested on how much you know about a particular subject. You are just there to have a chat for half an hour or so. So relax; listen to what's being said to you, and respond to it; and if you don't know what to say, be frank about that so the conversation can move on to some other topic that might be more productive.

● The interview isn't make or break

Finally, remember that the interview isn't the most crucial part of your application. Many interviewers are sceptical as to how valuable the interview actually is as a way of determining how well someone is going to do as a law student. I have certainly interviewed people who were completely disastrous in interview, but they were still admitted because the rest of their application – their reference and their exam results to date – was so outstanding, and they proved to be absolutely fine law students. So if you don't have such a good interview, it's not a disaster: there is lots of other information about you available to the interviewers that they can take into account in judging your application.

There are some other words of advice I'd like to give you, warning you against adopting certain disastrous ideas or habits of thought that seem to be particularly popular among people going to university, and which can result in your not doing so well in interview. But because the advice isn't just relevant to your upcoming interview, but will also be relevant for when you actually go to university, I'll deal with it separately in another letter. Read this one, think about it, and I'll be in touch again very soon.

Best wishes,

Nick

Some Traps to Avoid

- From: Nicholas J. McBride [dearnick@pearson.com]
- To: Brown, Alex
- Subject: Some Traps to Avoid

Hi Alex,

As promised, here's a letter warning you about some bad mental habits that a lot of students your age fall into. I hope reading this letter will not only help you do well in interview, but also help you generally with your legal studies.

● Relativism

Right at the start of his book *The Closing of the American Mind,* Allan Bloom – a very great American academic – observed, 'There is one thing a professor can be absolutely certain of: almost every student entering the university believes, or says he believes, that truth is relative.'

It's understandable why students should take this position. Students, as a whole, want to be nice, open-minded and tolerant people; and this is, of course, greatly to their credit. Now – suppose that I tell you that the world is flat. There are only two ways you can react. You can tell me that I am wrong, implying thereby that I am stupid and badly educated – which isn't very nice. Or you can say, 'Well, all truth is relative, so I'm not in a position to tell you that you're wrong. For you the world is flat; for me, it's roughly spherical – but there's nothing for us to disagree about. We're both right, from within our different perspectives.' This seems a much nicer, open-minded and tolerant response and is thus much more attractive to students.

However, it's extremely silly to think that 'all truth is relative'. The reason for this is very simple. We know for certain that the statement 'all truth is relative' cannot be absolutely true, because if this statement were absolutely true then not all truth would be relative. So only two possibilities remain. Either the statement 'all truth is relative' is absolutely false – in which case we shouldn't accept it. Or the statement 'all truth is relative' is only true for some people, and is false for some other people – in which case, why should we accept that it's true? Either way, it's senseless to think that 'all truth is relative'. As the philosopher Roger Scruton observes, 'A writer who says that there are no truths, or that all truth is "merely relative" is asking you not to believe him. So don't.'

'Well,' you may say, 'It may make no sense to think that "all truth is relative" when we are talking about questions of fact. But surely when we are talking about values or morality, everyone has different opinions, and it's simply not possible to say that one person's opinions are correct and another person's opinions are wrong. So in the area of values or morality, it is true to say that "all truth is relative".' If you think like this, you've already fallen into another trap that I want to urge you to avoid: the trap of moral relativism.

Let's try to get you out of the trap by considering a concrete example. In his great novel *The Brothers Karamazov*, Fyodor Dostoevsky set out a number of documented instances of cruelty to children that occurred a couple of centuries ago in Russia. This is the last one:

> There was a general at the beginning of the century, a general with high connections and a very wealthy landowner . . . He had hundreds of dogs in his kennels and nearly a hundred handlers . . . [O]ne day a house-serf, a little boy, only eight years old, threw a stone while he was playing and hurt the paw of the general's favourite hound. "Why is my favourite dog limping?" It was reported to him that this boy had . . . hurt her paw. "So it was you," the general looked the boy up and down. "Take him!" They took him, took him from his mother, and locked him up for the night. In the morning at dawn, the general rode out in full dress for the hunt . . . surrounded by . . . dogs, handlers, huntsmen, all on horseback. The house-serfs are gathered for their edification, the guilty boy's mother in front of them all. The boy is led out of the lockup . . . The general orders them to undress the boy; the child is stripped naked, he shivers, he's crazy with fear, he doesn't dare make a peep . . . "Drive him!" the general commands. The huntsmen shout, "Run, run!" The boy runs . . . "[Get] him!" screams the general and looses the whole pack of wolfhounds on him. He hunted him down before his mother's eyes, and the dogs tore the child to pieces . . .

A true story. So – what do you think? Was it morally wrong for the general to do what he did? I hope you will say, 'Yes it was – and anyone who thinks otherwise is wrong.' If you do, then you have to concede that moral relativism is incorrect: it is possible to say that someone's values or opinions on matters of morality are wrong.

Now – if you're anything like the students I see when I interview them for places at my college, you'll probably say, 'Well, it's my personal opinion that it was wrong for the general to do what he did, and if I could have stopped him I would have. At the same time, I recognise that other people might think it was okay for the general to do what he did – and if they do, I can't say they're incorrect. They're entitled to their opinion.' But if you say this, then you are contradicting yourself. If you genuinely think, 'It was wrong for the general to do what he did' then you must also think that the statement 'It was okay for the general to do what he did' is incorrect. But if you do think that that statement is incorrect, then you must think that you, I or anyone else would be making a mistake if we said that it was okay for the general to do what he did.

The truth is that moral relativism cannot be seriously defended. It's an affectation, adopted out of a laudable desire not to be offensive or cruel by telling other people that what they are doing is bad or morally wrong. Indeed, it's a self-refuting affectation because the people who adopt it would be the first to insist that it is morally wrong to be offensive or cruel to other people – and that anyone who thinks differently is simply wrong.

● Not taking human rights seriously

Imagine the following conversation between two people, A and B:

A: Would it be wrong for me to torture you for fun?

B: Of course it would.

A: Why?

B: Well, I have a human right not to be tortured.

A: What if you were a terrorist and you had information about an impending terrorist attack that will kill thousands of people. Would it be wrong for me to torture you to get you to tell me the details of the attack?

B: Er. . .

B is obviously not a moral relativist: he is happy to say that torture is wrong, and that he does have a human right not to be tortured. But B does not take the idea that there is a human right not to be tortured seriously. He hesitates on the issue of whether it would be wrong to torture a terrorist in order to prevent a terrorist attack. There are two possible sources of this hesitation; both of them are unjustified if we take seriously the idea that there is a human right not to be tortured.

(1) *Not wrong to torture the blameworthy?* B may be hesitating to say that it would be wrong to torture a terrorist in order to extract information about an impending attack because, while he is completely confident that it would be wrong to torture someone who is completely blameless and innocent (such as a terrorist's 5-year-old daughter), he is less confident about whether it would be wrong to torture someone who has been helping to plan the slaughter of thousands of people. But if there is a human right not to be tortured, then everyone has that right, the innocent and blameworthy alike. You cannot lose that right simply because you happen to be an evil person.

(2) *Society comes first?* The second possible source of B's hesitation may be a nagging thought that in the situation where we could prevent the deaths of thousands of people by torturing someone, surely the interests of those thousands of people must come before the interests of the person we are thinking of torturing. But again, if there is such a thing as a human right not to be tortured, this thought is unjustified. The whole point of human rights is that they place limits on what we can do to other people in the name of 'social welfare' or the 'public interest'. They assert the priority of the individual over society. (That is why Jeremy Bentham – who was the god-father of utilitarianism: the creed that tells us that sacrificing the interests of an individual is the right thing to do if the overall happiness of society will be increased as a result – was so hostile to the idea of human rights, declaring it to be 'nonsense on stilts'.) In the memorable phrase coined by the legal philosopher Ronald Dworkin, human rights are 'trumps' – if you have a human right not to be treated in a particular way, then that gives you the power to veto any proposal that you be treated in that way, no matter how overwhelming the public interest may be in the proposal being carried out. It might be argued against this that many of the human rights recog-nised in the European Convention on Human Rights (ECHR) are qualified in nature. So, for example, the right to freedom of expression recognised in Article 10 of the ECHR may be limited or abridged so far as is 'neces-sary in a democratic society, in the interests of national security, territorial integrity or public safety, for the prevention of disorder or crime, for the

protection of health or morals, for the protection of the reputation or rights of others, for preventing the disclosure of information received in confidence, or for maintaining the authority and impartiality of the judiciary.' Does this not show that what I've said in the previous paragraph is incorrect and that human rights can indeed be made to give way where the public interest demands it? The answer is 'no'.

To see why, we have to remind ourselves that human rights are enjoyed by everyone. Everyone has these rights because they are human beings and, as such, are endowed with a certain dignity that entitles them not to be treated as disposable commodities. If this is correct, the right to freedom of expression is not a genuine example of a human right. We don't have a right to freedom of expression because we are human beings. We have a right to freedom of expression because it is important for the health of our society that we be given a right to freedom of expression. History teaches us that democratic societies tend to flourish much more than undemocratic societies, and you cannot have a genuine democracy without giving people a right to freedom of expression. Given the social roots of the right to freedom of expression, it is hardly surprising that provision should be made for limiting this right where its exercise would work in an anti-social way. In contrast, the rights recognised by the ECHR that can be said to be genuine examples of human rights – the right not to be intentionally killed (Article 2), the right not to be subjected to 'torture or to inhuman or degrading treatment or punishment' (Article 3), the right not to 'be held in slavery or servitude' (Article 4), and the right to a fair trial (Article 6) – are completely unqualified, and cannot be set aside or limited when the public interest demands.

So if there is such a thing as a human right not to be tortured, then B should not hesitate: he should say firmly that, yes, it would be wrong to torture a terrorist to extract information from him about a terrorist attack, even if thousands of people will die if the attack is carried out. But it may be that B could not bring himself to say this. If that is the case, B must concede that there is, in fact, no such thing as a human right not to be tortured. Does that then mean that it would be okay for A to torture B for fun? No: even if B does not have a human right not to be tortured, it would still be wrong for A to torture B for fun. This is because if we weigh the pain B will suffer if A tortures him against the pleasure A will get from torturing B, B's pain will outweigh A's pleasure and make it wrong for A to torture B. (Of course, such a balancing exercise produces a quite different conclusion in the scenario where B is a terrorist and we need to torture him to prevent an impending attack.)

B is typical of many students that I come across, particularly at interview stage. They are more than happy to talk the talk of human rights, but when it comes to walking the walk, they stumble and fall. They happily condemn what happened in Auschwitz on human rights grounds. But after only a few minutes' discussion, they are all too willing to concede that, in fact, it might be acceptable to torture people, or conduct medical experiments on unwilling patients, or destroy thousands of lives in a nuclear holocaust, if doing so would serve the 'greater good'. Don't fall into the same trap: if you are going to say that people have a human right not to be tortured, follow through and insist that it is always wrong to torture someone, no matter what the circumstances are and no matter what good might be done as a result.

● Finding human rights everywhere

The finality of human rights – the fact that the existence of a human right that x not be done allows the holder of that right to veto any proposal that x be done, no matter how advantageous doing x might be – means that there is a constant temptation to invoke human rights as a way of establishing that it would be wrong to go ahead with a particular course of action.

So, for example, if you are opposed to a local authority's plans to create a housing estate near your village, it is very tempting to try to win the argument that the housing estate should not be built by asserting that building the estate would violate your and the other villagers' human rights. If you can make this assertion stick, then you've won the day. If the local authority attempts to argue that it would be in the public interest to build the housing estate, you can argue back that that is irrelevant: your and the other villagers' human rights trump any considerations of the public interest.

Students like to invoke human rights for the same reason: it provides an easy way of closing down the discussion of an issue that might otherwise prove too thorny for them to handle. So, for example, in the case I discussed in the previous letter, where Baby B has been placed in a hospital's last remaining free incubator, and Baby A is then wheeled into the ward for severely premature babies, and the issue is whether Baby A should be placed in Baby B's incubator, in place of Baby B, many students might feel tempted to short-circuit the discussion of what should be done by simply asserting that Baby B has a 'human right' to stay in the incubator.

Try to resist this temptation if it comes calling. Recognise what a difficult thing it is to establish that someone has a human right not to be treated in a particular way. Remember that human rights are based on the idea that all human beings are special, and as such deserve not to be treated like trash. This places a serious limit on when we can reasonably say that a proposed course of action will violate someone else's human rights. Choosing to replace Baby B in the incubator with Baby A because Baby B is black and Baby A is white would certainly violate Baby B's human rights because making such a choice involves a refusal to recognise that Baby B is just as special as Baby A. But it's hard to see how it could be argued that Baby B's human rights would be violated if we chose to replace Baby B in the incubator with Baby A simply because Baby A has a better chance of survival. Making that kind of choice does not involve any disregard, or contempt, for Baby B. (Though it may still be wrong to take Baby B out of the incubator, even if Baby A has a better chance of survival, for the reasons I discussed in my previous letter.)

Another way of making the same point about how difficult it is to establish that someone has a human right not to be treated in a certain way is to remember how *final* human rights are. That is, remember that if someone has a human right not to be treated in a particular way, then it would always be wrong to treat them in that way, no matter how beneficial the consequences of treating them in that way might be. This also places a serious limit on when we can reasonably say that a proposed course of action will violate someone's human rights. How many things that one person can do to another would you be willing to say are always absolutely wrong, no matter how beneficial the consequences of doing that sort of thing might be? I can only come up with eight:

1 executing someone else – that is, intentionally killing someone else after you have decided in a calm and collected state that that is what you are going to do;

2 torturing someone else;

3 having sex with someone without their consent;

4 intentionally sterilising someone without their consent;

5 experimenting on someone without their consent;

6 depriving someone of their liberty for an indefinite period;

7 intentionally destroying or getting in the way of someone's friendship with another;

8 treating someone with a contempt that is not based on an honest assessment of that person's character.

If I'm right, and there are no more than eight things that you can do to someone else that are always wrong, no matter what the circumstances, then there are only eight genuine human rights. And, of course, there are even fewer if, for example, it would in fact be justifiable in certain circumstances to torture someone, or intentionally kill someone.

● Assumptions about certainty in the law

Another common trap that I would counsel you against falling into is the belief that the law on every issue is always certain. This is simply not true: it's often very difficult to say what the law says on a particular issue. The sources of uncertainty in the law are threefold.

(1) *Gaps.* The law is full of gaps. That is, there are lots of areas and issues where we don't know what the law says, because Parliament hasn't legislated to cover that area or issue and the courts haven't yet been asked to decide what the law says on that area or issue. For example, suppose that I write a play that receives a great deal of acclaim. I subsequently allow the play to be performed at a theatre for six months, on the basis that I'm to receive 10 per cent of the box office. Suppose the play closes after two nights because the acting and the production received universally bad reviews in the newspapers. Could I sue the actors and the producer of the play for the money I would have earned had their acting and staging of the play been halfway competent? Nobody really knows: there's no statute governing the issue, and the issue has never come up to be decided by the courts. The law on this issue is therefore uncertain.

(2) *Vagueness.* Legal rules are often vague, making it very hard to know how they apply in concrete situations. So, for example, the Unfair Terms in Consumer Contracts Regulations 1999 provide that a term in a contract between a consumer and a business will be invalid if 'contrary to the requirement of good faith, it causes a significant imbalance in the parties' rights and obligations arising under the contract, to the detriment of the consumer'.

This is so incredibly vague it will often be very hard to tell whether a given term in a contract between a business and a consumer will be valid or invalid. For example, suppose that I hire a car from you, and the car hire contract provides that if the car suffers any damage for any reason while it is in my possession, then I am obliged to compensate the car hire company for the damage done. It's uncertain whether this term is valid or not under the 1999 Regulations.

(3) *Contradiction.* On occasion, the law is contradictory. One legal rule will point in one direction while another legal rule will point in another direction, and it's hard to know which legal rule one should follow. For example, let's suppose there are two children called Adrian and Brooke, and let's suppose that Adrian is under 18 and Brooke is under 13. Now – sections 9 and 13(1) of the Sexual Offences Act 2003 combined provide that Adrian will commit the offence of 'sexual activity with a child' if he intentionally touches Brooke and his touching is 'sexual'. Because Adrian is under 18, section 13(2) provides that in this situation the maximum punishment Adrian can receive is imprisonment for 5 years. However, section 7 of the Sexual Offences Act 2003 provides that if Adrian intentionally touches Brooke and his touching is 'sexual' then he will also commit the offence of 'sexual assault of a child under 13' – and the maximum punishment for committing that offence is imprisonment for 14 years. But this seems to contradict the effect of section 13(2). What is the point of Parliament having provided in section 13(2) that if Adrian intentionally touches Brooke in a 'sexual' way, the maximum punishment he can receive is 5 years' imprisonment if prosecutors can evade the effect of this provision by charging Adrian with an offence under section 7? This contradiction – or tension – within the Sexual Offences Act 2003 makes it very uncertain what the legal position will be if Adrian intentionally touches Brooke in a sexual way.

Thinking that the law is always certain can be damaging in interview if you dogmatically insist that a particular legal provision means x, and fail to acknowledge that it is actually difficult to tell what it means. It can also be damaging to you as a law student in answering problem questions. If you assume that the law on every issue is perfectly certain, your answer to a problem question will almost certainly be overly simplistic and fail to attend to all the issues raised by that question.

So try in your studies to embrace the idea that the law is uncertain on various issues and questions. Indeed, it would be a very good idea to carry around an

'Uncertainty Book' in which you can write down any issues or questions on which the law is uncertain and suggestions as to how that uncertainty might be resolved. This will prove invaluable for your exams, as examiners often set questions around areas of the law where the law is uncertain in order: (1) to test your ability to recognise that the law in those areas is uncertain; and (2) to see whether you can intelligently discuss how the courts might resolve that uncertainty if they are called upon to do so.

But don't go throwing the baby out with the bathwater. While you should embrace the idea that the law isn't always certain, you should reject the idea that the law is always uncertain. This idea – which is most closely associated with an American school of thought called the Critical Legal Studies Movement – is demonstrably untrue.

If I, being of sound mind, take a rifle, climb to the top of a tower in the middle of a square, and shoot dead someone walking around in the square below, I will have committed murder. If I contract to paint your house on Sunday, and I spend that Sunday watching football instead, you will be entitled to sue me for damages. If I am an examiner and I charge a student £1,000 to get an advance look at the paper that I have set, the exam board for which I'm working will be entitled to sue me for that £1,000 and anything that I've acquired with it. If a local authority has been allocated money by Parliament to improve transport facilities in its area, and it decides to use that money to buy cars for members of the party that controls the local authority, disaffected council tax payers will be entitled to bring an action for judicial review and have the local authority's decision set aside. There is as little doubt that these things will happen as there is doubt that apples that fall off trees will always fall towards the ground.

The idea that the law is always uncertain is, admittedly, very liberating for lawyers – it gives them a lot more freedom to fool around with legal rules and doctrines to achieve whatever results they want to achieve. But that feeling of liberation doesn't make the idea any more true. If I think I can fly, I may feel more liberated – but I still won't be able to fly. The truth is that if the law were always uncertain, then there'd be no point in our having a legal system at all. After all, what is the point of our having laws if they don't provide us with any effective guidance as to what we can and cannot do; if they don't provide us with any reliable information as to what actions we can bring against other people and in what circumstances; if they don't place any real limits on what the State may do to us? What are our laws for if not that? Fortunately, the law for the most part is certain and you should resist the temptation to think that the law is always uncertain, however dizzyingly exciting such a thought may seem.

Okay – that's enough advice from me for now. Again – good luck with your interview. Let me know how it goes.

All best wishes,

Nick

Some Advice Before You Start Your Studies

11

- From: Nicholas J. McBride [dearnick@pearson.com]
- To: Brown, Alex
- Subject: Some Advice Before You Start Your Studies

Hey Alex,

Thanks for your letter asking me if I have any tips for you before you go to university. Here they are:

● Read

You should read a lot of books before you go to university. You'll be reading a lot of material when you get there, so if you start reading a lot of books now, studying at university won't come as such a culture shock. Try to read books that you won't have much time to read when you're at university. So try not to spend too much time reading books that are about subjects that you'll be studying at university. You'll be able to read those books when you get there. Instead, you should try to read some good books that will give you tips on how you should approach your studies when you get to university, and absorb the lessons that they have to teach you so that you'll be ready to apply them from day one of your studies. Remember that you'll have so much to read once you get to university, you won't necessarily have time to read any books that give you tips on how you should approach your studies. So it's important to take advantage of the free time you have now to read such books. And remember what I said in my fourth letter to you about how important it is that you cultivate an interest in political and economic ideas if you are going to do well as a law student. I meet and teach so many students who are utterly bland and colourless in their views – and they are always rewarded with bland and colourless marks in their end-of-year exams. So take the opportunity between now and October to expand your mind a bit and spice up your views by reading interesting and challenging books of ideas, particularly on political and economic issues. Again, the Pre-U reading list on www.mcbridesguides.com may give you some useful ideas as to what books you should read.

● Listen

This is the most important tip I can give you – not least because if you don't take this piece of advice on board, everything else I have to say to you will be a waste of time. Listen to any advice that you are given. You are starting an entirely new subject and you will need a lot of guidance to make a success of your studies. Now – I'm not saying that all the guidance you will get will be helpful, but almost all of it will be – so keep your ears open and pay attention to everything your teachers have to tell you. In order to do this, you will need to do a couple of other things:

● Be humble

Try to realise that you have a lot to learn, and act accordingly. If your teacher tells you something about the law or gives you a bit of advice about your work, try to stop yourself thinking straightaway, 'That's ridiculous!' or 'That can't be true!' or 'She's talking rubbish!' or 'Well, I disagree' or 'Nobody's ever told me that before – he can't know what he's talking about'. These sorts of instant reactions are the brain's way of shutting up shop – of refusing to listen to what it is being told. Instead, try to keep an open mind. Try to recognise that you don't know everything and that what your teacher has told you probably has a lot of merit.

● Don't distract yourself

It's so important that you keep your focus while you are studying. So don't work in places where you can easily get distracted – especially by things like television or the Internet. If you are being taught in a small group or listening to a lecture, taking notes of what is being said helps keep your mind from drifting off to other places. Try to keep the rest of your life organised and in good shape so that you are not constantly worrying about other things when you should be working. Cut out of your life anything that is a bad influence or a source of constant distraction.

● Be self-critical

Remember that it easy when studying law to lull yourself into a false sense of security by adopting a superficial approach to your studies and thinking that that is all you need to know. Guard against this by asking yourself constantly: Am I going into this subject deeply enough? What don't I know – what do I still have to learn? Do the books I'm using look like the sort of books that top students would use? If not, what sort of books do top students use and how can I get hold of them? Is this book that I'm using inviting me to 'fly high' over the law by constantly skating over difficult issues? (Danger phrases to look out for are: 'Broadly speaking, . . .'; 'It's safe to assume . . .'; 'Generally, . . .'; 'Usually, . . .'.)

● Be positive

You will find studying law a very tough experience at times. You will be study-ing a whole new subject from scratch, one that is unlike any other subject you have studied before. You will be acquiring a whole new set of skills and taking what skills you have for making notes and writing essays to a whole new level. Doing this will be hard – but it is doable. The important thing is not to get discouraged, but to keep on going. Everyone who ever became really accom-plished in some skill or art started off as a beginner, and you are no different. So when you encounter difficulties in your studies, don't write yourself off and think that you aren't ever going to get anywhere as a law student – just keep on going and eventually things will come right.

● Speak up

If there's some point you don't understand about the law, don't be afraid to ask your teachers about it when you get the chance. Don't think, 'I don't want to embarrass myself in front of everyone else by making myself look stupid.' Chances are everyone else is having a problem with that point as well and they'll be grateful to you for speaking up and giving your teachers the chance to address it in front of everyone.

Similarly, if you are having a problem with your studies, don't be afraid to go to whoever is in charge of your studies to tell them about it and ask for their help. The problem you're having is probably one they have come across before and they'll be able to draw on their experience to give you some good advice. Don't be afraid to ask for and get as much help as you need. You have the right to freedom of speech. Exercise it.

● Be nice

Because of the work I do, from time to time I get contacted by sixth form students like you asking me questions about studying law at university. I always try to do my best to answer their questions – but am always amazed at how often it happens that after I've replied to a particular student, that they don't get back in touch with me to thank me for giving up some of my time to deal with whatever issue they were asking me about. And even among the students I know here, or students who have left university and are now making their way in the world, 'thank you' seem to be the hardest words of all.

Don't be like that. Be nice – thank everyone for helping you out, whether or not it's part of their job to do so, and they will be more willing to help you out in future. In small-group teaching sessions, be friendly, full of questions and radiate eagerness to learn. Your teacher will respond to this and will end up doing far more for you than he or she would if you were hostile and uncommunicative. Look out for your fellow students. If someone is going through a hard time, don't just ignore that – reach out to them, and help them out. Your kindness will be repaid in ways you can't imagine. Don't be secretive and competitive in your studying – let other students share in the fruits of your labours, and your example will encourage them to do the same for you, and for others. Always ask yourself – would I like it, if someone were to do that to me? If the answer is 'no', then don't do it.

● Try to fall in love with the law

This may sound like a strange piece of advice. But again it's common sense. If you are going to be successful in your studies, you are going to have to spend most of the next three years studying law. Now – imagine that the law is a person. If you were going to be spending most of the next three years living with a particular person, would you choose to live with someone you loved or someone you hated? Obviously, you'd choose to live with someone you loved. And the reason why is obvious too – if you had to spend most of the next three years living with a particular person, those three years would be far pleasanter if you loved that person than if you hated them.

In the same way, your next three years will be far pleasanter if you somehow manage to fall in love with the law. And how do you manage to do that? Well, again, how do you fall in love with someone? The answer's obvious – you spend a lot of time with them, getting to know a lot about them. In the same way, if you are going to fall in love with the law, you need to spend a lot of time with it, studying it and reading about it. With luck, in time you should find yourself falling in love with the law and getting excited about the idea of finding out new things about it. So – really commit yourself to your studies, and give law a chance to cast its spell on you. If it does, then your next three years will be a lot easier than if you start your studies half-heartedly, don't really give the law a chance, and as a result end up dreading every hour that you have to spend studying law.

Make the most of your time

There's going to be a lot to read and do if you are going to do well as a law student. So make the most of your time. Each day, work out some goals that you want to achieve that day. And then try your best to stick to your plan. If you succeed, then you'll get a great feeling of satisfaction – that you've done a good day's work. If you don't then review your day. Was your plan a bit too ambitious, or were you a bit too weak-willed to resist the lure of a 'quick coffee'? If the former, then adjust your plan for tomorrow. If the latter, then resolve to do better tomorrow.

Start thinking about the exams from day one

One difference between studying at school and studying law at university is that, as a law student, you have to start preparing for your exams almost as soon as you start studying. You can't afford to leave everything until six weeks before the exams – there is just too much information that you will need to assimilate and too much preparation that you will need to do for that to be a feasible option.

So start thinking about the exams as soon as you start studying. When you are reading a textbook, ask yourself: What points or issues are likely to come up in an exam? and pay special attention to those. When you are reading an article, try to condense its basic argument down to a few lines that can be reproduced in an essay in the exam. When you are writing an essay or answering a legal problem, don't write any more than you could write in an exam. When one of your teachers sets you some reading to do on a particular topic, before you even start going through the reading list, have a look at the past exam papers and see what sort of questions are set on that topic and direct your reading towards putting yourself in a position to answer those kinds of questions.

● Take time off from your studies

Don't spend all your time studying law. You don't want to get burned out from studying law every hour of the day. Try to ensure that you do something nice at the end of every day to reward yourself for the effort you've put in studying law during the course of the day, and make sure that one day a week you spend half of the day having a good time doing something other than law.

● Be kind

Finally, remember that the sort of skills that you will be acquiring as a law student – in particular, the ability to argue effectively in favour of a particular position – can, in the wrong hands, turn anyone into a deeply unpleasant individual. If we substitute the word 'legal' for 'philosophical' in the passage below from Robert Nozick's *Philosophical Explanations,* the passage still remains perfectly true:

> The terminology of philosophical art is coercive: arguments are *powerful* and best when they are *knockdown,* arguments *force* you to a conclusion, if you believe the premises you *have to* or *must* believe the conclusion, some arguments do not carry much *punch,* and so forth. A philosophical argument is an attempt to get someone to believe something, whether he wants to believe it or not. A successful philosophical argument, a strong argument, *forces* someone to a belief.

Acquiring the skill to make these kinds of coercive arguments can have a bad effect on an individual: they can start to enjoy being able to use this power to push other people around. And, as Nozick points out, that's just not 'a nice way to behave' towards other people. So make sure you ally your new skills with kindness. Don't argue points just for the sake of it unless you are doing it among consenting adults. And if you want to argue someone into doing something, remember that it's ultimately their life and their decision.

So – good luck with your studies! Let me know how you are getting on.

Best wishes,

Nick

PART 3

Studying Law

The Challenges
Ahead

● From: Nicholas J. McBride [dearnick@pearson.com]
● To: Brown, Alex
● Subject: The Challenges Ahead

Hi Alex,

I hope you've arrived safely at university and are settling in nicely. This can be a bit of a daunting time – especially for law students, who are taking on a subject completely different from any they have studied before. So I thought it might be helpful if I wrote you a letter setting out some of the unique challenges involved in studying law – so that when you find yourself struggling with a particular problem in your studies, you can take some hope and inspiration from the thought 'This is totally normal, and to be expected – the fact that I'm having a problem isn't my fault: that's just the way it is for law students. Moreover, this is a problem I will be able to deal with, in time – just like the thousands of law students who have come before me.'

● Change

This is, I think, the biggest challenge for law students – the need to change the way they think, the way they approach their studies, the way they write and argue. Law is a more personally transformative subject than any other you can study at university. You can study English, or history, or one of the sciences and still leave university pretty much the same person as you were when you arrived. In contrast, studying law – or, at least, studying law *properly* – leaves its mark on you. You leave university able to think more clearly, argue more effectively, reason more carefully and with greater insight than you could ever do when you were at school. But in order to obtain the full benefit of what a legal education could do for you, you have to be willing to allow yourself to change. So be careful not to fall into the trap of thinking that whatever worked for you in your studies at school will also work for you when studying law at university. Be eager to take advantage of all the advice you will be given by your teachers as to how best to approach your studies. And constantly review your performance – both in working and in writing – looking for areas that you could change and improve.

○ Linguistic

One of the most important changes that you have to make in studying law is that you have to learn to speak like a lawyer. You have to become fluent in the specialised language that lawyers talk in. Let me give you an example. Here's a scenario that we meet fairly early on in the textbook on tort law that I co-author with Roderick Bagshaw. It's called *The Unfortunate Rock Star Problem*:

> Star goes everywhere with his Bodyguard. Driver carelessly runs over Star while Star is crossing the road. Envy – who suspects that Star is having an affair with his wife and who has been following Star to confirm his suspicions – takes advantage of the fact that Star is lying in the middle of the road to go up to Star and kick him in the head (something which causes Star to suffer severe brain damage). Bodyguard does nothing to stop Envy doing this, because he is unhappy with Star for sleeping with Bodyguard's latest girlfriend.

If you were asked right now to say who Star should be able to sue for compensation for his brain damage, you would probably say something like:

> (A) Well, I think he should definitely be able to sue Envy for compensation, because it was Envy's kicking Star that caused the brain damage in the first place. And Bodyguard should also probably be liable because it was his job to protect Star and he didn't do his job. But I don't think Star should be able to sue Driver because the brain damage didn't have that much to do with what Driver did.

Now – that's not what a lawyer would say. A lawyer would say something like this:

(B) Star should be able to sue Envy: his brain damage was caused by Envy's committing the *tort* of *battery* in relation to Star. Star won't be able to sue Driver. While Driver did commit the *tort* of *negligence* in relation to Star by carelessly running Star down (it being well established that drivers owe pedestrians in the vicinity a *duty of care*), Driver's *negligence* did not cause *Star* to suffer brain damage. While Star would not have suffered his injuries *but for* Driver's *negligence,* Envy's actions *broke the chain of causation* between Driver's *negligence* and Star's injuries; in other words, they amounted to a *novus actus interveniens*. Bodyguard probably presents the most difficult case. While Bodyguard did owe Star a *duty of care* – based on the fact that Bodyguard *assumed a responsibility* to Star – and Bodyguard did *breach* that *duty,* it could be argued that Envy's actions *broke the chain of causation* between Bodyguard's *breach* and the injuries suffered by Star. However, it is a well-established *principle* that a *defendant* will not be able to rely on a plea of *novus actus interveniens* in order to escape being held liable for breach of a *duty of care* if that would render his *duty* meaningless or nugatory; and this *principle* seems to apply here. If Bodyguard were not held liable for the harm suffered by Star here, he could never be held liable for any injuries suffered by Star at the hands of third parties which Bodyguard *negligently* failed to prevent.

All of the italicised words in (B) are legal terms of art that you, as a law student, have to learn how to use properly. In essence, you have to stop becoming someone who says (A) in response to the *Unfortunate Rock Star Problem* and become someone who says (B). So studying law presents much the same challenge as learning a foreign language does. And you have to meet that challenge in the same way that anyone who is learning a foreign language does – by immersing yourself completely in the language of the law, and not coming up for breath until speaking like a lawyer becomes second nature to you.

● Discouragement

But at first it's difficult. Just as you would if you were starting off speaking a new language, you stumble over the words; you don't say the right thing; you forget the order in which the words should go. And you know you are messing up even as you mess up. Law is a great subject for confronting you on a daily basis with conclusive evidence of your own incompetence in the subject. And if the law doesn't do it, other people will. Students who seem to have taken to the law much more quickly than you have and teachers who – quite rightly – point out the errors and omissions in your first attempts at writing a legal essay or answering a legal problem will inevitably make you feel like you aren't getting anywhere. It's very discouraging. And you start to think that maybe law isn't the right subject for you, after all. But you need to put all those thoughts behind you and remember that *this is normal.* It's inevitable when you are starting a totally new subject for the first time that you will go through these experiences. And you will get over it – it will just take time. So give yourself the time you need to become a more confident and accomplished lawyer and don't beat yourself up that you aren't proving yourself to be the next Clarence Darrow (Google him) within a few weeks of arriving at university.

● Insecurity

Donald Rumsfeld, the former US Secretary of Defense, took a lot of flak for saying – of possible connections between the Iraqi government under Saddam Hussein and terrorist activities – that, 'There are known knowns; there are things we know we know. We also know there are known unknowns; that is to say we know there are some things we do not know. But there are also unknown unknowns – the ones we don't know we don't know.' The Plain English Campaign awarded him a prize for most nonsensical statement of the year. But – as plenty of people have pointed out since – what Rumsfeld was saying was extremely clear (at least to anyone who bothered to listen to what he was saying, and wasn't automatically inclined to dismiss anything coming out of his mouth as the ravings of a deranged dingbat). And Rumsfeld's classification applies very well to law students.

There are things that law students know they know – for example, there are a few things you now know about law just from reading these letters that I've been writing to you, such as that there is such a thing as the 'rule in *Rylands* v *Fletcher*' (which I mentioned in my third letter to you). And there are things that law students know that they don't know, and that they need to find out. So for example, now that you've heard about the rule in *Rylands* v *Fletcher* you are aware that you don't know what the effect of the rule in *Rylands* v *Fletcher* is, or when it applies. But there are also a huge number of things that law students are unaware that they don't know. For example, you don't know that the rule in *Rylands* v *Fletcher* doesn't apply in Australian law – but you were also (until two seconds ago) unaware of the fact that you didn't know that because it would never have entered your head to wonder whether the rule in *Rylands* v *Fletcher* does or does not apply in Australian law. The study of law is full of 'unknown unknowns' – bits of legal information or arguments about the law where: (i) you don't know about them and (ii) you are unaware that you don't know about them. This is because there is a bottomless well of knowledge about the law. However much you may know about the law, there is always more you could know.

A minority of law students don't worry about this. There are things they know about law; there are things they know they don't know yet and have to find out – but that's as far as they are willing to go. They aren't that disturbed by the fact that there might be a huge amount of information about the law out there that they aren't even aware that they need to know about to do well in their exams. And, inevitably, they don't do well in their exams as a result. But most law students do worry a lot about whether they are studying law to the 'right' level, and whether they are missing out on a whole load of information that they need to know about but which they aren't even aware exists. Some students who worry about this kind of thing react to their insecurity about whether they know enough about the law by working themselves into a frenzy. They work, and work, and work, hoping that by reading and covering as much material as possible they can guarantee that they will know enough to do well in the exams. And they do well – but there is a healthier way to reassure yourself that you are studying law to the right depth. You know enough if:

1 you complete the reading lists that you are given by your teachers;

2 you are familiar with the areas of law covered in any lectures that you are given;

3 you are able to come up with some intelligent and interesting answers to essay questions that have been set in the exams in your subjects in previous years;

4 you are able to answer properly problem questions set in past papers.

Once you satisfy conditions (1)–(4), there's no need to worry about pushing yourself harder and harder to learn more and more about the law.

● Memory

Law students have to absorb and retain a lot of information – information about what the law says, about what particular cases decided, about various people's views of the law. In subsequent letters, I'll give you a few tips about how to study effectively in a way that will help you remember what you are studying. But the basic point is that the key to fixing things in your memory is to associate what you are trying to remember with things that are memorable. For example, chess players are able to remember thousands of different chess positions – but that's only because they can see patterns in the positions that link different pieces together, and it's those patterns which enable them to remember the positions. A chess player – no matter how good – would not be able to remember a position where the pieces on the board were scattered randomly around the board.

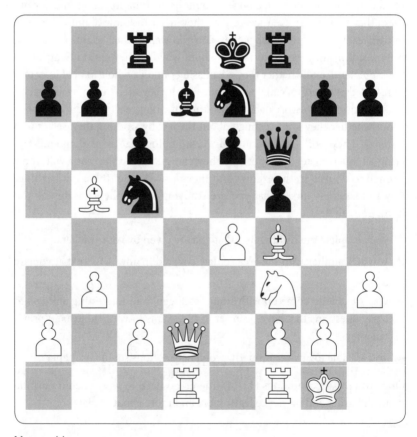

Memorable

Unmemorable

So searching for patterns or systems underlying what you are studying is an effective way of fixing what you are studying in your brain. Making use of information is another way of fixing that information in your head – you associate the information with the use you made of it. For example, go onto the Internet and search for a recipe for (say) beef bourguignon. Merely looking at the recipe and reading it over and over will not fix it in your head. But make the dish three or four times and you'll never have to look at the recipe again – your actions in shopping for the ingredients and cooking them will have placed the details of the recipe in your long-term memory. So using legal information as much as you can – in discussing the law with your fellow students, or in arguing hypothetical cases, or in answering past paper questions – is very effective way of making that information so much part of you that you'll never forget it.

● Legal fictions

The existence of legal fictions presents a particularly difficult challenge for students studying law. Peter Birks explains how a legal fiction works:

> Among the sillier Oxford stories is that of the Dean's dog. The college's rules forbid the keeping of dogs. The Dean keeps a dog. Reflecting on the action to be taken, the governing body of the college decides that the labrador is a cat and moves on to next business. That dog is a constructive cat. Deemed, quasi- or fictitious, it is not what it seems. When the law behaves like this you know it is in trouble, its intellect either genuinely defeated or deliberately indulging in some benevolent dishonesty.

So a legal fiction comes into existence when we have a legal rule which says (say): In situation A, you can do B. A judge would like to do B in situation C. But instead of *changing* the rule so that it says 'In situations A *or* C, you can do B', what the judge does instead is say that situation C is the same as situation A, when it isn't. The reason why judges do this is that they don't like to be seen to be changing legal rules, because it is popularly believed that the job of the judges is to *apply* the law and not *make* the law. If it were widely understood how much of our law is *made* by judges, then people would start expressing concerns about how judges are appointed and what they believe. So employing legal fictions makes for a quieter life for the judges – they can pretend simply to be applying the rules, while secretly manipulating their application through the use of fictions. Let's demonstrate this point with a couple of examples.

(1) The law on murder

The law on murder says that if you cause someone else's death by acting in a particular way, you will only be guilty of murder if you acted with an intent to kill or with an intent to cause grievous bodily harm. Now – suppose that Henry owns a plane and needs cash fast. So he has the idea of putting a bomb on the plane so that it blows up in mid-air. He figures that the explosion will be blamed on terrorists, and he will be able to claim on the multi-million-pound insurance policy that he has on the plane. Henry puts his plan into effect, and the plane does blow up, killing everyone on board. But the police find out that Henry put the bomb on the plane, and charge him with murder. The difficulty is that, when Henry put the bomb on the plane, he didn't intend to harm anyone. If everyone aboard the plane had escaped unharmed, then he would have been delighted – his only object in putting the bomb on the plane was to blow up the plane and cash in on the insurance policy. But the judges don't want to acquit Henry of murder in this situation. Now one way they could deal with this issue is by changing the law on murder so that it says that if you cause someone else's death by acting in a particular way, you will be guilty of murder if you acted with depraved indifference to the value of human life. That new rule would cover Henry's case perfectly, as well as all the other cases that were covered by the old rule. But the judges don't want to be seen to be changing the law on murder, so instead they convict Henry of murder by employing a fiction. They say that if you foresee that death is *virtually certain* to result from your actions, then you can be held to have acted with an intent to kill. This is a fiction because the fact that you appreciate that some consequence is virtually certain to result from your actions does not necessarily mean that you intend to bring about that consequence. A surgeon will foresee that it is virtually certain that the family of a man he was operating on will be profoundly upset when he tells him that he was unable to save the man's life; but it would be completely wrong (and extremely offensive) to say that when he tells them the terrible news, he is acting with an intent to upset them. But using this fiction allows the judges to convict Henry of murder – he foresaw that death was virtually certain to result from his actions, so he can be held to have had an intent to kill.

(2) The law on recovery for the careless infliction of pure economic loss

It used to be the case that if A carelessly caused B to suffer a form of pure economic loss – that is, a loss of wealth that doesn't result from B's being injured or his property being damaged – that B would not be allowed to sue A for compensation for the fact that A has made him worse off. B would just have to bear the loss himself. For example, if *Engineer* carelessly cut off the power to *Mogul's* factory so that the factory couldn't produce any goods for a few days, *Mogul* wouldn't be able to sue *Engineer* for compensation for the profits that he would have made from selling the goods that he would have produced during the period his factory was shut down. But in 1964, the judges – acting honestly for once – changed the law and said that if A carelessly caused B to suffer a form of pure economic loss, B could sue A for compensation for that loss if A had 'assumed a responsibility' to B not to be careless. So far, so good – but in 1995 a case called *White* v *Jones* came along where the courts wanted to allow a claimant (someone who is suing) to sue a defendant (in this context, someone who is being sued) for carelessly causing her to suffer pure economic loss, when there was no way it could be said that the defendant had 'assumed a responsibility' to the claimant. In *White* v *Jones,* the defendant solicitor had been employed to draw up a will under which the claimant would have inherited £9,000, but had carelessly taken so long to draw up the will that the testator (the person wanting to make the will) died before the will could be signed and witnessed. So the claimant lost out on her inheritance, and wanted to sue the defendant solicitor for compensation. But as there was no contact between the claimant and the defendant, it was impossible to say that the defendant had 'assumed a responsibility' to her in agreeing to draw up the will. He had 'assumed a responsibility' to the testator, but not to the claimant. However, the judges wanted to hold the defendant liable to the claimant. One way they could have handled the situation was to change the law as laid down in 1964 and say that 'If A carelessly causes B to suffer a form of pure economic loss, B will be able to sue A for compensation for that loss if A assumed a responsibility to B; but even if A has not assumed a responsibility to B, B might still be able to sue A, depending on the circumstances of the case. And in these circumstances, we think the claimant should be allowed to sue even though the defendant did not assume a responsibility to her.' But instead, what the judges did was that they employed a fiction. They said that they would hold that the defendant solicitor *had* 'assumed a responsibility' to the claimant in this case, even though it was clear that he had not.

Legal fictions are always bad news for the law, and law students. They are bad news for the law because they store up trouble in the future. For example, the fiction that you can be held to have had an intent to kill if you acted knowing that death was virtually certain to result from your actions creates problems in a situation where a mountaineer A, who is attached by a rope to a mountaineer B higher up on the mountain, slips and falls into a very deep crevasse. The only thing stopping A from falling to his death is the fact that he is attached to B, who is now unable to move because of the deadweight hanging off him. After a few hours of waiting fruitlessly for help to come, night starts to fall and the temperature drops dramatically. B knows that both he and A will die if they remain in their current positions. In order to save himself, he cuts the rope and A falls to his death. Is B guilty of murder? Under the rule adopted by the courts that you can be held to have intended to kill if you acted knowing that death was virtually certain to result from your actions, the answer might be 'yes'. But the judges don't want to find B guilty of murder, so in order to deal with this case they are forced either (1) to hold that they will not *always* find that someone had an intent to kill if they foresaw that death was virtually certain to result from their actions, and leave it unclear when they will and when they won't do this; or (2) to give B the benefit of some special defence (such as 'My actions resulted in more lives being saved than were lost') that may apply in other situations where we might not want it to apply.

Legal fictions are bad news for law students because they make the law harder to understand and apply. For example, when the judges held in *White* v *Jones* that the claimant could sue the defendant solicitor because the defendant had 'assumed a responsibility' to the claimant, the result of their deciding the case that way was to leave it completely unclear *why* they were *really* holding the defendant liable to the claimant. Their real reason for holding the defendant liable to the claimant could not have been that he had 'assumed a responsibility' to the claimant because he hadn't. So what was it about the case that motivated them to hold the defendant liable to the claimant? We can only guess. Maybe they thought that the defendant shouldn't be able to get away with acting unprofessionally. Maybe they thought that the claimant should be allowed to sue the defendant because the defendant had positively got in the way of her receiving an inheritance from her father by offering to help the father with setting up the inheritance and then doing nothing about it. Whichever explanation you go for has big implications for the relevance of *White* v *Jones* for other cases – but as we can't be certain which explanation to go for, we can't be certain how *White* v *Jones* applies in those other cases.

So – how should you approach legal fictions when you come across them? (A warning note: don't be overeager to find legal fictions all over the place. They exist, but they aren't *that* common.) Well, in *thinking about the law,* dig beneath the fictions and ask yourself – What is really going on here? Why are the courts stretching the law here? What is the real rule that the courts are giving effect to? In *writing about the law,* you have to respect and apply legal fictions in answering problem questions. So, for example, if you were asked to answer a problem question involving a situation like Henry's case, you should say something like 'Henry will almost certainly be held to have had an intent to kill when he put the bomb on the plane as he foresaw that death was virtually certain to result from his actions.' When writing essays, you should expose any relevant fictions and discuss why they exist, so as to demonstrate your superior understanding of the law. For example, if you were writing an essay on the law of murder, you might say that 'The willingness of the courts to find that a defendant had an intent to kill if he foresaw that death was virtually certain to result from his actions reflects, in some cases, their desire to find guilty of murder defendants who have caused others to die while showing a depraved indifference to the value of human life. Given this, there is a case for arguing that the law of murder should be reformed so that it can more straightforwardly give effect to this impulse of the courts, and that it should say that a defendant will be guilty of murder if he causes another's death in circumstances which demonstrate on the part of the defendant a depraved indifference to the value of human life.'

● The sources of law

The final challenge that you will come across as a law student is rooted in the sources of law in the UK. There are two principal sources of law – legislation (legal rules laid down by Parliament in *statutes*, or by ministers authorised by Parliament to create *statutory instruments*), and case law (decisions of the courts, determining what the law says in a particular case).

Case law is a particularly difficult source of law for students to handle. Where a case is deciding how a particular statute applies, or should be interpreted, in a particular case, there is generally no problem. But the courts are frequently called upon to decide what the law says in a particular case where no statutory provision applies. In such a case, lawyers say that the courts are determining what the *common law* – the law that applies to everyone, and that applies in the absence of any relevant statutory provision – has to say about that case.

The common law can be best compared to a coral reef – it is formed by, and emerges out of, the decisions of thousands and thousands of individual cases, with each case – each decision as to what the common law says in that case – adding to and altering the existing structure. But making sense of what those thousands and thousands of cases, taken together, amount to is very difficult. It represents an almost scientific challenge. You have thousands and thousands of data points, and you have to speculate as to what rule or rules best account for the existence of those data points. (This is why the letter I wrote to you on how to make speculative arguments is so important for law students, as making sense of the common law involves making precisely those kinds of arguments.) Indeed, it used to be fashionable to use the term 'legal science' to describe what lawyers did when they tried to make statements about what the common law did and did not say – though that usage has now fallen out of fashion, as it gives us exaggerated ideas about how certain we can be about what the common law actually says.

In determining what the common law says on particular issues, you will have lots of help – you will have textbooks and articles that give you their opinion of what the law says, lecturers and other teachers who have their views, and cases where judges helpfully try to make sense of what other cases that have been previously decided establish. But you will also be expected to think for yourself, and not just accept as Gospel truth other people's views about what the law says. And thinking for yourself may be the biggest challenge of all. Students emerging out of an educational system where they are told by the schools precisely what to write in their exams find the question 'What do *you* think?' very hard to handle. But make the effort to start thinking for yourself, and thinking critically about what other people have to say about the law, and you will soon get used to it.

It occurred to me, on looking at the last few paragraphs, that there are a few technical lawyers' terms (statutes, statutory regulations, common law) there that you are probably not familiar with at the moment. I have an idea for something I can do to help you with that . . . I'll be in touch soon.

All best wishes,

Nick

13

A Mini-Dictionary of English Law

- From: Nicholas J. McBride [dearnick@pearson.com]
- To: Brown, Alex
- Subject: A Mini-Dictionary of English Law

Hey Alex,

I've written something for you! It's a mini-dictionary of English law. It's designed to get you acquainted with a lot of the terms and concepts you'll come across this year. My hope is that reading this through will help minimise the disorientation that you might experience in beginning to read about law, and help get you talking and thinking like a lawyer as quickly as possible. I've highlighted the most important terms and concepts that you will need to know about for this coming year. (Incidentally, whenever you come across the abbreviation 'q.v.' – which is short for 'quod vide', which means 'which see' – that means that there is an entry in this dictionary for the term immediately preceding the abbreviation 'q.v.'.)

Act of Parliament. See 'Legislation', below.

Civil law. The term 'civil law' has a couple of different meanings.

First of all, the term 'civil law' is used by English lawyers to describe that part of English law that determines what rights (in the first sense of the word 'right' (q.v.)) private individuals enjoy against each other. Of the subjects you might study at university, tort law, contract law, land law, trusts law, family law, and labour law all belong to the field of 'civil law'. 'Civil law', in this sense, is opposed to 'public law' which is the area of law which specifically governs relationships between public bodies and private individuals, and 'criminal law' which governs when the government may punish someone for behaving in an anti-social fashion.

Secondly, 'civil law' is often used (along with 'Roman law') to refer to the law of the old Roman Empire, on which the legal systems of many countries on the European mainland are based. These countries are often known as 'civilian' or 'civil law' jurisdictions as a result. Because of the importance of civil law (in this secondary sense) for the development of legal systems on the European mainland, many universities offer courses in 'civil law' (or 'Roman law').

Claimant. Someone who commences litigation against someone else. Before 2000, someone who commenced litigation against someone else would be known as a 'plaintiff'. The person against whom litigation is brought has always been known as a 'defendant'.

Common law. The term 'common law' is used to refer to a few different things.

First of all, the term 'common law' is often used, loosely, to describe 'judge-made law'. This is law that does not derive from a statute, but from the decisions of the judges as to what the law says in concrete cases. Technically, such decisions only amount to evidence of what the law says – with the judge in his or her decision expressing his or her opinion as to what the law says (which opinion is then binding on the parties to the case, and creates a mini-law for their case). However, if it is clear that a particular opinion that the law says x would be accepted as correct by all the judges, then for the time being we can confidently say that the law does say x. And if the proposition x cannot be found in a statute then we say that it is a piece of judge-made law, and part of the 'common law'. Such propositions include: 'A promise will only be legally binding if something of value in the eye of the law is given in return for it, or if it is made in a deed'; 'Manufacturers of consumer products owe those who will ultimately use those products a legal duty to take care to see that those products are reasonably safe to use'; 'A decision of a public authority can be set aside as invalid and of no effect if no reasonable public authority would ever make such a decision'. There is no statute that says any of these things; but these propositions are still part of our law because they would be accepted as correct by the judges.

Secondly, the term 'common law' is sometimes used, more strictly, to describe areas of 'judge-made law' that derive ultimately from the decisions of judges in concrete cases heard by the courts of Common Law, in the days when the English legal system had separate courts of Common Law and courts of Equity. The Common Law courts would have general jurisdiction to hear all cases raising a legal issue. In contrast, the courts of Equity would only hear a case if – in the view of the Equity judges – there was a danger that applying the rules of the Common Law to the case would result in a serious injustice being done. So the courts of Equity acted as a corrective to the Common Law courts – either granting a remedy to a deserving claimant who would not be entitled to a remedy from the Common Law courts, or by ordering (on pain of going to prison for contempt of court if the order were disregarded) a claimant who would be entitled to a remedy from the Common Law courts not to pursue that remedy if it would be 'unconscionable' to do so. In the nineteenth century, the distinction between courts of Common Law and courts of Equity was abolished and from then on the rules of Common Law and Equity were supposed to be applied by a unified set of courts. But if a given bit of law has its origin in the decisions of the old courts of Common Law, lawyers will still mark that fact by referring to a 'common law interest' or 'common law action' or 'wrong at common law'; and if it has its origin in the decision of the old courts of Equity, lawyers will again mark that fact that by talking about an 'equitable interest' or an 'action in equity' or an 'equitable wrong'.

Thirdly, the term 'common law' is sometimes used as a catch-all term to describe those countries whose legal systems are ultimately based on English law. So the United States, Canada, Australia, and New Zealand are the major common law countries outside England and Wales. In contrast, so-called 'civilian' jurisdictions are those countries whose legal systems are ultimately based on 'civil law' (q.v.) – that is, the law of the old Roman Empire. Most countries in Europe count as 'civilian jurisdictions'. There is an entire subject – comparative law – that is devoted to comparing the common law approaches to various legal issues with the civilian approaches to those legal issues. Many universities offer their students the chance to interrupt their studies for a year to go to a civilian jurisdiction – usually France – to get acquainted with its distinctive system of law.

Contract. Many people would say that a contract is a promise that is legally binding. However, there are many occasions when a promise will be legally binding on an individual without there being any kind of contract involved. It would be better to say that contract law provides people with a facility for making undertakings to each other that will be legally binding, and that a contract is what two people enter into when they take advantage of that facility.

Courts. Below is a very simplified diagram setting out the names and relationships between the main types of courts that decide cases in England and Wales. The courts are arranged in a hierarchy, so that if you are unhappy with the result of your case, it may be possible to appeal to a higher court either to have the result in your case reversed in your favour, or to have the higher court order that your case be reheard by a lower court. The highest court in the land is the Supreme Court of the United Kingdom. (The highest court in the land was formerly known as the Appellate Committee of the House of Lords, but it was thought desirable on separation of powers (q.v.) grounds that there should not be any kind of link between the highest court in the land and the House of Lords, and that members of the highest court in the land should not have the power to sit in the House of Lords and contribute to its discussions of legislation. So the Constitutional Reform Act 2005 abolished the Appellate Committee of the House of Lords and put in its place the Supreme Court of the United Kingdom, which started hearing cases in 2009.)

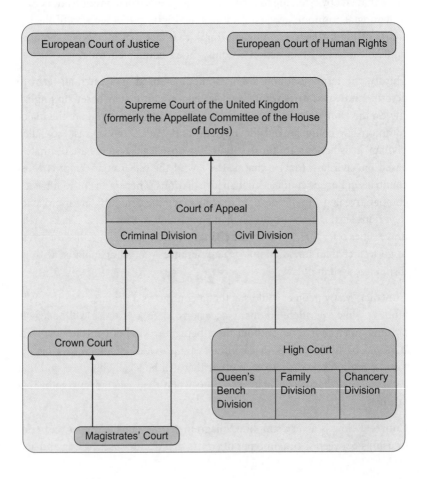

Criminal cases are heard in either the Crown Court or Magistrates' Court, with appeals from those courts ultimately going to the Court of Appeal Criminal Division, and from there (if the Supreme Court gives leave to appeal) to the Supreme Court.

Most of the non-criminal cases you will read as a student will have originated in the High Court. The Queen's Bench Division of the High Court typically hears cases involving disputes over land and claims for damages (q.v.). A sub-division of the Queen's Bench Division is the Administrative Court, which considers applications for judicial review (q.v.). The Family Division, as the name suggests, deals with all matrimonial disputes, and child custody cases. The Chancery Division deals with a wide range of cases, typically centred around issues that would have been dealt with by the old courts of Equity (q.v.). So issues relating to equitable claims or interests, companies, and intel-lectual property will be dealt with by the Chancery Division. Appeals against decisions of the High Court can be made to the Civil Division of the Court of Appeal, and from there (if, again, the Supreme Court gives leave to appeal) to the Supreme Court.

(A quick note on names: if Adam Smith were a High Court judge, he would be known as 'The Hon. Mr Justice Smith' or 'Smith J.' for short. If Adam Smith were a judge in the Court of Appeal, he would normally be known as 'Lord Justice Smith', or 'Smith L.J.'. However, if Adam Smith were in charge of the Court of Appeal Criminal Division, he would be known as 'Lord Chief Justice Smith', or 'Lord Smith C.J.'; and if he were in charge of the Court of Appeal Civil Division, he would be known as 'Lord Smith, Master of the Rolls', or 'Lord Smith M.R.'. If Adam Smith were a judge in the Supreme Court of the United Kingdom, he would be known as 'Lord Smith'.)

Standing over all of these courts are the European Court of Justice, and the European Court of Human Rights.

The European Court of Justice is the ultimate authority on all issues relating to European Union (q.v.) law and the UK courts must follow its decisions in deciding any legal cases that raise issues of European Union law. Any UK court is free to refer a case raising a tricky issue of European Union law to the European Court of Justice, which will give its opinion and then refer the case back to the UK court from where it came.

The European Court of Human Rights is the ultimate authority on how the European Convention on Human Rights (q.v.) should be interpreted. Under the Human Rights Act 1998 (q.v.), the UK courts are required to take into account the decisions of the European Court of Human Rights in determining whether someone's rights under the Convention have been violated. But they are, in theory, free to disregard those decisions where they think the European Court of Human Rights has got it wrong.

Crime. A crime is an act or omission which is punishable under the law in some way – either through imprisonment, or a fine, or an order to perform community service, or through some other sanction. It is often the case that the act or omission does not in itself amount to a crime; instead the act or omission will only amount to a crime if it is accompanied by a so-called 'guilty mind' or *mens rea*. For example, it is not a crime to take a bar of chocolate off a supermarket shelf and put it in your pocket; but it is if you do so dishonestly, and with the intent to keep the bar of chocolate for yourself or somebody else.

There are thousands of crimes recognised under English law. The crimes that make up the core of the criminal law are acts which involve someone's deliberately or recklessly violating someone else's rights (in the first sense of the word 'right' (q.v.)). Crimes of this type include murder, rape, assault, battery, theft, criminal damage to property, and fraud. Around this core are thousands of crimes that do not necessarily involve the violation of anyone else's rights, but involve some form of anti-social conduct that Parliament has thought it necessary to discourage by making it criminal. Such crimes include speeding, possessing dangerous drugs, false advertising, selling goods by weight without providing a price by metric unit, travelling on a train without a valid ticket, and possessing a firearm without a licence.

Damages. Damages are a monetary remedy (q.v.) that may be sued for in a case where someone has violated someone else's rights (in the first sense of the word 'right' (q.v.)). There are a few different types of damages.

The principal form of damages is compensatory damages. These are designed – as the name suggests – to compensate a claimant (q.v.) for some or all of the losses that he or she has suffered as a result of someone's rights being violated. They aim to put the claimant in the monetary equivalent of the position that he or she would have been in had the rights-violation not occurred; of course, they often fall short of achieving that aim.

English courts sometimes – though rarely – award exemplary damages against a defendant. These are designed to punish a defendant who has deliberately and outrageously violated a claimant's rights. Exemplary damages perform the same function as the criminal law, though without the controls that exist on when someone will be subjected to criminal punishment. For example, someone can only be held guilty of committing a serious crime (q.v.) if their guilt is established 'beyond a reasonable doubt'. In contrast, someone can be held liable to pay exemplary damages if it merely seems 'more likely than not' that he or she deliberately and outrageously violated a claimant's rights.

Delegated legislation. Delegated legislation is legislation that is created by someone – almost always a government minister – who has been given the power to make law by an Act of Parliament. The power to make delegated legislation is usually exercised by issuing what is called a statutory instrument.

(Delegated legislation that is of some constitutional significance is usually created by the Queen's issuing an Order in Council. (Of course, the Queen will do as her government advises.) The Terrorism (United Nations Measures) Order 2006 was created in this way. This gave the Treasury the power to freeze someone's bank accounts if there were 'reasonable grounds' for believing that he or she was involved in terrorist activities. This provision was later (and rightly) condemned by the courts as incompatible with people's rights under the Human Rights Act 2008 (q.v.).)

There were 3,327 statutory instruments issued in 2012, in contrast to 23 Acts of Parliament. The creation of law through statutory instruments undermines the existence of the rule of law (q.v.) in the UK: the fact that so many statutory instruments are issued each year makes it impossible to keep track of what the law actually says.

See also 'Henry VIII clause', below.

Duty (legal). Someone will have a legal duty to act in a particular way if they are required under the law to act in that way.

If A has a legal duty to do x, we can say that that duty is a private law duty if it was imposed on A for the benefit of a particular individual, B. In such a case, B is usually said to have a 'right' (q.v.) that A do x, and if A does not do x, B will normally be entitled to sue A for damages (q.v.).

A's legal duty to do x can be said to be a public law duty if A is a public body, and that duty was imposed on A to help ensure that A acts in the public interest. A breach of a public law duty is normally remedied through an application for judicial review (q.v.), though it may also amount to a crime (q.v.) for which A can be prosecuted.

Equity. See 'Common law', above.

European Convention on Human Rights. The European Convention on Human Rights ('ECHR' for short) was created by the 47 member states of the Council of Europe in 1950. Signatories to the Convention (which include the United Kingdom, as well as non-EU countries such as Russia, Switzerland and Norway) agreed to observe certain fundamental rights and freedoms, including the right to life (Article 2), the right not to be tortured or subjected to 'inhuman and degrading treatment' (Article 3), the right to liberty and security of person (Article 5), the right to a fair trial (Article 6), the right to respect for one's 'private and family life' (Article 8), and the right to freedom of expression (Article 10). Since its inception, the Convention has been supplemented by a number of Protocols. Signatories to Article 1 of the First Protocol undertake to respect people's rights to peaceful enjoyment of their possessions.

The European Court of Human Rights ('ECtHR' for short) was set up in Strasbourg, France, to monitor whether signatories to the Convention were in breach of their obligations under the Convention and to provide a satisfactory remedy in cases where someone had suffered loss as a result of a signatory's failure to abide by its obligations under the Convention. For example, a prisoner in the UK who was denied access to a solicitor could complain to the ECtHR that the UK government was violating his right to a fair trial, and if the Court found that the complaint was justified, it would order the UK to compensate the prisoner for the violation of his rights and to cease violating his rights. If the UK did not comply with this order, it would be in breach of its obligations under the ECHR, which would be embarrassing both at a political and public relations level. So in practice the UK does comply with orders of the ECtHR.

The need for UK citizens to take cases to the ECtHR has been lessened by the enactment of the Human Rights Act 1998 which imposes on public authorities a legal duty (q.v.) not to violate people's rights under the ECHR. A claimant (q.v.) who alleges that he has suffered loss as a result of a public authority breaching this duty may now take his case to be heard by an English court, which will grant a satisfactory remedy if – taking into account the ECtHR's interpretation of the ECHR – it is persuaded that the claimant's rights under the ECHR have been violated. The UK Parliament (q.v.) is exempt from this duty – if it were not, the traditional rule of Parliamentary sovereignty (q.v.) over the courts would have been abolished – but in cases where it is alleged that Parliament has passed legislation (q.v.) that violates people's rights under the ECHR, the courts have the power to issue a declaration of incompatibility, saying that the legislation is in violation of the ECHR. In such a case, political and public relations considerations could be expected to force Parliament to repeal the relevant legislation.

It is a common mistake of students (and journalists) to think that the ECHR has something to do with the European Union (q.v.). This is quite wrong: the ECHR has nothing to do with the EU. At the time I am writing this letter, the EU (as distinct from the member states of the European Union) is still not a signatory to the ECHR – though it is in the last stretch of negotiations to accede to the ECHR. In the past, this meant that the institutions of the EU were not bound by the ECHR, and were therefore not required to respect, for example, the freedom of speech of whistleblowers exposing corruption within the EU. To eliminate this loophole, the Lisbon Treaty gave effect to a Charter of Fundamental Rights that was binding under EU law both on the institutions of the EU, and the member states of the EU; though the UK insisted on a Protocol being inserted into the Charter which would stop the Charter applying to the UK's 'laws, regulations or administrative provisions, practices or actions'.

European Union. The European Union ('EU' for short) is an organisation of 27 European states, including the United Kingdom, bound together by a series of treaties (such as the Treaty of Rome 1957, the Maastricht Treaty 1992, and the Lisbon Treaty 2007), which commit the member states of the EU to maintain a single market within the borders of the EU (within which borders there is to be free movement of peoples, goods, services and capital) and to pursue common policies on a range of other areas, such as agriculture and fishing.

To achieve these objectives there exist a range of different European institutions. The EU is run on a day-to-day basis by the European Commission, which comes up with suggestions for legislation that might be created by the EU's legislature. The EU's legislature is made up of the European Parliament (which is, in turn, made up of elected representatives from all regions of the EU) and the Council of Ministers (which is made up of ministers from each of the member states of the EU, with the ministers making up the Council at any one point varying according to what the Council is discussing at that time).

The United Kingdom has been a member of the EU (at the time, the 'European Economic Community') since 1973.

Under the European Communities Act 1972, provisions in any treaty entered into by the member states of the EU automatically become part of English law (and override any inconsistent parts of English law) once the treaty is approved by the UK Parliament.

Any regulations created by the EU's legislature will automatically become part of English law (and automatically override any inconsistent elements in English law, irrespective of whether those elements pre-date or post-date the regulation in question), again as a result of the European Communities Act 1972.

The EU's legislature is also empowered to issue directives to the member states of the EU, requiring the member states to change their national laws so that the law on a particular point or issue is the same across the EU. For example, Council Directive 85/374/EEC directed each member state of the (then) European Economic Community to change its law so that the manufacturer of a dangerously defective product that did harm to someone's person or property would be held strictly liable for that harm (that is, without the need to prove that the manufacturer was at fault for the existence of that defect). That directive was implemented in the UK by passing the Consumer Protection Act 1987. (Directives are more usually implemented through the issuing of a statutory instrument, which is a form of delegated legislation (q.v.).)

If a member state of the EU fails to implement a directive correctly, it is required under EU law to compensate anyone who suffers financial loss as a result of that failure. Who says so? The European Court of Justice ('ECJ' for short) which so ruled in the case of *Francovich* v *Italy*. The ECJ, which is based in Luxembourg, is the ultimate authority on all issues of EU law. It interprets the treaties of the EU and the legislation issued by the European legislature, and decides such issues as whether a member state has failed to implement a directive correctly, or whether a particular aspect of the domestic law of a member state is inconsistent with an EU regulation or treaty provision. In theory, a member state of the EU is free to disregard an order issued against it by the ECJ (just as a member state of the EU is free to disregard a directive that has been issued by the European legislature) – but doing so would put it in breach of its obligations as a member of the EU, and put its continued membership of the EU in question.

Henry VIII clause. A 'Henry VIII clause' is a provision in an Act of Parliament (q.v.) that empowers a government minister to change the terms of an Act of Parliament or a statutory instrument (q.v.). (Such a provision is called a 'Henry VIII clause' because the Statute of Proclamations 1539 gives us a very early example of such a provision. That Act provided that Henry VIII's 'proclamations' had the full force of law 'as though they were made by act of parliament'.)

Examples of very wide Henry VIII clauses are provided by:

1 Section 1 of the Legislative and Regulatory Reform Act 2006 ('A Minister of the Crown may by order make any provision which he considers would . . . remov[e] or reduc[e] any burden, or the overall burdens, resulting directly or indirectly for any person from any legislation').

2 Sections 19–24 of the Civil Contingencies Act 2004, which provide that 'Her Majesty by Order in Council' (i.e. the government) may create 'emergency regulations' that have the effect of 'disapply[ing] or modify[ing] an enactment or a provision made by or under an enactment' if it is urgently 'necessary to make provision for the purpose of preventing, controlling or mitigating an aspect or effect of [an] emergency'. (An 'emergency' is defined as, among other things, 'an event or situation which threatens serious damage to human welfare in the United Kingdom or in a Part or region'.)

Human Rights Act 1998. See 'European Convention on Human Rights', above.

Judicial review. A claimant (q.v.) who brings an application for judicial review is asking a court to determine whether or not a public body exceeded its powers (in Latin, acted '*ultra vires*') in making a particular decision or in acting in a particular way or in failing to act in a particular way.

If the court finds that the public body is exceeding, or has exceeded, its powers in acting in a particular way, there are a variety of remedies (q.v.) that the court could award. In the case where a public body has made a decision that is *ultra vires* (for example, deciding to grant planning permission to a company to construct a supermarket), the court could issue an order of *certiorari*, quashing the decision. In the case where a public body has exceeded its powers by failing to act in a particular way (for example, by refusing to consider someone's objections to the construction of a new supermarket in a particular location), the court could issue an order of *mandamus*, ordering the public body to act in that way. In the case where a public body is continuously exceeding its powers by acting in a particular way (for example, by making a yearly grant to a company in return for its running a supermarket in a particular location), the court could issue an order of prohibition, ordering the public body to cease acting in excess of its powers.

There are a number of different reasons why a court might find that a public body has acted, or is acting, in excess of its powers. The public body may have misinterpreted the powers granted it by a particular piece of legislation (thereby making an error of law), or made an error of fact which made it think it was empowered to act in a particular way, when in fact it was not. The public body may have used the powers granted it by a particular piece of legislation for an improper purpose or may have exercised those powers in a way that no reasonable person would have exercised them. The public body may have exercised its powers without granting someone affected by them a fair hearing before deciding what to do, or the person making the decision as to how the public body should exercise its powers may have had a financial interest in the public body's exercising its powers in the way it did. Finally, the public body may have acted in a way that violated someone's rights under the European Convention on Human Rights (q.v.), something which it is barred from doing under the Human Rights Act 1998 (q.v.).

Virtually all public bodies are susceptible to having their decisions and actions challenged through an application for judicial review. The major exception to this rule is that no one can make an application for judicial review to ask the courts to quash an Act of Parliament on the ground, for example, that no reasonable person would have created such an Act, or that it violates someone's rights under the European Convention on Human Rights. (Though in the latter case, it is open to the courts to make a declaration of incompatibility between the Act and the Convention.) This is because of the doctrine of Parliamentary sovereignty (q.v.). No such bar to judicial review applies in the case of delegated legislation (q.v.). For example, if a minister creates a statutory instrument (q.v.) under legislation empowering her to do so, a claimant could make an application to the courts asking for the statutory instrument to be quashed on the ground that the minister exceeded her powers in creating that instrument, for one of the reasons set out above.

Jurisprudence. In ancient times, the term 'philosophy' was used to describe the study of the entire field of human knowledge. (The word 'philosophy' is derived from the Greek philos (meaning 'love') and sophia (meaning 'knowledge').) But then different branches of knowledge acquired their own titles – mathematics, physics, biology, chemistry . . . – and were hived off from 'philosophy', which simply came to describe 'whatever we study when we don't study mathematics or physics or biology or chemistry or . . .'. The same thing has happened to the term 'jurisprudence', which used to describe the entire field of legal studies (so that an undergraduate who obtains a law degree from Oxford is still said to obtain a BA in 'Jurisprudence'). But as different branches of the study of law have acquired their own titles – contract law, tort law, criminal law, public law . . . – those branches have become distinct from 'jurisprudence', which has simply come to describe 'whatever we study when we study law but don't study contract law, tort law, criminal law, public law . . '. As such, 'jurisprudence' as a subject is now concerned with theoretical issues affecting the other branches of legal study, such as: What is law? How do we tell what the law says on a particular issue? Can the law on a particular issue ever be certain? Is it ever justifiable to punish someone for acting in a particular way? What is the basis of the remedies that courts award when someone's rights (q.v.) have been violated?

Legislation. Legislation is law that has been deliberately created by a lawmaking body. There are two forms of legislation in English law. First: primary legislation, which is made up of laws contained in Acts of Parliament passed by Parliament (q.v.). Second: delegated legislation (q.v.), which is made up of laws created by someone (usually a government minister) empowered to make law by an Act of Parliament.

Some say that judges act in a legislative capacity when they decide cases where the law is uncertain: that they make new law in deciding the case. The better view would seem to be that judges hardly ever act as legislators. In other words, a judge hardly ever decides a case with the conscious intention, 'I will now lay down what the law will say on this particular issue from now on.' Instead, he will express his opinion on what the law says on that issue, and then wait to see if his fellow judges will accept his opinion. If they do, then his opinion will represent the law (for the time being). If they do not, then his opinion won't be worth the paper it was written on. But, unlike a true legislator, no judge acting alone has the power to affect what the law says.

Omission. English law draws a big distinction between acts and omissions. Roughly speaking, acts make people worse off; omissions merely fail to make people better off. If I run you over in my car, that is an act. If I fail to shout out a warning when I see that you are in danger of being run over by someone else, that is an omission.

Under English law, you have lots of rights (in the first sense of the word 'right' (q.v.)) that other people not make you worse off; but rights that other people make you better off are much rarer. You have a right against everyone that they take care not to do something that foreseeably would cause you physical injury. But if you are in danger of suffering some kind of physical injury, you will only normally have a right against someone that they take care to save you from that danger if you are in a special relationship with them. A complete stranger will not normally be under any kind of duty (q.v.) to save you from that danger. As a result he will not normally commit any kind of tort (q.v.) or crime (q.v.) if he leaves you to your fate.

Parliament. Under the UK constitution, the Parliament of the United Kingdom has the power to make law for the UK. Under the doctrine of Parliamentary sovereignty (q.v.), there are no restraints on how this power may be exercised.

The Parliament of the United Kingdom is made up of three parts:

1 *The House of Commons.* This is currently made up of 646 Members of Parliament ('MP' for short), each of whom represents a constituency within the UK and was elected to Parliament by that constituency. Almost all MPs belong to a party. The party that has an absolute majority of MPs makes up the government, with the leader of that party acting as Prime Minister.

2 *The House of Lords.* This is currently made up of 740 members, almost all of whom were appointed to serve in the House of Lords by the Sovereign, acting on the advice of the Prime Minister, who in turn allows the other parties in the House of Commons to nominate people to represent their interests in the House of Lords.

3 *The Sovereign.* The Sovereign is the UK's Head of State and is currently Queen Elizabeth II.

Parliament makes law by considering proposals to change the law, known as Bills. Bills are almost always introduced into Parliament by the government, though MPs are also given some Parliamentary time to offer their own Bills for approval by Parliament.

Normally, for a Bill to become an Act of Parliament, it has to be approved by all three parts of the Parliament of the United Kingdom. The Parliament Acts of 1911 and 1949 placed a limit on the power of the House of Lords to stop a Bill becoming an Act of Parliament by refusing to approve it. A Bill dealing with taxation, and a Bill that has been approved by the House of Commons in two separate sessions, can become an Act of Parliament without the approval of the House of Lords. The approval of the Sovereign – known as the Royal Assent – is always required for a Bill to become an Act of Parliament. In practice, the Sovereign never refuses to give the Royal Assent to a Bill that is presented to him or her for approval. However, the fact that the Royal Assent is required to turn a Bill into law is thought by some to be a residual bulwark against a government using its majority in the House of Commons to instal itself permanently in power as a dictatorship.

Parliamentary sovereignty. The 'doctrine of Parliamentary sovereignty' has two sides to it: the first deals with the relationship between Parliament and the courts; the second deals with the relationship between the current Parliament and future Parliaments.

The doctrine of Parliamentary sovereignty says, first of all, that the courts will be required to give effect to each provision in an Act of Parliament until that provision is repealed by a subsequent Act of Parliament; and this is so no matter how objectionable that provision may be. In other words, the courts are subordinate to Parliament.

The doctrine of Parliamentary sovereignty says, secondly, that any Act of Parliament can be repealed by Parliament, and that an Act of Parliament that has been repealed will no longer have any legal effect. In other words, Parliament cannot bind its successors. It follows from this that Parliament cannot place any hurdles in the way of a future Parliament repealing a given Act of Parliament, that would make that Act harder to repeal than it was to pass. In other words, Parliament cannot entrench legislation, protecting it against successor Parliaments that might want to repeal it.

The doctrine of Parliamentary sovereignty is fundamentally democratic in nature: it proclaims the supremacy of the elected legislature over unelected judges, and the current legislature – which represents the current views of the people – over previous legislatures. Given this, it might be wondered whether there should be an exception to the doctrine of Parliamentary sovereignty where a Parliament attempts to undermine democracy by, for example, passing laws against public demonstrations, or by passing laws that make it easier to engage in corrupt electoral practices – but (so far as we know) the courts would not make an exception to the doctrine of Parliamentary sovereignty in such cases. However, there are two major exceptions to the doctrine of Parliamentary sovereignty.

First, a provision in an Act of Parliament will not be given effect to by the courts if it is inconsistent with European Union (q.v.) law (as incorporated into English law by the European Communities Act 1972) unless Parliament has made it absolutely clear that it is to be given effect to even if it is so inconsistent.

Secondly, Parliament is free – within as yet unspecified limits – to pass legislation that will have the effect of changing the definition of what counts as an Act of Parliament. It remains uncertain whether this power can be used to entrench either other legislation ('An Act purporting to repeal the Human Rights Act 1998 will not count as a valid Act of Parliament') or the very legislation that has the effect of changing the definition of what counts as an Act of Parliament ('An Act that purports to repeal this legislation but does not command the support of 75% of the House of Commons will not count as a valid Act of Parliament').

Precedent. A precedent is a legal case that has been decided by some court in the past.

A binding precedent is a legal case that was decided by a court on the basis of some rule or principle which other courts must give effect to under the rules of precedent if they have to decide a case where that rule or principle applies. Under the rules of precedent:

1 Decisions of the Supreme Court of the United Kingdom (and the Appellate Committee of the House of Lords) are binding on all UK courts (q.v.) other than the Supreme Court of the United Kingdom unless and until they are overruled (declared no longer to be correct) by the Supreme Court (or have already been overruled by the Appellate Committee of the House of Lords).

2 Decisions of the Court of Appeal are binding on future Courts of Appeal, and all courts lower than the Court of Appeal, unless and until they are overruled by the Supreme Court (or have already been overruled by the Appellate Committee of the House of Lords).

A *persuasive* precedent is a case that was decided by a court on the basis of some rule or principle which another court is not bound to give effect to under the rules of precedent, but the legal wisdom and authority of the judges who decided that case is such that it is likely that other courts will accept that rule or principle as being correct.

The rules of precedent are rendered less important than you might think because of the fact that it almost always a matter of debate what rule or principle underlay a decision of a court in a particular case. So, for example, if the Supreme Court decides in *Doe* v *Brown* that Doe must pay Brown damages (q.v.), the Court of Appeal will be bound by that decision. At the same time, it will usually be a matter of debate what rule or principle underlay the decision of the Supreme Court in *Doe v Brown*. If this is so, it will be up to the Court of Appeal to decide for itself what rule or principle underlay the Supreme Court's decision in *Doe v Brown* and therefore what rule or principle it is going to be bound by under the rules of precedent.

Property. Lawyers use the term 'property' to refer to three different things, and are not always careful enough about distinguishing between them:

(1) They use the term 'property' to refer, first of all, to the things that can amount to property. These things are separated into two categories. First, tangible property. This category is made up of things that can amount to property that you can touch such as land, and cars, and computers, and CDs. Secondly, intangible property. This category is made up of things that can amount to property that you cannot touch. Intangible property always takes the form of a right (in the second and third senses of the word 'right' (q.v.)) of some kind. For example: copyrights (which give someone the right not to have their work copied by someone else), patents (which give someone the exclusive right to exploit a particular invention), rights to draw money from a bank account, and rights to sue someone for money.

(2) Lawyers also use the term 'property' to refer, secondly, to the interests that one can have in a thing that amounts to property. The greatest interest one can have in such a thing is legal ownership. But English law recognises many other interests that one can have in a thing, such as equitable ownership (otherwise known as a beneficial interest), a lease, and a charge. These interests can be traded, and can be held simultaneously in the same thing by different people. So a piece of land could be legally owned by A, but at the same time B has a beneficial interest in it (in which case A is said to hold the property on trust for B), and the land is leased out to C for a year, and D Bank has a charge over the land to secure the money D Bank lent A to acquire the land.

(3) Lawyers also use the term 'property' to refer, thirdly, to the rights (in the first sense of the word 'right' (q.v.)) that someone who has an interest in property will have that others not interfere with that interest. So someone who legally owns a thing will have rights against virtually everyone else that they not interfere with his ability to enjoy and exploit that thing. If B has a beneficial interest in a thing that is legally owned by A, B will have a right against A that A exploit that thing for B's benefit. If C leases a thing that is legally owned by A, C will have a right against virtually everyone else (including A) that they not interfere with her ability to enjoy and exploit that thing for the duration of the lease. If D Bank has a charge over a thing legally owned by A, it

will have a right against A that A sell that thing and use the money realised by the sale to pay off a debt that A owes D Bank. (D Bank will not, of course, seek to enforce this right unless it becomes worried about A's ability to pay off his debt to D Bank without selling the thing that D Bank has a charge over.)

Remedy. 'Remedy' is a catch-all term for the range of orders, awards, and sanctions that a claimant (q.v.) who brings a case to court may be seeking.

In a case where a claimant complains that a defendant has violated his rights (in the first sense of the word 'right' (q.v.)), the normal remedy that he will be seeking is damages (q.v.). But in a case where a defendant is continuously violating the claimant's rights, the claimant may also seek an injunction – an order of the court that the defendant stop violating the claimant's rights. (Disregarding such an order after it has been issued will amount to a contempt of court, which is a crime (q.v.) punishable by imprisonment.)

A claimant may bring a case seeking a declaration that he has an interest in a particular piece of property (q.v.) that is being held or exploited by the defendant, and that as a result he has certain rights against the defendant (in the first sense of the word 'right' (q.v.)).

A claimant may also bring an application for judicial review (q.v.) against a public body, seeking a range of remedies designed to ensure that that public body does not exceed its powers.

Right (legal). Confusingly, lawyers use the term 'legal right' to describe three different things:

1 The situation where the law imposes on B a duty to do x, and that duty is imposed on B purely for A's benefit. In such a situation lawyers say that A has a legal right that B do x. For example: 'A has a legal right that B not harass him', or 'A has a legal right that B take care not to injure him'.

2 The situation where the law gives A the power to perform a particular legal act, such as suing someone, or entering into a contract with someone else, or making someone your agent. In such a situation, lawyers say that A has a legal right to perform the act in question. For example: 'A has a legal right to sue B for damages', or 'A has a legal right to terminate his contract with B'.

3 The situation where the law protects to a limited degree some freedom or interest of A's against being interfered with by other people. In such a situation, lawyers say that A has a legal right to enjoy that freedom or interest.

For example: 'A has a legal right to freedom of speech', or 'A has a legal right to enjoy his property', or 'A has a legal right to bodily integrity'.

The fact that the word 'right' is used in these different ways creates room for confusion – either on the part of the person using the word, or the people he or she is speaking to. For example, suppose that Freddie is making a controversial speech at Nantwich University, and some student protestors are trying to shout him down. Freddie may try to silence the protestors by claiming (either to them or the police) that he has a 'right to freedom of speech', and that they should respect that. But in saying this, he is trying to pull a fast one. He does indeed have a 'right to freedom of speech' because the law – to a limited extent – protects his freedom of speech from being interfered with by the government. But that has nothing to do with the protestors. Unless the law gives Freddie a right (in sense (1), above) that the protestors not shout him down (which it does not, unless their conduct amounts to unreasonable harassment), the protestors are free, and should feel themselves free, to make as much noise as they want.

Rule of law. Academics use the term 'rule of law' in a number of different ways.

First, some use the term 'rule of law' to describe the conditions that have to be satisfied if a legal system is to work effectively as a legal system – that is, as a system for guiding people's behaviour by laying down rules for them to follow. Such people say that the rule of law demands that a legal system's laws be certain, consistent, prospective, easy to understand, easy to remember, easy to find out. It also demands that people generally must be inclined to obey the law, and there must exist effective remedies and sanctions that are applied to those who are not willing to obey the law.

Secondly, some think of the 'rule of law' as the antithesis of the 'rule of men' – as in the phrase, 'we live under the rule of law, not men'. According to this view, we can only say that we live in a country governed by the rule of law if: (1) our country's legal system places strict limits on when the State may use coercive force against someone; (2) those limits are normally observed; and (3) when those limits are violated, there exist effective remedies and sanctions that are applied against the State.

Thirdly, others think that if the ideal of living under the 'rule of law, not men' is to be achieved, the power to make law must be constrained, so that those who make the law are themselves subject to a higher law in the way they exercise their power. On this view, we can only say that we live in a country governed by the rule of law if – in addition to (1), (2) and (3), above – (4) there exist mechanisms in our country that work effectively to ensure that the power to make law is not exercised arbitrarily or irrationally or immorally.

Separation of powers. The French philosopher, Montesquieu (1689–1755), praised the British constitution for splitting the government into three different branches: the legislature (which makes the law), the executive (which enforces the law, and employs the power of the State within the limits placed on it by the law), and the judiciary (which interprets the law, and resolves legal disputes). This arrangement, he claimed, prevented governmental power being concentrated in the hands of any one person, or one group of people, and therefore helped to ensure that governmental power was not abused.

It seems obvious that Montesquieu's analysis of the British constitution no longer holds true (if it ever did). There is no longer an effective separation of powers within the UK of the type Montesquieu advocated. The fact that the leading figures in the government are drawn from the majority party in the House of Commons (and the fact that the House of Lords cannot block legislation that the majority party in the House of Commons is determined to introduce) means there is no longer any solid dividing line in the UK constitution between the legislature and the executive. The line is dissolved even further by the existence of delegated legislation (q.v.), which is legislation created by government ministers, and Henry VIII clauses (q.v.), which allow government ministers to rewrite Acts of Parliament after they have been passed. Turning to Montesquieu's third branch of the government, while the judiciary is theoretically independent of the executive under the UK constitution, the law reports contain very few cases where the courts have decided a case in a way that is seriously embarrassing for the government; there are, in contrast, plenty of cases where the courts have re-interpreted and twisted the law to avoid deciding cases in a way that would embarrass the government. In practice, the courts are careful not to exercise their powers in a way that might provoke a seriously adverse reaction from the all-powerful executive.

Statute. See 'Parliament', above.

Statutory instrument. See 'Delegated legislation', above.

Tort. A tort involves the violation of a legal right (in the first sense of the word 'right' (q.v.) that does not arise from a contract (q.v.) and which may be remedied through the award of damages (q.v.).

There are a large number of different torts recognised under English law, corresponding to the large number of legal rights that English law endows people with even before they have entered into a contract with someone else. The range of torts recognised under English law include: trespass to the person (touching someone else without justification (battery); threatening someone else without justification (assault); and locking someone else up without justification (false imprisonment); trespass to land (going onto someone else's land without justification); negligence (failing to take care not to injure someone or protect their interests when they had a right that you take such care); and defamation (damaging someone's reputation without justification).

So – that's my mini-dictionary of law! I'd recommend that you read this through a few times before you start studying law – once you are completely familiar with it, you should be able to hit the ground running when your studies begin. Having said that, it would be a good idea for you to buy a dictionary of law, as you will be coming across a lot of other strange words and concepts in the course of your studies that you will need to come to grips with. Elizabeth Martin and Jonathan Law's *A Dictionary of Law* looks really good, as does Leslie B. Curzon and Paul Richard's *Dictionary of Law*. If you have a lot of money, it might also be worth investing in *The New Oxford Companion to Law,* edited by Peter Cane and Joanne Conaghan.

Best wishes,

Nick

General Tips on Studying Law

- From: Nicholas J. McBride [dearnick@pearson.com]
- To: Brown, Alex
- Subject: General Tips on Studying Law

Dear Alex,

Now you are just about to start your studies, I thought I'd give you some general tips on how you should go about studying law. I'll give you some more detailed guidance later on how you should approach such things as reading textbooks, or cases – but for the time being, I just wanted to lay down general guidelines to help you study as effectively as possible.

● Never be passive

This is the most important tip. Never, ever be passive in studying law. For example, if you look back at the previous letter, and read it over again, you'll almost certainly be pretty passive in reading it. You're just reading it, without any particular agenda or set of questions in your mind – just letting me tell you whatever I have to tell you. As a result, it's unlikely that you'll remember that much of the details of what I wrote. (Be honest: you don't, do you? But that's okay – the point of the letter was not to help you remember anything, but just to get you comfortable with various key terms and concepts that you'll be expected to be familiar with as a law student.) I don't want you to study law like that. Always be thinking and questioning as you go through legal materials.

When you are studying a particular area of law, ask yourself: What problems is this area of law intended to deal with? How does it deal with those problems? Does it do a good job of dealing with those problems? Does this area of law create more problems than it solves? Could this area of law be improved? When you are studying a particular legal rule, ask yourself: Is there a better way of stating this rule? Why does this rule exist? How does it apply in practice? Are there any exceptions to this rule? When you are reading a textbook, ask yourself: How much of this information do I actually need to know? Is there a better way of presenting this information? Are there any issues the writer is skating over that I need to investigate further? When you are reading a case, ask yourself: What's the most straightforward and succinct way of summarising the facts of this case? On the basis of what I have read so far, how would I expect this case to have been decided? How was it decided? What were the key reasons for the decision? Did the judge make any interesting observations about the law (known as *obiter dicta* – words along the way (to the ultimate decision)) in his or her judgment? What do the academics think of this case? What do I think?

Approaching your studies with these sorts of questions in mind will make the process of studying law much more interesting and vital for you, and help to get the details of the law into your head. Remember: the more you use the information you come across and the more you are able to arrange that information into some sort of order, the more likely you will be able to remember that information. So if you ever find yourself *just* reading some legal material, give yourself a shake, take a five-minute break to clear your head, and come back ready to take a more active approach to your studies.

● The need to work smart

A fact which people who aren't lawyers find it hard to understand is that the law gets substantially bigger every year. Every year brings new cases, new statutes, adding to the detail and complexity of the law. As a result, the textbooks get bigger and bigger. For example, the 13th edition of *Winfield & Jolowicz on Tort*, published in 1989, was 650 pages long. The latest, 18th, edition, published 21 years later in 2010, is 1,336 pages long: over twice as long. I started studying tort law in 1989. So students studying tort law nowadays are expected to learn twice as I much as I had to for my exams – but in the same amount of time as I had to study tort law. One way to do this would be to work twice as hard as I did as a student. But that would be pretty difficult because I worked very hard myself. So that's not an option. Instead, what you have to do is work *smarter* than I did – get more out of the time you have to study than I ever did.

If you want to work smarter than I ever did, before you start working your way through a reading list that you have been given to read, look up the past exam papers that have been set on the subject you are studying, and see what sort of questions tend to be set on the area of law that your reading list is focused on. Use those questions as a guide to what you need to be focusing on in your reading. Read as much as you can that will allow you to deal with those questions before – if you have time – widening your focus and looking at issues and rules that tend not be the subject of questions in the exams.

A typical reading list will give you some chapters from a textbook to read, list some cases that you should look at, and then give you some references to articles written about the area of law you are looking at. When you go through the textbook for the first time, I don't think it's a good idea to take notes, or highlight anything – you'll just end up copying out the book, or highlighting virtually every line. (I did this as a student – I ended up just colouring virtually the whole of all my textbooks yellow.) Instead, work smart and just read the textbook through, without making notes or highlighting the text. But don't read the book passively – as you are reading through it, be thinking: What are the big issues that the textbook is highlighting? What are the key cases, and what do they say? Who are the big academic names in this area, and what do they think? Could I do a better job of writing this chapter? If so, how would I have done it?

Once you are through the textbook – and it shouldn't take long if you are reading it without taking notes or highlighting – you need to get onto the cases. Here, prioritise the most recent cases. This is for three reasons. (1) The most recent cases are the ones most likely to be relevant to the exam. (2) The most recent cases may well sum up for you the effect of the previous cases on the reading list, thus saving you the trouble of reading them. (3) The most recent cases are the ones least likely to appear, or to have been dealt with very well, in the textbook. Once you have got through the recent cases, you should then read some casenotes on the most important cases (you will be able to tell from the reading list what the most important cases are.) A casenote comprises a summary of, and comments on, a particular case – usually written by an academic, and occasionally by a practising barrister. I will tell you in a subsequent letter how to find out where to get casenotes on a particular case, but two journals in particular carry casenotes on all the important legal cases – the *Law Quarterly Review* and the *Cambridge Law Journal*. It is well worth reading casenotes on important cases in both of those journals, as a way of learning more about these cases, and getting some critical commentary on how those cases should have been decided.

Once you are through the cases, you will be onto the articles section of your reading list. Don't assume that all the articles on your reading list are going to be really good. Some of them won't be – but they have been put on your reading list because they seem relevant to the area of law that you are studying. When you are going through an article, the only real question you should be asking yourself is: Summed up as concisely as possible, what is this author actually saying? You need to be able to reduce the article down to a 5–10-line summary, setting out its basic argument – or you won't be able to retain it in your head. If it's clear that the article that you are looking at can't be reduced down in this way, then just skip through it, looking to see if there are any small, interesting points that you can pick up from it – but otherwise don't sweat over the article trying to figure out what it's saying. Instead: (1) Google the article to see if anyone else has been able to sum up its basic argument; and (2) if you get the chance, ask the person who set the reading list what they think the author of the article was trying to say.

Once you have gone through the articles you have been set, you need to go back to the textbook and go through it again, *this time* making notes of important-looking points that you think you will need to remember for the exam and that you aren't already familiar with from your other reading. If things have gone the way I hope and predict, your notes won't be that extensive – and certainly won't be as voluminous as they would have been had you made notes on the textbook on your first run through it.

If you've done all that, give yourself a pat on the back – you've got through the reading list! If you have time, do some research on the Internet to see if there are any further articles or other materials that look relevant and important for the area of law you are studying, and the sort of questions that might come up on that area of law in the exam. I'll give you some tips on how to do that in a subsequent letter.

◉ Your notes

So you should be making notes on:

1 the cases you read, and any casenotes you look at;

2 any articles you read;

3 details in the textbook that you aren't familiar with after you have done all your other reading and that seem important.

You should also be making notes on:

4 any lectures you attend; and

5 points made in small-group teaching sessions that you attend.

I'll talk about taking notes on (4) and (5) in another letter, but here are a few tips on taking notes on (1), (2) and (3).

Your notes on a particular case should start on a fresh sheet of A4 paper – so you never have more than one case on the same piece of paper – and should be structured as follows:

NAME OF CASE – CITATION – COURT
FACTS
OUTCOME
REASONS
COMMENTS

The facts of the case should be summarised as succinctly as possible. In summarising the facts, don't abbreviate the names of the parties – full names are more memorable than letters – but otherwise try to get the facts down to their essentials. The outcome of the case is simply the bare result – who won. The reasons you get from the judgments in the case. Don't try to summarise the whole of a judgment – just look for the key paragraphs where the reasons for the judge's decision are set out. Comments on the case could be your comments, or comments you have picked up from casenotes on the case, or your teachers.

Your notes on the articles you read should be structured as follows:

AUTHOR – TITLE OF ARTICLE – JOURNAL CITATION
BASIC ARGUMENT
ANY OTHER INTERESTING POINTS
COMMENTS

The comments on the article could be your comments, or points that have been made about the article by other authors.

Your notes from the textbook should be fun and interesting to put together and to go back to. Again, passivity is your enemy. If you are writing out chunks of text from the textbook, your mind is likely to switch off, your work will slow down, and nothing will be going into your head. Instead, you have to learn to be creative with your notes. Think about using diagrams and pictures to re-present the information in the textbook that you want to make a note of. Your presentation may not be that superior to what is in the textbook, but the creative act of imagining how to present this information in a new and different way, and your putting your ideas into practice, will help the information that you are making notes on to get into your head and stay there. This is particularly important when you are making notes on a particularly dry and technical area of law. It is vital that your notes not be dry and technical, but find some way of presenting the details of the law in an interesting and vital way. The effort you make to think of how to do that will pay off in spades in helping you recall that information later on.

● Being organised

You can't be successful as a law student unless you are organised. Make sure you have a system for filing your physical notes. It might be an idea to keep your notes on cases on a particular area of law separate from your physical notes on textbooks and articles, and to file the cases in alphabetical order, so as to make them really easy to locate in case you want to make a quick note of something you've read about a particular case. You will also be downloading a lot of documents – pdfs of articles and cases – from the Internet. Make sure again that your computer is set up to save those documents in an organised fashion. Create folders on your computer for the different subjects you will be studying. Within each of those folders it might be an idea to create a sub-folder 'Case file' to store pdfs of any cases you download relevant to a particular subject you are studying. Also create sub-folders for particular topics you will be studying in a particular subject (the headings on your reading lists and lecture handouts will be a good guide as to what those topics will be) to store away pdfs of articles, as well as soft copies of notes on textbooks and articles that you have made on a computer. And *make sure* you regularly save everything law-related on your computer onto memory sticks in case your computer crashes. If you are using a 'cloud' service such as Dropbox to store all your work on, it's still essential that you back up your work regularly to guard against the possibility of something going wrong with the cloud service.

You also need to organise your life as well as your notes. You won't get anywhere with your studies unless you give yourself a fair chance to spend extended periods sitting and studying. If you are constantly dashing off all over the place from one commitment to another, you won't get anywhere. So plan your weeks – figure out where you need to be and when and figure out what you are going to be doing in the spaces in between. Make up your mind in advance how you are going to be spending the time available to you to study. There are few things more conducive to creating stress and wasting time than wondering, 'What should I do now?' Make sure you know when you wake up in the morning what you are going to be doing that day, and focus on getting it done.

● Pulling it all together

If you follow all of the above advice, you should slowly start accumulating an impressive set of notes on the subjects you are studying. However, having a big file of notes on a particular subject can lure a student into a false sense of security that he or she really 'knows' the subject. No – having a big file of notes has put you into a good position to 'know' your subject, but you still need to pull the notes into one coherent whole.

One way American law students do this is to write an 'outline' of an entire subject they are studying. In other words, they write their own mini-textbook: but one which reflects the progress that you have made in your studies, and is geared towards addressing the topics and issues that have emerged as being important for you to master for the exams.

I think writing an 'outline' of a particular subject is a great way of getting the details of that subject into your head. But you mustn't forget that it's your performance on paper and not what's in your head that will determine how well you do in the exams. So, for me, practising past paper questions is an absolute *must* for any law student. You have to learn how to apply the knowledge in your head to concrete questions. And doing past paper questions – so long as you do them well – has exactly the same effect as writing an 'outline': by using the information in your notes to compose your answers, you help that information to become solidly locked into your head.

So those are my basic tips. I'll be in touch soon with some more detailed guidance on approaching textbooks, cases and so on.

All best wishes,

Nick

Using a Textbook

- From: Nicholas J. McBride [dearnick@pearson.com]
- To: Brown, Alex
- Subject: Using a Textbook

Hey Alex,

Okay – so this is the first of a series of letters about the specific sources of legal information that you'll be drawing on in your studies. We'll start with textbooks.

● The basic approach

As I said in the previous letter, when you go through a chapter or chapters from a textbook for the first time, your aim should just be to read it. If you take any notes, it should just be of key concepts, ideas, case names and statutory provisions that you will need to remember for later. What you have to avoid is getting stuck making very detailed notes that will slow your progress down, frustrate you, and prevent you ever getting onto anything else in the time available to you. But when you read a chapter or chapters from a textbook for the first time, you do actually have to *read* the textbook. That means going through it somewhere you can actually concentrate on the book and won't get distracted by other people or other things. So find somewhere that works for you to allow you to read without distraction – a library or your room (with the TV and computer *off*) or a comfortable chair in a coffee shop. But find somewhere. And when you go through the book, remember: keep asking – Why is this important? What are the key points here? What is this area of law about? What problems is it trying to solve? What are the key cases/statutory provisions?

After you have gone through everything else you are supposed to read, you should then return to the textbook with the benefit of all the knowledge you've picked up in the meantime. This time round you will make notes on various points that you come across in the textbook (1) that are important, and (2) that you are not already familiar with from your other reading. Past paper questions (which you should have looked at before you started any reading) and your lectures will provide a guide as to (1). On (2), try to avoid wasting time making notes of the obvious. For example, if you are studying contract law, you will soon find out that promises aren't automatically legally binding, and that usually something (consideration) has to be given in return for a promise to make that binding. Neither of those points is worth wasting a scrap of paper or a second of your time on noting: they are so foundational to the subject that you won't need to make a note of them to remember them. You will be reminded of them by everything else you read. That's one reason for leaving detailed notetaking from your textbooks to much later in your reading: it's only then that you are able to differentiate between points that are important but so obvious they're not worth noting, and points that are important but not so obvious or memorable that you'll be able to get away with not making a note of them.

And as I said in the previous letter, make sure your notes are fun and interesting; that you are constantly creating and thinking while making notes on your textbook. For example, I enclose the preface to the third edition of my tort textbook[1] – it's still relevant even though there's now a fourth edition in print. Have a look at it and think about how you would take some notes on it. At the end of this letter, you'll find one fun and interesting way that I thought the information in that preface could be re-presented for a student's notes.

● Further tips

(1) Don't rely too much on your textbooks

One of the most important differences between doing A-Levels and doing a law degree is the attitude you should have towards your textbooks. At A-Level, you could count on your textbooks to be correct and to tell you everything you needed to know to get a good grade in your exams. Neither of these things is likely to be true of the textbooks you will be looking at when doing a law degree.

---

[1] See Appendix B.

First of all, legal textbooks frequently get the law wrong or make statements or assumptions about the law that are debatable. So if a textbook says 'The law says x' you shouldn't necessarily think that the law does actually say x. Secondly, most textbooks do not tell you everything you need to know about the law to get a good mark in the exams. For reasons of space, most textbooks do not spend much time discussing how the law should be developed or reformed – and any discussion of such issues is likely to be quite superficial. For in-depth discussions of how the law should be reformed or developed, you need to look at monographs (short books on a single issue) or articles. In addition, most textbooks 'play safe' and spend almost all of their time simply reporting what the decided cases say; they spend very little time going beyond the cases and discussing what the legal position is in various hypo-thetical, problematic situations. But these are precisely the sort of situations you are likely to be confronted with in your exams.

So you should treat textbooks as fallible introductions to the various subjects you are studying. They get you started and give you some idea of terrain over which you are going to be moving – but it's dangerous to over-rely on them.

(2) Picking which textbook to make your principal guide

In any subject, there are going to be lots of different textbooks about that subject. Which one should you use? Your teachers will probably have a rec-ommendation, and if so, go with that. But in some cases, they will just list a variety of textbooks and leave it up to you to choose. So – how do you choose? Asking students in the year above you for their advice might be an idea – though watch out for slackers who recommend a really slim volume as telling you 'all you need to know' (if you want to do badly in the exams, that is); and also look out for someone who is just trying to sell you his or her text-books regardless of whether they were any good. Going to your university law library (or a good university bookstore with a wide selection of law books) and looking through the range of recommended textbooks to see if any of them catch your eye as being particularly readable and interesting would also be a good idea. Try not to select a textbook on price alone: £5 or £10 extra is a very small price to pay for getting a book that will make a major difference to the quality of your understanding of the law. Some textbooks that might appear on your reading lists or lecture handouts tend to be more oriented towards legal professionals – Treitel on *Contract* or Megarry and Wade's *Law of Real Property* are two examples. Don't be put off by the fact that they are mainly for professionals. The level of detail could really help you with your studies. However, if you use one of those textbooks you have to be prepared to skip past major chunks of text as not being relevant to your studies.

(3) Consult more than one textbook

So, let's assume you are now armed with your principal textbook. However, for the reasons stated in (1), above, it's dangerous to rely on just one textbook. No one textbook can be the font of all wisdom on a particular subject. (Though some textbooks come closer than others . . .) If you take virtually any legal textbook, there are going to be some chapters where the writers did a really good job and some chapters where the writers weren't quite on their game. So you shouldn't just ignore or write off the other textbooks that deal with the subject you are studying. If you have time, after you have done everything else you have to do, you should have a look at any other relevant textbooks stocked in your university library to see what they have to say about the particular area of law you are studying.

(4) Remember that textbooks get out of date

This point may be a bit too obvious to be worth making – but it sometimes catches inexperienced students out. There are some areas of law that change quite a lot over short periods of time – tort law and criminal law are examples – with the result that textbooks in those areas get out of date quite quickly. If you are studying one of these areas, be careful about using a textbook which is more than three or four years old – many of its statements about what the law says could be out of date. (Though if you are, as I advise, consulting a variety of textbooks, you'll soon detect any out-of-date statements.) And if you are buying a textbook second-hand – particularly from a student in one of the years above you – *make sure* that it hasn't been superseded by a later edition. If it has, then be careful. Certainly don't buy it if it is four or five years out of date. If it's only two years out of date – a lot of publishers now like to bring out new editions of legal textbooks every two years – then it might still be serviceable for your purposes; but certainly don't pay more than about £5 for it.

(5) Look at the footnotes

Don't ignore the footnotes in a textbook. They can often be the source of:

(a) very useful observations about the law which didn't fit easily into the flow of the main text and were therefore relegated to the footnotes;

(b) suggestions as to articles and other books that it might be helpful to read – and, if you are really lucky, summaries of what those articles and books say, thus saving the trouble of looking at them yourself;

(c) criticisms of other writers' views which will come in handy when trying to make up your mind whose views you agree or disagree with.

(6) Boredom

If you're getting bored reading a textbook what should you do? (Note that this is highly unlikely to happen if you adopt the above approach to going through the textbook.) The answer is: stop reading. If you're bored, you won't be taking anything in, and there's no point in carrying on reading when you're not taking in anything of what you're reading. Deal with the source of the boredom before you carry on reading. It may be that you've been working too long and your brain has decided it's had enough. In which case, take a break. Or it may be that the textbook is at fault: the writer hasn't made enough effort to make the bit of the textbook you are reading sufficiently interesting. In which case, search out another textbook that covers the same area but is more interesting. Or it may be that there's something on your mind that stops you focusing on what the textbook has to say. In which case, deal with the thing that's on your mind and then come back to the textbook. (Easier said than done in many cases, I know.)

That's all I have to say on going through textbooks. Reading cases is next . . .

Best wishes,

Nick

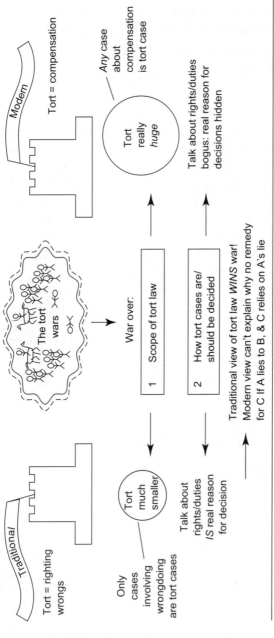
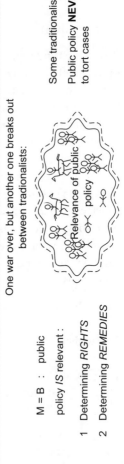

Reading Cases

- From: Nicholas J. McBride [dearnick@pearson.com]
- To: Brown, Alex
- Subject: Reading Cases

Hi Alex,

In this letter, I'm going to talk about one of the most important parts of a law student's legal education – reading and making sense of cases. Up until the twentieth century, most English law was case law – law that emerged from the concrete decisions of the courts. Out of thousands and thousands of cases, each presenting a set of facts and a question: 'What does the law say in this situation?', there emerged the body of rules and principles that is known as 'the common law'. The tidal wave of legislation in the twentieth century has reduced the importance of the common law, but large swathes of our law (especially administrative law and tort law) are still very much based on case law. So you will be expected to read cases and be able to discuss them in your legal essays and problem answers.

● Taking notes on a concrete case

Let's start with a concrete case: *Century Insurance Co Ltd* v *Northern Ireland Road Transport Board*. I'm sending you a copy of the report of the case in 1942 Appeal Cases.[1] Don't worry about what 'Appeal Cases' mean – I think I'll write you another letter about the whole history of law reporting, so that you can make sense of all the different sets of law reports. For the time being, let's

---

[1]See Appendix C.

just say that the 'Appeal Cases' (or 'A.C.' for short) report cases decided by the highest court in the UK legal system – previously the Judicial Committee of the House of Lords (or 'House of Lords' for short), and now the UK Supreme Court. So *Century Insurance* is a case decided by the House of Lords.

Now – if you were making a note on this case, you would start at the top of the page with the names of the parties, the citation of the case, and the court that decided the case. So –

Century Insurance v Northern Ireland Road Transport Board [1942] AC 509 HL

(Again, don't worry about why the year is written down as [1942], with square brackets, rather than (1942), with round brackets – I'll tell you about that in the next letter as well.) The next thing we want to make a note of is the facts of the case. Now – two points in particular need to be borne in mind in summarising the facts of the case.

First, we are NOT AT ALL interested in who the 'appellants' and 'respondents' in the case were. Technically, the 'appellant' is the person who lost in the court below and is now appealing against that decision. The 'respondent' is the person who is responding to the appeal, and hoping that the court will uphold the decision of the court below. But the technicalities of who was appealing and who was responding to the appeal are completely irrelevant to us. So your summary of the case MUST NOT make any reference to 'appellant' and 'respondent'. If you use those terms, you won't have a clue who you are actually talking about. What matters for our purposes is who is bringing the action (a claim for damages, a criminal prosecution, an application for judicial review) and who the action is being brought against. And ideally, we'd like to put actual names to those people as a summary of the facts is easier to write and easier to remember if we can put a name to the people involved.

Secondly, the headnote to the case will normally provide you with a good starting point for your summary of the case. If you turn to your copy of the report in the *Century Insurance* case, the headnote is the summary of what happened in the case and what was decided that is on the first page of the case (page 509). The headnote starts 'Under a contract with a petroleum company . . .' and ends '. . . entitled to be indemnified under the policy.' But you must not just copy out the headnote's summary of the facts of the case and adopt that summary as your own. The headnote will normally tell you enough about what happened in the case for you to produce a summary of the facts of the case, but the headnote's summary of the facts will probably be too long and overcomplicated for your purposes. You need to produce a summary of the bare essentials of the case.

As it happens, the headnote of the *Century Insurance* case isn't that great at making it clear what exactly happened in the case. We start off with a 'transport undertaking' which entered into a contract with a 'petroleum company' to deliver the petrol company's petrol in the transport undertaking's lorries. I'm already getting a bit irritated with the lack of names, so let's just try to see if we can put some names to some people here. For that we need to skip forward to the judgments for a more detailed account of the facts. As it happens, that more detailed account is set out on the very next two pages – pages 509–10 – but that starts unhelpfully by talking about 'The respondents' being 'insured by the appellant company'; and no names. So we need to go back to the first page and look at the title of the case to see who the appellant and respondents were – and we see that Century Insurance were the appellants and Northern Ireland Road Transport Board were the respondents. The Northern Ireland Road Transport Board must be the 'transport undertaking' but what's the name of the petrol company? Going back to page 510 we eventually find a reference to 'a consignment of three hundred gallons of petrol at the Larne depot of Holmes, Mullin & Dunn Ld.' That must be the petrol company. So – 'The Northern Ireland Road Transport Board entered into a contract with a petrol company, HMD, to deliver HMD's petrol in its lorries.' Fine. So what happened next? Back to the headnote to find out. According to the headnote, the Transport Board (for short) undertook to do various things for the petrol company – but we know now that the petrol company isn't involved in the case, so that might not be worth making a note of. Okay. So what happened next? This is what the headnote says –

> While one of the lorries belonging to the undertaking, in respect of which a policy had been issued by an insurance company against liability to third parties arising from damage to property caused by its use by the undertaking, was being used to deliver petrol at a garage in accordance with the agreement, the driver, while transferring petrol from the lorry to an underground tank, struck a match to light a cigarette and threw it on the floor, causing a conflagration and an explosion.

Okay – how could we sum this up? We know the 'undertaking' is the Transport Board. The 'insurance company' is almost certainly Century Insurance. So: 'Century issued an insurance policy to the Transport Board (TB) under which it would cover any liabilities incurred by TB to third parties arising from damage to property caused by . . .' Hmm . . . the next bit of the head-note says 'its use by the undertaking'. What does the 'its' refer to? Looking at the sentence 'its' seems to refer to 'one of the lorries belonging to the under-taking. So: 'Century issued an insurance policy to the Transport Board (TB) under which it would cover any liabilities incurred by TB to third parties aris-ing from damage to property caused by TB's use of its lorries. When one of TB's lorries was being used to deliver petrol to a garage, the driver – while transferring the petrol from the lorry to the garage's tanks – struck a match to light a cigarette, threw it on the floor, and caused an explosion.' Fine – and then what happened? The headnote says:

> Claims in respect of consequent damage having been made against the undertaking, the insurance company contended that they did not fall within the scope of the policy

Putting this in another, less abrupt, way: 'TB was sued for the damage caused by the explosion. It sought to claim on its insurance policy, but Century said it wasn't liable under the terms of the policy.' But this isn't completely satis-factory as a summary of the facts. We don't know *why* Century said it wasn't liable. To find that out, we again need to flip over the page to the more detailed statement of the facts in Viscount Simon's judgment, and look through it for something that will tell us why Century thought they weren't liable under their insurance policy with the Transport Board. And at the bottom of page 510, we find that:

> One of the grounds on which the appellants resisted the claim of the respondents under the policy was that, in view of the terms of an agreement of October 11, 1934, between the respondents' predecessors, the Irish Road Transport Co., Ld., whose undertaking they acquired on April 30, 1937, and Messrs/Holmes, Mullin & Dunn, Ld., the liability for the damage did not rest on the respondents.

Ignoring all the stuff about the Irish Road Transport Co, which doesn't seem relevant at all, the important thing to take away from this is that Century said they weren't liable under their insurance policy with the Transport Board because the *Transport Board* wasn't liable for the damage caused by the explo-sion. So: 'TB was sued for the damage caused by the explosion. It sought to claim on its insurance policy, but Century said it wasn't liable under the terms of the policy because TB wasn't liable for the damage caused by the explosion.' Putting all this together, here's our summary of the facts:

The Northern Ireland Road Transport Board entered into a contract with a petrol company (HMD) to deliver HMD's petrol in its lorries. Century issued an insurance policy to the Transport Board (TB) under which it would cover any liabilities to third parties incurred by TB arising from damage to property caused by TB's use of its lorries. When one of TB's lorries was being used to deliver petrol to a garage, the driver – while transferring the petrol from the lorry to the garage's tanks – struck a match to light a cigarette, threw it on the floor, and caused an explosion. TB was sued for the damage caused by the explosion. It sought to claim on its insurance policy, but Century said it wasn't liable under the terms of the policy because TB wasn't liable for the damage caused by the explosion.

Now – if you compare this summary with the summary of the facts in the headnote, I think you'll agree that our summary is much clearer and more straightforward. And all the work we have done trying to get the facts clear in our head will be helping get those facts into our head for the long term, so that we'll never forget what happened in the *Century Insurance* case. (This is one of the reasons why it's good to read cases in their original reports rather than packaged up in a cases and materials book – sometimes it's not good for you to have someone else do all the hard work for you. Having said that, there are some cases where the facts are so hard to make sense of that you'll need some help from academic authors to get an idea of what actually happened in the case.)

So now we have the facts straight, let's pause for a second and think – what do we think the result should have been? The whole case turns on whether the Transport Board was liable for the damage caused by the explosion that happened when one of its drivers, who was delivering HMD's petrol to a garage, lit a cigarette and threw the match away. Thinking about this is helpful for three reasons. First, doing this sort of thing helps educate your legal instincts – it gets you thinking like a lawyer instead of just being a passive recipient of legal information. Secondly, it helps you test the legal knowledge you have picked up so far from your textbook reading – can you remember enough to make an educated guess as to what the outcome of the case would have been? Thirdly, it gives you 'some skin in the game' (as the saying goes): if you have already taken a side in the case, it makes the judgments much more interesting to read and get through.

So – we've got our facts straight and we've had a think about what the outcome of the case should have been. The next job is to make a note of what the outcome actually was. Again, the headnote will tell us this, in the bit of the headnote which comes after '*Held*'. There it tells us that the House of Lords found that Century was liable under its insurance policy with the Transport Board: the Transport Board was liable for the damage caused by its driver because (1) he was employed by them at the time of the explosion and (2) he was acting in the course of his employment when he carelessly caused the explosion.

Now that we have noted the outcome of the case, we can turn to the judgments. When we go through the judgments, we are looking for *added value*. We are looking for anything in the judgments that adds something of value to what we already know about the case. So, for example, we are not looking for bare statements that the employee in *Century Insurance* was acting in the course of his employment when he lit his cigarette and threw his match away. We already know that. We are looking for explanations as to *why* the court held that he was acting in the course of his employment when he did this.

So – we skip past pages 510 and 511, as they just deal with the facts of the case, and we already have those straight. We move past page 513, as that contains the barristers' arguments in the case, and we're not really interested in those. We just want to get onto the judgments – and they start with Viscount Simon's on page 514. So let's start noting that. As we go through the judgment, we are looking for statements of principle or observations about the law. We are not really interested in quotations from other cases – we want to know what the judges said in *this* case. So whenever you see a judge quoting from another case, you can skip past that bit of the judgment. Don't feel bad about not reading it. It's an essential skill for getting through cases quickly – the ability to skip the bits you don't need to know about and focus on the really important parts. It's a skill that students take time to develop, which is why they are so slow in reading cases initially. But once you get the hang of it, you get through a serious number of cases in a day. (And, of course, if you never read cases you will remain for the rest of your life a real slowcoach in reading cases – not a great thing to be if you are practising lawyer who needs to master a lot of legal information very quickly.) What I want you to do is to set aside this letter and just look at Viscount Simon's judgment and make some notes on the judgment. Then come back here, and look at my summary. Just to make sure you don't look at mine before you've done yours, here's a picture of Viscount Simon to provide a break in the text before I launch into my summary of his judgment. Now – go away and only come back when you have done your summary.

Okay – here's my summary:

Viscount Simon

First issue (who was driver employed by?):

M can be generally employed by X but because of arrangements between X and T, M can at the time he was careless be held to have been T's employee, so as to make T liable for M's carelessness.

Test for whether X or T was employer at time M acted depends on who had power to control what M did.

→ Employee in this case was under Transport Board's control: never lent their lorries and drivers to HMD.

Second issue (was driver acting in course of employment?):

driver's duty to watch petrol as it flowed from lorry into tank, and it was while he was watching that he lit cigarette

– so was acting in course of employment: plainly negligent in discharging duties he was employed to perform.

And that's it. How did you do? If your summary is quite a bit longer, don't worry about it. As I said, it takes time and practice to learn how to note cases properly. Just by trying to make a summary of Viscount Simon's judgment, you are taking a first step down that road towards becoming an expert on noting cases.

In looking at my summary, I want you to observe in particular how I've noted Viscount Simon's judgment. My notes are written in an abbreviated style, with no attempt to write in full grammatical sentences. And they are presented in a broken up form with dashes and arrows to indicate the chain of reasoning. While we are not particularly looking for a fun or interesting way of making notes on cases, we are looking to ensure that our notes are easy to follow and take in at a glance. So avoid big chunky paragraphs of text – break the text up so that the eye can slip over your note like a skier slaloming down a mountain.

Having noted Viscount Simon's judgment, you can move on to the following judgments and note them as well. But remember that you are always looking for *added value*: so if a judge says essentially the same thing as a judge whose judgment you have already noted, then there's no point in making notes of the second judge's decision. It doesn't add anything to what has already been said. There's actually only one more substantive judgment in this case (from Lord Wright), and it doesn't seem to add very much to Viscount Simon's judgment. There is one passage that looks like it might add something, on the issue of whether the Transport Board's driver was acting in the course of his employment when he lit his cigarette and threw his match away. The passage goes as follows:

> The duty of the workman to his employer is so to conduct himself in doing
> his work as not negligently to cause damage either to the employer himself
> or his property or to third persons or their property, and thus to impose

the same liability on the employer as if he had been doing the work himself and committed the negligent act. This may seem too obvious as a matter of common sense to require either argument or authority. I think what plausibility the contrary argument might seem to possess results from treating the act of lighting the cigarette in abstraction from the circumstances as a separate act. This was the line taken by the majority judgment in *Williams* v. *Jones* (2), but Mellor and Blackburn JJ. dissented, rightly as I think. I agree also with the decision of the Court of Appeal in *Jefferson* v. *Derbyshire Farmers, Ld.* (3), which is in substance on the facts indistinguishable from the present case.

But in fact it's very hard to see what point is being made here. Remember the iron rule of lawyering that I talked about in my second letter to you – *express yourself clearly or die*. Here Lord Wright has not expressed himself clearly, so his judgment must die and remain unnoted by us.

So let's put the whole case note together and see what it looks like:

Century Insurance v Northern Ireland Road Transport Board [1942] AC 509 HL

The Northern Ireland Road Transport Board entered into a contract with a petrol company (HMD) to deliver HMD's petrol in its lorries. Century issued an insurance policy to the Transport Board (TB) under which it would cover any liabilities to third parties incurred by TB arising from damage to property caused by TB's use of its lorries. When one of TB's lorries was being used to deliver petrol to a garage, the driver – while transferring the petrol from the lorry to the garage's tanks – struck a match to light a cigarette, threw it on the floor, and caused an explosion. TB was sued for the damage caused by the explosion. It sought to claim on its insurance policy, but Century said it wasn't liable under the terms of the policy because TB wasn't liable for the damage caused by the explosion.

The House of Lords found that Century was liable under its insurance policy with the Transport Board: the Transport Board was liable for the damage caused by its driver because (1) he was employed by them at the time of the explosion and (2) he was acting in the course of his employment when he carelessly caused the explosion.

>

Viscount Simon

First issue (who was driver employed by?):

M can be generally employed by X but because of arrangements between X and T, M can at the time he was careless be held to have been T's employee, so as to make T liable for M's carelessness.

Test for whether X or T was employer at time M acted depends on who had power to control what M did.

→ Employee in this case was under Transport Board's control: never lent their lorries and drivers to HMD.

Second issue (was driver acting in course of employment?):

driver's duty to watch petrol as it flowed from lorry into tank, and it was while he was watching that he lit cigarette

– so was acting in course of employment: plainly negligent in discharging duties he was employed to perform.

With that note in your files, you'll never have to look at the case again.

● Casenotes

Casenotes are different from your case notes; in other words, your notes on the cases you have been told to read. Casenotes, as I explained in my letter giving some general tips on studying law, are summaries and comments on cases – usually written by academics for journals such as the *Law Quarterly Review* and the *Cambridge Law Journal*. Casenotes are hugely useful. They can provide you with a handy summary of the facts of a very complex and convoluted case. They also provide you with a bit of critical perspective on a case, which it can often be difficult for a student to achieve on their own. And at a time when, frankly, a lot of judges write in such a boring and prolix way, they can provide with you with a shortcut to understanding what exactly were the key points of the judgments in the case. So I would strongly recommend that you get used to reading casenotes, particularly on the most important cases on your reading list that are the most likely to be relevant to essay questions in the exam paper.

So how do you find a casenote on a case? Suppose you are looking for case-notes on the case I mentioned in my very first letter to you – *A* v *Secretary of State for the Home Department* (the 'Belmarsh case'). How you find some casenotes on that case depends on whether you have access to Westlaw or not. If you have access to Westlaw, then go to Westlaw's home page, click on 'Cases' and type in 'A v Secretary of State for the Home Department' in the box for 'Party names'. That name is pretty generic, so you might also want to type 'Belmarsh' into the 'Free text' box so as to help narrow the search down. Press 'Search' and Westlaw will then bring up the details of a quite a few cases where *A v Secretary of State for the Home Department* matches your search.

You'll know from your textbook that the case was reported in 2005, so you should scroll down the list of cases, looking for cases decided in 2004–5 (with some reports of cases, they come out a year after the case was actually decided), with the right name and the right sort of keyword headings underneath the name. Eventually you'll find the case – it's number 39 on the list that Westlaw has brought up for me. Click on the 'Case analysis' link underneath the name of the case, and then in the left hand menu click on 'Journal Articles'. This will bring up a list of all the journal articles that deal with *A v Secretary of State for the Home Department*. Only a few of these will be the casenotes we want. Casenotes are written very shortly after a case has been decided. So we want to scroll down the list of journal articles until we get to some that have been written in 2004–5, and we are looking in particular for short articles (two to four pages) written in the *Law Quarterly Review* ('LQR' for short) and the *Cambridge Law Journal* ('CLJ') – they are our primary source of casenotes.

After a bit of scrolling we eventually find a journal article entitled 'Proportionality and discrimination in anti-terror legislation' which has the citation 'C.L.J. 2005, 64(2), 271–3' and an article entitled 'Rights brought home?' which has the citation 'L.Q.R. 2005, 121(Jul), 359–364'. The briefness of both of these articles makes us hopeful that these are the casenotes we want. Click on each of these links and you will be taken to a page with a brief outline of what the article says. Click on the link under the author's name, and you will be taken to the complete article, which you can download onto your computer by clicking on the little envelope at the top right hand corner of the screen. (Not all journal articles mentioned on Westlaw are available online through Westlaw, but articles in the CLJ and LQR are.) With those two notes safely downloaded onto your computer, you can explore the other journal articles to see whether any of the other articles published around 2004–5 contain useful casenotes. Journals particularly worth looking out for are the *Oxford Journal of Legal Studies* ('OJLS', for short)(though that tends not to publish casenotes), the *Modern Law Review* ('MLR'), *Public Law* ('PL') (specialising in the area of law dealt with in the Belmarsh case – control of government action), and the *Conveyancer and Property Lawyer* ('Conv') (useful for casenotes on land law or trusts law). But don't spend too long doing this – it's easy to get lost in a blizzard of journal articles, and to start fooling yourself that you are actually achieving something by looking through these articles and downloading them to your computer when you haven't actually started reading any of them. (The philosopher Arthur Schopenhauer once observed that many people mistake the act of buying a book for actually reading it, and the same could be said of the act of downloading an article.)

If you don't have access to Westlaw, you'll have to do a physical search of the journals in your university law library, again focusing on the *Law Quarterly Review* and the *Cambridge Law Journal* before having a look through other journals. Pick out the volumes for 2004 and 2005 and simply look at the 'Table of cases' at the front of these journals to see where the case you are looking for is mentioned. But make sure you don't end up reading a casenote on the wrong court's decision – you want to find casenotes on the House of Lords' decision in the *Belmarsh* case, not the Court of Appeal's!

Now – a few words of caution. First, you won't be able to find casenotes on every case you are told to read. Casenotes on cases decided before (say) 1980, and cases decided very recently are thin on the ground. If you want to get any critical commentary on pre-1980 cases, you have to look at the textbooks and proper full-length journal articles. To see what a textbook has to say about a particular case, just look in the 'Table of cases' at the front to see where the textbook deals with that case. To see whether there are any full-length journal articles dealing with the case you are interested in, Westlaw is again the best place to search – though it is very important, again, that you place a strict time limit on how long you search for articles on a case. Critical commentary on very recent cases will be hard to come by. The best way of seeing if there is anything 'out there' on a particular case that has just been decided is to do a Google search for it. Occasionally, barristers' chambers or academics will rush out a blog entry on a case that has just come out. A lot of legal publishers now run 'update websites' to accompany the textbooks that they publish and those websites might be worth looking at for comments on recent cases. So, for example, the website that accompanies my tort book (www.mylawchamber. co.uk/mcbride) contains twice-yearly updates on recent tort cases.

Secondly, as I said earlier, casenotes tend to be written very quickly after a decision in a particular case has been handed down, and they also – by convention – tend to be quite short. Neither of these things exactly help academics produce intelligent commentary on the cases they are writing about. (Though they can generally be relied on to summarise the case well.) So don't believe everything you read in a casenote, and try to get a balance of views by reading more than one casenote on a particular case.

● Further tips

Here are four more tips on reading cases:

(1) Dissents

Students often ask whether they should take notes on dissenting judgments in cases – that is, judgments where the judge disagrees with his colleagues who are deciding the case (and who are in the majority) as to what the outcome of the case should be. I think it depends. If you are reading a recent-ish case – say, one decided after 2000 – then I think it's important to read any dissenting judgments, so as to help you see how the case could have been decided and help you get some sort of critical perspective on the majority's decision. If the case is older than that, then I think it's only important to read the dissent if: (1) the textbooks make it clear the dissent is important; or (2) the judge who is dissenting is always worth reading (Reid, Diplock, Denning, Hoffmann, Bingham, Brown, Sedley are the only post-1945 judges who come to mind as being good value for money whatever case they are deciding).

(2) Remembering cases

Students often find it a challenge to remember cases. Cases are a lot like small, shiny beads. If I told you to hold out your hand and I poured 50 such beads into it, it's doubtful whether you'd be able to keep hold of more than 10 of them. All the rest would simply bounce out of your hand and fall onto the floor. But if I ran a string through 50 beads and tied the two ends of the string together, you'd have no problem keeping hold of all of the beads in one hand. In fact, all you'd have to do is hold one of the beads, and all the rest would be under your control.

Cases are the same. If you try to remember them individually, the likelihood is that you'll only remember one-fifth of them. But string them together and you won't forget a single case. So how do you string cases together? Well, what you've got to do is come up with a story that helps explain why the cases were decided the way they were. Say you've got fifteen cases to remember and those cases were decided over forty years. There are a number of different stories that you could tell to try to link these cases together.

You could try to find some basic principle which explains the outcome of the cases. If you can, then you've got a story that can link all of your cases – even the ones that don't give effect to the principle in question. You could say, 'Almost all of these cases give effect to the following principle . . . For example, in case A . . . Similarly, in case B . . . This is also true of case C . . . However in cases X, Y and Z the courts chose not to give effect to this principle. For example, had the courts given effect to this principle in case X, we would have expected them to find in favour of . . . But they didn't . . . Similarly, in case Y . . .'

A more radical version of the same story would identify a fundamental conflict in the law – with roughly half of your 15 cases giving effect to one principle and the other half giving effect to a completely different and opposed principle. A 'battle of the cases' story line can prove very effective at helping you to remember a large number of cases because battles are always interesting and therefore memorable. But don't invent battles where none exist – the story that you come up with to link your cases must actually work. Otherwise the story will have no plausibility and will be extremely hard to remember – just as it's hard to remember the details of a crazy dream where all sorts of people were acting in odd ways.

Alternatively, you could try to find some *political links* between the cases – seeing them as reflecting various basic political views: either *libertarian* (the only thing the State should do is to protect us from being harmed by other people) or *utilitarian* (the State should take steps to maximise the net welfare or happiness that exists in society as a whole) or *right-wing liberalism* (the State should generally act to maximise everyone's freedom to live their lives as they want) or *left-wing liberalism* (the State should generally act to minimise inequalities of income and opportunity in society) or *perfectionism* (the State should encourage people to live morally worthwhile lives) or *communitarianism* (the State should protect, elaborate, and give effect to the shared understandings, practices and traditions that are essential features of our community).

A third possible story line is to link your 15 cases to one 'master' case, which all your 15 cases have 'descended' from. For example, a very effective story line that would link your 15 cases together might go: 'In *Roe* v *Doe,* the House of Lords decided that . . . Applying this decision has created huge problems for the courts ever since. In case A, the courts applied *Roe* v *Doe* to find . . .

But in the very similar case B, the courts came to a very different conclusion, holding that . . .' and so on.

So – if you want to remember lots of cases, remember them in *groups,* where each group of cases is linked by a story that helps explain why they were decided the way they were. Remembering cases in this way will not only work wonders for your ability to recall cases in the end of year exams, it will also, of course, help deepen your understanding of, and interest in, the law. Which is all to the good.

And of course, don't miss out on any opportunity to use cases. Talk about them with your fellow lawyers. Participate in moots where you will be called upon to use cases. Write as many essays and problem answers as you can – even if no one else ever sees them. Take advantage of any chance you get to talk about or write about cases you have studied. The more you use cases, the more deeply they will penetrate into your memory.

(3) Casebooks/Cases and materials books

Generally speaking, I'm not a fan of casebooks or books that gather together a lot of 'cases and materials'. They are useful when you don't have ready access to a law library, but I don't think that even as huge as they generally are, they cover as much material as you would want to be familiar with for the exams, and I do think it's more helpful to your long-term memory of the cases not to be presented with them on a plate. The acts involved in: (1) settling down to try to make sense of the facts of the case, (2) finding out what the case decided, (3) trying to figure out why the judges decided the case they did, (4) determining which bits of the case you are going to make a note on, and which can be safely ignored – all these things help get the case into your memory, and help you start thinking about it and using it.

(4) *Ratio decidendi*

If you've read any introductory books on studying law, you may have been expecting me to give you some advice in this letter on how you discover the *ratio decidendi* of a case. (Just in case you haven't read any introductory books on studying law, the *ratio decidendi* – or *ratio* for short – of a case is the rule of law that underlay the decision in that case.)

In practical terms, the only time you'll ever have to worry about finding the *ratio* of a case is after you've left university and you've started practising law.

If you are arguing a case in court, you may well be called upon to discuss what the *ratio* of a case was. For example, suppose there is a *dictum* in a previously decided case that is unhelpful to your argument. If you can establish that the *dictum* was *obiter* – that is, not essential to the outcome of the case (in other words, not part of the *ratio* of the case) – then you can invite the court deciding your case to disregard that *dictum*. Alternatively, suppose there is a *dictum* in a previously decided case that is very helpful to your argument. In that situation, you will want to establish that that *dictum* was part of the *ratio* of the case – with the result that the court before which you are arguing your case may be bound to apply it.

But as a law student, you'll never have to spend time determining what the *ratio* of a case was. You obviously need to know what the judges' reasons were for deciding a case in a particular way, but you don't need to know how to take the further step of determining from those reasons what we can say was *the* reason for the decision. So I'm not going to waste your time (and mine) discussing such things as how you determine what the *ratio* of a case was when three judges all decided the case in the same way but they all gave different reasons for their decision. Instead, I'll finish now and write to you in a few days about the different kinds of reports that we find cases in. This is pretty important for you to know – it'll help you to make sense of the systems for citing cases that lawyers use.

All best wishes,

Nick

A Brief History of Law Reporting

- From: Nicholas J. McBride [dearnick@pearson.com]
- To: Brown, Alex
- Subject: A Brief History of Law Reporting

Dear Alex,

I thought it might be quite useful to give you a very quick history of how cases have been reported in this country, so as to help you make sense of the system for citing cases that lawyers use.

● The Law Reporters

For our purposes, we can begin with the Law Reporters – brave souls who would sit in the various courts and write reports of the decisions in the cases they were listening to. These reports would be put together into volumes published under the name of the reporter or reporters who had composed them. You can find lists of the names of these reports on Wikipedia (search for 'Nominate reports') or by going to http://www.justis.com/support/jlinktext-english-reports.html.

If you scroll down the list of names of reports, you'll come to Ellis, Blackburn and Ellis' Queen's Bench Reports and Ellis and Blackburn's Queen's Bench Reports. The 'Blackburn' in the title was Colin Blackburn (1813–1896), who was eventually made a judge – and became one of the most distinguished judges in English legal history. It was Blackburn J who in 1866 formulated the 'rule in *Rylands* v *Fletcher*' that I've had occasion to mention before, and who made seminal contributions to the shaping of the English law of contract in cases like *Taylor* v *Caldwell* (1863), *Smith* v *Hughes* (1871), *Hughes* v *Metropolitan Ry Co* (1877), and *Foakes* v *Beer* (1884).

Blackburn may have owed his appointment as a judge to the esteem in which the reports that he wrote with Thomas Ellis were held. Not all such reports, or their reporters, enjoyed such a great reputation. The reports written by Isaac Espinasse (1758–1834) were generally regarded as not wholly reliable: in *Small* v *Nairne* (1849), Lord Denman CJ said that 'Espinasse's Reports . . . were never quoted without doubt or hesitation'. This may have been due to the fact that he was very deaf: the great English lawyer Frederick Pollock (1845–1937) joked that Espinasse only heard half of what was said in court, and he reported the other half. An example of this is provided by Espinasse's report of the decision in *Stilk* v *Myrick* (1809), on whether seamen who had been promised a bonus if they – as they were already contractually obliged to do – sailed a ship back to its home port, could sue for the bonus. Espinasse's report can be found in the sixth volume of his reports, on page 129: so 6 Esp 129. If you compare Espinasse's report with the report published by John Campbell, on page 317 of the sixth volume of *his* set of reports – so 6 Camp 317 – you will see that their accounts of the reasons for the court's decision to turn the seamen's claim down are very different. Espinasse has Lord Ellenborough saying that 'public policy' demanded that the seamen's claim be turned down. Campbell has Lord Ellenborough saying that the seamen's claim should be turned down because they had not given anything in return (a consideration) for the promise to pay them the bonus if they got the ship safely home. Campbell's report is regarded as more accurate, even though Espinasse was actually the lawyer for the seamen in the case. (The lawyer for the defendant was William Garrow, whose name and criminal practice has been used as the basis of the BBC series *Garrow's Law*.)

All the reports produced by the Law Reporters were eventually put together into one set of English Reports (or 'E.R.', for short). So the sixth volume of Espinasse's reports, and the sixth volume of Campbell's reports, can both be found in the 170th volume of the English Reports. This gives us two alternative citations for the case of *Stilk* v *Myrick*, depending on whether you are referring to the report of the case by Espinasse, or the report by Campbell:

Stilk v *Meyrick* (1809) 6 Esp 129, 170 ER 851

Stilk v *Myrick* (1809) 2 Camp 317, 170 ER 1168

You'll see that Espinasse and Campbell couldn't even agree on how to spell the name of the defendant; again Campbell has prevailed on this point.

All of the cases that are in the English Reports are now available online. Simply go to: www.commonlii.org/uk/cases/EngR/ and start searching for whatever case you want. So if you click on 'S' (under 'Decisions beginning with . . .') and scroll down for long enough, you will eventually come to the two alternative versions of the decision in *Stilk* v *Myrick*. Click on the name of a case and you will be taken to a copy of the report, which you can then download onto your computer by right-clicking on the report and selecting 'Save as . . .'

● The Official Law Reports

The Law Reporters operated from the thirteenth century until the middle of the nineteenth century – that's why there are so many volumes of the English Reports. But by the middle of the nineteenth century, the powers that be decided to formalise the process of law reporting in this country. The Incorporated Council of Law Reporting ('ICLR', for short) was founded in 1865, and started producing official reports of the most important decisions decided by the 'Superior and Appellate Courts in England and Wales'. These reports – known as the 'Official Law Reports' – are still the most authoritative and complete law reports that lawyers operating in England and Wales have access to. Each case in the Official Law Reports comes complete with a headnote, a summary account of the barristers' arguments in the case, and – of course – the judgments in the case.

The Official Law Reports are split into different series. The two most important that you need to know about are:

1 The Appeal Cases Reports (or 'A.C.' for short). These contain reports of the decisions by the highest court in England and Wales – previously the House of Lords, but now the UK Supreme Court.

2 The Queen's Bench or King's Bench Division Reports ('Queen's' or 'King's' depending on who is on the throne at the time) contain reports of important decisions of the Court of Appeal and selected first instance decisions (where one judge, sitting alone, hears a case for the first time). These are referred to as 'Q.B.' or 'K.B.' for short.

It took a little while for the ICLR to settle down on how it wanted to present its Official Law Reports. For example, contrast the way these two cases – both dealing with the issue of when A's consent to being injured by B will give B a defence to being criminally prosecuted for injuring A – are normally cited:

R v *Coney* (1882) LR 8 QBD 534

R v *Donovan* [1934] 2 KB 498

Both cases are in the same series of Official Law Reports – the Queen's Bench/ King's Bench Division Reports – so what accounts for the difference in the way they are referred to?

Well, when the Official Law Reports were first starting, the ICLR decided that a volume of reports of cases decided in a particular year would be given a unique number. So the volume of QB reports for 1882 had the number 7; the same volume of reports for 1883 had the number 8; the same volume of reports for 1881 had the number 6. So with the start of every new year, the number on the volume of the reports of cases decided in that year would go up by 1. And because, at that time, each volume of reports had a unique identifying number, the year of the case was not so essential to identifying where the case was reported – and that's why the year in the citation for *R v Coney* is in round brackets. All you need to know is that *R v Coney* is on page 534 of the 8th volume of the Queen's Bench Division Reports, and you can find it.

But at some point, pretty early on, the ICLR realised that if they carried on giving each successive volume of official reports a unique identifying number, then by 1982, they would be on the 108th volume of Queen's Bench Reports – and the numbers for each volume would get unfeasibly large. So they scrapped that system and identified volumes of reports exclusively by the year in which they were issued. That's why the year in the citation for *R v Donovan* is in square brackets – you have to know the year of the volume in which that case is reported in order to locate the volume. The number '2' that comes after '[1934]' merely indicates that it is in the second volume of King's Bench Reports issued in 1934.

● The All England Reports and the Weekly Law Reports

The next big development in law reporting was the publication of the All England Reports (or 'All E.R.' for short), from 1936 onwards. The problem with the Official Law Reports was that they were so good, they took some time to produce. A case will frequently only be reported in the Official Law Reports a year after it has actually been decided. The All England Reports – which were published on a commercial basis by Butterworths (now Butterworths LexisNexis) – were intended to give practising lawyers a quicker way of accessing reports of cases that had been recently decided. The reports came out every week – about ten cases per week – and because they did not include the barristers' arguments, the turnaround time between a case being decided and its featuring in the All England Reports was much quicker than it was for the Official Law Reports. And because the All England Reports were reporting about ten cases per week, by the end of the year, they had reported on far more cases than a lawyer could find in the equivalent year's Official Law Reports. The sheer volume of cases being reported each year through the All England Reports meant that each year's reports had to be split at first into two volumes, and then three, and eventually four. But the cases were – just as with the Official Law Reports – identified just by the year in which they were reported, with a volume number after the year to identify which volume of All England Reports for that year the case could be found in. So, for example, *R* v *Brown* – another case which deals with the same point of law as *Coney* and *Donovan* – was reported in [1993] 2 All ER 75. This simply means the case is on page 75 of the second volume of the All England Reports issued in 1993.

The comprehensiveness and convenience of the All England Reports meant they were a big success, and the ICLR eventually decided it wanted a bit of Butterworths' action. So from 1953, it started to issue the Weekly Law Reports ('W.L.R', for short), which operated in exactly the same way as the All England Reports. So in the Weekly Law Reports, *R* v *Brown* can be found in [1993] 2 WLR 556 (with it coming out in the Official Law Reports a year later in [1994] 1 AC 212). The fact that *R* v *Brown* came out in the second volume of the Weekly Law Reports for 1993 is of some significance. Because the ICLR publishes both the Official Law Reports and the Weekly Law Reports, it knows in advance which cases that it is publishing in the Weekly Law Reports will eventually also be published in the Official Law Reports. Cases which will eventually be coming out in the Official Law Reports – because they are so important they deserve the Rolls-Royce treatment that the Official Law Reports provide – go into the second, third or fourth volumes of the Weekly Law Reports. Cases which are not going to be reported in the Official Law Reports – because, while noteworthy, they aren't regarded as that hugely important – go into the first volume of the Weekly Law Reports. So if you see a case cited as [2013] 1 WLR xxx, then you know that the ICLR does not regard that case as important enough to go into the Official Law Reports. But they occasionally get it wrong, with the result that they park a case that is actually really important in the first volume of the Weekly Law Reports. An example would be the case of *Re Selectmove* [1995] 1 WLR 474, which is a major decision on when A will be contractually bound by a promise not to sue B for money that B owes A. However, most of the time they get it right, and they got it right with *R* v *Brown* – a major decision which was put in the second volume of the Weekly Law Reports because it was also going to come out in the Official Law Reports.

I think it's fair to say that whatever competition existed between the Weekly Law Reports and the All England Reports has been decisively won by the Weekly Law Reports: 'the Weeklies' are far more popular and more regularly cited than the 'All Englands'. The reason is partly to do with comprehensiveness: the Weeklies seem to cover many more cases than the All Englands. And it's also partly to do with accessibility: you can access all the cases in the Weekly Law Reports (and in the Official Law Reports) on Westlaw; whereas for the All England Reports you need to use Butterworths' own (and not terribly user-friendly) website. However, occasionally there will be a case that turns out to be noteworthy that doesn't appear in the Weekly Law Reports, but does get into the All England Reports. So you do still need to be familiar with the All England Reports.

● Specialist reports

The All England Reports and Weekly Law Reports report on a lot of cases decided in England and Wales; but only a fraction of the total number of cases decided in any one year. Reports of other cases not to be found in the Weeklies or the All Englands may be found in series of reports that specialise in particular areas of law. Particularly important are the Lloyd's Law Reports (cited as [year] Lloyds Rep xxx), which specialise in reports on contract law, commercial law, and shipping law; and the Criminal Law Review (cited as [year] Criminal LR xxx), which does not carry full reports of any cases but does contain detailed summaries of, and comments on, a comprehensive range of cases dealing with criminal law and punishment. The Criminal Law Review is available online, on Westlaw, but the Lloyd's Law Reports are not unless your library has taken out a subscription to them. You won't need to worry about any other specialist law reports unless you are specifically referred to them.

● Neutral citation

The advent of the Internet – and the increasing availability of reports of decided cases on the Internet – created a problem for law reporting in this country (as in other countries). How can you refer to the decision in a case where that decision has been published on the Internet, which has no years and no page numbers? The solution was to invent a system of neutral citation, where every case was given a unique identifying citation, which referred to the year in which it was decided, the court, and when it was decided. This system of neutral citation came into force from 2002 onwards. Since then cases, have been given citations like the following:

[2004] UKHL 35 – which means the case was the 35th case decided by the House of Lords in 2004.

[2011] UKSC 24 – the 24th case decided by the UK Supreme Court in 2011.

[2010] EWCA Civ 135 – the 135th case on civil law or public law decided by the Court of Appeal in 2010.

[2010] EWCA Crim 135 – the 135th case on criminal law decided by the Court of Appeal in 2010.

[2011] EWHC 351 (QB) – the 351st case decided at first instance on an issue of civil or criminal law.

[2011] EWHC 351 (Admin) – the 351st case decided at first instance on an issue of public law.

So now any case you come across in the Official Law Reports, or the Weekly Law Reports, or the All England Reports, will have an alternative, neutral citation. And the sheer volume of cases that are decided nowadays means that you may be referred to some cases that *only* have a neutral citation. This means that these cases have not been reported anywhere else. Fortunately, these cases will almost certainly be available online, on Westlaw. Less fortunately, when you download the reports of these cases, all you will get is a transcript of the decision – so you will need to figure out what happened in those cases and what was decided without the assistance of a helpful headnote.

I think I've said enough now to help you make sense of all almost all references to cases that you will come across on reading lists, or in your reading. But just in case you get into any further difficulties, there is always the Cardiff Index to Legal Abbreviations (available at www.legalabbrevs.cardiff.ac.uk). If you come across an abbreviated reference to a set of Law Reports that mystifies you, you can always find out what the abbreviation means by using this very handy website.

All best wishes,

Nick

Looking at Statutes

○ From: Nicholas J. McBride [dearnick@pearson.com]
○ To: Brown, Alex
○ Subject: Looking at Statutes

Hey Alex,

After two letters about case law, just one on reading statutes. Students usually find reading statutes extremely boring. Unlike cases, statutes tend to be very dry and technical. As a result, it is hard to work up any enthusiasm for reading a statute, and it's even harder to remember a statute once you've read it. I'm not going to pretend that I have any magic method for taking the pain out of reading statutes, but following the approach below will inject a little bit of interest into the job of reading a statute, and make the job of remembering what that statute says a little bit easier.

○ The basic approach

Suppose you have been told to read a statute, or some sections from a statute. (You may not be familiar with the term 'section', so I'll briefly explain. Every Act of Parliament is made up of sections, or 's.' for short. A section in an Act of Parliament is usually divided up into sub-sections, where each sub-section is denoted by a number in brackets. So if you want to refer to sub-section 1 of section 1 of the Guard Dogs Act 1975, you would simply write 's.1(1) of the Guard Dogs Act 1975'.) Of course, you shouldn't just read the statute – you should also make some notes about the statute.

Now, in making notes on the statute, you shouldn't try to summarise what the statute *says*. There's a very good saying that 'You can't paraphrase a statute'.

In other words, if you attempt to summarise what a statute says, your summary will always omit some crucial details. And if you attempt to avoid missing out any crucial details in making your summary, you will usually simply end up copying out the statute. And copying out the statute is the last thing you want to do. Copying out a statute is such a passive activity that you will simply get bored, your brain will shut up shop and you won't take anything in of what the statute says.

So – how should you make notes on a statute? The answer is – by *thinking* about it while you are reading it. As you are going through a particular statute, ask yourself – Why was this statute enacted? How does this statute apply in concrete situations? Why does the statute go as far as it does? Why doesn't the statute go further? Is this statute in need of reform? And make notes on anything that is relevant to those kinds of questions. Doing this sort of thing will help make going through a statute more interesting, help you to see what issues are raised by the statute, and help cement the details of the statute into your mind.

● The approach applied

Let's now apply this approach by looking at the first five sections of the Theft Act 1968. We'll look at one section for each of the questions you should be thinking about in going through a statute.

(1) Why was the statute enacted?

Section 1(1) of the Theft Act 1968 (title: 'Basic definition of theft') provides that:

> A person is guilty of theft if he dishonestly appropriates property belonging to another with the intention of permanently depriving the other of it; and "theft" and "steal" shall be construed accordingly.

Why does the law criminalise the dishonest appropriation of property belonging to another when that property was appropriated with the intention of permanently depriving that other of it? Why doesn't the law simply allow the owner to sue for his property back – why does the criminal law have to get involved here at all? Use your textbook, your brain, any relevant articles you have read, and any relevant *dicta* in any relevant cases you have read to come up with some answers to these questions, and make notes of the answers in the appropriate place in your case file. No doubt the answers to these questions are pretty obvious. However, the important thing is that by asking these questions, you are thinking about s.1(1) of the Theft Act 1968 instead of just passively reading it.

(2) How does the statute apply in concrete situations?

Section 2 of the Theft Act 1968 (title: 'Dishonestly') provides that:

(1)   A person's appropriation of property belonging to another is not to be regarded as dishonest–

    (a)   if he appropriates property in the belief that he has in law the right to deprive the other of it, on behalf of himself or of a third person; or

    (b)   if he appropriates the property in the belief that he would have the other's consent if the other knew of the appropriation and the circumstances of it; or

    (c)   (except where the property came to him as trustee or personal representative) if he appropriates the property in the belief that the person to whom the property belongs cannot be discovered by taking reasonable steps.

(2)   A person's appropriation of property belonging to another may be dishonest notwithstanding that he is willing to pay for the property.

In thinking about how the statute applies in concrete situations, you should come up with a number of different hypothetical scenarios, and see how the section applies in each of them. Try to think up the scenarios yourself and make them as memorable as possible by using the names of people you know about, preferably doing things that they would never do in real life. (These kinds of scenarios will stay longer in your memory than scenarios that might have been supplied to you by a textbook.) Here are some examples of scenarios you might come up with:

1   Peter realises that a DVD in a shop has been wrongly priced as being for sale for £1.59, rather than £15.99 (which is what other identical DVDs are being sold for in the shop). He takes the DVD up to the counter and pays £1.59 for it.

2   Hannah finds a wallet that has been dropped in the street by Siobhan. There is a £20 note in it. She hands the wallet in at a nearby police station but keeps the £20 note as a 'finder's fee'.

3   Megan, a student living in college, makes a cake for everyone on her staircase using ingredients that she has found in the fridge that everyone on the staircase uses to keep their food in. None of the ingredients belong to her, but she figures that as everyone on the staircase is going to get to eat some of the cake, the rightful owner of the ingredients won't mind her using them.

4   Hugh owes Beka £5 but is refusing to pay up. Beka takes one of Hugh's DVDs out of his room when he isn't looking and auctions it on eBay. Someone pays her £10 for the DVD. Beka keeps £5 and slips the remaining £5 into Hugh's wallet when he isn't looking.

5   Maryam has read a textbook on 'Natural Law' which says that 'no law is valid if it is contrary to the will of God'. Believing that God desires all living creatures to be free, she releases Clare's parrot into the wild.

Having come up with some such scenarios, work out when s.2 will apply to acquit someone of being dishonest in these scenarios – and when it won't. (To do this, make use of your textbooks, any relevant articles, your brain and – importantly – any cases that have helped clarify how s.2 of the Theft Act 1968 is to be applied.) In your notes, make a note of these scenarios, how s.2 will apply in those scenarios, and the reason it applies or does not apply in each.

It may be pretty obvious how s.2 will apply in the above scenarios. But the point of going through them isn't to anticipate potential problem questions that you might be asked in the exam – questions which will probably pose more tricky issues than the scenarios set out above. The point of going through these scenarios is to get a solid grasp of how s.2 of the Theft Act 1968 applies in concrete situations. This will help you to remember how s.2 works. This, in turn, will help you apply s.2 with confidence when you are faced with trickier problem questions about s.2 in the end-of-year exam.

(3) Why does the statute go as far as it does?

Section 3(1) of the Theft Act 1968 (title: 'Appropriates') provides that:

> Any assumption by a person of the rights of an owner amounts to an appropriation, and this includes, where he has come by the property (innocently or not) without stealing it, any later assumption of a right to it by keeping or dealing with it as owner.

You will have discovered in the course of your reading that the case law seems to suggest that merely touching an item of property will amount to an 'appropriation' of an object. So think about why the definition of 'appropriation' goes that far (if it does). In other words, why should merely touching an item of property potentially amount to a criminal act? Or was s.3(1) never intended to have that effect – have the courts misinterpreted it?

Again, make notes on the answers to these questions using your textbooks, any relevant articles, any relevant *dicta* in any relevant cases, and your brain. Asking and answering these questions will help you to remember what s.3(1) says; deepen your understanding of, and interest in, s.3(1); put you in a good position to think about whether s.3(1) needs to be reformed; and put you in a great position to answer any essay questions that might be set on s.3(1) in the end-of-year exam.

(4) Why doesn't the statute go further than it does?

Section 4 of the Theft Act 1968 (title 'Property') provides that:

(1) 'Property' includes money and all other property, real or personal, including things in action and other intangible property.

(2) A person cannot steal land . . .

(3) A person who picks mushrooms growing wild on any land, or who picks flowers, fruit or foliage from a plant growing wild on any land, does not (although not in possession of the land) steal what he picks, unless he does it for reward or for sale or for other commercial purposes.

For purposes of this subsection 'mushroom' includes any fungus, and 'plant' includes any shrub or tree.

(4) Wild creatures, tamed or untamed, shall be regarded as property; but a person cannot steal a wild creature not tamed nor ordinarily kept in captivity, or the [carcass] of any such creature, unless either it has been reduced into possession by or on behalf of another person and possession of it has not since been lost or abandoned, or another person is in the course of reducing it into possession.

In considering why the 1968 Act doesn't go further than it does, s.4 raises a host of questions related to that issue. Dead bodies don't normally count as 'property' – so why doesn't the law of theft cover someone's taking away a dead body? Is it because there are already other areas of law that criminalise this sort of conduct? Information doesn't normally count as 'property' – so why doesn't the law of theft cover the situation where someone sneaks an advance peak at an exam paper, or gives out advance copies of an exam paper to his friends? Why can't someone steal land? (Note, however, that you can in certain situations – s.4(2) is quite long and to save space I have cut it down.)

What would stealing land involve? Is this sort of conduct covered by some other area of the law? Why are you potentially guilty of theft if you pick wild mushrooms on someone else's land for reward but not if you pick them to deprive the owner of the land of the opportunity to pick them himself? Is doing something for reward worse than doing something out of malice?

The point of asking and trying to answer these kinds of questions should be obvious by now. Doing this will: help cement the details of s.4 into your memory; deepen your understanding of – and therefore interest in – s.4; put you in a good position to think about whether s.4 needs to be reformed; and put you in a great position to answer any essay question that you might be set on s.4.

(5) Is the statute in need of reform?

Section 5(1) of the Theft Act 1968 (title: 'Belonging to another') provides that:

> Property shall be regarded as belonging to any person having possession or control of it, or having in it any proprietary right or interest (not being an equitable interest arising only from an agreement to transfer or grant an interest)

Your reading will have told you that s.5(1) means that someone can be convicted of theft for stealing his own property. This happened in one case where a man left his car with a garage to be repaired, and after it had been repaired, he drove the car away without paying for the repairs. Because the garage had possession and control of the car at the time the car-owner drove the car away, the courts held that the car 'belonged' to the garage under s.5(1) at the time it was driven away, with the result that the car's owner could be convicted of stealing it.

The fact that you can be found guilty of stealing your own property naturally prompts the question of whether the Theft Act 1968 is in need of reform. Is it right that someone can be convicted of stealing his own property? Should the law of theft go beyond protecting the ownership of property and help protect people's possession of property? Asking these questions and trying to answer them (again, with the help of your textbooks, any relevant articles, any relevant *dicta* in any relevant cases, and any thoughts you yourself might have) will help deepen your understanding of – and therefore interest in – the law of theft as a whole and its functions and put you in a great position to answer essay questions either specifically on s.5 of the Theft Act 1968, or on the law of theft as a whole.

● Three more points

So – that's the basic approach you should adopt in reading statutes (or statutory instruments, for that matter). I don't have any further tips for you on how you should approach the job of reading a statute. However, there are three more points that I want to make.

(1) Statute books and the exams

Almost all universities now allow their law students to take statute books into their exams so that they can consult them in the course of answering problem questions or writing essays. Given this, you may wonder if there is any point doing work which is geared to helping you to remember what particular statutes say. I think there is. The more time you spend in the exam looking through a statute book trying to find out what a particular statute says and trying to figure out how it applies, the less writing time you will have in the exam. You want to maximise the amount of writing time you have in your exams – so it is very important that by the time you do your exams, you have a good knowledge of all the statutes that you will need to know about for the exams.

(2) Only look at statutes that you are going to be examined on

While I normally encourage you to do more reading than you are actually asked to do by your teachers, this doesn't apply to statutes. There is no real point in knowing about a statute that isn't going to figure in the exam – so unless you have been told about or asked to read a particular statute, the chances are that it's not worth knowing about and you shouldn't bother looking it up.

(3) Statutory interpretation

Again, if you've read any introductory books on studying law, you may have been expecting me to say something in this section on various techniques that can be used to interpret statutes, such as the 'literal rule' (where words in a statute are interpreted according to their plain meaning) or the 'mischief rule' (where words in a statute are interpreted in light of the problem or evil that the statute was trying to address) or the 'golden rule' (where the courts try to avoid interpreting words in a statute in a fatuous or stupid way). Again, I'm not going to waste your time by talking about such things. If a particular word in a statute is ambiguous or needs to be interpreted, your textbooks will give you sufficient guidance as to how that word has and should be interpreted. You won't need to worry about what rule you should apply to interpret that word. This is something you may need to worry about if you are a practising lawyer advising people on how a new statute applies – but for the time being, you have better things to worry about.

I will be in touch again soon about reading articles in the course of your legal studies.

Best wishes,

Nick

Reading Articles

- From: Nicholas J. McBride [dearnick@pearson.com]
- To: Brown, Alex
- Subject: Reading Articles

Hey Alex,

It's important that you read lots of articles written by legal academics. Other than writing legal essays yourself, there is no better way of improving your legal essay writing skills than to read legal articles. They provide you with models of how to argue properly when you are writing an essay, and are a fertile source of ideas and arguments that you can draw on or react against in writing your essays. So – here are my tips on getting the most out of reading articles.

● The basic approach

Okay – so you are going to read a particular article. What should be your basic approach? Go through the article twice.

The first time, you are trying to get an idea of what the article is basically saying – what the overall point of the article is, and what arguments are being made (or dismissed) in order to make that point. The second time, you should look through the article to see if it has anything interesting to say about any particular cases, you can then make a note of these observations in your case file, under the name of the case in question.

Your aim in going through the article for the first time should be to enhance your understanding of the law, thereby helping you to critically evaluate the law and write good, solid essays about it. Your aim in going through the article for the second time should be to enhance your knowledge of the law,

233

thereby helping you to appreciate the full range of legal issues raised by a specific legal problem.

● The first run-through

When I say 'run-through' I mean it. *Hustle* through the article. Don't make notes as you go through it – that will just slow you up and make you feel miserable. Read the article at speed, asking the following key questions all the time:

1 What is this article basically saying?

2 What arguments are being made in favour of the article's basic point?

3 What are the arguments against the article's basic point, and how does the author dismiss them?

4 What do I think of the author's arguments? Those are the only things you want to know on the first run-through.

Once you've read the entire article through, getting an idea of what it has to say (if it has anything to say) on these issues, then take a fresh A4 piece of paper and make some notes about the article from memory, organised around these key questions, referring back to a specific part of the article only if necessary to refresh your memory. Let's now look at the above four questions in more detail.

(1) What is the article basically saying?

In making a note on question (1), try to reduce the basic message of the article down to five or six lines at most. If you can't do that, then it's doubtful whether the article is going to be that much help: either it is very unclear in what it wants to say, or you are very unclear about what it wants to say, and either way the article's not going to be of much help to you. If you have a nagging feeling that you have completely missed the point of what the article has to say, Google search it to see what other people have to say about it, or ask your fellow students what they thought of it, or ask your teachers what they think its basic message is.

(2) and (3) What are the arguments being made/being dismissed?

In making notes on questions (2) and (3), use numbers to identify the different arguments that the author makes in favour of his/her basic point, and the reasons why an author thinks that an argument that might be made against his/her basic point should be rejected. If the author is making four arguments for what he/she wants to say, then your notes should reflect that and number those arguments 1–4. Numbering the arguments helps you get clearer about what the author is actually saying – instead of a mish-mash of jumbled assertions, you have four crisp (and make sure that when you make a note of the author's arguments, you express them as crisply as possible) arguments on which the worth of the article will depend.

(4) What do I think?

In making notes on question (4) (and in reading the entire article) . . .

. . . Be aggressive

In the excellent film *Searching for Bobby Fischer* (highly, highly recommended), Laurence Fishburne's street speed chess player intimidates his opponent with some trash talk:

> What's that? . . . Is that the best you got? Is that the best you got? Uh-huh . . . you ain't got nothin' . . . No . . . that ain't it . . . Hmmm . . . that ain't it either . . . You're going to have to do much better than that, boss. . . Much better than that . . . C'mon, show me something . . . show me something, grandmaster . . .

That is *exactly* the sort of mentality I want you to adopt on going through an article for the first time. You should be hustling through the article, challenging it to 'show me something' – to tell you something interesting about the law. If the article doesn't seem to have anything worthwhile to say (which may well be the case), don't be afraid to conclude that it doesn't actually have anything worthwhile to say. Maybe check first with some other people to see if the article was actually saying something, but you missed it. But if no one can clearly express what the article was trying to say, then throw it aside as a failure. (Well, not literally – just put it back on the shelf, politely.) It's no good and not worth noting.

You should adopt the same aggressive mentality in making notes on question (4), which requires you to evaluate the arguments that the writer makes in favour of his/her basic point, and seeing whether the writer does a good job of dismissing the arguments against his/her position. Don't let the writer walk all over you with his/her claims. Resist. Ask yourself: Do the writer's arguments stand up? Are they circular? Are they based on a false premise? Are they illogical? Don't assume the arguments are any good. Be aggressive: test the writer's arguments out, and see if they collapse under scrutiny.

Don't be afraid to say, 'That ain't it . . . that ain't it either . . .' to the author, no matter how revered they might be.

● Some harsh words about articles

As an aid to helping you adopt the sort of mentality about articles that I want you to adopt, it might help you to know the current state of play within universities on writing articles. I've already mentioned – in my letter on 'Choosing a University' – that how much money a university (and the particular faculties within the university) receives by way of research funding from the Higher Education Funding Council for England (HEFCE) depends on how highly its research is rated under the 'Research Excellence Framework' (or 'REF', for short). Under the REF, each university's faculty that wants research funding from HEFCE will submit articles and books (no more than four, and preferably four) written by members of the faculty for evaluation by panels of academics, and each faculty's 'research output' will be given an overall star rating: four stars, three stars, two stars or one star. The more stars a faculty gets, the more money it gets from HEFCE.

In the preface to the first edition of his book *Unjust Enrichment,* Peter Birks recalls some advice that he was given at the start of his career by Barry Nicholas, the distinguished Roman lawyer and principal of Brasenose College, Oxford where Birks was teaching (my old college, as well): 'Teach, do not worry about writing, nobody wants to hear from you till later.' Birks admits that the advice 'seems to come from a world which is no more'. And that is largely due to the REF. There is now intense pressure on academics to produce 'research outputs' that can be used to earn research funding from HEFCE. In the greatest assault on academic freedom that the UK has known since the seventeenth century, some faculties convene their own internal panels to evaluate their employees' work; thus none too subtly conveying the message that their academics can either shape up and start producing 'outputs' that other people think are worthy of four stars, or they can ship out and be replaced by other, more conformist, academics. And academics looking for promotion or a better job elsewhere know that they won't get anywhere unless they have a good 'research profile', so they also put pressure on themselves to churn out books and articles (with a strong bias towards articles as they are quicker to write) in the hope that some of them will hit the four-star jackpot.

So academics have now been turned into journalists. In large part, they write not because there is anything they passionately want to say, but because the nature of their job requires them to write. And the result – at least within law departments – has been a significant degrading of the quality of academic writing. This is absolutely no reflection on the quality of the academics producing this work. It is just a reflection of four aspects of the way life is under the REF.

First, a lack of passion kills. If an academic is writing about a topic not because he or she is desperately interested in it, but because he or she thinks that this would be a good topic to write about for REF purposes, then that will show through in the writing. The ideas will be boring, and boringly expressed.

Secondly, an academic who is pretty good is probably capable of producing two really good books and about ten really good articles in the course of his or her academic lifetime – so twelve pieces in all. For an academic who is a genius (and they are very rare), you can probably double that – twenty-four pieces over a lifetime. But the REF – and the pressures associated with the REF – demand a much higher rate out of output from academics: nominally, four pieces every four years, but in reality (because not every piece of work will be evaluated as four star-worthy) at least eight pieces every four years. The result is that even good academics end up producing works which are, frankly, forgettable – they are only capable of producing a limited number of pieces that are of very high quality, but are being made to write far more than that.

Thirdly, it takes time to produce high-quality work. You need time to think ideas out, and time to consider how best to express those ideas. But the pressure to churn material out means that a lot of academics are never given, and never give themselves, the time to produce high-quality work. It's far better for an academic's career to spend three years writing eight articles, than spend three years working on one book – especially as in terms of 'research outputs' an article counts as being as significant as a book.

Fourthly, good ideas for books and articles are hard to come by. That's the major reason why even good academics are limited in how many high-quality books or articles they can hope to produce in their academic lifetime. So academics who are under pressure to produce material have to cast around for ideas as to what they might work on. In doing this, it is very tempting for legal academics to focus on *recent developments in the law*. Recent developments – new cases and new legislation – make for tempting research fodder because they are easy to write about, and so long as you get in early enough, no one else will have written about them and stolen your thunder. So the last ten years or so have seen a proliferation of articles about recent developments in the law. A lot of this work is good, and a lot of it useful for students trying to come to terms with a particular area of law – but man, it's boring as hell as well. Other academics get tempted to focus on *law and . . .* – that is, to write articles that seek to link law with some other subject. (Sedley LJ once wrote a parody of such articles entitled 'Law and plumbing' – it's available online for free if you Google search it.) The more obscure the other subject is, the better for the academic as it's less likely that anyone else will have written about the relationships between that subject and law and made it more difficult to say anything else about those relationships. Again, these articles tend to be really boring and pretty irrelevant to anything that really matters. Finally, a third group of academics feed off other people's good ideas – they write articles summarising and criticising ideas that other people have come up with about the law. This is very flattering for those other people (who can then convince their faculties that their work is having the sort of 'impact' that merits a high star rating), but ultimately 'My response to Professor X's theory' type articles descend into a morass of technicalities and fruitless point scoring that doesn't actually help anyone.

So it's entirely appropriate for you to approach any article you are reading in a sceptical spirit. You shouldn't assume that the article *must* be good and *must* be worth reading: the institutional pressures under which academics now sadly work mean that isn't the case. So hustle through the article, always asking 'show me something' – and if it doesn't: forget it.

● The second run-through

Okay – let's assume you've read a particular article, and made a note on it on a piece of A4 paper, summing up the basic point of the article and the key arguments made in favour of that point. Now you can go through the article again, this time looking to see whether it has any points to make about particular cases that you have already made a note on. What you are looking for are:

1 (good) accounts of what happened in the case and how it was decided;

2 explanations why the case was decided the way it was; and

3 criticisms of the decision in that case, or the way it was decided.

It may also be that the article mentions a particular case that you don't yet have a note on. If the case seems interesting enough, then use what the article has to say about that case as the basis for creating a note about that case.

Once you've completed the second run-through, you can put the article aside and not bother looking at it again. You've got what you need from it, and it's time to move on to something else. If you come across a subsequent article that trashes the article you've just noted, then obviously go back to your A4 note on the original article and make a note of the subsequent article's criticisms (also making a note of whether you think those criticisms are valid or not), so that all the relevant notes on that article are all in the same place.

● Finding more articles to read

The reading lists that your teachers give you will refer you to a few articles relevant to the areas of law you are studying, but it is always worthwhile looking around to see whether there are any other relevant articles 'out there' that might be worth a look. Try the following:

1 Go onto Westlaw, click on 'Journals', and type in a few key terms related to the area of law you are looking into, or want to research, into the 'Free text' box and then press return. Get ready to turn up *a lot* of articles that will have *no* relevance to what you are looking for – but there may be a few downloadable articles that will be helpful.

2 HeinOnline provides a wonderful database of legal journals, particularly from the United States. If you have access to that, then click on 'Law journal library' on the left-hand menu, and then type some key terms into the 'Search' box and set HeinOnline to search 'Text'. You will again turn up a huge amount of irrelevant material, but there may be a few things out there that will be helpful.

3 'SSRN' stands for the Social Sciences Research Network. A lot of legal academics now post on SSRN articles that they are working on. Go to SSRN (www.ssrn.com) to see if there is anything on the area of law you are interested. Click on 'Search' and type in some key terms into the 'Search terms:' box, making sure that SSRN is set to search 'Title, Abstract, Abstract ID or Keywords'.

4 Doing a Google search for key terms related to the area of law you are studying may well turn up some relevant materials.

5 One problem with doing (1)–(4) is that it is unlikely to turn up details of papers that have been written for published collections of essays on various legal topics. Information about what is 'out there' in such collections has traditionally been difficult to track down. If you know the title of a particular collection of essays, then Amazon or the publisher of the collection may give you a list of essay titles – but it will be almost always the case that you don't even know of the existence of a particular collection

of essays. One partial solution to this problem is the Index to Common Law Festschriften (collections of essay in honour of a particular figure, distinguished in the legal world). You can find this at http://magic.lbr. auckland.ac.nz/festschrift/. However, most published collections of legal essays are not *festschriften* (literally, 'celebration writings') and so don't fall within the Index. The Index is also not particularly user-friendly. In order to try to begin to fill this hole in our abilities to know what is 'out there' in the field of research on legal topics that might interest us, I created on my website (www.mcbridesguides.com) the 'PCC Law Library Database'. This basically lists all the significant legal essays published in collections of essays that are held in the Pembroke College Cambridge Law Library. So if you are working on a particular area of law, look up the corresponding list of essays relating to that area of law on the database, and look through the list to see if there are any essays that seem to relate to the particular issue or topic that you are interested in. If there are, then you can look up the essay in your own library, if it has the collection of essays in question. If it doesn't then you can always request your library to obtain the collection in question, or see if there is a pdf of the essay available on the Internet (either on SSRN, or via a Google search).

Looking for material on the Internet can be very time-consuming and involve you in making huge numbers of searches for different combinations of keywords. In order to stop this happening, I would advise that you set yourself a time limit of three minutes to search a particular source of legal material – whatever you can't find within three minutes probably isn't worth wasting your time on searching for it.

I hope this is helpful. The last section makes me think I should write to you about the various legal materials that are available on the Internet for you to use. I'll get back to you about that as soon as possible.

Best wishes,

Nick

Using the Internet

● From: Nicholas J. McBride [dearnick@pearson.com]
● To: Brown, Alex
● Subject: Using the Internet

Hi Alex,

This letter can be short and sweet. For lots of useful law-related links to help you with your studies, go to my website www.mcbridesguides.com and click on 'Useful links'.

Happy exploring, and I'll be in touch soon!

All best wishes,

Nick

Your Teachers and You

- From: Nicholas J. McBride [dearnick@pearson.com]
- To: Brown, Alex
- Subject: Your Teachers and You

Hey Alex,

So far, the letters I've been writing about how you should approach studying law have focused on the work you'll be doing in your own time: reading textbooks and cases, looking at statutes, making notes on articles, and using the Internet. This letter will be about how to get the most out of the guidance and teaching you receive in the form of lectures and small-group teaching sessions.

● A preliminary point

Before I get onto that, I want to emphasise one point. I once read somewhere that the difference between school and university is that at school you are a pupil and at university you are a student. Pupils learn by being taught, while students learn by studying – by finding out things for themselves. The distinction holds especially true of law students – as I said in a previous letter, law is probably the most self-taught subject that you can study at university. So you shouldn't rely too much on lectures and small-group teaching sessions as a vehicle for finding out about the law. You should rather regard lectures and small-group teaching sessions as providing you with opportunities to pick up useful titbits of information and to test out your blossoming legal skills.

But you mustn't misunderstand me. I don't want to encourage you to skip lectures and the small-group teaching sessions that have been laid on for you.

While they are not an essential component of your legal education, they provide a very useful service that you should take full advantage of. But please remember that it is how much work you put in on your own – or in conjunction with your fellow students – that will determine how well you do in your exams, not how many lectures you have been to. If you are spending 60 per cent of your 'working time' as a law student at lectures and small group teaching sessions, and only 40 per cent of the remaining time working on your own or with your fellow students – then you are in trouble. You are not giving yourself enough of an opportunity to develop as a law student by working away at the law yourself, rather than having it spoon-fed to you by your teachers. A healthier distribution of your working time that you should aim for is: spend 70 per cent of your 'working time' studying on your own, or with your fellow students, and only 30 per cent of your time attending lectures or small-group teaching sessions.

● Lectures

Okay – let's get on with some guidance as to what you should be doing in lectures. Basically, you should be looking to make notes of points that will make useful additions to your secondary materials and your cases and statutes files. So keep your ears open for:

(1) *Summaries of cases.* These can be really useful, particularly if the lecturer is talking about a case which is very difficult to understand. Lecturers will usually work really hard to make cases comprehensible to the students that they are lecturing to – if only because it's really embarrassing for a lecturer to speak to an audience that is looking at her with blank incomprehension. If a lecturer is explaining a case and some aspect of his or her explanation seems particularly obscure, do not hesitate to stick your hand up and ask him to express himself more clearly. Some lecturers don't like to be interrupted by questions. But you shouldn't care about that – your lecturers are working for you, not the other way around. If you want to ask a question, you have a right to ask it and have it answered. Having said that, if you start asking too many and too obscure questions, you should also remember that your fellow students also have a right to hear what the lecturer has to say without unnecessary interruptions.

(2) *Summaries of articles.* Again, these are very useful – a really good summary of what an article says can make the actual article a breeze to read through subsequently. I should emphasise that if an article has been summed up very effectively in a lecture, I wouldn't advise skipping the article in your subsequent reading, on the basis that you already know what it says. However effective the summary, it is only a summary and there may be more in the actual article that you may find worth taking a note on – perhaps a summary of a case, or an interesting argument.

(3) *Evaluations of the law.* It is always useful to note what your lecturer thinks of a particular area of the law – and what arguments she makes in support of her views.

(4) *Aids to remembering cases.* You should also be looking to take notes on any 'story lines' that you can make use of to remember a string of cases, following the advice I gave you in my letters on reading cases and looking at statutes. So – make notes of any general principles that the lecturer has identified as underlying a number of cases, or any speculations that the lecturer has as to why a number of cases were decided the way they were.

You shouldn't be looking to make notes on the following:

(1) *Statements of basic legal rules.* Suppose your lecturer says, 'A defendant will have the *mens rea* of murder if he has an intention to kill or an intention to cause grievous bodily harm.' There's absolutely no point in your making a note of that. Your textbook reading will tell you that – so why wear out your hand trying to scribble this piece of information down in the middle of the lecture? It would be better to put your pen down and give your hand a rest and wait for the lecturer to tell you something that you won't necessarily find in a textbook.

This takes me on to a more general point. If your lecturer on a particular subject is consistently not telling you anything that you couldn't find in a textbook, then you should consider stopping going to his or her lectures. This is for a very simple reason: you can read faster than your lecturer can talk. So you would make better use of the hour that the lecture will last reading a textbook rather than attending the lecture. You will find out more in that hour by reading the textbook than you will by attending the lecture.

(2) *History.* Lecturers often like to preface their discussion of a particular area of law with a quick run-through of the history of that area. So, for example, if you are being lectured by your tort law lecturer on the law on 'Occupiers' Liability', he may well spend a bit of time talking about what the law said before the Occupiers' Liability Acts of 1957 and 1984 were enacted. Making notes on this is a complete waste of time. You are interested in what the law says now, not in what it said 50 or 20 years ago. You are interested in what reforms should be made to the law as it is now, not in what reforms were made to the law as it was 50 or 20 years ago.

Having said that, history does have its place. As I've said before, it can help you to remember a string of cases if you see them as part of some historical trend or pattern. Arguments that a particular reform to the law has proved unsuccessful and that the law should return to where it was before that reform was implemented are always interesting and worth noting. But if the lecturer is talking about the history of a particular area of law for no other reason than as a way of introducing that area of law, or because he or she is loath to abandon a set of carefully composed lecture notes that have been made completely redundant by a recent reform, then put your pen down and give yourself a rest.

When a lecture is over, take the notes that you have made on the lecture and use them to make fresh notes in the appropriate places in your files of notes. This will serve a number of useful purposes. First, your lecture notes are likely to be quite scruffy and messy – making fresh notes will mean you don't have to rely on your lecture notes. Secondly, making fresh notes will help you remember in the long term what was said in the lectures. Thirdly, making fresh notes will give you a chance to look over your lecture notes and see how many of the lecture notes you made actually seem, on reflection, worth entering into your files. If the answer is 'Not many', you are taking too many notes in the lectures and you need to be more discriminating in your note taking.

● Small-group teaching sessions

That's all I have to say about taking notes in lectures. What about small-group teaching sessions? Any university will arrange for these to take place throughout the year, in parallel with the lectures, as a way of checking the progress you are making as a law student and giving you an opportunity to raise any concerns or questions that you might have about the subjects you are studying. The advice I can give you on these sessions is quite limited because I have no idea what format they will take. However, whatever format they take, the following advice should always hold good:

(1) *Be prepared.* You won't get anything out of your small-group teaching sessions if you aren't prepared for them. If you're not prepared for a small-group teaching session, then it will turn into a small ordeal for you. You'll be lost, confused, and praying desperately that you aren't called upon to speak – and every minute of the session will seem like ten minutes. Why put yourself through that kind of torture? Come prepared and then you can make the most of the session and actually get something out of it. And if you're not prepared – for whatever reason – it's far better to admit that and ask if you can come along to a later session than put yourself through the agony of sitting in the session, pretending to be better prepared than you are.

(2) *Ask questions.* Try to take advantage of any small-group teaching session that you attend to get whoever's holding the session to answer your questions about the area of law that you'll be focusing on in the session. So come to the teaching session armed with a list of questions that you want answered. Make sure you have actually got a list – don't rely on your memory to tell you that you have such and such a question to ask. The pressure of a small-group teaching session means that your memory will often fail you.

(3) *Take your books and notes along.* That last point takes me onto a separate point. A small-group teaching session isn't a memory test – so take your textbooks and your notes along to the session so that you can consult them in the course of a general discussion of a particular legal point.

(4) *Make notes.* When I hold small-group teaching sessions with first-year students, I notice that a lot of them don't take notes when I'm talking to them. This could be because they think that what I'm saying is rubbish. However, I find that hard to believe. More likely explanations are either: (i) they think that they'll be able to remember what I'm saying without making a note of it; or (ii) they think that I'd be offended if they took my eyes off me and started writing in their notebook while I was talking.

Neither of these things is true. On (i), unless a student is blessed with an absolutely exceptional memory, he or she will not be able to remember very much of what was said in a small-group teaching session unless he or she has made good notes of what was said. On (ii), there is no way any of your teachers will be offended if you make notes on what they are saying as they are saying it. They are far more likely to be offended if they make some really brilliant argument and their students just stare at them and don't make any notes to help them remember the pearls of wisdom that have just been scattered before them.

As to what you should be making notes on, what I said in connection with lectures also applies here – you should be looking to make notes of points that will make useful additions to your topic and case files. And when the small-group teaching session is over, you should take your notes and use them to enter a set of fresh notes at appropriate points in your topic and case files.

(5) *Exercise your right of freedom of speech.* I've already made this point in an earlier letter, but I'll repeat it here: do not be inhibited about speaking up in small-group teaching sessions. If there is some point you are unclear on, do say: 'I don't understand this, could you help me?' You're not going to get another opportunity to get some help on clearing up that point – so why not take advantage of it?

Don't be put off asking a question because you think, 'I'll look like an idiot if I ask about that.' You probably won't: your question is likely to be a really good one, and everyone else in your teaching group will profit from having your question answered. And even if you do look like an idiot, so what? It's good for you to make yourself look like an idiot once in a while. It'll stop you being arrogant – which is never an attractive quality. It'll make everyone else feel better about themselves – they'll think, 'Oh, at least I'm not doing as badly as Alex'. And it'll make everyone else feel a bit more comfortable about asking questions themselves – they'll think, 'Well, it might be a bit embarrassing to ask this question, but at least I won't be as embarrassed as badly as Alex was.'

(6) *Make the most of the opportunities that small-group teaching sessions give you.* Suppose that you are being taken for small-group teaching sessions in a particular area of law by Professor White, who is a renowned scholar in that area of law. Use your time with Professor White to get her to talk about her views – not only her views about the area of law she specialises in, but also her views of what other academics have to say about that area of law.

Suppose alternatively that you'll be expected to submit an essay in advance of a particular small-group teaching session with Professor Black – the session will then be used to talk about people's essays and how they might be improved. Try to make your essay the best it can possibly be so you can take full advantage of any feedback you will get from Professor Black in the session on how your essay might have been improved. Don't come up with an average piece of work which will be returned to you with some really obvious criticisms that even you knew could be made of your essay.

Again, suppose that in a small-group teaching session with Professor Green you'll be considering what the law says in a particular fact situation. Prepare well for the session by thinking of as many points as you can that might be made about that situation. Then in the session, make those points – and learn from what Professor Green has to say about them. Also use the opportunity provided by the small-group session to get some guidance from Professor Green about how one should approach the task of writing about problem situations in the exams – what are the examiners looking for you to do? What are they not looking for you to do?

Remember that the more you put into a small-group teaching session, the more you will get out of it. Even if you are being taught by an academic who has zero interest in teaching you, he or she will not fail to respond to the interest you show in getting the most out of your session with him or her. He or she will soon 'warm up' and start giving of his or her best to you.

(7) *Be nice.* This is a point that I've made before, but I'll make it again – be warm, bubbly and enthusiastic in your small-group teaching sessions. No one enjoys teaching a surly or uncommunicative student and even the most dedicated teacher will soon lose interest in doing anything for you if you persistently come to his or her small group sessions with a bad attitude. Of course, if you're feeling down on a particular day when you have a small-group teaching session, it's okay to make that clear – but your normal attitude in going into a small-group teaching session should be positive, friendly and outgoing.

That's enough advice from me. Hope your studies are going well. Keep in touch – I hope you'll let me know how you are getting on.

All best wishes,

Nick

Your Fellow Students

● From: Nicholas J. McBride [dearnick@pearson.com]
● To: Brown, Alex
● Subject: Your Fellow Students

Dear Alex,

I talked in the previous letter about the need to be aware that you aren't being taught on your own – and mentioned a couple of ways in which the way you act can either disrupt or help your fellow students' education. I thought it might be an idea to write you a letter about how you should deal generally with your fellow students. Here are three pieces of advice:

● Kindness and consideration

The bottom line is that you must always treat your fellow students with kindness and consideration. Remember that as a law student you are being equipped with a set of skills – the ability to argue effectively in favour of a particular point of view, the ability to see clearly any flaws in a particular line of reasoning, the ability to determine when someone should be forced to act in a particular way – that, in the wrong hands, will make you someone who is not particularly nice to know. You must ensure that the skills you are acquiring are tempered with kindness and consideration so that those skills work to help other people, and aren't used to drag them down.

So if one of your fellow students is making an argument that strikes you as flawed in some way, don't stick the boot in and tell them they are talking rubbish. If you want to say anything, try to help them discover for themselves what the problem might be with their argument by asking them a question ('But what about x?') that will make them think about the weak point (as you see it) in their argument. If they still persist in their views – and they can't convince you that their views are correct – then leave it: there's no point in continuing the discussion.

And when you are with other students in a small-group teaching situation, and you get the chance to ask some questions of your teacher, try to share the questions around, and don't hog the floor. It would be a good idea if the students in your group met together beforehand to review the issues you all want to discuss and get some clarification on, so that everyone gets as much as possible out of the session when it happens.

● Study groups

I'm not sure whether trying to form study groups with your fellow students is a good idea. In principle, it's good to share ideas, and work through problem questions, and develop lines of argument for essays together – but the problem is that forming an official study group is fraught with problems. The problems are mainly one of exclusion – telling people that your study group doesn't have room for them, and dealing with members of the study group who aren't contributing very much, or are actually a negative influence on the group. So I think a better idea is to form informal associations with two or three like-minded souls, whom you can meet when required to discuss ideas, or to try to clear up some difficult area of law.

● Competition

Some students get very competitive in their studies: they try to ensure that they will do better than others by doing as little as possible to help others with their work. Try to avoid falling into this mentality. Unless you are a genius, you will do better working with others than you can do working in isolation from everyone else. Even doing something as seemingly one-sided as helping someone who is struggling to understand a particular area of law will actually end up helping you with your work, because having to explain that area of law in the clearest possible terms will help make that area of law clearer in your mind, and force you to confront any confusions about that area of law that you suffer from.

All best wishes,

Nick

Making the Most of Your Time

- From: Nicholas J. McBride [dearnick@pearson.com]
- To: Brown, Alex
- Subject: Making the Most of Your Time

Dear Alex,

This is the final letter I'll write to you about the process of studying law. The final topic I want to write to you about is time. Time is the most precious thing you have as a law student. As a student, you have so much to do (both in studying law and in doing other things at university) and so little time in which to do it. So time is like gold for a student, and you should treat it accordingly – don't waste it. I've already given you some tips on how to maximise the time available to you, in trying to get through a reading list as quickly as possible, and in researching additional articles and materials that will help you with your work. But here are some further tips.

● Timetables

Draw up a timetable of your weekly, or fortnightly, schedule and look at it. Work out a plan of what you are going to be doing and when by way of studying and other activities. There may be on your timetable some gaps in your schedule where you have a lecture, then nothing for an hour, and then another lecture. Don't waste that hour – work out in advance what you are going to be doing at that time. (Reading some cases? Photocopying some articles? Looking on the Internet or through your faculty's library for useful materials?) There will also be long stretches of time on your timetable that are free – particularly at weekends. Again, decide in advance how you are going to use that time, so when that time comes round, you will know exactly what you are supposed to be doing and get on with it. Of course, if something else comes up that you have to attend to, then do that – but the important thing is not to drift, and to waste time thinking, 'What shall I do now?'

● Checklists

Make a checklist at the start of the day of your objectives for that day. Doing this has a number of benefits. It encourages you to get on with things and get everything on the checklist ticked off by the end of the day. Getting through your checklist will give you a sense of satisfaction and allow you to get to sleep without worrying about your work. And if you find yourself regularly not being able to get through everything on your daily checklist, that will force you to think – Are your plans for the day too ambitious, or are you unable to get through your checklist because you are wasting too much time?

● Tablets

When I was a student (1988–1992), it was unusual for a student to have a personal computer. Nowadays it's standard. I wonder if the same thing will happen soon with tablet computers – that it will be standard for students to carry around a tablet with them, as well as having a desktop computer back in their room. I recently bought a Kindle Fire, and find it invaluable for making the most of my time. I load it up with pdfs of articles I have to read, and when I have a spare moment (such as when I am travelling), I get my Kindle out and start reading. You can do the same thing on an iPad. So if you have the money, think about investing in a tablet computer so that you are carrying around a library with you that you can look at when you have an odd hour or half hour free between commitments.

● Work avoidance

I am the world's No.1 champion work avoider. If there is something I have to do, I will do anything to avoid having to knuckle down and get on with it. I'm always flicking through the channels on the TV next to my computer on which I'm typing this, checking out newspaper sites on the Internet for blogs or the latest news, and fiddling with iTunes to find a good album or piece of music to accompany the work I have to do. This is because most of the time what I have to do is write, and writing is difficult. Filling up a blank page with words that have to come out of your own head is tiring, and frequently dispiriting when the right words don't come. So I try to put off the unpleasant moment where I have to get down to writing as long as possible. Try to recognise when you are doing the same thing – wasting time to avoid having to do something that is going to be hard to do. Recognise what is happening and pull yourself out of it. *Just start* doing what you are trying to avoid doing, and you'll soon find that whatever you are doing is not so bad, and that it actually feels good to be getting on with what you have to do – and before you know it, you'll have it done. But you do have to *just start*.

● FOMO

The fear of missing out is a great source of timewasting. You've been working away in the library for a full 20 minutes and someone comes along and says 'Fancy a coffee?' There is no way that you should be taking a break after just 20 minutes, but FOMO kicks in and you end up saying 'Why not?' You have an essay to do on a particular evening, but a group of your friends are planning to go out. You should stay in, but FOMO makes you think, 'Well, I could go out for a couple of hours, and then really get stuck into the essay when I come back.' You need to be working at least four evenings in seven during the week to do well in your studies, but FOMO means you are out five evenings a week. You really have only scope for involvement in one or two university societies or activities, but FOMO means that you end up doing three or four extra-curricular things every week. The difficulty with FOMO is that it does have some rational basis – you *could* be missing out on something amazing if you don't go out, or you don't get involved with a particular sport or other activity in which you have some talent. So FOMO is never going to go away. The key to dealing with FOMO is to make FOMO work *in favour* of sticking to your studies, and not getting needlessly distracted. Instead of fearing missing out on what could happen *right now* if you went out tonight, or got involved with this society, start to think about what you might miss out on *in future* if you lose focus on your studies and end up doing less well in your exams than you could have done. Don't end up like a few of my former students, who are now stuck with permanent feelings of what might have been had they worked harder at university and got the sort of grades that would have enabled them to walk into any job they liked. So cultivate long-term FOMO to counteract any short-term FOMO that might encourage you to fritter away your time at university on doing virtually anything other than studying law.

● Holidays

As a university student, you can't regard your holidays as holidays – you have to make the most of the chances they provide to consolidate the knowledge you have acquired so far, and prepare for any upcoming exams. But the Christmas and Easter vacations contain a whole host of potential distractions – seeing your mates from home, going away with your new friends from university, spending time catching up with your family (who may not understand how hard you have to work as a university student), maybe earning some money doing a part-time job, and just generally relaxing and enjoying the comforts of being back at home. The best way of dealing with any pressures you might feel during your holidays to take time off from your studies is to have a plan. During the vacation, act as though you have a day-time job: your day-time job is to study law. So get up in the morning, ready to start work at 9 am, working through to lunchtime, and then start again at 1.30 pm and work through to 5.30 pm. After that, your time is yours to do with whatever you please. If you do that every day in the vacations, then you should be able to make everyone happy.

Talking of exams, I think it's about time I gave you some advice on preparing for exams – so that'll be the next set of letters. Until then . . .

All best wishes,

Nick

PART 4

Preparing for
Your Exams

Writing Essays

- From: Nicholas J. McBride [dearnick@pearson.com]
- To: Brown, Alex
- Subject: Writing Essays

Hey Alex,

Thanks very much for the copy of your first ever legal essay! I'll try to get round to commenting on it in a bit, but in the meantime, here are ten rules for writing essays that you should always observe.

● (1) Don't be lazy

This is the most fundamental rule. Writing good essays involves a lot of effort. A really good essay will look as though it was effortless to write – but that is an illusion, produced by the fact that a really good essay will be effortless to read. Being able to write a good essay is a skill, just like being able to play the piano is a skill – and just as you can't learn to play the piano overnight, neither can you write good essays just like that. Learning to write good essays takes time, and self-discipline, and constant practice – and all that is hard. And that is the single most important reason why a lot of students never learn to write good essays – they are not willing to take the time and put in the work required to acquire that skill. But it is vital for your long-term future that you not follow their example. How you do in your exams will depend crucially on how good you are at writing essays. And how you do in your exams will affect everything about your future – what sort of job you can get, how happy you will be in your work, how much money you will earn, who your friends will be in the future, whether you will get married and, if so, to whom. It's incredible to think that all of that depends on whether you are, or are not, willing to observe the rules set out below. But it does.

● (2) Answer the question

This is the second most fundamental rule. It seems such a simple and straight-forward rule, and such an obvious one as well – but it is amazing how often students fail to observe this rule. I was talking some time ago to a colleague of mine about her experience marking essays that students had written for a par-ticular exam. She must have marked over 200 students' papers. She told me that only three of those students actually tried to answer the question in writ-ing their essays. Incredible, but true. But the fact that so few students actually bother to answer the question in writing an essay gives you a big advantage: if you make the effort in writing an essay to actually answer the question, your essay will automatically look really good compared with everyone else's.

So – suppose you are given the following essay to write:

'The law on homicide is in a mess.' Discuss.

This is what we call a *discursive* essay – an essay that asks you to evaluate a particular area of the law. This is the most common sort of essay you might be asked to write. (The other kind of essay that you might be asked to write is a *descriptive* essay – an essay setting out the key elements of a particular area of the law. An example of a descriptive essay would be: 'When will one person be held liable in tort for failing to rescue another?')

So – this essay is asking you to say whether or not the law on homicide (which deals with when someone will be criminally punished for causing another's death) is in a mess or not, and to present some arguments in favour of your view. And that's precisely what you should do – make up your mind whether or not you are going to say that the law on homicide is in a mess, and then come up with some arguments in favour of your point of view. But many stu-dents don't do that – they don't answer the question. Instead, they turn their essay into a descriptive essay and spend 90 per cent of their time setting out what the law on homicide says. (They usually excuse themselves for doing so by first saying, 'Before we can address this issue, it is first necessary to set out the law on homicide . . .' Whenever you find yourself writing 'it is first necessary . . .', ask yourself: Am I drifting off the point here? The answer will almost always be 'yes'.) They then realise that actually they were supposed to be writing a discursive essay on whether the law on homicide is in a mess and try to rescue the essay by saying in the very last paragraph 'So, as we can see, the law on homicide is [is not] in a mess . . .' when that is the very last thing we can see from what has been said so far. Of course, in writing an essay on whether the law on homicide is in a mess, you are going to have to talk about what the law on homicide currently says, but in the context of a discussion of whether the law on homicide is in a mess. So a good response to the following question might start:

> The law on homicide is in a mess – it is unclear, inconsistent, and serves no rational purpose.

And then all you need to do for the rest of the essay is come up with examples of the law on homicide's being unclear, inconsistent, and serving no rational purpose. You don't need to set out the whole of the law on homicide to do this – you just have to switch a flashlight on elements of the law that help demonstrate your overall point.

This second most fundamental rule – that in writing an essay, you should answer the question – has a sub-rule: in writing an essay, you should *only* answer the question. Don't drift off the point for a second. If you are set an essay on a particular topic, and given some reading to do on that topic, there is a great temptation to try to refer to all the things that you have been told to read on that topic in your essay. Resist that temptation: only bring into your essay cases and articles that are relevant to the point you are making in your essay.

If you approach an essay thinking, 'I should mention the case of *X* v *Y*, and I must get in somewhere a reference to Professor Z's interesting argument that . . .' then you are flirting with disaster: it's very likely that your essay will just turned into an unfocused, messy hodgepodge of observations and arguments. When you are writing an essay on a particular topic, work out what you are going to say in response to the question that has been set and then focus like a laser on making out what you want to say. It doesn't matter if a lot of interesting stuff that you've read about is left unsaid – the agony of not being able to show off to the reader just how much you know about your subject is the price you have to pay for writing a really good essay.

● (3) Write clearly

Again, this is such an obvious rule, but it is very rare for students to make the effort to observe it. An infallible way of telling whether you are writing clearly enough is to employ what I call the 'friend test'. Imagine that a friend has asked you the question that you are responding to in writing your essay. Would your friend understand what you are saying? If the answer is no, you have failed the friend test and you are not writing clearly enough.

The two most common causes of unclear writing are: being in a hurry, and over-complication. Students often fail to write clearly because they are in too much of a hurry to take the time to make some sense of what they want to say. This is particularly the case, I find, when students write about cases. For example, consider the following:

> An example of the courts forcing people to act in good faith is the *Interfoto* case, where the defendants did not have to pay the extra charge because they had not been warned about it.

Would anyone reading this have much of a clue as to what happened in the *Interfoto* case? What makes this sort of bad writing completely unforgiveable is that it is just so unnecessary – there is absolutely no reason why the student who wrote this had to rush over the facts of the *Interfoto* case. They could easily have written:

> There are many cases which can be interpreted as examples of situations where the courts have required people to act in good faith when contracting with other people. For example, in the case of *Interfoto Picture Library* v *Stiletto Visual Programme*, the defendants hired some slides from the claimants. The small print in the claimants' standard terms said that if the defendants did not return the slides on time, they would have to pay the claimants £5 per slide for every extra day they kept them. This term was not brought to the defendants' attention. The defendants returned the slides 13 days late and were sent a bill for £3,000 as a result. The Court of Appeal held the defendants did not have to pay the bill. One way of looking at this case is that the Court of Appeal took the view that the claimants had acted in bad faith in failing to draw such an onerous term to the defendants' attention, and should not be allowed to profit from this.

Isn't that much clearer? But don't think it's clearer just because I wrote it. You don't need to be particularly clever to write as clearly as this: the only reason our student didn't write this is that he/she wasn't willing to take the time to do so.

As I've just said, the second reason why students often fail to write clearly is that their essays are over-complicated. They try to make points that are far too subtle and difficult to make out convincingly. The best essays are quite simple in what they have to say. You should be able to reduce what you want to say in your essay down to a five- or six-sentence 'soundbite'. If you can't, then your essay is too complicated to be worth writing, and you should rethink your essay. Some academics might be horrified at this advice, but they aren't trying to do what you have to do. They have the luxury of writing an article on a particular topic, or an entire book. In an exam, you will probably have about 45 minutes or an hour to write a convincing essay on a particular issue. You can't afford to act like an academic in that sort of situation. The following advice – given by an Oxford Fellow, Bruce McFarlane, to a student in 1956 who was just about to sit his history exams – has always struck me as completely correct:

> It's no use treating an examination as if it were the Last Judgment; your scrupulous weighing of the pros and cons, your unwillingness to decide, would be admirable . . . if you were writing serious history. [But you're] not supposed to be doing that; you're supposed to be showing how clever you are or aren't, and it's absolutely suicidal to be modest, unsure, diffident or muddled . . . You've got to have a fairly simple, fairly plausible, intelligible "attitude" and you've got to plug it confidently.

So if you have to write a discursive essay on a particular topic, try to think of a simple and straightforward 'line' (but still interesting) that you can take in response to that essay question and avoid like the plague any temptation to depart from that line or overcomplicate it. Similarly, if you have to write a descriptive essay on a particular area of the law, try to think of a very straightforward and simple way of setting out the law – for example, presenting the law as the product of a clash of two competing principles or philosophies, or presenting the law as giving effect to one or two very simple ideas.

And when you write your essay, do everything you possibly can to make it easy to follow. Ensure the first paragraph explains what you are going to say in the rest of the essay. Don't make your essay into the equivalent of a conjuring trick where what you are saying is only revealed (ta-da!) at the end of the essay. If you have three points to make, number them: (1) . . . (2) . . . (3). And make sure it's clear that these are three different points, and that points (1) and (2) aren't the same points just written in different ways – don't force the reader to do the work of figuring out why points (1) and (2) are actually different points. If your essay has a number of different parts (for example, one part of your essay sets out a number of different arguments in favour of the overall point you are making, while another part considers an argument that is commonly made against the point you are making and shows why that argument doesn't stand up), then use headings to distinguish the different sections of your essay.

● (4) Use concrete examples

A great aid to writing clearly – and also writing succinctly – is to use concrete examples. For example, suppose you have been set the following essay:

> "There is no reason why constitutional conventions should not have the force of law; in fact, some constitutional conventions already do." Discuss.

(Just in case you haven't covered constitutional conventions yet, examples of constitutional conventions are:

1 that the Monarch will only dissolve Parliament 'early' on the advice of the Prime Minister;

2 that the Monarch will not refuse assent to a Bill that has been passed by both Houses of Parliament;

3 that the Prime Minister will resign or seek a dissolution of Parliament if his party loses a vote of confidence in the House of Commons;

4 that a member of the Cabinet will not question the correctness of a decision reached by the Cabinet as a whole without first resigning his position as a member of the Cabinet;

5 that the Prime Minister will not disclose to other people the advice he/she has received from the Monarch at one of his/her weekly meetings with the Monarch;

6 that if the current Speaker of the House of Commons is a Conservative MP, the next Speaker will not be a Conservative MP.)

Suppose, in writing the descriptive part of the essay (whether some constitutional conventions have the force of law) – which I would advise you to do first (there's no reason why, in considering the issues raised by an essay title, you should consider them in the order in which they have been raised by the essay title if it would make more sense to do them in a different order) – you want to argue:

1 Constitutional conventions do not have the force of law because the courts will not award any remedy or impose any kind of sanction in response to the mere fact that a constitutional convention has been departed from.

and

2 If the courts do award a remedy or impose a sanction when a constitutional convention is departed from that is because the person who has departed from that convention has in doing so breached some

independent rule (such as that statutory powers should not be exercised in a way which is wholly unreasonable, or that people should not disclose information imparted to them in confidence) that does have the force of law.

This is pretty abstract stuff that can be made a lot easier to understand by bringing it down to earth through a concrete example. For example, you could consider what could happen if the Prime Minister leaked to a newspaper information about what the Queen had told him at their last weekly meeting, and make the point that if the Prime Minister were successfully sued for damages by the Queen, that would not be because he had breached a constitutional convention in leaking the details of their conversation to the newspapers, but because in leaking that information he breached an independent legal rule that says that if A tells B something in confidence, then A is not allowed to disclose that information to a third party unless it is in the public interest to do so.

Again, suppose in writing the discursive part of the essay (whether constitutional conventions should have the force of law) you want to argue that constitutional conventions should not have the force of law, because:

1   If the courts were to award a remedy or impose a sanction in response to the breach of a constitutional convention, there are only four different kinds of remedies/sanctions that they could award/impose: (i) criminal punishment; (ii) an award of damages; (iii) an injunction; (iv) a declaration that failing to observe the convention was unlawful.

2   It would be unthinkable – for various constitutional reasons – for the courts to respond to the breach of a constitutional convention in ways (i), (ii) or (iii).

3   If the courts merely responded to the breach of a constitutional convention by issuing a declaration that failing to observe the convention was unlawful, the courts would be brought into disrepute – it would look like the courts were powerless to back up their words ("this action is unlawful . . .") with concrete action (". . . and we forbid you to do it on pain of being sent to prison if you disregard our order"), or did not seriously mean what they said ("we're saying that this action is unlawful, but not so unlawful that we want to do anything about it").

This is quite a complex point to get across, but focusing on some concrete examples could really help to make what you are saying a lot clearer. For example, you could make out point (2), above, by considering a hypothetical situation where the Prime Minister has refused to resign on losing a vote of confidence in the House of Commons, and show that even if constitutional conventions did have the force of law, the most the courts could possibly do in that situation would be to issue a declaration that the Prime Minister was acting unlawfully in refusing to resign.

The essay on constitutional conventions demonstrates another reason why concrete examples can be so useful. You can sometimes make a particular concept or idea immediately intelligible by drawing an analogy with a real-world situation. For example, students sometimes find it difficult to understand what a 'convention' is and what it might mean for a 'convention' to have the 'force of law'. But this difficulty can normally be immediately solved by pointing out that in football, there is a custom that if your team has kicked the ball out to allow an injured player to be treated, once play has resumed with the opposing team taking a throw-in or a goal kick, the opposing team will give the ball back to your team. This custom is like a constitutional convention – it is a practice that is normally observed, and on the few rare occasions that it is not observed, the failure to observe it is severely disapproved of by everyone else. And the question of whether a constitutional convention should have the force of law is analogous to the question of whether the referee in a football game should have the power to punish a side that fails to give back the ball to the other team after the other team has kicked the ball out of play in order to allow an injured player to be treated. So using homely concrete examples like this can be a very good way of making the points you want to make a lot clearer to the reader.

● (5) Write something interesting

To get a really good mark for an essay, particularly an essay written in an exam, you will have to write something interesting. Boring may get you a 2.1 – but it won't get you a First.

So if you are writing a descriptive essay, make the effort to come up with an interesting way of setting out the area of law you've been asked to write about. Think about:

1 centring your description of the law around a concrete example that you can constantly refer back to;
2 using a table or tables to set out the key elements of the law; and
3 organising your description of the law around some core principles that (you will argue) the law gives effect to.

But whatever you do, don't just repeat what is in the textbook. That is boring – you have got to come up with something that is better than what is in the textbook. (Which is actually not as hard as it sounds.)

And if you are writing a discursive essay, make the effort to come up with an interesting 'line' in response to the question. In doing so, it's worth thinking about adopting a *contrarian* position, where you adopt a line of argument which goes against the current, fashionable trend of thinking. An essay that takes that kind of line will automatically be much more interesting than an essay which just repeats the well-worn arguments that everyone else has been making for years, and, as a result, have a much better chance of getting a First than the second kind of essay. (If you don't believe me, I strongly recommend you either read Alan Bennett's play *The History Boys* or watch the DVD.)

But don't be contrarian just for the sake of it. Only adopt a line of argument that goes against the current orthodoxy if you actually believe in that line of argument – if your essay lacks conviction, that will be pretty clear and your essay will suffer for it. Also be aware that the person marking/reading your essay may well be a true believer in the current orthodoxy, and will take some convincing that your argument is correct. So make sure, if you do adopt a contrarian position in your essay, that you take time to consider the strongest possible arguments in favour of the current orthodoxy and then show how those arguments do not stand up. Note that I said: 'the strongest possible arguments . . .' If you try to pull a fast one and put up some really weak (what are called 'straw man') arguments against your position, that isn't going to impress anyone and your easy knock-outs will be rewarded with a pretty poor mark.

Two qualifications need to be made to what I've just said. First, don't adopt a contrarian position in writing an essay if doing so will require you to do the impossible. For example, let's go back to the essay on whether the law on homicide is in a mess. Okay – now everyone thinks that the law on homicide is in a mess, so it would make for an interesting essay to argue that the law on homicide is in fact in perfect working order. However, it's impossible to argue that effectively, because to do that you would have to go through the entire law on homicide and argue that every single element of the law makes perfect sense. It's just not possible to do that in an essay. You could maybe do that in a book – but in an essay there simply isn't the space to make your essay convincing. So if you are going to do an essay on whether the law on homicide is in a mess, you won't have a choice about what line you will take in response to that question. You will have to argue that the law is in a mess – and make your essay interesting through the points you come up with to show that the law is in a mess.

Secondly, don't adopt a contrarian position in an exam essay if the question expressly excludes you from adopting such a position. For instance, a few years back, I was pretty confident that my tort students would get an essay asking them to talk about what's called the 'rule in *Rylands* v *Fletcher*' (which basically says that if you bring a dangerous thing onto your land, and it escapes, and does damage to your neighbour's land, you'll be liable for that damage even if you weren't at fault for the escape). There had been a very big and recent case on that rule, and examiners often set questions around recent developments in the law. (We'll talk about that some other time.) Not many people think very much of the rule in *Rylands* v *Fletcher*, so I gave the students some arguments in favour of the rule, so that they could write an interesting essay on it if it came up, instead of a boring '*Rylands* v *Fletcher* is rubbish' essay. So – come the day of the exam, there was indeed an essay on *Rylands* v *Fletcher* on the paper, but it was a quote from an Australian judge saying that the rule in *Rylands* v *Fletcher* should be abolished and then after that, the question said something like, 'In light of this, critically assess the decision of the House of Lords in *Transco plc* v *Stockport MBC*' (which decision had upheld the existence of the rule in *Rylands* v *Fletcher* in English law). So anyone wanting to say that the rule in *Rylands* v *Fletcher* was a good thing was left nowhere to go – the examiner was basically saying, 'I want you to trash the rule in *Rylands* v *Fletcher* (and the decision of the House of Lords in *Transco*) for 45 minutes.' So it just wasn't possible to write a contrarian essay in response to that particular question.

If your essay is going to be non-contrarian in nature and argue in favour of a position that pretty much everyone agrees with, you can still make it interesting enough to stand out from the crowd by making as strong a case in your essay as you can against the position you are arguing for, and then demolishing that case. So, for example, suppose that you are writing an essay which is aiming ultimately to argue that prison doesn't work (whatever that means). The most interesting way of doing this essay is to set out as carefully as you can the strongest arguments that can possibly be made for the position that prison works, and then do a really great demolition job on those arguments. Again, remember that this kind of essay will only be as strong as the arguments that you set out to demolish, so don't succumb to the temptation to confine yourself to considering the weakest arguments against your position.

One final point about writing interesting essays: if you are writing a discursive essay to be marked by a supervisor or a tutor, or simply for practice, it's essential that you go beyond the reading list, and have a look to see whether there are any other articles or short books that you haven't been referred to, but are relevant to the essay. The more ideas and arguments you expose yourself to, the more likely it is that you will be able to come up with an interesting line in response to the essay question that you have been set. If you just stick with what you've been told to read, then it's not very likely that you will have anything interesting to say in response to the essay question – you'll just be repeating what you've read in articles that are really well known and familiar. So the very first thing you should do when you've been asked to write a discursive essay on a particular topic is do a Google search of terms relevant to the essay and see what's 'out there' on the Internet that might be relevant to your essay. Of course, you'll turn up a lot of irrelevant stuff – but just an hour's searching should turn up some very useful material. And following all the other advice I gave you, in my letter on reading articles, on how to find other articles relevant to your studies should help you turn up further material that is relevant to the essay you are planning to write.

● (6) The first paragraph is vital

Your first paragraph has a bigger influence on what final mark you get for an exam essay than any other part of the essay. To see why this is, you've got to understand a bit about how essays are marked.

The final mark you get for an exam essay will be a percentage mark – usually, 70 per cent or more is a First Class mark, between 60 per cent and 70 per cent is a 2.1, between 50 per cent and 60 per cent is a 2.2, and beyond that it will depend on the particular university you are at what the boundary is between a Third and a Fail. (Of course, I hope you'll never have to worry about where that boundary is.) Now – while the mark you get is a percentage mark, the examiner won't mark your essay by giving you points as he/she reads your essay, and then give you a percentage mark by seeing how many points you got compared with a notional maximum number of points that you might have got for your essay. No – this is how it works.

The examiner will form a view on reading your essay whether it is a First Class essay, a 2.1 essay, a 2.2 essay, or worse than that. Having formed this view, the examiner will then ask him/herself: was it a high or a low First/ 2.1/2.2/whatever? And if he/she thinks it was a First Class essay (it answered the question, was interesting, had good arguments), but not a high First (but it didn't blow my mind), you'll get 71 per cent or 72 per cent. If on the other hand, he/she thinks it was not only a First Class essay but a really high First (it was the best essay I've ever read on this subject), you could get 80 per cent – 85 per cent for an essay like that. (Only God gets more than 85 per cent for an essay – don't ask why; that's just the way it is.) Similarly if he/she thinks it was a 2.1 essay (it was okay, not very interesting), but a low 2.1 (the arguments seemed to be a bit flimsy, failed to mention a couple of relevant cases) then you'll get 62 per cent or 63 per cent for that. If, on the other hand, he/she thinks it was a high 2.1 (the arguments were pretty solid, and the essay mentioned the relevant cases) then you could get 68 per cent or 69 per cent for that.

Now – note that there is an absolute gulf between getting 70 per cent and 69 per cent for an essay. Someone who gets 69 per cent for an essay might think – argh, I only just missed a First. Wrong: you didn't just miss a First; you were never in with a chance of getting a First. And that's because the overall impression that the examiner got from your essay was that it was not First Class quality. It was a 2.1 at best. It was a really good 2.1 essay – but it was never going to be a First. So whether you get a First or not depends on what overall impression the examiner forms of your essay. And the first paragraph is the most important paragraph of your essay in shaping the overall impression that the examiner forms of your essay.

To see why this is so, let's go back to the essay on whether the law on homicide is in a mess. Let's just look at two alternative first lines:

(A) 'The law on homicide is in a mess – it is unclear, inconsistent and serves no rational purpose.'

(B) 'To address this issue it is first necessary to set out the law on homicide.'

I can tell you for a fact that an examiner reading line (A) will immediately think: 'This is going to be a First Class essay.' And an examiner reading line (B) will immediately think, 'Ugh – 2.1 at best.' It should be pretty obvious why this is. Line (A) tells the examiner: this candidate is going to answer the question, they know what they want to say, and they are going to give me some good arguments in support of their answer. Line (B) tells the examiner: this candidate doesn't really know what to say in response to the essay question and is trying to avoid having to answer it by fleeing to the safety of a boring description of the law.

Now – first impressions are hard to budge. If the examiner starts off thinking that your essay is a First Class essay, then you'll have to do something seriously wrong somewhere in the rest of the essay to dislodge that first impression and end up getting a 2.1. If you keep your nose clean and do what you promised to do in your first line – that is, highlight some elements of the law on homicide that establish that it is unclear, and inconsistent, and serves no rational purpose – then you will get a First at the end of the essay. (Whether it's a high First or a low First depends on how great the execution of the essay is.) If, on the other hand, the examiner starts off thinking that your essay is a 2.1 essay, then you're going to have do something seriously impressive in the rest of the essay to dislodge that first impression and get him/her to start thinking that maybe your essay is a First Class essay after all.

That's why the first paragraph is absolutely vital. And that's why most of the time you spend writing practice essays should be spent on learning how to write impressive opening paragraphs – that is, an opening paragraph that makes it clear how you are going to respond to the essay title and sets the stage for the rest of the essay by introducing the key ideas that will underlie your response. Some examples:

'The doctrine of consideration is in need of reform.' Discuss.

The philosophy underlying the doctrine of consideration is simple enough: only promises that form part of a commercial deal – what we can call 'bargain promises' – should be enforced. It is essential that the courts enforce bargain promises if our society is to enjoy any kind of sophisticated market economy. In contrast, a gratuitous promise – for example, A's promise to pay B £100 on his next pay day, or his promise to pay B £100 a year for the rest of her life to reward her for saving his life, or his promise to waive part of a debt that B owes him – is economically 'sterile' and there is consequently no public policy reason why it should be enforced. Critics of the current state of the doctrine of consideration reject the idea that only bargain promises are worth enforcing. They fall into three camps. (1) 'Social critics' argue that gratuitous promises that have been relied upon should be enforced, in certain circumstances. (2) 'Libertarian critics' argue that gratuitous promises that were intended to be legally binding should be enforced. (3) 'Economic critics' argue that there are some gratuitous promises that it is important to enforce for the purpose of ensuring the smooth running of our market economy. I will argue that none of these criticisms of the current state of the doctrine of consideration are valid.

>

'Prison works.' Discuss.

The catchphrase 'prison works' is capable of being interpreted in a number of different ways. (1) The prospect of being imprisoned is a more effective deterrent to crime than any other form of punishment available to us. (2) Imprisoning people for serious offences is a more effective way of cutting crime rates than any other form of punishment available to us. (3) Imprisoning people for serious offences is a more cost-effective way of cutting crime rates than any other form of punishment available to us. I will argue that while claim (1) is true, it is also immaterial whether or not (1) is true. I will go on to argue that while claim (2) is untrue, that is also immaterial. What actually matters is whether claim (3) is true. I will argue that claim (3) is not likely to be true. So while prison may 'work' at some level, it does not work at the level that matters to us – cutting crime rates in the most cost-effective manner possible.

When will one person be held liable in tort for failing to rescue another?

The normal rule in English law is that if I fail to save you from harm, you will not be able to sue me in tort for compensation for that harm – no matter how easy it might have been for me to rescue you. However there are a number of well-established exceptions to that rule. If: (1) I put you in danger of suffering that harm, or (2) I stopped someone else saving you from that harm, or (3) you were harmed by a child or an animal that was initially in my control, or (4) I 'assumed a responsibility' to you to save you from that harm, or (5) you were on my land at the time you suffered that harm, and you suffered that harm because my land was in a dangerous condition, then I will be held liable to compensate you for the harm you suffered if I failed to take reasonable steps to protect you from that harm. There have been attempts to expand the categories of exceptions to the 'no liability for omissions' rule to cover the case where: (6) it was my job, as an employee of the State, to save you from harm. So far there is only tortious liability in situation (6) where I intentionally chose not to save you from harm, knowing that I was required to do so under the terms of my employment: in such a case you could sue me for committing the tort of misfeasance in public office. But in cases where I carelessly failed to save you from harm, the current state of the law is that there is no tortious liability (though there may be liability under the Human Rights Act 1998) in situation (6): the general rule of 'no liability for omissions' applies.

● (7) Make sure your essay stands up to scrutiny

Again, a pretty obvious rule which is routinely ignored by students. Don't make any old point or argument in your essay – make sure that the points and arguments that you do make do not suffer from any obvious flaws. Always ask yourself – Is what I am saying true? What objections could be made to what I'm saying? Do those objections stand up?

For example, take the interpretation of the case of *Interfoto Picture Library* v *Stiletto Visual Programme* that was set out a few pages back. According to this interpretation, in that case the Court of Appeal refused to allow the claimants to charge the defendants £5 a day per slide for returning their slides late because the claimants had acted in bad faith in inserting that charge for late return into their contract with the defendants. But if you were relying on that interpretation of the case to argue that the courts require contracting parties to act in good faith towards each other, you should be asking yourself: Is that interpretation of the *Interfoto* case correct? What objections could be made to it? Do those objections stand up?

So someone who objected to the above interpretation of the *Interfoto* case might argue:

> The Court of Appeal in the *Interfoto* case *didn't* say to the claimants, "Well – you sure pulled a fast one on the defendants, sneaking that term into the contract; but we're not going to allow you to get away with that – we're going to find that that term is unenforceable and of no effect." Instead, they said, "Sadly for you, you never even managed to get the term as to payment for late return of the slides into your contract with the defendants. That term wasn't actually validly incorporated into your contract with the defendants because the defendants didn't think that such a term would be part of their contract with you: while they were happy to deal with you on your standard terms, they never thought that such an onerous term would be part of those terms, and you never told them that it was." So the *Interfoto* decision had nothing to do with sanctioning bad faith behaviour – the Court of Appeal in that case was giving effect to the much more basic idea that you can't be bound by a contract term which you didn't agree to, and which you didn't give the appearance that you were agreeing to.

Does this objection stand up? If it does, then you can't use *Interfoto* as support for the idea that the courts require contracting parties to act in good faith towards each other. You'll have to cast around for some other, stronger, authorities in favour of that view. And if you think you've found them: test them out. Ask again – is there a more plausible interpretation of these cases? Doing this is hard work, but it is essential that you do this work if you are going to construct a solid argument that will stand up to scrutiny.

In testing the arguments that you are making in favour of a particular position that you are taking, look out in particular for whether they are circular or incomplete or based on a false premise. (You may want to look again at my letter on logical arguments at this point.) For example, suppose that you are criticising the law for saying that a teacher does not have a duty to take any steps to stop a child being bullied as she goes home from school. To try to make your discussion of the issue clearer, you wisely follow my earlier advice and introduce a concrete example where B is being consistently bullied on her way home by other people in her class, and A, the class teacher, knows about this but has done nothing to reprimand or discipline the bullies. Now you want to find a way of criticising the law for not holding A liable for failing to protect B. Don't just seize on any old argument in favour of saying the law is deficient. Try to find one that isn't flawed in some obvious way.

Suppose, for example, that you are thinking of arguing:

> The law in this area is deficient because the law should say that A has a duty to take steps to stop B being bullied.

Unfortunately, that's a circular argument. It simply assumes that the point you are trying to establish – that A should have a legal duty to protect B – is correct. Alternatively, you might think of arguing:

> The law in this area is deficient because B has a right not be bullied.

However, this argument is incomplete. B does have a right *against the bullies* not to be bullied, but that does not establish that she should have a legal right that A take steps to protect her from being bullied. Maybe you'll try to argue:

> The law in this area is deficient because A should protect B from being bullied.

Sadly, again, that argument is incomplete because while we can accept that A should protect B from being bullied, that does not – all on its own – establish that the law should step in to encourage A to do the right thing by imposing a legal duty on her that requires her to take steps to protect B from being bullied. Trying a different approach, you could try to argue:

> The law in this area is deficient because A should protect B from being bullied, and the law should encourage us to do the right thing.

However, that argument seems to rest on a false premise. It is not at all clear that the law should always encourage us to do the right thing. We don't have laws against adultery, or being rude to people, or letting your children down, or failing to rescue strangers who are drowning. Finally, we come to an argument that actually seems to work:

> The law in this area is deficient. The law should encourage us to do the right thing where doing so will not have any seriously adverse consequences. That is the case here: A should protect B from being bullied, and encouraging A, and other teachers, to do the right thing in this sort of situation will not have any seriously adverse consequences.

This argument isn't circular or incomplete. However, you still have to test it out to see whether it rests on a false premise. You've got to ask yourself whether imposing a legal duty on someone like A to protect someone like B from being bullied may in fact have some seriously adverse consequences.

● (8) Don't avoid a fight

Students sometimes seem to think that if they mention any arguments that run counter to the point that they are trying to make in their essay, that will somehow undermine and weaken their essay. So they just concentrate on the arguments that support their case, and ignore any opposing voices. The truth is quite different: if you don't mention any obvious arguments that run counter to the general thrust of your essay, that will look like a sign of weakness. It will look like you are avoiding dealing with those arguments because you know you have no response to them. A strong essay will make the arguments in favour of its position, and then consider the arguments against its position and demolish those opposing arguments. And again – don't try to pull a fast one by introducing some weaknesses into your opponent's position that will make it much easier for you to dismiss him/her. Doing so will only weaken your essay.

● (9) Pay attention to the details

There's a saying: 'Don't sweat the small stuff.' That is: don't get worried about small things. Please, please do sweat the small stuff when you are writing an essay. Little slips in spelling, grammar, and punctuation can create a terrible impression and result in your getting a lower mark than the content of your essay deserves.

So – it's 'Act of Parliament' not 'act of parliament'. And 'it's' always means 'it is' or 'it has'. So never write 'it's' if you don't mean to say 'it is' or 'it has'; write 'its' instead. It's the European Court of Human Rights that ultimately decides whether someone's rights under the European Convention on Human Rights have been violated, not the European Court of Justice. Avoid run-on sentences – sentences that squash together two or more different sentences into the same sentence – they make you look illiterate. (See what I did there?) Don't refer to Hoffmann LJ's decision in *Stovin* v *Wise* – his decision in that case was given in the House of Lords, not the Court of Appeal, and so it was Lord Hoffmann's decision, not Hoffmann LJ's. If you want to refer to the major reason for the decision in a case, talk about the princip*al* reason for the decision. If you want to refer to the idea or theory underling the decision in a case, talk about the princip*le* underlying the decision. Defendants in tort cases are sued – they are not prosecuted. An unsuccessful defendant in a criminal case is found guilty of committing a particular offence; he is not held liable for committing that offence.

● (10) Don't plagiarise

I can't believe I have to say anything about this, but as plagiarism is a growing concern for university authorities, I guess I should. Plagiarism involves stealing someone else's ideas and passing them off as your own. The 'someone else' is normally an academic who has published a book or an article. Plagiarising an academic's work usually involves either: (1) copying out chunks from his/ her book or article into your essay without acknowledging that those chunks did not come from your head, but came from someone else's published work; or (2) setting out an idea or concept that he/she came up with without acknowledging the source of that idea or concept. Plagiarising someone else's work is just dumb, dumb, dumb – and not just because you might be caught out and embarrassed, or worse.

Let's take the first form of plagiarism – writing an essay by copying out chunks from a book or article that someone else has written. This is not going to help you in the long run. As I said before, writing essays is a skill that requires a lot of time and practice to acquire. Copying out chunks from someone else's work is not going to help you acquire that skill. So any essay that you write that contains substantial sections from someone else's work is just a waste of time – you may have saved yourself some effort by lifting someone else's work, but you are guaranteeing that when you are asked to demonstrate your essay writing skills in the exams, you will have nothing to show.

As for the second form of plagiarism – stealing an idea or concept from some-one else's work and passing it off as your own – again this is just pointless. No one is expecting you to write something wildly original in an essay. There is absolutely no reason for you to want to pretend that some idea or concept came from you, rather than someone else. You will get just as much credit for acknowledging that you came across that idea or concept in an article or book written by some academic – at the very least, it shows that you have done some reading around the subject and been able to appreciate someone else's work.

So those are my ten rules for writing essays. It might be an idea to write out the rules – just the rules, not the explanations of the rules – on a bit of a card, that you can have with you whenever you write an essay, so as to remind you of what you ought to be doing in writing an essay.

Before I finish, I just have one last word of advice. I can't claim any credit for this bit of advice (no plagiarism here!) – it was actually a suggestion of a colleague of mine here at Pembroke College, Professor Loraine Gelsthorpe, which struck me as being very sensible. She suggested that in writing practice essays for exams, students should not write them on computers, but should instead write them longhand.

The idea behind this is that writing essays in longhand is a very different skill from writing essays on a computer. If you write an essay on a computer, you can write a sentence, see what it looks like, delete bits of it if you are unhappy, and try it again. You can also insert text into the middle of an essay, if you think a particular point needs expanding, or you suddenly realise that you should have mentioned a particular case at a particular point in the essay. And you can move text around the essay if you think that it would be more appropriate to have a particular section appear earlier or later on in the essay than it currently does.

You can't do ANY of this if you write an essay longhand. You have to work out what you want to say, and how you want to say it, before you start writing – because once you start writing, there is no going back. So you have to make sure that your essay plan is a good one before you put pen to paper. Now writing an essay on a computer doesn't encourage you to acquire this skill – you don't need to have a particular plan when starting writing an essay on a computer: you can just start writing, see how it goes, let a plan emerge as you go along, and revise the text in light of your emerging understanding of what the essay should look like. But it's essential that you do acquire this skill because you're going to need it for the exam, where – unless you have special circumstances – all your essays have to be written longhand.

However, for the time being I would suggest that you continue to write your essays on a computer to enable you to get into the habit of writing some really good, effective essays. Once you've shown yourself able to do that, then I would advise abandoning the computer and writing your essays longhand to acquire the special skills required to write really good, effective essays in exam conditions.

If you want to read anything else on how to write good, effective essays, you should definitely get hold of the excellent *A Short Guide to College Writing* (fifth edition) by Sylvan Barnet, Pat Bellanca, and Marcia Stubbs. It's also worth reading George Orwell's essay on 'Politics and the English language' (now freely available on the Internet). You should also have a look at Chapters 9 and 10 of Thomas Dixon's excellent book *How to Get a First*.

Okay – I'll be in touch soon about the essay you sent me.

Best wishes,

Nick

A Sample Essay

● From: Nicholas J. McBride [dearnick@pearson.com]
● To: Brown, Alex
● Subject: A Sample Essay

Dear Alex,

I've now had a chance to read over the essay you sent me. I think if you've had a chance to read the rules for writing essays that I set out in my previous letter, you'll see a number of respects in which your essay could have been better. I've got three comments in particular.

First, the essay title was '"The 'but for' test for causation is neither a necessary nor sufficient test for causation. It should be abandoned." Discuss.' You didn't take a clear line on what your response to this title was. Whenever you are given a quote like this to 'discuss' you have to make up your mind: are you going to argue that the quote is correct, or that it is incorrect? Instead, what you did was take the line that some people might argue that the 'but for' test is an important test for causation, but other people argue that it does not work well in certain situations. In fact, calling that a 'line' is doing it too much credit: it's not a line, it's a fudge. You have to aim for complete clarity in your essays. That is scary, I know: the clearer your position, the easier it is for someone to shoot you down. But this is the game you chose to play when you opted to study law. Remember the first rule of lawyering: express yourself clearly, or die.

Secondly, your essay didn't have any headings, or anything to break it up. I know you were taught at school to write without using any headings, but it isn't helpful at this level. Using headings makes it easier for your reader to digest and understand what you are saying. And using headings helps you keep your essay on track and discourages you from wandering off into making unhelpful digressions.

My third point is that you didn't use your legal knowledge particularly well in the essay. You dwelled far too long on the facts and decisions in particular cases, without any regard for whether that was important for helping along the argument of your essay. (But given the fact that your essay didn't have that much of an argument, this was probably understandable.) I know it's tempting when you've worked so hard to understand a particular case or set of cases that you would want to show off your knowledge of that case or cases, but you have to resist that temptation like mad. You must subordinate everything to making out the arguments in favour of the basic point you are making in an essay. The art of writing good essays is as much about knowing what to leave out as it is about knowing what to put in.

Okay – that's enough about your essay. Here's how I would have approached the essay. I haven't had time to really polish it up (I would have liked to have a few more references to particular legal academics' views in the essay) but it should give you a good idea of how you could and should have approached the essay.

'The "but for" test for causation is neither a necessary nor sufficient test for causation. It should be abandoned.' Discuss.

In this essay, I will argue that while the 'but for' test for causation (that D's tort will only be held to have caused C to suffer a particular loss if that loss would not have occurred in the way it did but for D's tort) is not a necessary nor sufficient test for causation, it should not be abandoned.

The 'but for' test in action

Let's begin with a few examples of the 'but for' test being used to demonstrate that the defendant's tort did not cause the loss of which the claimant is complaining, with the result that the defendant was *not* held liable for that loss. In *Barnett* v *Chelsea & Kensington Hospital Committee*, the defendant doctor negligently failed to diagnose that three workmen who had turned up to his hospital were suffering from arsenic poisoning, from which they subsequently died. It was held that the defendant's negligence had not caused their deaths: they would have died anyway, even if the fact they were suffering from arsenic poisoning had been diagnosed. In *Calvert* v *William Hill Ltd,* the claimant lost a huge amount of money placing bets with the defendant bookmakers. The defendants – having been previously requested to do so by the claimant – had agreed to close down the claimant's bet-making facilities with them, but had failed to do so. It was held that the defendants had owed the claimant a duty of care not to accept his bets, but it was further held that the defendants' breach of that duty of care had not caused him any relevant loss: if he had not been able to place bets with the defendants, he would have placed the same bets with someone else and lost the same amount of money as he did with the defendants.

Not necessary

In some cases, the 'but for' test does not have to be satisfied before a defendant will be held liable for a particular loss that the claimant has suffered:

(A) Overdetermination cases

In these types of cases D1 and D2 have each committed a tort in relation to C, and C has suffered some kind of loss as a result. Each tort would have been sufficient on its own to produce the loss that C has suffered, so each of D1 and D2 can argue that 'Had I not committed my tort, C would have still suffered the loss that she did.' Such an argument will always fail: D1 and D2's individual torts will always be held to have caused C to suffer the loss that she did, and C will be entitled to sue each or both of them in full for compensation for that loss. For example, in *Baker* v *Willoughby,* D1 negligently injured C's leg so that it became practically useless to C; four years later D2 shot C in the same leg in the course of a Post Office robbery, so that the leg had to be amputated. D1's claim that 'Had I not negligently injured C's leg, C would have lost the use of his leg four years later anyway, so I can't be liable for the loss of the use of the leg for more than the four years before it was shot' was rejected by the House of Lords. D1's tort was held to have caused C to lose the use of his leg for the rest of his life, not just for the four years before C was shot.

I will discuss below whether the overdetermination cases reveal some underlying flaw in the 'but for' test of causation; but the justice of not applying the 'but for' case in overdetermination cases is plain. In a case where C has suffered a loss which D1's tort or D2's tort would have been

>

sufficient to produce, it would be obviously unjust to allow each to rely on the other's tort to escape being held liable to C.

(B) Lack of proof cases

The same sort of consideration led the House of Lords in *Fairchild* v *Glenhaven Funeral Services* to rule that in a case where C contracts mesothelioma in her lungs as a result of being exposed to asbestos by two tortfeasors – D1 and D2 – but scientific uncertainty makes it impossible to tell which exposure caused the mesothelioma, and makes it impossible even to assess the probabilities that it was D1's rather than D2's exposure which caused it, C will be allowed to sue both D1 and D2 for her mesothelioma. But unlike the overdetermination cases, in *Barker* v *Corus,* the House of Lords ruled that D1 and D2's liabilities would be proportionate to the amount of asbestos they exposed C to – so they would be liable on an aliquot, rather than in solidum measure. This ruling was overturned, so far as mesothelioma cases were concerned, by the Compensation Act 2006. However, *Barker* will still apply to any other *Fairchild*-type cases which do not involve mesothelioma. There is currently a debate over whether – in light of the Supreme Court decision in *Sienkiewicz* – *Fairchild* does apply to any other cases of uncertainty over causation that do not involve mesothelioma. It is submitted that it does apply in a case like *Cook* v *Lewis* where two hunters negligently fire towards the same area, and a gamekeeper in that area is hit by one shot, and it is impossible to tell from which hunter's gun the shot came (or to say that it was more likely than not that it came from one hunter than another). In such a case, it is submitted, each hunter will be liable for 50 per cent of the gamekeeper's injuries. The injustice of allowing the gamekeeper to go without a remedy when we know one tortfeasor was responsible for it outweighs the injustice of holding a tortfeasor liable for an injury that he may not have caused at all.

Not sufficient

Even in cases where the 'but for' test is satisfied, a given defendant may still be held not to have caused the claimant to suffer the harm of which the claimant complains.

(A) No material increase in risk cases

There are situations where the claimant's harm will be merely a coincidental result of the defendant's tort. An example is provided by *Chester* v *Afshar,* where the defendant doctor failed to warn the claimant of the

2 per cent risk of paralysis that was involved in her having a particular operation. That was negligent, and unfortunately for everyone involved, that risk materialised after the claimant's operation. The claimant's paralysis would not have happened but for the doctor's negligence: had he warned her of the risk, she would have delayed the operation to think it over further and when she eventually had it, the probability would have been overwhelming that she would not have been paralysed. However, the paralysis was merely a coincidental result of the defendant's negligence: it was just bad luck that the one time he failed to warn a patient of this risk, the risk materialised. The failure to warn had no effect on the size of the risk. In *Chester,* all of the Law Lords agreed that the fact that the defendant's negligence did not materially increase the risk that the claimant would be injured made her claim problematic: the fact that the 'but for' test was satisfied was not enough to entitle her to recover. However, three of the Law Lords thought that on policy grounds, the normal rule that a merely coincidental result of a defendant's tort will not be held to have been caused by that tort should be set aside.

(B) Break in the chain of causation

Even if the claimant's loss would not have resulted but for the defendant's tort, the defendant's tort will still not be held to have caused the loss if something happened after his tort that also contributed to the claimant's loss in such a way that it broke the chain of causation between the defendant's tort and the claimant's loss. For example, if D beats C up so that C is lying unconscious in the street, and T takes advantage of that to steal C's wallet, D's battery will not be held to have caused C to lose his wallet, even though C's wallet would not have been stolen but for D's beating C up: T's deliberate, voluntary, informed and unreasonable decision to steal C's wallet will have broken the chain of causation between D's battery and the loss of C's wallet.

Abandon 'but for'?

The fact that the 'but for' test is neither a necessary nor sufficient basis for finding that the defendant's tort caused the claimant harm is no reason for abandoning it. The 'but for' test expresses a fundamental point about why tort law cases give rise to causation issues. If you have committed a tort in relation to C, you have something to answer for, and something to make up for. But if your tort has made no difference to C's health or wealth or standing in the community then you don't have very much to

>

make up for. You might still be required to make some token gesture of regret for the mere fact of committing your tort through paying C nominal or vindicatory damages, but that is all you can be required to do where your tort has made no essential difference to C. It is only where your tort has had an adverse effect on C that C can call you to do more for him, to make up for the consequences of your tort, and put him in roughly the same position as he would have been in had you never committed your tort.

Some thinkers on causation would acknowledge this point, but would argue that the 'but for' test should be abandoned as an inaccurate guide as to when a tort can be said to have made a difference to the position of the victim of that tort. For example, some argue that the 'but for' test on causation should be replaced with the 'NESS' test, according to which D's tort will be held to have caused C to suffer a particular loss if D's tort was a necessary element in a set of circumstances that were sufficient to bring about the loss that C has suffered. My view is that these calls are misplaced and that the NESS test does not do a better job than the 'but for' test at identifying in what situations someone's tort can be said to have made a difference to the current position of the victim of that tort. For example, in a case where D1 and D2 independently put poison in C's fish tank, and D1 puts 100 units of poison in the tank, and D2 puts 0.1 units of poison in the tank, and the fish in the tank could only be affected by the poison if more than 60 units were put in the tank, the NESS test implies that D2's putting poison in the tank has caused C's fish to be poisoned – as there is a set of circumstances (D1's putting 59.9 units in the tank, and D2's putting 0.1 units in the tank) where D2's putting 0.1 units of poison in the tank would have been sufficient and necessary to bring about the result that C's fish were poisoned. This seems wrong. D2 did wrong by putting poison in the tank, but his wrong had no effect on C. As a result, D2 does not have anywhere near as much to make up for with C than D1 does. The 'but for' test recognises that, but the NESS test does not.

Have you ever heard the story about Michelangelo and the angel? One of Michelangelo's friends was admiring a sculpture of an angel that Michelangelo had carved, and asked Michelangelo what was his secret for creating such an amazingly life-like sculpture. Michelangelo replied, 'I saw the angel inside the block of marble and I carved until I set him free.' For me, that story expresses an important lesson about writing essays. A great essay will make you feel like it was just waiting to be written. All the author did was serve as a channel for getting that essay out of the ether and down onto paper. You should aim in your essays to try to achieve the kind of naturalness and flow and inevitability that will make the reader think, 'It never could be any other way' (which are the final words on the Beatles' *Sgt Pepper* album). Whenever your essay starts getting really gnarly and complicated, stop and think – What am I doing wrong here? Because you are doing something wrong. You just have to put your finger on it, and stop doing it and get back to writing something clearer, simpler and cleaner.

All this talk about essays makes me think that it might be an idea to give you some tips on writing dissertations. A lot of universities now make their students write dissertations as part of their course, or at least give their students the option of doing one of their papers in the form of a dissertation. The trouble is, I've never written a dissertation in my life. But I know a guy who has, and he'll be able to give you some tips. In the meantime, I'll think about what advice I could give you on answering problem questions – the other main type of question, other than essay questions, that you will be expected to answer in your exams.

All best wishes,

Nick

Writing a Dissertation

26

- From: Jason Varuhas [dearnick@pearson.com]
- To: Brown, Alex
- Subject: Writing a Dissertation

Dear Alex,

Nick has asked me if I could give you some tips on writing a dissertation. I'm more than happy to help out. Many of the tips that Nick has given you in his letter on writing an essay – for example, in respect of writing style – will come in handy when you come to writing a dissertation. However, dissertations differ in a number of respects from essays. For example, they are markedly longer (generally between 8,000 and 15,000 words). You will have a longer period of time to write the dissertation (perhaps the whole academic year). The dissertation will probably not be designed to assess what you have learned over a course, but is rather a self-directed project. You will be required to conduct your own research in order to write a dissertation, and you may be asked to decide upon your own dissertation topic. In general, you will likely have greater freedom to shape your approach to the topic and your line of argument than in a course or exam essay. There is also a greater expectation that your piece of writing will put forward original ideas and arguments, and entail original research.

What follows are a number of key points that you need to bear in mind if you ever have the pleasure of writing a dissertation.

Picking a topic

The first task is to decide upon a topic. This decision is of the utmost importance, because it will shape the destiny of your entire project. Now you may have a topic set for you. In this case, you will probably still find the points in this section helpful, not least because set topics can deliberately be framed in broad terms to allow students the freedom to take their own distinctive 'angle' on the dissertation topic. For example, a topic such as the following allows for a range of different angles to be taken: 'Parliament ought to be sovereign. Discuss.' The process of deciding the 'angle' you take or the 'focus' of your dissertation will likely be similar to the process someone goes through in selecting and refining a topic for themselves.

Interests: yours and others'

The topic should be one that interests you. If a topic bores you, you may find it difficult to motivate yourself to spend long hours researching it and thinking about it. In contrast, if you are interested in a topic, you are more likely to find the process stimulating and will get more out of it (and probably produce a better dissertation). Two further points. First, note that an interest in a subject is not the same as feeling passionate about a subject. There is no rule against researching something that you have strong feelings about. However, there is a greater risk that you may not bring an objective mind and scholarly approach to your research. It is generally the case that people write their best work about topics they find intellectually stimulating and interesting, but which they come to with no strong views one way or the other. Second, if you are set a topic that does not initially appeal to you: give it a chance. Most topics become far more interesting once you get 'stuck in' and you may find your own 'angle' on the topic which you find stimulating. If the topic still does not appeal to you, then simply treat the dissertation as a means to an end, get on with the job, and do the best that you can; at the very least it will be a character-building exercise, and you will learn a great deal from the process, whether you are enthused by the topic or not.

In selecting your topic it may be worth thinking about whether there will be a wider interest in your topic. A good piece of work is a good piece of work regardless of whether there is a wider audience for it. However, consideration of whether there is likely to be a wider audience for your work is relevant if you would like to eventually submit your dissertation or a revised version of it for publication, say, in a student law review. Thus, you may want to consider whether and how your proposed topic links in with contemporary academic debates, whether it addresses a significant issue which is likely to come before the higher courts, or whether it relates to ongoing debates about possible legislative reform. However, don't spend too much time speculating about whether a topic is likely to be of wider interest. If a dissertation presents an original, thought-provoking and well-researched argument it ought to be of interest to others who are academically minded, regardless of the specific subject-matter it addresses, while the most important thing is what *you learn* through the dissertation process.

Originality

A critical consideration in deciding upon your topic is the degree to which any given topic affords the opportunity for original thinking and research. This is important because, all things being equal, you will receive a higher grade if your dissertation evinces original thought; the grading system rightly places a premium not only on your ability to understand legal materials but also your ability to formulate and develop new ideas and arguments. More generally, research which advances legal knowledge is clearly far more valuable than research that does not.

Having stressed the importance of originality, it is important to emphasise that you ought to have realistic expectations of yourself. No one expects an undergraduate dissertation to present some novel theory that will unify the whole of the law of obligations, or settle disputes about the basis of law. You can produce good, original and thought-provoking research without revolutionising legal thought. Indeed, there are dangers in seeking to be too profound, in that you may end up 'overreaching', and confusing yourself and your audience.

There are various sources of originality. You may choose to analyse a novel legal development which has not yet been the subject of serious analysis, such as an emergent line of cases or a new statute. You can adopt a new approach to analysing an established area of law, such as an historical analysis of how the body of law has developed over time, or a comparative approach which considers how different legal systems approach the same legal issue. You may contribute an innovative line of argument to a pre-existing legal debate, or provide an original critique of an established line of academic thinking about a particular subject.

Viability

However interesting and original a topic, it must also be viable. The viability of a topic is determined by whether it is possible to write a good dissertation on that topic given certain parameters, the most important being time frame and word limit. To illustrate this point let us consider the following possible topics:

1 A critical evaluation of the law of damages across the law of torts.

2 A critical evaluation of the law of damages in the tort of false imprisonment.

3 A critical evaluation of the damages principle in *R (Lumba) v Secretary of State for the Home Department* (a case in the field of false imprisonment which holds that where the claimant suffers an unlawful imprisonment on the facts, and therefore establishes liability for false imprisonment, they may nevertheless be denied substantial damages if the defendant – often a public officer or public authority – in theory had the power to detain them lawfully).

Assuming a word limit of 8,000 words, topic (1) ought to be rejected as simply not viable. Any attempted analysis of the law of damages across the whole of tort law, including negligence, nuisance, defamation, the trespassory torts, the economic torts, and statutory torts, could only be done very superficially, and therefore very badly, within 8,000 words. Further, it would take far longer than one academic year to conduct the research required for this topic, bearing in mind the time you need to dedicate to other courses and extra-curricular commitments.

Therefore the choice is between (2) and (3). In making this choice, we face an inevitable trade-off between 'breadth' and 'depth'. This trade-off ought in general to be resolved in favour of depth, and thus in favour of topic (3). You will usually find that what, on the surface, may appear to be the narrowest of topics will end up raising a plethora of complex and interesting issues, and that the broader your topic, the more difficult it will be to engage in the topic as thoroughly as you might a narrower topic.

Let us take topic (2) as an example. The law of damages within false imprisonment is a large body of law. It includes rules and principles relating to compensatory damages, exemplary damages and nominal damages, including those rules and principles which govern when each type of damages ought to be awarded and the assessment of quantum. That this is a large body of law will cause significant problems within an 8,000-word dissertation. On the one hand, there is a risk that you will spend a significant portion of the dissertation describing what the law of damages is, leaving yourself too few words to conduct a thorough critical examination of the state of the law. In this way you will have deprived yourself of the opportunity to demonstrate to the examiner your capacity for original criticism. On the other hand, in seeking to leave yourself enough words in which to do a thorough job of critically evaluating the relevant rules and principles, there is a risk of presenting an overly simplistic description of those rules and principles, for example by passing over the reality that the law is not clear in certain respects. Not only is superficial description of the law a cause for concern in itself, but analysis based on an account of the law which passes over its nuances and complexities is unlikely to be convincing.

Reading and talking

In order to identify a potential topic or range of potential topics and test it/ them against the above guidance, you must know something of the substance of the topics under consideration. It is, therefore, important that you do some general reading around the topics before settling upon one. You might want to read relevant parts of a leading textbook, the leading case in the field or a significant recent case, and/or two or three leading articles. This will help you to determine whether you are interested in the topic, and will also help you to start thinking about the line of argument you might take in the dissertation.

Importantly, the more you know about a field, the more you will be able to refine and narrow your topic. So, you may start with a general interest in the law of damages in tort, then, after reading a number of articles or cases, find that you are particularly interested in the law of damages in false imprisonment. From a little further research you may discover that the case of *Lumba* raises very interesting and significant issues, and has not yet been the subject of serious analysis in the literature, leaving the door open for an original contribution.

You will also find it helpful to talk to people about your topic, in particular your dissertation supervisor, who will be able to offer you some 'inside knowledge' of the field. They may be able to advise you how much has been written on your proposed topic, suggest how you might narrow your topic, and/or suggest some initial readings. Although your supervisor is your first port of call, you may also want to test out your proposed topic and line of argument on a range of people with some knowledge of the relevant legal field, including fellow students. This advice – about talking to people – is equally relevant to the process of researching and writing the dissertation. Some of the most significant insights I have had in relation to my research have come during a 'stop and chat' (to quote Larry David) in the corridor or over a coffee with a friend.

At the end of this process of talking, reading and reflecting you should have a clear research question, to which your dissertation will seek to provide an answer. Illustrative examples are: (1) 'Should the law of negligence recognise that public authorities owe duties to take reasonable steps to protect an individual where the relevant authority knows of a real and immediate threat to that individual's life from the acts of a third party?'; (2) 'Should exemplary damages be available for a breach of contract?'; and (3) 'Should the law require a newspaper to give prior notice and an opportunity to comment to an individual before the paper publishes a story about that individual?'

● Finding an approach to the topic

Intimately connected to the task of deciding your topic, and of ongoing relevance as you research and write the dissertation is your *approach* to your topic (in more technical terms, your *methodology*). An awareness of different approaches is important for several reasons. First, your approach will often provide the original element of a dissertation. Second, you need to have a clear idea of the approach or approaches you are taking in order to articulate clearly your central lines of argument. Third, although the matter cannot be discussed in detail here, different approaches entail different techniques and different potential pitfalls, and it is important that you are aware of the salient features of any particular approach so that you implement the approach rigorously and avoid any pitfalls. Before going on I should note that, while it is important that you are aware of your approach, it is equally important that you do not become fixated upon it, otherwise you may never get on with the tasks of researching and writing the dissertation.

This letter is not the place for a detailed exposition of the different approaches that may be taken to legal research. However, it is worth briefly outlining a few different approaches in order to illustrate the variety of approaches open to you. I focus particularly on doctrinal and theoretical approaches as these are the most common approaches to legal research.

Doctrinal approaches

The most prevalent form of legal research is 'doctrinal'. This approach involves the examination of legal 'doctrine' – doctrine being the body of rules and principles based in legal sources such as legislation and judicial decisions. Usually a doctrinal researcher is concerned with one body of doctrine, such as the law of contract or administrative law, and typically a particular sub-body of doctrine within these general fields, such as the law of expectation damages or of legitimate expectations.

The first task of a doctrinal scholar is to state what the law is.

This may seem an easy task on the face of it but it will require the researcher to locate all of the relevant case law, read those cases and distil the rules and principles enunciated therein, and sort that collection of rules and principles into a coherent and intelligible order, so far as one exists. In undertaking this task, you must be open to the possibility that the law, shaped as it has been by many hands over many years, may in certain respects lack coherence or consistency; if this is the case you ought to say so. A common challenge in doctrinal research is that it can often be the case that the law is not clear in some respect – for example because of apparently conflicting precedents, or because an issue has not been squarely addressed by the courts, leaving scope for argument and original analysis as to what the best account of the legal position is.

There may also be different ways of sorting and categorising the law, and scope for original argument as to which way is best, while we may wish to categorise the law differently for different purposes. For example, you might provide a statement of the law according to the nature of legal obligations, for example separating tort from contract on the basis that contract is based on consent whereas tort is an obligation imposed by the law. Another person might structure their statement of the law in a different way – for example according to the subject-matter that the law addresses, such as the law as it relates to ships or to the media.

The second task of the doctrinal scholar is one of critical analysis, and in particular critical analysis by reference to established legal values, such as coherence, consistency, rationality, and justification. For example, you might criticise a Supreme Court judgment in the field of false imprisonment because it is inconsistent with an important line of House of Lords precedent which was not considered or which you believe was misinterpreted by the Supreme Court; you might criticise the judgment on the basis that it creates an incoherence in the law by establishing a new rule that cannot be reconciled with other long-standing rules within false imprisonment; or you might criticise the decision on the basis that the reasoning adopted by the Court is unconvincing – for example because it is based on arguments that on closer analysis conflict with one another, or premised upon assumptions which can be shown to be false.

Theoretical approaches

Another common approach to legal research is 'theoretical'. Theory is a difficult idea to pin down, but one useful way of thinking about it is in terms of levels of abstraction. When we are engaged in theoretical research we are seeking to explain or evaluate the law from a bird's eye view, and therefore will be less engaged with the messy detail of particular legal rules and principles. The bird may be flying higher above the doctrinal landscape, such that our analysis is far removed from doctrine and we are considering the law in much more abstract or philosophical terms. For example, we might ask what the possible rationales are for having a law of vicarious liability in tort, or why damages should ever be an appropriate legal remedy. The bird may be flying lower, in which case our theory will engage more closely with doctrine. For example, a dissertation may argue that we can explain the significant doctrinal features of the tort of false imprisonment by reference to the distinctive underlying function of the tort, which is to afford strong legal protection to the fundamental right to liberty. Note that although the dissertation will be more engaged with doctrine, it is concerned with 'significant features' of doctrine, such as whether liability is in general strict or fault-based or whether the tort is actionable without proof of loss, rather than the outcomes of particular cases or the intricate details of particular rules.

Other approaches

There are many other possible approaches. You might undertake *comparative* research. For example, you might consider how different legal systems approach analogous legal issues, assessing the degree of divergence or convergence among the relevant legal systems, and seeking to understand why, for instance, different approaches may have emerged, given distinctive contextual features within each jurisdiction. You may take an *interdisciplinary* approach, using insights from other disciplines to help analyse legal issues. Thus, we might consider research into behavioural psychology in assessing the claim that the prospect of damages liability for defective products may incentivise product manufacturers to take more care in the production of their goods. You might take an *historical* approach, considering how changing social, economic and/or political conditions have shaped the development of a particular body of legal doctrine over a particular period of time. Or you might prefer a *contextual* approach, considering how legal rules operate in context. For example, a researcher may want to examine whether and how public officials take into account human rights law in exercising their powers, discretions and duties. This sort of research will usually require *empirical* research such as conducting interviews with officials, or spending time at a public authority observing bureaucratic behaviour.

Combining approaches

In a great many dissertations a number of approaches will be utilised. For example, we will need to know what the law is, using orthodox doctrinal techniques, before we are able to develop a theory to explain the law. In conducting a critical analysis of a new rule enunciated in a recent Supreme Court decision, we may wish to look at the approach taken to the same legal issue in other comparable common law jurisdictions, such as Australia or New Zealand. The courts in these jurisdictions may have adopted a different rule, and you might find that the courts' reasoning helps to demonstrate the weaknesses of the UK Supreme Court's approach. You may wish to critically examine a court's reliance on the argument that the imposition of a duty of care on a police authority will help to incentivise good practice within the police forces. On the one hand, you may criticise the court's reasoning on the basis of established legal values, for example on the basis that the use of policy arguments may undermine the coherence of the law of negligence. On the other hand, you may also wish to criticise it on the basis of empirical studies which demonstrate that the effects of imposing liability on police forces are not at all clear, suggesting that the court's assumption that imposition of a duty will have positive behavioural effects may be misplaced. Thus different approaches can be combined to powerful effect. However, it is important to remember that in order to avoid confused analysis you need to have a clear idea of when you are utilising one approach or the other.

Positive and normative analysis

Lastly, I ought to draw your attention to one significant distinction which cuts across all of the aforementioned approaches and with which all legal researchers ought to be familiar. That is the distinction between *positive* and *normative* analysis. Put simply, positive analysis is an analysis of what the law *is*. Examples of positive analysis include (1) the doctrinal task of describing what the law of false imprisonment is, and (2) the development of a theory which seeks to explain the law of false imprisonment at a certain level of abstraction. Normative analysis is an analysis of what the law *ought* to be. In other words, it is a prescriptive form of analysis, seeking to argue for what the law should be ideally. Examples of normative analysis include (1) the argument that the damages principle in *Lumba* ought to be rejected because it affords insufficient protection to liberty, and (2) the argument that courts ought not to be given the power to strike down legislation passed by Parliament because this would be inconsistent with democratic principles. Importantly, an 'ought' cannot be derived from an 'is'. Thus, it does not follow from the fact that the damages principle in *Lumba* is the law of England at the moment that it represents a sound or justifiable principle, such that it *ought* to be the law of England. Equally, when you are conducting positive analysis, such as articulating a theoretical explanation of the law, you must be careful not to allow your explanation to be captured by your normative views of what the law ought to be, as this would be to confuse two different tasks – explanation and prescription. This is not to say that positive and normative analysis cannot feature in the same dissertation; they almost always will. For example, you might engage in a doctrinal analysis of a body of case law and find that conflicting rules emerge from two lines of authority, and then go on to articulate a normative argument as to which rule you think ought to be preferred. The important point is to keep clear in your mind and in your dissertation when you are engaged in positive analysis and when you are engaged in normative analysis.

● Researching the dissertation

So let's assume you now have your topic and an idea of the general approach you want to take to it. The time has come to begin the process of researching and writing the dissertation. I will discuss researching and writing the dissertation separately – research in this part and writing in the next – as some structure has to be imposed on the discussion. However, it is worth recording that it is somewhat artificial to address the two separately. The two processes are inherently intertwined (as I say below, the writing process is a core aspect of the research process), and while you must begin the research process before you start writing, putting pen to paper by no means marks the end of the research process.

Sourcing material: one thing leads to another . . .

When faced with the task of researching a new topic, it can be difficult to know where to begin. It is easy to respond by procrastinating. This ought to be avoided. In my experience, the best way to get into a topic, particularly if you are unfamiliar with it, is to begin with reference works. These include textbooks, legal encyclopaedias such as *Halsbury's Laws of England,* or research handbooks, such as the *Oxford Handbook of Empirical Legal Research* or the *Oxford Handbook of Comparative Law*. Thus, your first step might be to go to the library and round up a number of the leading textbooks and reference works in your field.

Just as valuable as the material in the text of these reference works – if not more valuable for your purposes – are the references in the footnotes. Within the footnotes you might find references to books which specifically address your topic, which you can then look up and read. From reading the relevant chapters in a number of reference works you will start to see which journal articles are frequently cited and relied on by the authors. Some textbooks even have a list of further reading at the end of each chapter, which can be a useful resource for locating relevant articles and books. You can seek out articles, either by looking up the paper copies of the journals in the library or searching online resources such as Westlaw or HeinOnline. From reading the reference works and scouring the footnotes you will similarly get a clear idea of the leading cases in your field of research, which you can then look up in the law reports or in legal databases such as Westlaw or LexisNexis.

One thing will lead to another. From each book, article, or case you look up in the course of your initial 'research sweep' you will learn more about your topic and find references to further relevant material. You will also start to get a feel for resources which are likely to be a source of further relevant material. For example, if you are researching a topic in constitutional or administrative law, you will no doubt begin to see that many of the articles written on your topic appear in specialist public law journals such as *Public Law* and *Judicial Review,* while some appear in generalist journals such as the *Modern Law Review* or the *Cambridge Law Journal*. You can then use Westlaw or LexisNexis to conduct keyword searches of past volumes of these journals, or you can go to the library shelves and flick through the contents pages of past volumes to see if you can spot anything of interest.

As your research goes on, you will find that you move from general reading around a subject to distinct 'streams' of research, each of these streams correlating with sub-topics in your dissertation. For example, part of your dissertation may address how the area of law you are looking at has developed over time, which will require you to locate and read the most important cases decided in the field. Another aspect of your dissertation may be a critical comparative analysis of the area of law you are concerned with, meaning that you will need to read relevant cases from other jurisdictions. Yet another aspect of your dissertation may be a consideration of different theoretical explanations of that area of law, such that you need to locate and read articles and books written by leading theorists in the field.

It is important to emphasise that there will often be material that is relevant to your topic which is not contained in textbooks or in articles written within your field of research. Indeed, an important source of originality in a dissertation will be the inclusion of original research. For example, there may be cases which bear on your topic which have not been analysed in the existing academic commentary and which have been missed in later court decisions, or there may be literature in other fields, such as political science, which might help you to analyse your topic in an original way. A key to conducting this sort of original research is to figure out where to look.

If you are seeking out relevant political science literature, you can start with reference works in political science, such as the *Oxford Handbook of Political Science,* and move on from there. If you are searching for cases, you will probably need to run keyword searches on electronic legal databases, and carefully analyse the results for relevant material. There are other facilities on electronic databases which can be helpful. For instance, if you uncover a relevant case on *Westlaw* it is possible to bring up a screen which lists later cases which have applied or distinguished that case. There may be specialist law reports which report cases in your field of interest, have reasonably detailed tables of contents, subject indexes and helpful headnotes, and which you can spend an afternoon flicking through at the library. For example, if you are researching an area in constitutional or administrative law, the *Administrative Court Digest,* which provides summaries of public law cases, would be useful; while if you are researching European human rights law, the *European Human Rights Reports* would be an important resource.

While the most common sources in conducting legal research will be primary materials such as cases and legislation, and secondary materials such as textbooks and journal articles, you should bear in mind that the sources that you ought to consult will vary with your approach and the subject-matter of your dissertation. For example, if you are conducting historical research, you may have to visit archives, such as the National Archives, to go through historical papers, such as letters or newspapers, read autobiographies or biographies of important figures from the period you are researching, and/or read cases and academic commentary from the relevant time period. If you are conducting research into the meaning of provisions of a statute, you may have to consider background material, such as policy documents prepared by the government department which was responsible for proposing the legislation, the record of the Parliamentary debates on the Bill (known as 'Hansard'), and the reports of Parliamentary Committees which scrutinised and heard evidence on the Bill. Some legislation implements reports produced by bodies such as the Law Commission or *ad hoc* special inquiries set up by the government. Helpfully, much of this material is published online on governmental or Parliamentary websites.

An important and challenging aspect of the research process can be keeping up with current developments. You cannot rely on textbooks or articles to provide an up-to-date statement of the law or repository of academic commentary; as soon as a textbook or article is published, it is almost invariably out of date. New judgments are constantly being issued, new statutory measures enacted, new government reports produced, and new academic commentary published. It is critical that you do not miss out on an important development such that your dissertation appears incomplete, while a new case or article might greatly aid your argument.

There are various ways to try to keep up to date. As regards articles, you can periodically check the latest issues of the leading journals in your field, while there are various updating services which you can sign up to and through which you will be sent an email when a new issue of a selected journal is published. In terms of textbooks, it is now very common for textbook writers to publish online updates or small hardcopy supplements which detail the most recent developments in the field. It is worth noting that new editions of a textbook may come out while you are writing your dissertation, and it is important to refer to the most recent edition. In terms of cases, a very helpful resource is the *Weekly Law Reports,* which reports the most recent and important judgments and is published on a weekly basis, such that there is only a short lead time between the issuance of a judgment and its appearance in the *Reports.* Similarly helpful are the 'recent decisions' lists on the Bailii website, and the 'decided cases' section of the UK Supreme Court website – you can find the relevant links by going to the 'Useful links' section on Nick's website (www.mcbridesguides.com).Various update services are available, for example through electronic databases such as Westlaw, which usually give you the option of subscribing to content based on your interests. Although many posts on legal blogs resemble sound-bite journalism rather than academic scholarship, they can be useful in drawing your attention to recent developments in your field – again, Nick's website will give you some relevant links. You can also sign up to relevant Twitter feeds, such as that of the UK Supreme Court (@UKSupremeCourt).

From this discussion it ought to be apparent that to conduct effective legal research you will need to know how to use a law library and how to use electronic databases. It is important that you seek out and get the training that you need. A linked point is that librarians and IT helpdesks are there to help you and, although they cannot do the research for you (regrettably), you should not hesitate to ask for help if you are having difficulty locating books on fifteenth-century tort law or struggling to find an obscure case on Westlaw.

Focus, reflection and when to stop reading

So far we have discussed how you might go about locating relevant sources. What follows are a few tips you should bear in mind when it comes to reading the material you have located.

First, it is important to read key materials, such as leading cases in your field of research, *for yourself,* and not rely on secondary accounts in articles or in textbooks. Each person understands material slightly differently and each person reads material for a different purpose. A textbook writer is concerned to state the most important rules and principles within a particular field of law. This is different from your task, which is to answer a specific research question. There may be material in a particular case that is relevant to your topic which is not flagged up in textbook discussions of the case; the textbook writer may not have considered the material relevant to his or her task, or possibly overlooked the material. Furthermore, you can only truly understand a body of law if you have spent time reading the relevant cases for yourself, and taken time to form your own understanding of the rules and principles they entail. This sort of deep understanding will ultimately shine through in your dissertation and can only increase your grade.

Second, it is imperative that you read with focus. In other words, when you are reading an article or case you should constantly be thinking about how the material you are reading is relevant to your overarching research question. Linked to this point is that you should try to make notes of points in the article or case that are relevant to your topic. It is all too easy to spend days and days reading material, find a number of really important points in the material, and then not remember where you saw those points or simply forget the points because of all of the information you have taken in. When you are reading, you will often find that you have your own important observations on the material, which you will ultimately wish to include in your dissertation. It is critical that you note these points down. In this respect, it is a good idea to have a dedicated Word document in which you record any important ideas you have while reading.

Third, take time to reflect. Each time you read a case or article, you need to afford yourself sufficient space and time to properly digest and think about what you have read – particularly if the case or article is of particular significance to your project. You need to think about the relevance of the material to your topic, the implications it has for your argument and, if it is salient, how you might integrate it into your dissertation. During periods of reflection, you may feel like you are not achieving a great deal because you are not physically doing anything and you are not producing tangible outcomes. However, these periods of reflection are fundamental aspects of the research process; no one has ever produced a great piece of scholarship without engaging seriously with their source materials and thinking deeply about their subject. Indeed, deep reflection is a fundamental characteristic of academic scholarship, which marks it out from other types of writing.

Fourth, you need to know when to stop reading. It is difficult to give concrete advice on this issue because the decision to stop reading will require the exercise of your own judgment. However, a few points may help you to make the call. In making your judgment, it is important to bear in mind the reality that there will always be more to read and you could, in truth, go on reading for years. It is also important to bear in mind that you need to afford yourself enough time to reflect on all of the material you have read, how it all fits together and relates to your argument, and to write the dissertation. A reasonable litmus test for when you ought to stop reading might be when the readings start to get repetitive, because you are coming across the same sorts of arguments and observations being made over and over again by different authors. Put another way, you ought to stop reading when you become acutely conscious of 'diminishing returns' – i.e. the marginal benefit you derive from each extra piece of reading is getting less and less.

● Writing the dissertation

So you have a topic, you have an approach, and you have made progress with your research. All that is left to do is write the dissertation. In this part I will provide some tips on structuring the dissertation, and important aspects of the writing process. Nick's letter on essay-writing addresses a number of topics that are also relevant to writing a dissertation, including the importance of writing clearly, paying attention to details and not avoiding a fight (i.e. ensuring your argument is balanced). In the interests of avoiding repetition I will not be addressing those points again here, and I would recommend that you read Nick's letter together with what follows.

Structuring the dissertation

Superficially, the structure of a dissertation appears to be a formal aspect of writing; it is about the form that the argument takes rather than the substance of the argument. Nonetheless, there is a strong interrelationship between the structure of your argument and its power to convince. Rational arguments that are likely to convince a reader generally follow a rational structure, and confused arguments which are likely to baffle a reader generally follow a confused structure.

As you go through the initial research process and you reflect upon what you have read, you will find that you have a collection of arguments that you wish to make. Your task is to forge these arguments into a coherent and rational structure. One way of forging this structure is to think about the sub-questions or sub-topics you need to address in order to answer your overarching question.

Let's say your overarching research question is a normative inquiry into why Parliament ought to be the ultimate arbiter of human rights issues, rather than the courts. At first blush, you might say that to convincingly establish this argument you need to demonstrate that

1 there are good arguments against the judiciary having the power to finally determine human rights issues;

2 that arguments in favour of the judiciary having this power are not convincing;

3 there are good arguments for why Parliament ought to be given this power; and

4 arguments against Parliament having this power are not convincing.

Now it may be that these broad divisions provide a natural way of sorting your collection of arguments into the sections. You might then possibly go on to identify sub-sub-topics within each sub-topic and further divvy up your arguments.

On the other hand, the way you first identify your sub-questions or sub-topics may not provide a natural template for your structure. Going back to our example, if you find that all of your arguments – or a significant proportion of them – cut across sub-topics (1)–(4), it may lead to a great deal of repetition if you address the same arguments in different sections, and it may be difficult to decide where particular arguments ought to be housed. It may also be artificial to split your discussion of important lines of argument across different sections. For instance, if you find that many of your arguments in favour of Parliamentary supremacy also serve as strong arguments against judicial supremacy, it might be artificial to deal with these arguments in different sections. You may thus find that another way of stating your sub-topics or sub-questions may provide a more natural template for your structure. For example, instead of defining your sub-topics according to type of argument (e.g. arguments for Parliamentary supremacy or against judicial supremacy) you might define them according to subject-matter. Thus you might say that to make out your overarching argument you need to (a) consider the relative democratic legitimacy of Parliament and the courts; (b) consider the relative institutional competence of Parliament and the courts; and (c) compare and contrast the practical consequences, negative and positive, of each different model. You might find that categorising your arguments into a structure which mirrors these sub-topics helps to resolve the problems of repetition and artificiality. Sorting your arguments in this way does not mean that the task of making out propositions (1)–(4) is no longer relevant, only that you will seek to establish these propositions in the course of considering each subject matter.

Structure changes over time. The way you think you might structure your argument after your initial research sweep may be quite different from your final structure, and you need to be flexible enough to allow your structure to evolve for the better. Returning to our Parliamentary supremacy example, you may at first contemplate a structure modelled on sub-topics (1)–(4). However, as you continue your research, you may find that groups of arguments related by subject-matter, such as democratic legitimacy or practical consequences, clearly start to emerge, such that subject-matter becomes a viable basis for your structure, and boasts the benefit of solving the problems you might have been having with the structure based on (1)–(4).

The use of headings and sub-headings is critical in structuring a piece of writing that is between 8,000 and 15,000 words. Indeed, a good litmus test for whether your dissertation follows a rational structure will be whether an observer familiar with your field of research can garner a rough idea of your overarching argument from a list of your headings. A common question asked by students is how many headings you ought to have and how many levels of headings are permissible. You will have to rely upon your own common sense. For example, it seems fairly obvious that you will be more likely to use three levels of headings (i.e. major headings, sub-headings, and sub-sub-headings) in a 15,000-word dissertation than in an 8,000-word piece of writing. In terms of the frequency of headings, a general piece of guidance is that you should avoid having so many headings that it disrupts the flow of your argument, while you should only generally be using headings, or at least major headings or sub-headings, to demarcate divisions between *groups* of arguments, grouped according to some feature such as subject-matter, rather than to separate single arguments.

Aspects of the writing process

So you have a preliminary structure for your dissertation, but when should you start filling in the detail? *As early in the process as is possible.* There is a common tendency amongst students to postpone the beginning of the writing process until they feel they have read everything relevant to their topic. One can understand the tendency but it ought to be consciously resisted.

One of the most important reasons for beginning the writing process as early as possible is that it is an integral part of the research process. In your mind, your arguments may be crystal clear and utterly convincing. However, it is inevitable that, when you try to commit them to paper and reason them out fully, you will begin to see gaps that need to be filled, issues that are more complex than you originally thought, and weaknesses in your argument that need to be addressed. It is typically the case that each of these issues will require you to get back to the grindstone and conduct further, more detailed, and more focused research, possibly in fields you may not have otherwise thought you needed to research. If you delay the beginning of the writing process for too long, you risk not allowing yourself sufficient time to conduct the further research required to get your argument up to scratch.

Another closely linked reason not to delay writing is that you need to afford yourself adequate time to reflect on what you have written if you are to produce top-quality scholarship. Draft sections which at first appear difficult to fault may, upon further reflection or upon completion of further research, require refinement or a complete re-write. Indeed, it is hardly ever the case that the first draft of any part of the dissertation will end up, in its original form, in the final version. It may take reasonably long periods of reflection, time away from the dissertation, and discussions with others about your research for you to recognise weaknesses in your argument, which aspects of your argument are redundant or add little, ways in which your argument may be further strengthened, or how your argument might be presented more tightly and succinctly. In this way, the writing process is an iterative process, and each successive draft should entail a further refinement of your argument. You may feel that discarded arguments and drafts which end up needing a complete re-write denote wasted time and effort. This is not the case. Those discarded arguments and abandoned drafts are part and parcel of writing scholarly work. If we all managed the perfect argument the first time round, writing a dissertation would not be much of a challenge (and there would be a lot more good scholarship out there than there is!).

Strive to write with focus. Always bear in mind the task at hand: that you are seeking to convincingly answer your research question. Every word, sentence and paragraph that you write ought to be geared to that task. Common temptations which can work against focused writing include the temptation to include material because you personally have found the material interesting or stimulating, or the temptation to demonstrate the breadth of the research you have done or that you understand a difficult idea. You ought to resist these temptations because succumbing to them will not help to make your dissertation more convincing; indeed the inclusion of material that is not relevant will probably annoy the reader, disrupt the flow and momentum of your argument, and most significantly, entail the squandering of words that could have been used for original analysis and argument, and that would have helped you to more convincingly address your research question. Someone once usefully described this insight to me as separating 'your story' from 'the dissertation story'. You will learn a great deal over the course of the research process, but you should only include material that advances your argument.

A dissertation is not a whodunit novel. You should not keep your reader in suspense as to the conclusions you are arguing towards or why you are advancing particular arguments, holding this information back for a thrilling finale in the last few pages. You should always signal to the reader why you are making a particular set of arguments, the conclusion you are arguing towards, and how this set of arguments advances the dissertation's central argument. This helps the reader to follow your line of argument; no reader enjoys wading through a great deal of written material with no idea as to why they are being asked to read it or where the analysis is going. This advice applies to the dissertation as a whole and also to sections of the dissertation.

Thus in the Introduction to the dissertation you should clearly state the over-arching argument you are advancing and the conclusion you are arguing towards: in a dissertation considering whether Parliament or the judiciary should be supreme over human rights issues, you should state clearly in the Introduction whether you will be arguing that Parliament or the judiciary ought to be supreme. Equally, in each major section of the dissertation, you should include a relatively brief introduction stating what you will be arguing in that section and why.

Make your argument. It is not uncommon for students to get bogged down setting out the views of other commentators on a particular topic, with the consequence that their own 'voice' is lost and the dissertation resembles a review of relevant commentary rather than a clear and coherent argument. As a general proposition, the views of other commentators ought not to be the centrepiece of your dissertation. Rather, your argument should be the centre-piece, and you ought to discuss or criticise the views of other academic com-mentators *in the course of* advancing your own argument.

Define key concepts. If a particular concept, which is open to various inter-pretations, such as 'democracy' or 'rights', is fundamental to your overarching argument – for example, if you are advancing a rights-based conception of the democratic state – you ought to stipulate definitions of these concepts. Otherwise the examiner might infer that you have not done the relevant research and thinking required to properly define these terms. Further, your argument will inevitably be weakened to the extent that reliance on unde-fined terms plunges it into ambiguity.

Footnoting is a key feature of dissertation-writing that distinguishes it from a short course or exam essay. When should you footnote? In general, footnotes should be used only to make necessary citations rather than to provide addi-tional text. If a footnote includes text that is more than a couple of lines long, you will need to consider whether the inclusion of that text is necessary for your argument. If it is, it should go in the main text; otherwise it should prob-ably be cut out. An exception applies where (1) the text is important to your argument but (2) including it in the main text would seriously disrupt the flow of your argument. Examples of when it is necessary to footnote include the citation of authority in support of a legal proposition in the main text, and citation of an article or book from which you have sourced an idea or concept referred to in the main text. It may also be permissible to use foot-notes for illustrative purposes. For example, in the main text you might state: 'Many have argued against the availability of exemplary damages for breach of contract'. In the footnote you could list a number of the articles or books that propound this argument.

Students often ask what style they should follow in referencing cases or articles. Some law schools have their own style guide which you will be required to follow. Others do not. In the latter case the key is to ensure your referencing style is consistent, and that you include sufficient information to enable readers to easily locate the material you are citing. It will probably be a good idea to have a look at and possibly follow the citation style adopted in one of the leading journals, such as the *Cambridge Law Journal* or *Law Quarterly Review*. A last point on referencing is that, if you are citing a case or an article for a specific point, which you often will be, you ought to provide a pinpoint citation such as a reference to the paragraph number of the case in which the point is made or the relevant page number of the article. This will make it easier for the reader to locate the relevant passage you are referring to and reassure the examiner that you have in fact read the material you are citing.

A final piece of advice before you get started: the dissertation is first and foremost a learning process. No one is born an expert researcher or with the gift of polished prose. Skills of research, writing and argumentation can only improve with experience. The dissertation provides you with an opportunity to gain such experience. Make the most of it.

All the best,

Jason Varuhas

Discussing Problem Questions

- From: Nicholas J. McBride [dearnick@pearson.com]
- To: Brown, Alex
- Subject: Discussing Problem Questions

Dear Alex,

A problem question presents you with a set of facts and asks you to discuss what legal conclusions we might be able to draw from those facts.

What sort of legal conclusions we are seeking to reach in doing a problem question will depend on what kind of subject the question relates to. When you are doing a criminal problem question, you will usually be expected to look at a set of facts to determine who, if anyone, has committed a crime on those facts. When you are doing a tort problem question, you are usually looking to see what remedies, if any, are available to someone who has suffered some kind of harm. There are a number of different issues that you might be expected to address in doing a contract problem question: it could be asking you whether a particular promise is legally binding, or whether someone can get out of a deal that has now proved to be a bad deal for them, or what remedies are available to someone who wants to hold someone to a deal, or what the parties to a deal are required to do for each other, given the nature of that deal and its terms. And so on, across the range of different subjects you will study at university.

In what follows, I will give you some general guidance on how to do problem questions. I must emphasise that the general guidance below does *not* apply in the case where you are a doing a tort or criminal problem question. There are specific methods for doing tort or criminal problem questions, and

I'll explain those later on in this letter. But I'll start by setting out a general approach to doing legal problem questions.

● General guidance

The most basic word of advice I can give you on doing problem questions that are not tort or criminal problem questions is: *identify the issue or issues that the examiner wanted you to discuss in answering the question.* Issue spotting is a crucial talent that you need to develop if you are going to do problem questions well. Here are a couple of different approaches to issue spotting that you might want to adopt in doing a problem question. (I emphasise again that what I am about to say does *not* apply to tort or criminal problem questions – nothing I say in this section is of any relevance to doing those kinds of questions.)

(1) Get inside the head of the examiner

One way of issue spotting is to ask yourself – why did the examiner think this was a *good* problem question to set? What sort of difficulties did the examiner think that this problem question gave rise to? For example, consider the following mini-problem:

> Henry was infatuated with Jenny and would do whatever she told him to do. She used her influence to get him to make a loan to her friend, Clara, who was setting up a hairdressing business. Clara's business is now in severe financial trouble. Advise Henry.

Why did the examiner think this was an interesting question to set? He or she could hardly think that there was an issue here over whether Henry could get out of (or, in lawyer's language, rescind) the contract of loan between him and Clara, as it's fairly obvious that he could (provided Clara knew or ought to have known that Henry was only lending her the money because Jenny wanted him to – which she almost certainly did). No – there must be something more here that the examiner wanted you to address. And in fact there is: Can Henry sue Jenny for compensation for the loss that he is likely to suffer as a result of lending money to Clara? That's the issue you would need to focus on if you were doing the above question.

In trying to get inside the head of the examiner in order to see why he or she thought their problem question was a *problem*, it is useful to approach the question on the basis that *every word counts*. Ask yourself – why did the examiner write the problem question in the way he or she did? For example, in the above question, why didn't the examiner make it that Henry was infatuated with Clara and Clara used her influence over him to get him to lend her money for her business? Why is Jenny in this problem question? In thinking about that, you would quickly come to the conclusion that Jenny is actually crucial to the resolution of the issue that the examiner wants you to address in doing this question. However, I should enter two words of caution here. The first is that not every word *actually* counts. For example, the fact that Clara was setting up a *hairdressing* business, as opposed to some other kind of business, is not really relevant – it's just there for colour. So you should only *presume* that every word counts. The second point is that examiners sometimes plant red herrings in their problem questions – words that are designed to mislead the less able students into thinking that the problem question raises a particular issue when in fact it doesn't. I strongly disapprove of this practice, but it does happen. So you have to be tough-minded in spotting issues in a problem question – if you think a particular feature of the problem question is irrelevant to its outcome, then stick by your judgment and don't second guess yourself. (Though you may want to explain why that feature of the problem question is irrelevant – I address this point later on in this letter.)

(2) What do the parties want?

Another way of spotting the issues raised by a problem question is to ask – What do the parties want? This will usually give you a good clue as to what sort of issues the problem question has been set up to raise. For example, in the mini-problem set out above, if Henry wants anything, he wants to get his money back. Henry won't be able to get his money back from Clara because she's evidently got no money. If he wants to get his money back, he has to go against Jenny and find some way of arguing that she should compensate him for the loss he has suffered on his deal with Clara. So focusing on what Henry wants allows us to spot the issue that the examiner really wanted us to address in doing this problem question.

Once you have identified the issues raised by the problem question (and it would be a good idea to start your answer by saying something like 'This question raises three issues: (1) . . . (2) . . . (3) . . .' to make it clear what those issues are), then you need to discuss what the law says about those issues. Some academics advocate that you do this by identifying the *rule* that governs that issue, and then *apply* the rule to that issue, and in light of that reach a *conclusion* as to what the law says on that issue. This is the so-called 'IRAC' method of answering problem questions – spot the Issue, state the Rule governing the issue, Apply the rule, and reach a Conclusion. I'm not much of a fan of IRAC because: (1) it is not often clear whether there *is* a rule that governs the particular issue you want to resolve; and (2) there may be more than one rule that is relevant to the resolution of a particular issue. For example, the real difficulty that the problem question about Henry gives rise to is whether there exists any rule that would allow Henry to sue Jenny for compensation for inducing him to make a bad loan to Clara. There is a rule that wrongdoers should compensate the victims of their wrongs, but even if that rule doesn't apply here it may still be the case that there is another rule that will help Henry out.

My preferred approach to discussing the issues raised by a problem question is to focus on the possible *legal arguments* that are relevant to those issues, and work through those arguments – explaining whether they are valid or invalid. For example, in the problem question involving Henry, having first identified the issue you are going to discuss as being whether Henry can sue Jenny for compensation for inducing him to make a bad loan to Clara, you should then go on to say that there are two possible bases for Henry's claim: (1) that Jenny committed a legal wrong in using her influence over Henry to get him to lend money to Clara; and (2) that even if Jenny's use of her influence didn't amount to a legal wrong, she is still liable to compensate Henry for any losses suffered by him as a result of getting him to act in a particular way. And you would then discuss whether either of these arguments is valid or not. So the first argument turns on whether there is any legal support for the idea that someone who possesses influence over someone else has legal duties not to exercise that influence to the detriment of the person being influenced. The second argument turns on whether there is any legal support for the idea that if A induces B to act in a particular way, and B suffers loss as a result, A can still be held liable for that loss even if A didn't do anything wrong to B in inducing B to act in the way B did. Answering the problem question properly will require you to address both of these points, through detailed discussion of the law as it stands at the moment.

So that's the general approach that I think you should adopt to doing legal problem questions. There are a few more general tips that I want to give you on answering problem questions, but first I'll keep my promise to set out the specific approaches you should adopt in doing a tort problem question and a criminal problem question.

● Doing tort problem questions

The basic approach that you should adopt in doing a tort problem question is this:

1 Identify a claimant (someone who wants to sue someone else for compensation).

2 Identify a defendant whom that claimant might be interested in suing.

3 Identify a cause of action (tort or rule of liability) under which the claimant might try to bring a claim against the defendant.

4 Consider whether, given what has to be established for the claimant to bring a claim under that cause of action, the claimant has a good claim against the defendant.

5 If the claimant does not have a good claim under that cause of action, go to step (6). If the claimant does have a good claim under that cause of action, go to step (7).

6 Go back to step (3) and identify another possible cause of action that the claimant might have against the defendant. If you have exhausted all possible and plausible causes of action that the claimant might have against the defendant then go to step (7).

7 Go back to step (2) and identify another possible defendant whom the claimant might be interested in suing, and repeat steps (3), (4) and (5) in relation to that defendant. If you have exhausted all possible and plausible defendants that the claimant might want to bring a claim against then go to step (8).

8 Go back to step (1) and identify another possible claimant, and repeat steps (2), (3), (4) and (5) in relation to that claimant. If you exhausted all possible and plausible claimants that might want to bring a claim in the problem question you are considering, then stop writing.

This is all a bit abstract, so let's apply this approach to a particular problem question:

> Jeffrey, a world famous violinist, decided to put on a concert to raise funds for his local school, Sunshine College. He hired out a hall owned by the local council for the night of the concert. Admission was free but notices outside the hall informed concertgoers that they would be
>
> **>**

invited to make a financial contribution to Sunshine College at the end of the concert. Concertgoers were also warned that 'No responsibility is accepted for the safety of concertgoers' person or property while they attend the concert'. It turned out that far more people wanted to attend the concert than there were seats in the hall and many people had to stand crowded together at the back of the hall while Jeffrey performed. Matilda, an 80 year old, turned up late and, as no one offered her a seat, she had to stand at the back of the hall. She soon fainted due to the heat and cramped conditions and twisted her ankle in the fall. Donald, a music lover who came to the concert but never intended to donate anything to Sunshine College's funds at the end of the concert, wandered round the hall in an attempt to find a seat and in doing so slipped on a patch of oily water which was in one corner of the hall; he grazed his knee as a result. Jeffrey had arranged with the council that their cleaning contractors – Easy Clean – would clean the hall before the performance but no one in the council had bothered to tell Easy Clean, and Jeffrey had been too busy on the day of the concert to notice that the hall had not been cleaned. The concert was a resounding success and £8,000 was collected at the end of the concert. The money was collected by Wendy, a friend of Jeffrey's. Wendy then promptly disappeared with the money.

If you follow the approach to doing tort problem questions set out above, your problem answer will be structured as follows, with the following headings:

Matilda's claim for compensation (for fainting and twisting her ankle)

(1) Claim against Jeffrey

(1a) in negligence

(1b) under the law on occupiers' liability

(2) Claim against Sunshine College under the law on occupiers' liability

Donald's claim for compensation (for grazing his knee)

(1) Claim against Jeffrey

(1a) in negligence

(1b) under the law on occupiers' liability

(2)   Claim against Sunshine College under the law on occupiers' liability

(3)   Claim against Easy Clean in negligence

Sunshine College's claim for compensation (for loss of the £8,000)

(1)   Claim against Wendy in conversion

(2)   Claim against Jeffrey in negligence

There are three points I want to make in particular about this method of doing tort problem questions.

1   *No issue spotting.* Under this approach, you don't need to do any issue spotting. All you have to do is identify a claimant, someone they may want to sue, and – and this is the crucial bit – a tort or rule of liability under which they might bring their claim. Then all you have to do is apply the law on when one person can bring a claim for that tort or under that rule of liability to the situation you are considering. It is the law which will tell you what the issues are that you need to be considering – you don't have to spot them yourself. So when you are doing a tort problem question, let the law guide you as to what you should be discussing. Don't try to decide for yourself what you need to be talking about: just let the law take you home.

2   *But lots of issue weighing.* Having said that, you need to decide how much time you are going to spend on each of the issues raised by the problem question. The key here is to dispose quickly of the issues that can be straightforwardly resolved, and invest most of your time on the tricky issues that require a lot of discussion of the relevant authorities and academic opinion. Five minutes spent writing about one such tricky issue will get you far more credit with the examiner than five minutes making a point about the law that is so obvious it could be made in one or two lines.

3   *The need for rigour.* This takes me onto the third point, which is the absolute need to be completely rigorous in doing tort problem questions. If you are not going to miss any issues, you have to consistently follow the step-by-step approach to doing tort problem questions set out above *and* you have to apply the law rigorously in determining whether a particular

claimant can bring a claim against a particular defendant. This is the primary reason why students find tort problem questions much more difficult than any other problem questions, even though the fact that they don't have to spot any issues should make tort problem questions much easier than other problem questions. Students find it very, very hard to be rigorous in answering tort problem questions. But you have to learn: a lack of rigour in doing a tort problem question is always fatal, without exception.

● Doing criminal problem questions

The basic approach that you should adopt in doing a criminal problem question is this:

1 Identify a defendant (who might be charged with having committed a criminal offence).

2 Identify an offence that he might have committed.

3 Consider whether he has committed the *actus reus* of that offence. If he has, or arguably has, go to step (4). If he has not, go to step (6).

4 Consider whether he has the *mens rea* of that offence. If he has, or arguably has, go to step (5). If he has not, go to step (6).

5 Consider whether he has a defence to being found guilty of committing that offence. If he does, then go to step (6). If he does not, then conclude that he will probably be found guilty of committing that offence, and go to step (7).

6 Conclude that the defendant will probably not be found guilty of the offence you are considering, and go to step (7).

7 Go back to step (2) and identify another offence that that defendant might have committed and repeat steps (3), (4) and (5) in relation to that offence. If you have exhausted all possible and plausible offences that that defendant might have committed, then go back to step (1) and identify a different defendant who might be charged with having committed a criminal offence, and repeat steps (2), (3), (4) and (5) in relation to that defendant. If you have exhausted all possible and plausible defendants, then stop writing.

Again, this is a bit abstract so let's apply this approach to a concrete criminal problem question:

Albert was HIV+. No one other than Albert and his doctor was aware of that fact. Albert had always fancied Britney, who was engaged to Charlie. One night Albert and Britney were at a party together, and Albert spiked Britney's orange juice with very strong alcohol. Britney got very drunk and told Albert that she was scared that Charlie had been unfaithful to her. Albert lied to Britney, telling that he had found out that Charlie had slept with Britney's best friend, Debra, a week ago. Albert suggested that Britney get her revenge by having sex with him. Britney said, 'Okay – but only if you use protection and pay me £300 cash in advance.' Albert didn't have the money, but approached his very rich friend Ernest, who was also at the party, and told him, 'Look – I'm in a tight spot. I sold some cocaine to a friend of mine and he was caught by the police, and he's threatening to tell them I was his supplier unless I pay him £500 tonight.' This was untrue. Ernest – who has often bought drugs from Albert – went to a cashpoint and withdrew the £500 needed, which he then gave to Albert back at the party. In the meantime, Albert bought a pack of condoms from a machine, using counterfeit coins to buy them. Albert then gave Britney £300, telling her, 'Don't tell Ernest I gave you this – I borrowed some money off him recently by telling him I was strapped for cash, and he wouldn't like it too much if he heard I'd been flashing this much money around.' Britney then had sex with Albert. Unfortunately, the condom they used was defective and Britney is now HIV+.

If you follow the above approach to doing criminal problem questions, then your answer to this question will be structured as follows, with the following headings:

Albert

(1) Maliciously administering noxious substance with intent to injure, aggrieve or annoy

(2) Fraud (by lying to Britney)

(3) Fraud (by lying to Ernest)

(4) Theft of £500 given him by Ernest

(5) Fraud (by using counterfeit coins)

(6) Rape

>

(7) Causing a person to engage in sexual activity without consent

(8) Malicious infliction of grievous bodily harm

Britney

(1) Handling stolen goods

There are three points I want to make about this method of doing criminal problem questions.

1 *No issue spotting.* Again, if you follow this method of doing criminal problem questions you won't need to spot any issues. Rigorously asking whether the defendant had the *actus reus* and *mens rea* of the offence you are considering, and whether the defendant had a defence will highlight for you all the issues that the examiner meant you to consider in setting the problem question. But you will again have to decide how much time you will spend on each issue (spending more time on the tricky issues than the obvious ones) and . . .

2 *The need for rigour.* You have to be rigorous. You can't afford to get the law wrong in stating what the *actus reus* or *mens rea* of a particular offence is, and you can't afford to jump around and consider whether the defendant has the *mens rea* for a particular offence before you consider whether he or she has committed the *actus reus*. Once again, a lack of rigour will inevitably prove fatal.

3 *Limitations.* While the basic approach to doing criminal problem questions in this way is sound, it should be noted that there are times when you have to make a slight adjustment in applying it. First, there are some offences that you can't divide neatly into having an *actus reus* and a *mens rea* – gross negligence manslaughter (committed when (1) A breaches a duty of care; (2) A's breach causes B's death; (3) A's breach is so serious as to be worthy of punishment) and constructive manslaughter (committed when A commits an unlawful and dangerous act which causes B's death) are two good examples. But in those cases, you simply apply the definition of the offence. Secondly, when you are considering whether a defendant has committed an offence *as an accomplice,* you can't ask whether the defendant has committed the *actus reus* and *mens rea* of that offence, but must instead apply the rules on when someone can be held to have committed an offence that someone else committed on the basis that he was an accessory to that

offence. (But if you are going to consider whether a defendant is guilty of an offence as an accomplice, make sure you first consider whether some other defendant is guilty of that offence as a principal offender!)

● Further words of advice

Now that I've laid down the basic guidelines for doing *all* problem questions, here are some further tips for doing *any* problem question.

(1) Uncertainty in the law

Don't be afraid of admitting that the law on a particular issue is uncertain. Sometimes a problem question will be set precisely because it raises issues on which the law is uncertain. As I said in my letter to you on 'Some Traps to Avoid', uncertainty in the law is due to vagueness, gaps, or contradictions in the authorities. So long as you can argue convincingly that the law on the issue you have to consider is uncertain because of one of those three factors, then you shouldn't be at all afraid to say that it's difficult to know how the problem question would be resolved. Having said that, you shouldn't rest content with simply saying that the law as it applies to your problem question is uncertain because it might say *x* or it might say *y* – you should then go on to explain: (i) what the answer would be to your question if the law said *x* and what the answer would be if the law said *y*; and (ii) whether you think the law *should* say *x* or *should* say *y*, and why.

(2) Uncertainty in the facts

> A is thinking of buying a particular car. B tells A that if A buys the car, B will service the car for free every year. A buys the car.

Whether B is bound by his promise to service A's car will depend crucially on whether B was making his promise with the object of inducing A to buy the car. So if B was selling the car, then B would be bound. But if A and B were friends, and B made the promise over a drink in the pub, and B was relatively indifferent as to whether A bought the car or not, then B would not be bound by his promise. The examiner hasn't supplied you with that information. So you have to say, 'We need more information as to the circumstances under which B made his promise before we can determine whether B is bound by his promise.' But don't just say that – explain what information is required, and what the legal position would be in the various different scenarios in which B might have made his promise.

(3) The importance of being straightforward

In answering a problem question, just focus on the facts that have been set and don't make any unlikely suppositions as to what might have been going through the actors' heads when they acted as they did. For example, in the criminal problem question above involving Albert, the examiner has not said that Albert was aware that the condom he used in having sex with Britney was defective – so answer the question on the basis that he wasn't aware. It's highly unlikely that the examiner deliberately meant to leave that issue open for you to discuss what the position would be (i) if Albert was aware; and (ii) if Albert was unaware. So why make more work for yourself – and overcomplicate, and possibly screw up, your answer – by considering possibility (i)? One way of helping you decide whether or not you were 'meant' to consider a particular possibility is to ask yourself, 'If I don't consider this possibility, will the examiner think "I can't believe they didn't consider that issue!"?' If the answer is 'no', then don't consider it. Remember that problem questions are, by and large, set so that the best answers to those questions will be easy to identify. So the best answer is unlikely to rest on some very subtle and obscure interpretation of the facts.

(4) Negative outcomes

It can be just as important, in answering a problem question, to show that you are aware that applying the law to a particular question will result in a negative outcome, as it is to show when you are aware that applying the law to a particular question will result in a positive outcome. What I mean by that is that sometimes a question will be set in order to test you on whether you can see that a particular claim *can't* be brought in that situation, or whether you can see that a particular defendant *isn't* guilty of a particular offence. For example, when Britney has sex with Albert without knowing of his HIV+ status, the examiner might have been expecting you to consider (however briefly) whether or not Albert committed the crime of rape in having sex with Britney. The fact that the cases are clear that Albert did *not* commit rape in this situation is irrelevant: the examiner wants to know whether you know that. On the other side of the divide, my plan for answering the tort problem question on Jeffrey's violin concert doesn't consider whether anyone might be able to sue Sunshine College on the basis that they are vicariously liable for any torts committed by Jeffrey. This is because it seems so obvious that Jeffrey isn't an employee of Sunshine College that it's highly unlikely the examiner who set this problem intended someone answering this question to make that point. When it comes to negative outcomes, it can be difficult to judge whether the examiner wanted you to show that you were aware that the law did *not* make anyone liable in a particular situation. If in doubt, err on the side of caution and mention the fact that a particular actor is not liable – you can only get marked on what you write on the page, and you won't get credit for points that you saw but thought were too obvious to mention.

(5) Obvious points

But where a point is obvious, don't dwell on it. It is tempting, when you see a point that you are sure of, to make the absolute most of it before going onto more uncertain terrain – but once a point is made and established, you won't get any credit for writing any more about it.

(6) Headings

It is *so* important, in writing a problem answer, that you use headings to organise your answer. This helps you keep track of what issues and points you have considered so far, and – more importantly – what you still have to consider. And it helps the examiner see what issues and points you have dealt with, and encourages him or her to give you proper credit for dealing with them. Do everything you can to show off how good your answer is – don't make the examiner do *any* work to see that you have provided a proper, comprehensive answer to the question set.

(7) Statutes

You will almost certainly be allowed to take a statute book into the exam with you. Given this, *do not* – I repeat, *do not* – copy out any provision from the statute book in doing a problem answer. You won't get any credit for doing so, and you will waste valuable time. Simply get on with applying the provision in the statute book to the situation you are presented with, and in your answer refer just to numbered sections or sub-sections from the statute book to make it clear which bit of a statute you are referring to, or applying. For example, here's a bit of a model answer I wrote for my students to a problem question which raised the issue, among other things, as to whether A could sue B, the owner of a dog ('Rex') which had a tendency to attack people wearing red, under the Animals Act 1971:

> In order to sue B, as the keeper of Rex (because owner: s. 6(3)(a)), A has to show (because Rex does not belong to a dangerous species) that his bite marks were a result of Rex having a characteristic that: (1) meant that he was likely to cause the kind of harm that A suffered, or that if he caused A that kind of harm, it was likely to be severe (s. 2(2)(a)); (2) was not normally found in dogs, or only normally found at certain times or in certain circumstances (s. 2(2)(b)); (3) was known to B. There seems no problem arguing that all these conditions are satisfied. Rex's tendency to attack people wearing red meant that he was likely to cause A the kind of harm that A suffered; it was an unusual characteristic for dogs to have; and it was known to B.

(8) Cases

There's an old story about either the Oxford or Cambridge Law Faculty (I can't remember which) that students were told to underline the names of cases they mentioned in their problem answers so as to make it easier for the examiners to mark their answers – the more cases they mentioned, the higher their mark! Of course, things are very different now, but it couldn't do any harm to underline the names of the cases you mention in your problem answer, just to make it clear how many you have actually mentioned . . . And talking of names of cases, sometimes you just won't be able to remember the name of a particular case that you want to refer to. That's absolutely fine: simply mention some other feature of the case to identify it. So, for example, *Felthouse* v *Bindley* (1862) is a case which always seems to be sitting just beyond the reach of my memory when I want to refer to the case which helped to establish that you can't accept an offer of a contract through silence. But if the name of that case eludes you as much it does me, it's perfectly fine to refer to it instead as 'the case where the uncle offered to buy his nephew's horse'.

(9) Advise the parties

Oftentimes a problem question will say 'Advise the parties' or 'Advise X'. (Our first problem question, involving Henry, did precisely that.) When a problem questions tells you to 'Advise X', it is *not* telling you that you should write in your answer, 'I would advise X that . . .'. What it means is that you should answer the question looking at it from X's point of view – that is, you should consider what claims, if any, X can bring; or what offences X might have committed. It follows that a question that instructs 'Advise the parties' isn't saying anything – there is no particular angle or point of view from which you should approach the question, and you should simply answer it straight-forwardly, adopting the approaches set out in this letter.

● Essays or problem answers?

My students sometimes ask me, 'If we have a choice in the exam between doing an essay or a problem question, which should we go for?' It's tricky.

I think it's easier to write an essay that will get a high mark than a problem answer that will get a high mark. (I'm talking here about discursive essays, which are the principal kind of essays you might get asked to write in an exam.) The reason for this is that the general standard of essay writing among students is so low that an essay that is well-written, interesting and well-argued will be seized on by the examiner with tears of gratitude and awarded with a very high mark.

In contrast, to get a high mark for a problem answer it's essential that you cover all the issues raised by the problem question and don't make a mistake in discussing those issues. If you miss even one issue or misstate the law on one point, that will drag your mark down. So I often compare writing a problem answer with defusing a bomb – one false step and it's all over. And when I'm marking a problem answer that has started off well, I often find myself holding my breath – I'm in such suspense to know if the writer is going to be able to get to the end of the answer without it all going horribly wrong. In contrast, if you make one weak argument in an essay that is otherwise of a high standard, the examiner will usually be indulgent and think, 'Well, so what if he or she made one weak argument? The overall standard was so good, this should definitely get a high mark.'

Given that, you might think my advice to my students would be to choose to do an essay over a problem answer every time. But there is a downside to that choice. It's this: marking an essay involves a lot more judgment on the part of the examiner than marking a problem answer. So if you write an essay, you're always taking a bit of a chance with what mark you get for it. It may be that your essay is, objectively, really good – but it's given a poor mark because it rubbed the examiner up the wrong way or because the examiner was in a bad mood when he or she marked it. In contrast, if you write a problem answer that covers all the issues raised by the question, does so in an intelligent way, doesn't misstate the law, backs up every legal statement by reference to a case or a statute – you can be sure you are going to get an excellent mark for your answer, whoever the examiner is.

To sum up, then: it's easier to guarantee a high mark for a problem answer than it is for an essay – you can never be sure that an essay you write will get a high mark. But, on the other hand, it is easier to get a high mark for an essay than it is for a problem answer.

So – what should you do if you have a choice between writing an essay and a problem answer? If you are confident that you could write a better essay than a problem answer (or vice versa), then obviously go for the essay (or problem answer, as the case may be). If you are so talented that you think you could do both really well, go for the essay if you don't think there's much chance that what you say will rub anyone up the wrong way. (You'll just have to take a chance on the examiner not being in a bad mood when he or she marks your essay.) If, on the other hand, what you have to say is quite controversial and might annoy the examiner if he or she takes a different view, there's no point in taking a chance – do the problem answer instead.

All best wishes,

Nick

Coping with Stress

- From: Nicholas J. McBride [dearnick@pearson.com]
- To: Brown, Alex
- Subject: Coping with Stress

Hey Alex,

Sorry to hear you've been getting stressed out, worrying about the upcoming exams. Please do bear in mind the following points: I hope they will help you feel a bit better about things.

The first thing I want you to remember is that it's not worth worrying about these exams: even if they don't go well, you're only in your first year at university and will have other chances to make up for how you've done. So try not to build them up in your mind as this huge make-or-break thing, because that's simply not the case.

And be positive! Don't run yourself down and start thinking that you're not going to be able to deal with these exams. Of course you are – there's absolutely no reason why you shouldn't be absolutely fine taking these exams, just like thousands of other people up and down the country who will be taking exams very similar to yours this summer. Don't build them in your mind into a bigger, or harder, thing than they are. Reassure yourself of this by having a look at the exam questions that were set in previous years. At first sight, they may look pretty intimidating and un-doable. But on a second look, you should find a way 'in' and figure out a good answer to most of the questions. This should calm you down a bit and help you to see that the forthcoming exams are the equivalent of a steep hill that you have to walk up and over, not a towering mountain.

And if you are feeling stressed out about things, whatever else you do, don't shut yourself away. There's a great temptation to think that no one else wants to know, or cares, how you're feeling and that even if they do, there's nothing they can say to you that will help you. Again, that's simply not the case. So it was good that you wrote to me – but also reach out to your personal tutor, and whoever's the main person in charge of your studies and see if they've got anything to say to you that will provide you with some help or reassurance. Also make it clear to your friends how you're feeling – they may feel the same way, and it will make you feel better to know that you're not on your own in this, and it will also make them feel better to know that they aren't alone either.

And don't forget to relax! One of the damaging things about stressing about exams is that it makes you feel guilty about taking time off to socialise with your friends, or go to the cinema, or just go mad clubbing. Any time you think about doing something like that, a little stress-related voice in your head will say, 'I CAN'T do that – I can't waste my time like that when I've got so much to do.' But you *can* and you *won't* be wasting your time. If, in a desperate attempt to obtain a washboard stomach, I decided to spend an entire day doing sit-ups, I wouldn't end up with a decent set of abs – but I would end up doing my abdominal muscles some severe damage. To exercise your muscles effectively, you need to give them a rest every now and then, to allow them to recover from the work you've been making them do. It's the same with your brain – it needs regular periods of downtime, if it's going to work effectively. So it's really important that between now and the exams, you regularly take some time off your studies and do something completely different. Don't allow your feelings of stress to put you off doing this.

Those are all fairly obvious points, all of which I hope you will take on board. But many students do follow all of the above advice, but still feel really high levels of stress. Why is this? I think part of the reason is that they don't understand where stress comes from, and so are ill-equipped to deal with it effectively. So – let's address this issue and see what comes of it. Why do people get stressed? Well, I think the answer is that people get stressed about things that are important to them but that they can't control. Stress is a reflex reaction to feelings of powerlessness over things that are important to you. You can test out whether this is true by simply thinking about your own feelings of stress. You're not getting stressed about whether you'll wake up late on the first day of the exams, or stressed that your pens won't work in the exams. That's because at the moment you are able to do something to something to stop those things happening: you can set loads of alarm clocks to wake you up on the morning of your first exam, and you can take loads of pens with you into the exam. But you *are* getting stressed over whether you'll 'freeze' in the exams and not do yourself justice, or whether the 'right' questions will come up in the exam. These are things that you have no control over, and that's precisely why you're getting stressed out about them.

This means that stress is a predictable emotion. You will be tempted to feel stressed if you feel powerless over something that is important to you. So stress isn't something that just happens – it happens for a reason. And if that's right, then it follows that you can take steps to avoid getting stressed about things. To demonstrate this point, let's take an easy example: you don't feel stressed *at the moment* about the possibility that you might wake up late on the first day of the exams. That's because you don't feel powerless to do something about that *at the moment*: you still have the chance to buy about five different alarm clocks that will guarantee you wake up at the right time on the first day of the exams. But if you have only one alarm clock in your room *the night before the exam,* then you may well start to feel extremely stressed about the possibility that that alarm clock will let you down and you'll wake up late. So avoid putting yourself in that situation of feeling powerless by buying an extra alarm clock *now* (if you don't have one), as a back-up, so that the night before the exam, you won't have anything to worry about. Similarly, concentrate on doing what you can do *now,* while you still have the chance, to work on things that will help you in the exam, like improving your essay writing and problem answering techniques, or your knowledge of the law. If you work to improve those things *now,* you won't spend the night, or the week, before the exam stressing over the fact that it's too late to learn how to write a decent essay or problem answer, or stressing over the fact that there are still huge holes in your knowledge of the law that you can't now make up because you've run out of time. These particular feelings of powerlessness are easily avoidable if you do something *now* to ensure that you simply won't have an occasion to feel them when the time comes.

Another reason why students feel high levels of stress is that they allow their feelings of stress to grow out of control. There are two main reasons why stress has a tendency to grow over time. The first is that stress encourages you to waste your time. Instead of using the time left to you before the exams to improve your chances of doing well in the exams by working on the things that you still can do something about, you instead spend your time worrying about things that you can no longer do anything about, or about things that you could never have done anything about. The second reason why stress grows is that when you realise how much time you are losing to stress, if you are unable to let go of your feelings of stress, then you will start experiencing feelings of powerlessness in respect of your stress (it's important to you to get rid of it, because it's using up your time unproductively, but you can't get rid of it), and as a result you'll start getting stressed about feeling stressed. And then you'll get stressed about feeling stressed about feeling stressed. And in this way a vicious upward cycle of stress develops.

Don't allow this to happen to you. Your feelings of stress can only grow if you allow them to distract you from what you have to do right *now,* which is *focus* on the things you can do between now and the exams to improve your position for the exams. So make a list of practical things you can do between now and the exams to help yourself do well in the exams, and concentrate on getting those things done. And, as you are doing these things, try to shut out any voices that may go off in your head, saying, 'But what about . . .?' and 'There's no point . . .' There *is* a point, and there is *nothing else* that you need to think about other than getting through your list of things that you can do to help yourself. Focus on that, and your feelings of stress won't be given a chance to grow.

If you follow all this advice, then you should feel *a lot* less stressed, both now and in the future, than you seem to be at the moment. But – and this is the final point I want to make – following the above advice will help you avoid *unnecessary* stress, but it won't mean that you'll *never* feel worried about things. There will always be some things that are important to you, and that you can't control. For example, if a firm offers you a job when you leave university, but makes the offer conditional on your getting a 2.1 in your final year exams, none of the advice above will help you avoid feeling *some* stress about whether you will get the 2.1 you need. That's because whether you get a 2.1 in your final year exams won't be completely under your control: the examiners will have the final say on that. If you want to avoid stressing about that kind of thing, the only way to do that is simply to let go of the worry. Try to train your mind to think along the following lines: 'I can't ultimately control whether the examiners will recognise all my efforts with at least a 2.1, so there's no point worrying about it. If I get a 2.1, all my worrying will have been for nothing. If, in spite of everything I've done to prepare for the exams, things don't work out and I don't get a 2.1, then there will have been nothing I could have done about that, and so again all my worrying will have been for nothing. So – I'll just let go of the worry and try and think of something else.' Some people find it helps while they try to think along these lines to do something symbolic to represent letting go of the worry – like writing the worry down on a piece of paper and burning the paper, or letting it float away on a stream. It sounds crazy, I know, but apparently it does help.

So – to sum up:

1 Get a sense of perspective: don't get worried about things that actually aren't that important.

2 Be positive: don't think of the obstacles you face as being bigger than they are, and don't think of yourself as being smaller than you are.

3 Don't lock yourself away: reach out to other people if you are feeling troubled – they want to help you.

4 Don't forget to relax.

5 Do what you can to improve your position between now and the exams so that you won't feel stress later on over things that you could have done something about earlier, but can't now do anything about.

6 Don't feed your feelings of stress by allowing them to distract you from doing the things you can do now to help yourself do as well as you can in the exams.

7 Try to let go of any remaining worry you feel about the things that you absolutely positively cannot do anything to affect: realise that there is no point worrying about the things you have absolutely no control over.

I hope all this helps you a bit. If you want to read anything further that might help you feel a lot calmer about things, I'd recommend the *Discourses* of a Greek philosopher called Epictetus. You may well think that a disabled slave who lived almost 2,000 years ago won't have much to say to you – but you'd be surprised. The U.S. Army makes its soldiers study Epictetus to train them to cope with stressful situations they may find themselves in (such as being captured and imprisoned by the enemy) – so you may well get something out of reading him as well. This is from the first chapter: 'What, then, is to be done? To make the best of what is in our power, and take the rest as it naturally happens.' Reading the *Discourses* helps you to do that: I strongly recommend it.

Be thinking of you,

Nick

Tips on Revising

● From: Nicholas J. McBride [dearnick@pearson.com]
● To: Brown, Alex
● Subject: Tips on Revising

Hi Alex,

Thanks for your e-mail. I'm glad you're now feeling a bit less anxious, and determined to get down to some serious revision for the exams. Okay – here are my tips on how to make the absolute most of the time remaining to you. You should be aiming in your revision to do two things: (1) get the details of the law, and ideas about the law, into your long-term memory; (2) improve your essay-writing and problem-answering techniques.

Both of these are crucial to your being successful in the exams. If you can't write good essays and problem answers, then you won't do well, no matter how much you might know about the law. If you don't know anything about the law, or have nothing to say about it, you won't be able to write good essays or problem answers, no matter how good your technique is.

You already know from everything I've already told you how to improve your essay-writing and problem-answering techniques: practice, practice, practice. But what's the best way of getting information about the details of the law, and ideas about the law, into your long-term memory? As I told you in my letter on 'The Challenges Ahead', the answer is: use the information, over and over again. This is just common sense. If you need to learn the layout of a town, you could spend hours and hours staring at a map of the town, trying to burn it into your brain. But why make it so hard on yourself? – Just walk around the town a few times, and you'll learn the layout of the town without even trying. Why do people who move to France learn in months to speak French far more proficiently than schoolchildren who can spend years trying to learn French and forget everything they've learned in half the time it took them to learn it? The answer is: people who move to France are using the language all the time, and that helps them pick it up so much more quickly than children who are taught French by being made to study it, rather than use it.

So if you can find ways in your revision of constantly using information about the law, that information will go into your head without your even realising it, or your having to try to remember it. But what ways are there of doing this? Well, that's what I'm here to tell you.

● The primary revision method

Your primary way of revising for the exams should be – writing answers to essay questions and problem questions that have been set in your university's exams in previous years. What you should do is this. If you want to revise a particular topic in, say, criminal law, look at the last five years' criminal law exam papers (they should be available in your University library, if not online), see what sort of questions have been set on that topic, pick a couple of questions that are fairly representative of the sort of questions that tend to be asked on that topic, research the hell out of them, both by using your existing notes and looking up new material (either in books in your Law library, or online), and then write some really good answers to those questions. As a revision method, this has some huge advantages:

1 The past paper questions alert you to what you really need to know about the topic you are revising, and so direct your revision to the most important issues relating to that topic.

2 Exams in some subjects tend to have the same sort of questions come up year after year – so if you can figure out how to answer a good selection of questions that have been set in previous years, that can really set you up to turn in some brilliant answers to the questions that are set in your exam.

3 In researching how to answer the past paper questions that you have chosen to do, you are using the information that your researches turn up because you will be constantly thinking about how the information that you are looking at relates to the questions you are going to answer; using the information in this way should help it get into your long-term memory.

4 In writing out answers to past paper questions, you will again be using the information that your researches have turned up, this time in the course of

writing your answer, and using the information in this way will again help it get into your long-term memory without your really trying.

5 By writing out answers to past paper questions, you will be improving your essay-writing and problem-answering techniques.

This last point illustrates why answering past paper questions should be your primary revision method. No other revision method combines the two things you should be aiming for in your revision – to get information about the law into your long-term memory, and improve your essay-writing and problem-answering techniques.

● Supplementary revision methods

Doing past paper questions is an effective way of getting information about the law into your long-term memory, but it's not the only way. I'd also recommend that you think about employing some of these other methods in the course of your revision. You'll note that all of them are geared around the idea of learning information by using it:

(1) Definitions

In some of your subjects, you will need to learn definitions. For example, if you are studying criminal law, you need to learn the definitions of all the offences that you are studying as part of your course. To learn a definition, first of all write it out as clearly as possible. For instance, if you are trying to learn the definition of the elements of the offence of maliciously wounding or inflicting grievous bodily harm, contrary to s. 20 of the Offences Against the Person Act 1861, this is not a clear definition:

> *Actus reus*: wounding or inflicting grievous bodily harm
>
> *Mens rea*: maliciously

This is not clear enough: we all know what wounding means, and we can all have a pretty good idea of what grievous bodily harm means, but what is 'inflicting' and what is 'maliciously'? A clearer definition will go something like this:

> *Actus reus*: wounding or causing grievous bodily harm
>
> *Mens rea*: intending to cause some physical harm, or being subjectively reckless as to whether your actions will cause some physical harm

Once you've got a clear definition, write it down in the middle of a piece of A4 paper (turned on its side), and then get jazzy with it! Have the facts and names of cases coming off the central definition to illustrate and support the key terms (for example, what case established that 'inflicting' means 'causing'? what cases said there was a difference? do these cases survive at all?). Draw the facts of the cases, if possible, rather than write them down – the added creativity involved in drawing should help fix the facts into your head. Around the edge of the paper, write down (or draw) some hypothetical situations and say whether an s.20 offence would be committed in those situations. Before you know it, and without even trying, the central elements in the definition will be fixed into your head.

(2) Cases

I've already given you some tips on remembering cases. But just to recap briefly, you will most effectively remember cases if you can arrange them into some kind of pattern. So think of issues or ideas relating to a particular subject that you are studying, write the issue or idea down in the centre of a piece of A4 paper (turned sideways), and then try to arrange as many cases as you can around that issue or idea. So, for example, the issue might be 'Is Parliament sovereign?' Write that down in the centre of a piece of A4 paper (turned sideways) and then think about all the cases that you've come across (and look for more that you haven't yet come across) and try to arrange them (with drawings or key words to illustrate their facts, or what they say) under a set of answers to the key question. So think about what cases take the line: 'An Act of Parliament will always be valid unless it is repealed by another Act of Parliament'; and what cases take the line: 'An Act of Parliament will not be valid insofar as it purports to bind future Parliaments, or change the rules governing how an Act of Parliament is passed'; and what cases take the line: 'An Act of Parliament will not be valid insofar as it contains provisions that violate the rule of law'; and what cases take the line: 'An Act of Parliament will not be valid insofar as an earlier Act provides that it will not be valid, and that earlier Act has not been expressly repealed by Parliament', and arrange the cases around the central issue 'Is Parliament sovereign?' according to what answer they support.

(3) Filling gaps in your knowledge

Make a list of issues or questions that you are hazy about, arrange the list into a rough order of importance, research the hell out of those issues or questions starting with the ones at the top of your list, and then write mini-essays or textbook entries about those issues or questions. Again, the process of researching and writing will help get the details relating to the issue or question you are working on into your long-term memory without your really trying. When you are doing this, concentrate in particular on issues or questions that tend to crop up regularly in the exams (for example, What counts as a non-natural use of land for the purposes of the rule in *Rylands* v *Fletcher*? or, When will someone's consent to having sex/being touched be so vitiated that they will not be regarded as having consented to have sex/be touched at all?) because they are issues on which the law is very uncertain or problematic. Use the past paper questions as a guide to help you with this.

● The importance of having a plan

Work out a revision plan for between now and the end of the exams. This is very important, for a number of reasons:

1 Having a plan will help ensure that you cover everything you need to cover between now and the exams. Haphazardly revising whatever you're in the mood for on a particular day will likely leave you with some big gaps in your knowledge and understanding.

2 Having a plan will give you a stimulus to work. You won't be able to put off revising a particular topic to another day if you can see that doing this will have knock-on effects on what else you will have time to revise before the exams.

3 Having a plan will help you not to panic about your revision. If you start thinking about everything you need to do between now and the exams to prepare for the exams, you will tend to feel overwhelmed and helpless. You need to stop thinking about everything you have to do, and just focus in on what you have to do today to get ready for the exams. Having a plan helps you to do this – it gets your mind off the bigger picture and helps you just to think about what has to be done today. Plus, having a plan is reassuring – it helps you to think that you know what you are doing, you are in control, and the possibility for things going wrong has been minimised.

So, sort out a plan for yourself. But to make a plan, you have to be prepared. You have to think about what topics you want to revise. You have to have gone through the past paper questions, and picked out some representative questions that you are going to attempt. You have to have thought about what other revision methods you are going to employ, and how you are going to use them. So take three or four days to do this, and then spend a day putting together your plan of attack.

In making your revision plan, make sure that you don't overload yourself. Don't give yourself four or five tasks to accomplish each day if you have no chance of getting through that many tasks. And leave yourself some room for things to go wrong. Have some free days scheduled where you can catch up on any aspects of your revision plan for which it turned out that you didn't have time. And on each day of your plan, give yourself some free time that you can cut into if a particular task is taking longer than expected, or more interesting than you might have expected! (Though if you follow my advice, I hope all your time spent revising will be relatively interesting.)

● The importance of taking time off

Remember what I said in my previous letter about the importance of taking time off, and not working your brain all the time. If you spend all your time revising, then you'll burn yourself out, and approach the exams feeling tired, jaded and listless – when you need to feel enthused and sparky. And it's important that when you do take time off, you make sure you enjoy it – that you do something nice for yourself, and don't spend the time worrying about the exams, or feeling guilty that you are taking time off from your revision.

Now – the best way of ensuring that you do take adequate time off from your revision, and of ensuring that you have some quality time off that is free from worries or guilt feelings, is to build your time off into your revision plan. Set yourself goals, and plan what rewards by way of spending some time off revising you will give yourself for achieving those goals. If you build your time off into your revision plan in this way, you'll help ensure that you do get adequate time off from revision, and your breaks from revision will start to seem like something you are entitled to enjoy in recognition of how hard you've been working, rather than a guilty or worry-filled treat.

● Work together

Where you can, work with other people in your revision:

1 *Picking questions.* Get together with your fellow students to work out together what sort of questions you should be focusing on in your revision. Two minds are better than one, and they may have some useful

advice for you (and you may have some useful advice for them) as to what sort of topics might come up in the exams.

2 *Send your written work around.* If you've written an essay or problem answer, send it to them for their comments and advice. This will help to ensure that you work hard at making the essay or problem answer as good (and in particular, as clear) as possible, and reading your essay or problem answer and thinking about whether it is correct, and sending you comments on it, will provide your fellow students with another useful (because it involves using information) method of revising.

3 *Share information.* If you've come across in the course of your revision a really useful article on a particular subject, then let other people know about it. You'll benefit from your generosity when someone else finds something useful that you haven't heard of.

4 *Ask each other questions.* You and your fellow students should get into the habit of asking each other questions that have cropped up in the course of your work and that you don't know the answer to. Maybe someone else in the group knows the answer. If no one does, then you could collaborate on looking into it. Either way, your group's knowledge of the law will be improved.

● Predicting what will come up on the paper

Wouldn't it be great if you could get an advance peek at what the questions will be in this year's exam? Well, you can't. But you can make some educated guesses as to what might come up in the exam, and prepare for those questions to come up in your revision. Here are some tips on spotting what sort of questions are likely to come up in the exam.

1 *Past papers.* Look at the past papers that have been set over the last few years on the subject you are revising. Is there an issue that tends, time and time again, to form the basis of a question in the exam? If so, be prepared for a question on that issue to come up again.

2 *Last year's paper.* Pay particular attention to last year's paper. Examiners tend not to set the same sort of essay questions two years in a row, so if there was an essay question on last year's paper on a particular issue, it's not likely you will get a similar essay question this year. So preparing for such a question to come up will normally be a complete waste of time. But only normally. There are some papers where the same sort of questions get

set time and time again. In which case, last year's paper will be as good a guide as any as to what is likely to come up in this year's paper.

3 *Recent developments.* Examiners are human beings. When an examiner sits down to write an exam, he or she can often feel very jaded and uninspired. Lacking in ideas for good essay and problem questions, he or she will often turn to recent cases and articles for inspiration. So, in your revision, pay a lot of attention to recent developments in the subject you are revising.

A case decided in the past year is far more likely to form the basis of a problem question in the exam than a case that was decided five years ago. An article that was published in the past year is far more likely to supply a quote for an essay question than an article that was published five years ago. An issue that has made the newspapers in the past year is far more likely to form the basis of an essay question or a problem question than an issue that was dominating the headlines five years ago.

So make sure that your revision concentrates a lot on improving your knowledge of:

(i) recent cases relating to the subject you are revising (and what academics have to say about them);

(ii) recent articles on the subject you are revising (don't limit yourself to the articles you have been told to read: explore the journals and recently published books for articles that the examiner might have come across);

(iii) recent issues relating to the subject you are revising that have made the news.

● Some common questions

Now to address some questions that my students tend to ask me when I suggest they revise in the above way:

(1) Revision notes

'I've tended to revise in the past by just making summaries of my notes – shouldn't I do the same for my Law exams?' The answer is: 'No'. When I was a student, I used to make revision notes, and I hated the time I spent making them, and I'm not sure I got anything out of them. Drawing up revision notes – by which I mean bare summaries of your notes, rather than anything more creative – is a really ineffective way of revising. It's boring, which means your brain isn't taking much, if anything, into its long-term memory, and it doesn't help at all with improving your essay-writing and problem-answering techniques, which is 50 per cent of the battle so far as getting ready for exams is concerned.

(2) Essay plans

'If I am attempting to write an essay in response to a past paper essay question, would it be okay if I just wrote an essay plan rather than a complete essay?' The answer is: 'In an ideal world – no.' If you have time to write a full essay, then do that. There is a huge difference between being able to draw up an essay plan and actually being able to execute it. Writing essay plans won't get you ready for the task of writing full essays in the exam. However, if you don't really have time to write a full essay, then an essay plan is better than nothing – but make sure that you always, always write a full first paragraph for the essay. As I've said before in my guidance on writing essays, the first paragraph of an essay is crucial: so make sure you get as much practice in as possible at writing really good, effective, attention-grabbing first paragraphs.

(3) Timed answers

'If I am attempting to answer a question, should I write my answer in the time I'd have to write it if I were doing it in an exam?' The answer is: 'Not at the moment.' At the moment, we are looking to improve your essay-writing and problem-answer techniques. To do that, you need to take time – a lot of time – over your essays and problem answers, trying to make them as good as possible. It would be a good idea to work out how much you can write in 45 minutes or an hour (depending on how long you get to answer each question in your exams) and learn to write to that kind of length – but so far as learning how to write an answer in 45 minutes or an hour is concerned, leave doing that until the run-up to the exams. At the moment, we have to focus on quality. So if you are aiming to write an answer to a particular question, give yourself a couple of days to do it – one day to research, one day to write. Really take your time to make it as good as possible.

(4) Scope of revision

'Do I have to revise everything relating to a particular subject, or are there some topics or issues that I can disregard?' The answer is: 'It depends.' If the exam in a particular subject will require you to answer four questions, then you only have to know enough to be able to do four questions on the day. To ensure that this is the case, you will generally only have to revise six topics or issues that regularly crop up in the exam – you can dump everything else. However, it may be that a particular exam tends to mix up in its questions a lot of different topics or issues – in which case, you will probably have to cover everything to make sure you are covered in the exam.

Okay – that's enough from me. Good luck with your revision, and let me know how you get on in the exams!

Best wishes,

Nick

Last Advice Before the Exams

30

Hey Alex,

The very best of luck for your exams! I'll be thinking of you! As for whether I've got any last minute words of advice, I do have a few things I want to say to you – but first, a word of warning. You've probably had loads of advice from your teachers as what to do in the exams. If any of my advice contradicts what they've told you, then ignore my contradictory advice. They will know far better than me what's the best approach for you to adopt in the exams – after all, they are going to be marking them. That said, here are a few tips for you to bear in mind in doing your exams.

● Timing

Spend equal time on all the questions you have to do in the exam. Suppose, for example, that you have to answer four questions in three hours, which gives you about 45 minutes for each question. Make sure that you don't spend more than 45 minutes on each question. Do not succumb to the temptation to spend 'just five more minutes' on any question. The extra marks you will pick up by spending 'just five more minutes' on the question will be dwarfed by the marks you will lose by spending only 40 minutes on the next question. Be disciplined. If the 45 minutes for doing a particular question are up, finish your sentence and then move on to the next question. Leave about a page space between your answers to allow you to add extra material to any of your answers if you have time at the end of the exam.

Writing essays

I've said this before, but I'll say it again – if you are writing a discursive essay (discussing a particular area of the law's merits or demerits), make sure your essay has a point and that you make that point clear right at the start of the essay and that you spend the rest of the essay making that point out. If you find yourself writing things like, 'First, it is necessary to discuss the history of this area of the law' or 'A brief survey of the cases reveals how complicated this area of the law is' or any other phrase that invites you to engage in a boring and pointless run through the case law in the area, stop and think: Surely there's a better way of doing this?

Plan your essays

Don't rush into doing any essay. Even if you think, 'Yes, this essay is on something I know about. I can do this essay!' – stop and think: What's the best way, the most effective way, the most impressive way of doing this essay? Your first instincts as to how to do the essay are usually going to be wrong. Stop and think: Is there a better way, a more effective way, a more impressive way of doing this essay? Five minutes spent thinking and planning at the start of your writing time will pay far more dividends than five extra minutes spent writing.

The importance of first impressions

Remember what I told you in my first letter on writing essays: pay extra special attention to the first paragraph and make sure it's a winner. Make the examiner think, on reading the first paragraph, 'This is going to be a first class essay'. If you can do that, you will be far more likely to get a first class mark for your essay than you will if the examiner thinks after your first paragraph, 'This is going to be a second class essay'. I cannot emphasise too strongly how important it is that you start your essay in an interesting and arresting way. Just read what Thomas Dixon has to say in his excellent *How To Get a First*:

> Speaking from the point of view of someone who regularly marks . . . exam essays, I cannot tell you how welcome it is to pick up a script and find that its author has made an effort to engage your attention, arouse your interest, provide you with a thought-provoking, arresting or unexpected opening paragraph or two. If this attention-grabbing opening is followed by or includes an account of a key scholarly dispute to which the essay relates, and a brief map of the essay itself, then, speaking for myself, I will be so

overwhelmingly grateful that I will be predisposed to give the essay a first if
I possibly can.

And he is not just speaking for himself: he is speaking for all examiners who
mark essays, everywhere.

● Leave your weakest answer to last

The law of first impressions – that first impressions are hard to dislodge – applies
also to the whole of your answer paper. Say you have to do four questions in
your exam. You have picked your four questions, but you feel that your answer to
one of the questions is going to be significantly weaker than your other answers.
Leave your weakest answer to last. If, in your first three questions, you have established yourself in the mind of the examiner as a top student, that might make her
inclined to overlook or go easy on any failures or omissions in your last answer.
Who knows? Maybe she will surmise that your last answer was weaker than the
others because you were exhausted or running into time trouble, and out of sym-
pathy give you a higher mark for your last, weak answer than she would have
done had you written that answer first, before any of the others.

Another reason for leaving your weakest answer to last is this. Suppose that
at your university a first class script is one which gets a mark of 70 per cent
or above. And suppose that you have to do four questions in your exam, and
the exam is marked out of 100, with each question being marked out of 25.
Suppose that for your first three questions, you get marks of 18, 19 and 18 –
so, 55 in total. This will only leave you needing a mark of 15 on the last question to get an overall first class mark for your paper. The examiner would
have to have a heart of stone to give you a mark of 13 or 14 out of 25 for that
last question, when you only needed a mark of 15 to get an overall first. So
even if your last question, objectively, deserves a mark of 13 out of 25 because
it's so weak, it's likely that the examiner will bump up the mark to 15 to get
you over the first class boundary. So – that's another reason for leaving your
weakest answer to last. Your opening strong answers can actually give the
examiner an incentive to inflate the mark for your concluding, weak answer.

● Try to finish with an essay

This was one of the first tips for the exams I was ever given as a student (by
Professor Hugh Collins) – but it's a tip that is subject to the preceding bit of
advice, that you should always leave your weakest answer last. If your answers

to all of the questions on the paper are likely to be equally strong, you should aim to finish with an essay. The reason for this goes as follows. Suppose you have to do four questions in your exam, and you have decided to do two essays and two problems. Try to make one of the essay questions the last question you will answer. The reason is that if you are running into a bit of time trouble, an essay can be compressed to fit the remaining time available without too much loss of quality. In contrast, a problem answer is less susceptible to being compressed. As a result, it's much harder to write a problem answer to a high standard in a shortened period of time.

● General guidance on problem answers

Don't make your problem answers over-complicated. Don't make ridiculous assumptions/arguments as to what the actors thought/why the actors did what they did. Always have in mind the sort of answer the examiner would have had in mind when setting the question: relatively straightforward, addressing five or six key issues with reference to the relevant case law, easy to mark when done right.

● Never stop thinking

I wish I had £10 for every time a student has told me, 'I can't believe the marks I got in the exams. I thought I did really well in the exam on X law, but I got my worst mark for that. And I thought my exam in Y law was a disaster, and I got my best mark in that subject.'

It's so common for students to say this, there must be a reason for it. There must be a reason why students do worst in the papers they think they've done the best in, and why they do best in the papers they think they've done the worst in. After many years of pondering this mystery, I think I've got the answer. How you do in the exams is related to how hard you think during the exams.

If you're having a really torrid time in an exam and really having to fight to do well, then you are being made to think very hard. In writing problem answers, you are so desperate to find anything relevant to say that you start seeing points that you might otherwise have missed. In writing essays, you work very hard to make some intelligent points, hoping that your doing so will redeem what is, in your eyes, an otherwise disastrous performance.

In contrast, if you are sitting a paper that seems very straightforward to you, your brain tends to switch onto 'auto-pilot' and you stop really thinking about what you are doing in the exam. In writing your problem answers, you get sloppy and complacent and start to miss some relevant issues. Your essays tend to be more directed towards what you think the essay question is about rather than what it is actually about.

The end result is that you will get a much better mark for your performance in the exam where you had a really tough time than you will for your performance in the exam that seemed very straightforward to you.

The lesson you should draw from this is not to switch off during the exam. If the exam seems very straightforward, be on your guard. Stop and think: Are there some issues I'm missing in doing this problem question? Any relevant cases that I haven't thought about? What is this essay really about? Is there some way I could improve on the essay I was thinking of writing on this topic? Never stop thinking along these lines.

● Style

Use headings, numbers and underlining throughout to make your exam as easy to mark and to follow as possible. If you can remember to do so, write on every other line only. This will make it very easy for you to insert corrections into your answers if you need to do so.

● In the exam

Try to remain calm, especially at the start of the exam when you experience the shock of seeing a lot of brand new questions for the first time. When doing a problem question, don't panic. Just think – 'I have covered the material that will allow me to do this question. I just have to be calm and I will see the issues raised by the question and I will remember what cases and statutes are relevant to those issues.' When thinking about how to approach an essay, just think – 'I have thought about this before. I just have to be calm and the ideas will come as to what points I should make in my essay and how the essay should be structured.'

Jot down any ideas/cases/issues as they come to you on a bit of rough paper: don't rely on your memory to bring them back to you when you need them – under stress you will be particularly prone to the phenomenon of being completely unable to remember something that you were thinking about just two minutes ago. On the same lines, it might be a good idea at the start of the exam to scribble down quickly any key rules or names of cases that you are very likely to need to use in the exam. You then won't have to worry about forgetting these rules or names in the course of the exam.

After the exam

When the exam is over, leave the exam paper in the exam hall. There's absolutely no point in taking it away with you and looking at it and worrying about what you should have said. By then it will be too late. And try to avoid getting into any extended discussions about what you wrote in the exam – again there's no absolutely no point. Just a simple 'It went okay' should suffice. Certainly don't do what I did after my contract law exam in Oxford, when I foolishly went through the paper with one of my lawyer friends who had also sat the exam. He said that he had done a particular question. 'I didn't do that question,' I said. 'It was obvious it was all about *The Super Servant (No 2)* and I hadn't revised that case.' 'What's *The Super Servant (No 2)*?' my friend replied. The rest of his day was ruined – and so was mine.

Whatever happens, be philosophical

Even the best of students can get unlucky in the exams. You may prepare really well for the exams but then get caught cold by a really unfair exam and end up getting a mark that your efforts simply didn't deserve. This can happen. Examiners are human and can foul up, just like the rest of us. My advice is – try to be philosophical and put it behind you. You've just got to believe that everything will work out well for you in the end, and this bit of what looks like bad luck will at some point in the future turn out to be a real blessing. I've found that to be true in my own life, and that of many people I know – and I have no doubt it'll be true of you as well.

But let's hope it won't come to that and that your examiners will do a good job and you will receive the credit you deserve! Good luck with the exams, Alex – and let me know your results when they come through.

Best wishes,

Nick

PART 5
Moving On

Preparing for What's Next

- From: Nicholas J. McBride [dearnick@pearson.com]
- To: Brown, Alex
- Subject: Preparing For What's Next

Hi Alex,

Congratulations on getting through your exams! We'll have to see how you've got on with your marks, but I think it's time you started thinking about the future. You may think it's far too early for that, while you've still got a couple of years plus to go before you graduate – but in fact you need throughout your time at university to be (1) *positioning* yourself to pursue whatever career you'll want to pursue once you leave university; and (2) *researching* what you want to do after university. And the 'down time' that you enjoy after the exams is the ideal time to start that process going. So I'll talk in this letter about these two aspects of preparing for life after university: positioning, and researching.

● Positioning

You've already started this process by taking your first set of exams. Your exam results are very, very important in terms of putting yourself in a position to be able to do whatever it is you want to do when you graduate. The competition for good jobs is increasingly tough nowadays, and you have to have decent grades in order to give yourself a chance in that competition. The days of people being able to leave university with a 2.2 and land a very good job at a very good firm are over. But it's increasingly the case that achieving very good marks in your exams is the minimum that employers are looking for when giving out the kinds of jobs that you might be going for when you graduate. You also have to think about, and start working on:

(1) Extra-curricular activities

Employers want to see that you are a well-rounded individual with a range of different interests, not someone who is just focused on studying law to the exclusion of everything else. So allow yourself to get passionate about spending time doing things other than law, and pursue those passions. But the emphasis is on *doing*. No one is going to be impressed by your saying that you are passionate about watching boxed sets of *Scrubs* or that you spend all your spare time listening to Justin Bieber. Get passionate about doing things that get you out of your room. And don't worry about whether what you are doing is 'interesting' or not – the fact that you are passionate about what you are doing automatically makes what you are doing interesting.

(2) Commercial awareness

This is a very important quality that law firms look for in people applying for jobs – but one which law students generally have to work on to develop. 'Commercial awareness' is an awareness of how businesses operate, what objectives they seek to pursue, and how best those objectives might be achieved in any given situation. There are a variety of ways of developing commercial awareness. Working in a business in your holidays, and trying to develop a deep understanding of how the business is run, why it's run in the way it is, and how it might be run more effectively, would be one way. Keeping abreast of the business news, and doing a bit of research to get behind the headlines – for example, trying to understand why a particular merger might make sense to the players involved, and whether it does actually make sense, all things considered – would be another way. The latest editions of the books written by Chris Stoakes should also be helpful: *Commercial Awareness* and *Know the City*.

(3) Verbal reasoning

Big law firms nowadays often make job applicants do a verbal reasoning test as part of the application process. It's important that you do well on this kind of test, because you can't rule out the possibility that if you fall below a certain mark, your application will be automatically turned down by a computer without a human being ever getting to see all the wonderfully interesting aspects of your application. So if you are going to be applying for a job with a big city law firm you need to get used to these tests beforehand. You can find a number of free to access verbal reasoning tests online – the University of Kent very helpfully provides a number of such tests (and other kinds of tests such as numerical, and non-verbal, reasoning tests) at http://www.kent.ac.uk/careers/psychotests.htm.

(4) Negotiation skills

Another skill that law firms might be looking for in potential recruits is negotiation skills – the ability to achieve an acceptable agreement with someone who may be pursuing goals that are very different from, or even opposed to, yours. Law students tend to be very weak on these skills because when you study law you are – for the most part – working on your own, and not with others. Moreover, in studying law, you are learning how to persuade other people to agree with a fixed position that you have adopted by making rational arguments in favour of that position. This is hugely different from learning how to move towards an as yet undefined position that will turn out to prove mutually acceptable to you and to the other people with whom you are dealing. There are a number of online introductions to developing negotiation skills, as well as a number of books that you could buy and read (just search for 'negotiation skills' on Amazon). But there is a big difference between knowing something in theory and being able to apply it in practice. So look out for opportunities to enhance your negotiation skills. For example, get involved with a university society or event that requires the organisers to use negotiation skills in dealing with suppliers or the university. Try to get yourself elected onto a committee to learn how to operate in that sort of arena. If there is an institute of mediators – who try to see if a settlement can be achieved between parties who are involved in some kind of civil dispute without their having to go to court – write to them to see if they would be willing to allow you to sit on a mediation to see how a skilled mediator sees if the parties between whom he or she is mediating can achieve any common ground.

(5) Mooting

If you have any aspirations to be a barrister, it's essential that you get involved with mooting – arguing hypothetical cases in front of a 'judge' (normally a graduate student or law academic) who decides the legal issue being argued over, and, more importantly, decides who has done the most impressive job of presenting their case. Your university law society should run regular mooting competitions – if it doesn't, then press for them to start. You can find guides to mooting online (and examples of moots on YouTube). The small introductory guide to studying law, *Learning the Law,* has a chapter on mooting; and there also some specialised books on the subject (search for 'mooting' on Amazon). More generally, if you are interested in becoming a barrister, it would be well worth looking at the latest editions of Wolfe and Robson, *The Path to Pupillage: A Guide for the Aspiring Barrister,* or Kramer, *Bewigged and Bewildered? A Guide to Becoming a Barrister in England and Wales* for further guidance on the best ways of positioning yourself to get where you want to go in what is an increasingly competitive and overcrowded area of legal practice.

(6) Contacts

While contacts are not so important for obtaining training contracts with law firms, or pupillages with sets of barristers' chambers – the competition for those things tends to be very meritocratic – if you are interested in getting into the charitable sector, or working for an international organisation, or a non-governmental organisation, then contacts tend to be very important, sadly. So put yourself in positions to make as many useful contacts as possible. Attend speaker meetings where the speaker is doing the kind of thing you would like to do, and see if you can get a chance to talk to them. Work for a university newspaper, or a student law journal run by your university, and interview people who are doing the kind of interesting work you would like to be doing. Join university societies that are likely to provide opportunities to meet people who might be able to help you get onto the first rung of your chosen career ladder when you leave university.

(7) Further study

If you want to work as a solicitor, it isn't very important to go on to do a postgraduate degree, such as a Masters in Law (LLM), or some other kind of Masters degree, or the Oxford Bachelor of Civil Law (BCL) degree. But competition for places at barristers' chambers is now so intense that it's increasingly important to have done (and done well in) some form of postgraduate study if you want to catch the eye of their application committees. Many international, and non-governmental, organisations also require that their recruits have done a postgraduate Masters degree. So if you want to do the kind of work for which a postgraduate degree is important, it's vital that you keep your grades up at the kind of level that will enable you to be accepted to do such a degree – and at the kind of institution that will command a great deal of respect from prospective employers.

● Researching

Doing the kinds of things listed above to put yourself in a position to do whatever it is that you will want to do when you leave university may also help you get a bit clearer as to what you want to do when you leave university. If the idea of becoming more 'commercially aware' is anathema to you, then life at a big city law firm probably isn't going to be for you. But if you're the kind of person I think you are – someone who is interested in lots of different aspects of law, and lots of different potential careers – then you are going to have to make some choices as to (1) what sort of career you are going to pursue and, having made that choice, you are also going to have to make some choices as to (2) where you want to work.

Fortunately for you, there are now a large number of websites that can help you with both (1) and (2). You should check out the following sites:

thegatewayonline.com – the website for the student business and careers newspaper *The Gateway*. Check out the special law issue (issue 52) in the 'Newspaper' section of the site.

lawyer2b.com – the website that accompanies *The Lawyer* magazine.

lawcareers.net – a hugely useful source of information about law jobs.

targetjobslaw.co.uk – again, very useful as source of information about law jobs.

chambersstudent.co.uk – the same again.

rollonfriday.com – *lots* of insider information about law firms.

barcouncil.org.uk – the Bar Council's official website.

lawsociety.org.uk – the Law Society website: scroll all the way down and click on 'Becoming a solicitor'.

jobs.thirdsector.co.uk – click on 'Careers advice' for guidance on jobs working for charities or non-governmental organisations.

Your university careers service should also be a very helpful source of information, as well as giving you tips on constructing your CV and filling out application forms. You should also look out for any law fairs held at your university and talk to as many people as possible at those. But nothing substitutes for getting a taste of what it's actually like to work as a solicitor, or a barrister, or in whatever other career you are thinking of. So far as solicitors are concerned, this involves doing a *vacation placement* at a law firm; and in the case of barristers, a *mini-pupillage* at a set of chambers. As a law student, you would usually be looking to do one or two vacation placements and/or mini-pupillages in the summer holidays after the end of the second year of your studies. (But the deadline for applications for summer vacation placements and mini-pupillages is usually much earlier – as soon as your second year Christmas holidays begin, start looking into making applications, and consulting the websites of individual firms and sets of chambers for deadline details.) Competition for these opportunities is very intense – I'm often told it's usually harder to get a vacation placement with a big city law firm than it is to get a training contract with them. So be prepared to make *lots* of applications – and don't get disappointed if you don't get anywhere with them; and certainly don't think that means you'll never be able to work as a solicitor or a barrister. Instead, think about casting your net more widely: perhaps applying to do a few days' work in a firm in the area where your family lives; or trying to spend some days visiting courts and sitting in the public galleries, observing the barristers and getting some idea of what it's like to work as a barrister. Doing these kind of things can often show a more impressive degree of commitment to, and interest in, working as a lawyer than someone who has easily picked up a couple of vacation placements or mini-pupillages.

I hope this is helpful and that once you leave university, you'll find yourself doing something you really love. Good luck with everything, Alex!

All best wishes,

Nick

Some Final Words
of Advice

○ From: Nicholas J. McBride [dearnick@pearson.com]
○ To: Brown, Alex
○ Subject: Some Final Words of Advice

Hi Alex,

It's great to hear from you again, after such a long time. I'm glad that things are working out for you – your plans sound very exciting. I really appreciated what you said – that all the advice in my letters had helped you a lot with your studies, and helped put you on the path that you're currently on. Given that, I thought you might like one last letter with some advice that I hope will come in helpful in the future. After all, I am almost twice your age – and age does have its advantages, perspective and experience being two of them. And if I can do anything to help you avoid making the mistakes I've made, then that would make me very happy. So – a few last words of advice:

● Don't ever lose sight of what matters

Life has a way of distracting you from what really matters. We get sucked into thinking that we need to attend to this or that problem or task, and soon forget the big picture of what's important and what we're meant to be doing. We see this on a daily basis with lawyers – the day-to-day challenges of life as a lawyer means that soon nothing else matters but the day-to-day challenge, and any sense of their life having some overarching meaning or importance is lost. And law academics are the worst of all. Almost all such academics are now on a treadmill of churning out article after article without having any sense of what all this effort and activity is actually *for*. Don't ever be like that – try always to think of your life in terms of being a *vocation*: something that you are called to do. If you can't think of your life in that way, then something's gone wrong and you need to readjust and find a new bearing for the course of your life that will allow you to think of your life as having some meaning and importance and value.

● Keep challenging yourself

Life also constantly tempts us to take things easy, and stop pushing ourselves to achieve more, and do better than we did yesterday. Resist that temptation and never stop challenging yourself to improve. At the moment, this won't be a problem – you're just starting out in your career, and you'll need to push yourself in order to get anywhere. But someone as talented as you will eventually get to the position where you won't have to change or work hard to achieve your goals – and at that point you'll have a choice. Either you fold your hands and rest up and take it easy, and atrophy. Or you push yourself on, and grow.

● Be honest with yourself

You can't challenge yourself to change and improve unless you are honest with yourself about where you are falling down at the moment. We all have a tendency to lie to ourselves about ourselves – to think that we were right to do something that was actually quite wrong, or to absolve ourselves from responsibility for a particular failure by thinking to ourselves that it was 'inevitable' or 'natural' that we would do what we did. Try to see these rationalisations for what they are, and set them aside in favour of a more penetrating understanding of how we should have acted, or of our responsibility for the fact that things went the way they did.

● Avoid self-righteousness

A huge obstacle to being honest with yourself is self-righteousness: the temptation to believe that because what you are *doing* is particularly virtuous or just, *you* are particularly virtuous or just. It doesn't work like that: people can do the right thing without being particularly righteous themselves. (The philosopher Immanuel Kant gave the example of a merchant who gives the correct change to his customers because he fears that he will lose business if he gets a reputation for short-changing his customers.) This is something you will particularly have to look out for, given the kind of work you hope to be doing in future: don't ever let the quality of the work you do make you puffed up or proud of yourself.

● Don't go with the flow

The last four pieces of advice can all be summed up in a very easy phrase: '*don't* go with the flow'. Of course, today's society is more likely to advise that you should 'go with the flow'. This *is* good advice when we are talking about things that are done best when you think least about *how* you are doing them – putting a golf ball into a hole, or playing a guitar, or dancing, or making someone laugh. You'll tend to screw up doing these kinds of things if you become self-conscious, and start to dwell on all the things that you need to do to get from point A to point B. So in doing these things, the best advice is to get out of your own way, and go with the flow of what comes naturally. *But* outside these contexts, the advice to 'go with the flow' is almost always disastrous. It's easy to hate people who treat you badly, and hard to forgive them – so if you 'go with the flow', you'll end up hating when forgiving is the right thing to do. I can tell you from experience that there won't be a single good thing in your life that you won't be tempted at some point to walk away from, like it was the most natural thing in the world – so if you 'go with the flow' you'll end up depriving yourself of everything good in your life. It's easy to go along with the consensus that everyone else has arrived at, and hard to stand against the crowd – so if you 'go with the flow' you will go along with the majority view, even when the majority view is disastrously mistaken. So outside situations where self-consciousness would just result in your getting in your own way, *don't* go with the flow – but instead be suspicious of any urgings from either inside or outside you that you should just do what comes naturally.

● Be honest with other people

This may seem like an odd piece of advice for a law student as lawyers are identified so closely with liars in popular consciousness. But lying to other people is always corrosive – of your relationships with those people, and your ability to think well of yourself. In talking to other people, try to steer clear of the platitudes and clichés that make it easy for you to lie because no one is that clear what exactly it is you are saying. And never, ever engage in the kind of 'management speak' – for example, 'I hear what you're saying' or 'These changes will add value to our client experience' – which is designed to allow people to be dishonest about what they think, or what they intend to do, or what is important to them. As George Orwell observed in his great essay 'Politics and the English language', 'The great enemy of clear language is insincerity. When there is a gap between one's real and one's declared aims, one turns as it were instinctively to long words and exhausted idioms, like a cuttlefish spurting out ink.' You have been trained, as a law student, to write and express yourself clearly. So if you catch yourself later in life writing or expressing yourself obscurely – think about why you are doing that, and whether you haven't fallen into the trap of misusing your talent for language to conceal rather than to reveal; to obfuscate rather than to communicate.

● Be careful with your words

On the subject of communication, the career you are now entering on will involve a *lot* of talking. Anyone involved in a career that involves a lot of talking should bear in mind two things. (1) It's very difficult to talk a lot without screwing up once in a while and saying the wrong thing. (2) We live in a society that is incredibly – almost hysterically – intolerant of people who happen to have said the wrong thing. In order to avoid (1) getting you into trouble with (2), try to cultivate a more deliberate, measured way of expressing yourself, which will allow you to check and weigh your words before they come out of your mouth and can't be taken back.

● Embrace your limitations

Reinhold Niebuhr's 'Serenity Prayer' – which was subsequently adopted by Alcoholics Anonymous – goes as follows: 'God, grant me the serenity to accept the things I cannot change, the courage to change the things I can, and the wisdom to know the difference.' So long as you can say that you have done your best in relation to the things that you had the power to change, then that's all that matters. If you have done your best to bring about a particular change, and someone else gets in the way of that happening – that's on them, and really has nothing to do with you. Resenting them for what they did is just pointless – it makes you feel bad, poisons your relationship with them, and doesn't do anything to help bring about the change that you did your personal best to achieve. Someone who realised this too late was President Richard Nixon. The day after he resigned the Presidency in disgrace – under threat of being indicted for helping to cover up the White House's involvement in criminal activities against Nixon's opponents – Nixon gave a farewell speech to his staff. The speech – apparently delivered without any preparation – is one of *the* great speeches of the twentieth century, and in it Nixon achieved a level of wisdom and insight that had signally eluded him up until then. One of the final lines of the speech expresses precisely the point I want to make here: 'Always give of your best, never get discouraged, never be petty; always remember, others may hate you, but those who hate you don't win unless you hate them, and then you destroy yourself.' If you attempt to do anything worthwhile in this world, there will always people who will get in your way, and a lot of the time they will succeed in frustrating what you want to do. But that's their problem, and don't allow it become your problem by hating them for getting in your way.

● Be kind

The author Henry James is quoted as saying: 'Three things in human life are important: the first is to be kind; the second is to be kind; and the third is to be kind.' I think this is a particularly important point for law students to remember, skilled as they are in the unkind arts of exposing stupidity and compelling people to agree with them. Remember that you don't have to use those skills all the time, and that using them to humiliate someone who hasn't been taught how to think or argue properly is unacceptable.

Okay – that's it from me, Alex. I hope everything goes really well for you.

All best wishes,

Nick

APPENDIX A

A Proust Questionnaire[1]

1 What is your idea of perfect happiness?

2 What would you like to be doing in five years' time?

3 Which living person do you most admire, and why?

4 What is your greatest fear?

5 What is your main fault?

6 What is your favourite thing to do?

7 What is the most important thing you would like to say you had done by the time you died?

8 When and where were you happiest?

9 What is your idea of perfect misery?

10 Who is your favourite writer?

11 What was the hardest thing you have ever had to do?

12 What is your most treasured possession?

13 What do you consider to be your greatest achievement?

14 What country would you most like to visit, and why?

15 What would you like to be doing in 20 years' time?

16 What fault in other people are you least able to tolerate?

17 What talent would you most like to have, and why?

18 What is your favourite memory?

19 If you could change one thing about yourself, what would it be?

20 Which historical figure do you most identify with?

---

[1] See the end of Letter 4. But Is Law the Right Subject for Me?

APPENDIX B

Preface: The Tort Wars

(from McBride and Bagshaw, *Tort Law,* 3rd edn (Pearson Education, 2008))

● The current division

The academic community of tort lawyers is now divided into two rival camps.[1] Much of the larger camp is made up of academics who take what we might call the *modern* view of tort law. According to this view of tort law,[2] in tort cases the courts determine whether A should be held liable to compensate B for some loss that A has caused B to suffer. According to this view, then, tort law is simply the law on compensation – it tells us when one person will be held liable to compensate another for some loss that he or she has caused that other to suffer.

Throughout the 1960s and 1970s, it was assumed without question among academic tort lawyers that the modern view of tort law was correct. There was universal agreement that, in the words of Lord Bingham, the 'overall

---

[1] Or possibly three. There is a school of thought that, unlike any other area of law one can possibly think of (such as contract law, or family law, or company law, or international law), tort law does not actually refer to anything in particular. According to this *nihilistic* view of tort law, nothing unites the various legal rules and principles that are customarily discussed in tort law textbooks. For some reason, this view seems quite popular among academics from the University of Cambridge: see Weir 2006, ix ('Tort is what is in the tort books, and the only thing holding it together is the binding'); Howarth & O'Sullivan 2001, 1 ('[it is] particularly difficult to present a rational or logical classification of [tort law]'); M&D, 90 ('Expecting structure, order or theoretical consistency from our courts or any underlying theory for tort recovery is perhaps asking too much from them'). It is hard to know whether these authors intend such statements to be taken seriously: why would they spend their time writing about a subject which – according to them – does not exist?

[2] Stevens 2007, at 2, calls this view of tort law, the 'loss model' of tort law.

object of tort law is to define cases in which the law may justly hold one party liable to compensate another.[3] There were, of course, disagreements among the tort academics as to *why* people were held liable 'in tort' to pay compensation to someone else. Some argued that the object of such awards was to pass losses that were suffered by individuals onto businesses and insurance companies, so that those losses could then be spread throughout the community through price rises and premium increases, thus minimising the social impact of those losses. Others argued that in holding people liable to pay other people compensation, tort law was concerned to minimise the 'cost of accidents' by encouraging people who could most cheaply avoid an accident occurring to take the precautions required to stop that accident occurring. And a third group argued that in making compensation awards, tort law was simply concerned to protect those who had suffered a loss which they did not deserve to suffer. But these disagreements masked an underlying consensus – a universal agreement among tort academics that the modern view of tort law was correct.

That consensus began to break down in the mid-1980s – round about the time the authors of this book went to Oxford to study law. In Canada, a legal philosopher called Ernest Weinrib wrote a series of articles arguing that tort law was concerned with *corrective justice* – which, for our purposes, can be taken as a fancy name for 'remedying *wrongs*'.[4] At roughly the same time, the greatest modern scholar of English private law – Professor Peter Birks, Regius Professor of Civil Law at the University of Oxford – started to take an interest in the classification of legal obligations, as part of his work on the law of unjust enrichment. He began to argue that tort law, as a subject, is not centred around a particular *response* – that is, compensation.[5] Rather, tort law focuses on a particular *event* – the commission of a *civil wrong* – and describes the varying ways in which the law responds to that event.[6] Out of the work of these two academics emerged a very different view of tort law from that which

---

[3] *Fairchild* v *Glenhaven Funeral Services Ltd* [2003] 1 AC 32 at [9].

[4] See Weinrib 1995 for the most complete statement of Weinrib's views on tort law, and law generally.

[5] It is noticeable that the first part of the US Third Restatement of Tort Law is explicitly centred around a response: 'Liability for Physical and Emotional Harm'. (The second part, 'Economic Torts and Related Wrongs', also seems based on the response of compensation for economic harm.) It is not clear how successful this approach will be: Peter Birks regarded any response-based approach to describing the law of tort as doomed to be incoherent, repetitive, and incomplete.

[6] See Birks 1983, 1985, 1995, 1997a.

held sway in the legal academy in the 1960s and 1970s, and one which is now endorsed by a significant minority of tort academics.[7] According to this view of tort law, in tort cases, the courts determine whether A has committed a wrong in relation to B, and if he has, they determine what remedies will be available to B. To put it another – exactly equivalent – way, in tort cases, the courts determine whether A has violated B's rights in acting as he did, and if he has, they determine what remedies will be available to B.

We can call this view of tort law, the *traditional* view of tort law.[8] Traditional, because up until about 40 years ago, it had *always* been thought that tort law was all about protecting people who had suffered a wrong, people whose rights had been violated.[9] Up until about 40 years ago, Lord Hope's statement in *Chester* v *Afshar* that 'the function of the law [of tort] is to enable rights to be vindicated and to provide remedies when duties have been breached'[10] would have been regarded as a statement of the obvious. But no longer: those who endorse the modern view of tort law would in all likelihood dismiss a statement such as Lord Hope's as narrow and naïve.

● Why this disagreement matters

It is as impossible for a tort law textbook to be neutral on the issue of whether the modern or traditional view of tort law is correct as it is for a science textbook to be neutral on the issue of whether the Earth is flat or spherical. The issue is too fundamental for neutrality to be an option. Whether the modern or traditional view of tort law is correct affects:

1 *The reach of tort law.* One of the reasons for the popularity of the modern view of tort law among tort academics is that it makes their subject so excitingly huge. On the modern view of tort law, tort law has the potential to intervene and provide a remedy in any situation where A has caused B to suffer some kind of loss. That is, after all, the function of tort law – to determine whether it would be 'fair, just and reasonable' to allow B to sue

---

[7] See Goldberg & Zipursky 2001, 2006; Coleman 1993, 2001; Calnan 2005; Stevens 2007; Beever 2007.

[8] Stevens 2007, at 2, calls this view of tort law, the 'rights model' of tort law.

[9] For example, the full title of the 13th edition of Sir Frederick Pollock's *The Law of Torts* (published London, 1929) was 'The Law of Torts: A Treatise on the Principles of Obligations Arising From Civil Wrongs in the Common Law'. See also Goodhart 1938.

[10] [2005] 1 AC 134, at [87] (endorsed by Baroness Hale in *Gregg* v *Scott* [2005] 2 AC 176, at [216]).

A for compensation, and if it would be, to allow B to sue A for compensation. So, on the modern view of tort law, any situation where one person causes another to suffer some kind of loss is one which tort academics are entitled to discuss with a view to deciding whether a remedy should be granted or not in that situation.

In contrast, the traditional view of tort law places severe constraints on the scope of tort law's jurisdiction. On the traditional view, if A has caused B to suffer some kind of loss, B will not be entitled to sue A in tort for compensation for that loss unless she can first show that A violated her rights in acting as he did. If she cannot do this then tort law has nothing to do with her and it cannot be invoked to help her out. As we will see later on in this Preface, this hurdle – of having to show that A's conduct violated B's rights – can be very difficult to surmount. And if it cannot be surmounted, that is the end of B's case so far as tort law is concerned. No matter how beneficial it might be to grant B a remedy in this situation, there is nothing to talk about so far as tort law, and the tort academics, are concerned.

2   *What goes into tort textbooks.* On the modern view of tort law, the task of a tort textbook is to set out all the situations where B is entitled to sue A for compensation for a loss that A has caused her to suffer. In contrast, if the traditional view of tort law is correct then a tort textbook need only concern itself with cases where B is entitled to sue A for compensation because A has violated her rights. On the traditional view of tort law, cases of what we will call 'compensation without wrongdoing' – that is, cases where B is entitled to sue A for compensation for a loss that A caused her to suffer without, however, violating B's rights – fall outside the scope of a tort textbook.

3   *How we think about the way cases are decided.* As anyone who has ever read a few tort cases will know, the way judges decide cases supports the traditional view of tort law. In a case where A has caused B to suffer some kind of loss and B is seeking some remedy against A as a result, the judges do not say – 'Well, let's weigh up the pros and cons of awarding B a remedy here. On balance, we find that it would be desirable to allow B to sue A for some compensation here, so it is duly ordered that A should pay B £10,000.' Instead – just as the traditional view of tort law would lead us to expect – the judges first of all look to see if A violated B's rights in acting as he did. If he did then they will normally grant B a remedy; if he did not, B's claim will fail. *Ubi ius, ibi remedium* – where there is a right, there is a remedy. If there is no right, there is no remedy (so far as tort law is concerned).

This fact about the cases creates a problem for the modern view of tort law. How can the modern view of tort law be correct when the way tort law cases are decided makes it so obvious that the traditional view of tort law is correct? The preferred solution for those academics who adopt the modern view of tort law is to argue that when the judges *say* that they are granting B a remedy in a given case because A violated her rights, that is not the *real reason* for their decision. In order to discover the real reason, one must discard all the nonsense in the cases about 'rights' and 'duties' and 'unmask' the real 'policy concerns' that motivated the courts' decision.[11] This is another reason why the modern view of tort law is so exciting, and therefore popular among tort academics. It *is* exciting to think that you have found out what is really going on – that the courts are pursuing a secret agenda in the cases and you know what that agenda is. But it must always be remembered that exciting is not necessarily true. It may be exciting to think that President Kennedy was assassinated by the CIA and the Mafia. But it is not necessarily true.

At any rate, whether the traditional view of tort law is correct or not should have a big impact on the way we think about the way tort cases are decided. If the traditional view is correct, then we have no reason not to take the judges seriously when they deny a claimant a remedy in a tort case on the ground that the defendant did not violate her rights in acting as he did. If the traditional view of tort law is wrong, and tort law is not in fact

---

[11] Two notable examples of this kind of thinking were provided in two consecutive issues of the *Cambridge Law Journal* by the tort academic turned politician, David Howarth. In *Gorringe* v *Calderdale MBC* [2004] 1 WLR 1057, the claimant was injured when she drove her car into a bus. Had she been driving more slowly, she would have avoided the bus. The claimant sued the defendant local authority for failing to put up a warning sign by the side of the road, telling her to slow down. Lord Hoffmann, giving the leading judgment, dismissed the claimant's case on the ground that the defendant local authority had not owed her a duty to save her from the consequences of her own foolishness. According to Howarth 2004, at 548, the real reason for the decision was Lord Hoffmann's 'extremist hostility to the very idea of negligence liability.' In *Sutradhar* v *Natural Environment Research Council* [2006] 4 All ER 490, the claimant was poisoned from drinking water contaminated with arsenic. He sued the defendants in negligence for compensation – they had surveyed the water in the area where the claimant lived but did not test it for arsenic; had they done so, the arsenic would have been detected and steps would have been taken to protect people like the claimant from suffering arsenic poisoning. The House of Lords upheld the Court of Appeal's decision to throw out the claim, on the ground that the defendants – not having had any kind of contact or developed any kind of relationship with the claimant – had not owed him a duty to take steps to save him from suffering arsenic poisoning. According to Howarth 2005a's note on the Court of Appeal's decision, at 25, 'The court's real worry in *Sutradhar* seems to have been the 699 other claimants waiting in the wings and that their success might put a large hole in Britain's international development budget.'

concerned with vindicating a claimant's rights, then in tort cases where a judge denies a claimant a remedy on the ground that the defendant did not violate the claimant's rights in acting as he did, that cannot be the real reason for the judge's decision. The fact that the defendant did not violate the claimant's rights cannot be sufficient reason to deny her a remedy in tort. Something else must be going on – and we need to find out what it is.

4 *How we judge whether a case was correctly decided.* Finally, whether the traditional or modern view of tort law is correct will have a big impact on how we approach the issue of judging whether a given tort case was correctly decided. For example, in *Bradford Corporation* v *Pickles,*[12] the defendant blocked off a stream of water flowing under his land so that the water could not flow into the claimants' reservoirs. The claimants sued the defendant in tort. They lost: as they had no right to receive the water that flowed under the defendant's land, the defendant did nothing wrong to the claimants in blocking that water off. Was this case correctly decided?

If we adopt the traditional view of tort law then we will approach this issue by asking whether the House of Lords in *Bradford Corporation* v *Pickles* was right to say that the claimants had no rights over the water flowing under the defendant's land. If the House of Lords' decision on this issue was correct, then *Bradford Corporation* v *Pickles* was correctly decided: the defendant did not violate the claimants' rights in acting as he did, and so the claimants could not have been entitled to a remedy in tort against the defendant. If, on the other hand, we adopt the modern view of tort law, then that cannot be the end of the matter. So what if the defendant did not wrong the claimants in acting as he did? The traditional view of tort law is wrong: recovery in tort is *not* conditional on its being shown that the defendant violated the claimants' rights in cutting off the water to their reservoirs. Instead, we should look at the pros and cons of awarding a remedy here, taking *all* the circumstances of the case into account.

● What we think

So it is simply impossible to write a tort textbook without either endorsing the modern view of tort law or the traditional view of tort law. Too much depends on which view is correct. So where do we stand? We endorse the traditional view of tort law, and wholly reject the modern view of tort law. We do so for two reasons.

---

[12] [1895] AC 587.

1 *Process*. As has already been observed, *the way* tort cases are decided supports the traditional view of tort law. In a negligence case, the courts ask: did the defendant breach a *duty* of care owed to the claimant? In a case where a claimant is suing a defendant in nuisance because the defendant blocked something from coming onto the claimant's land, the courts ask: did the claimant have a *right* to receive the thing that the defendant obstructed from coming onto the claimant's land? Admittedly, in other tort cases, the courts tend not to inquire into whether the claimant had a right that the defendant not act as he did, or whether the defendant owed the claimant a duty not to act as he did. However, that is because if the defendant did what the claimant is alleging he did ('He hit me'; 'He unjustly slandered me'; 'He lied to me'; 'He sold his goods pretending they were made by me') it will be so obvious that the defendant violated the claimant's rights in acting as he did that the issue is not worth going into. In tort cases where there *is* an issue whether the defendant violated the claimant's rights even if he did what the claimant alleged he did, the courts *always* ask, as a precondition of awarding the claimant a remedy: If the defendant did what he is alleged to have done, did the defendant's actions violate the claimant's rights/did the defendant breach a duty owed to the claimant? Of course, it is *possible* that all this talk of 'rights' and 'duties' in the tort cases is a fiction – a 'device' that the courts employ to achieve some goal that they would rather not tell everyone they are pursuing. But it is not *likely*.

2 *Outcomes*. The traditional view of tort law explains the *outcome* of tort cases far better than the modern view. Take, for example, this imaginary case.[13] Suppose that John is a stockbroker and he secretly hates Paul because he wishes he could go out with Paul's girlfriend, Mary. One day John finds out that Biocorp – a public company – is about to announce that it is insolvent. John sees his chance to do Paul down. He rings Paul up and says, 'Paul – don't tell anyone I've told you this, but I hear on the grapevine that a company called Biocorp is about to announce that it has discovered a vaccine for AIDS. Buy as many Biocorp shares as you possibly can – the price will rocket as soon as this news gets out.' Paul instantly rings Mary up to tell her the good news. As a result, Paul invests £50,000 in Biocorp, and Mary invests £10,000. They both lose all their money when it is announced that Biocorp is insolvent.

---

[13] Zipursky 1998a can claim the credit for being the first to point out the huge hole in the modern view of tort law that the law's treatment of this case creates.

Now – anyone who knows anything about tort law will be able to tell you that Paul will be able to sue John in tort for compensation for the fact that he has lost his £50,000; and that Mary will *not* be able to sue John. This is not a matter of dispute: this is a very easy case.[14] The traditional view of tort law has no problem explaining this result. When John lied to Paul he violated Paul's rights, not Mary's. So Paul is entitled to a remedy in tort in this case – compensation for the loss that he suffered as a result of John's lying to him – but Mary is not. John did not violate Mary's rights in acting as he did, so tort law does nothing for her. On the modern view of tort law, the fact that Mary is not entitled to sue John for damages here is very hard to explain. John is a bad man, and the courts are not normally overly concerned to limit the liabilities of bad men. But here they do – they only allow Paul to sue John, not Mary. Why? At the very least, if the modern view of tort law were correct, one would not expect this to be such an easy case for tort lawyers to resolve. One would expect some voices to be raised in the decided cases in favour of allowing Mary to sue John. But there is nothing – for tort lawyers, nothing could be more obvious than that Mary cannot sue John here. Only the traditional view of tort law explains why it is so obvious to tort lawyers that Mary has no claim in this situation.

So – the traditional view of tort law explains *both* the way tort cases are decided, *and* the outcome of those cases. The modern view of tort law finds it difficult to cope with either task. Only one conclusion can be drawn: the traditional view of tort law is correct; the modern view of tort law must be rejected as heresy. As the great physicist Richard Feynman would tell his students, 'It doesn't matter how beautiful your theory is, it doesn't matter how smart you are. If it doesn't agree with experiment, it's wrong.' In judging whether a particular view of tort law is correct it is irrelevant how popular or unpopular that view is. The truth is not a matter of majority vote. The *only* way to determine whether a given view of tort law is correct is to ask: is it consistent with the reality of what happens in tort cases? The traditional theory of tort law passes this test; the modern view of tort law does not. In the war that now prevails among tort academics over the nature of tort law, we are firmly on the side of those academics who endorse the traditional view of tort law, and have written this textbook on that basis.[15]

---

[14] It is so easy that it is very hard to find a case to demonstrate that Mary cannot sue John here.

[15] Readers who are interested in pursuing this debate are referred to the opening pages of Chapter 3 ('Tort Law and Its Critics'), as well as the Appendix to this book, where we deal with Professor Jane Stapleton's criticisms of the traditional view of tort law. Student readers who are coming to tort law for the first time are advised not to read these passages until they have at least read Chapers 1 and 2 of this book and gained a bit more knowledge of tort law and its terminology.

● The relevance of public policy to tort law

While we unequivocally reject the modern view of tort law, we disagree with those who have taken their dislike of the modern view of tort law to such an extreme that they deny that considerations of public policy should have any role to play in the operation of the tort law system.[16] To explain: those who endorse the modern view of tort law take the view that if A has caused B to suffer some kind of loss, A should be held liable in tort to compensate B for that loss if, all things considered, it would be desirable to make A pay B such compensation. On this view, considerations of what is in the public interest – or, in other words, considerations of public policy – have a crucial role to play in determining whether A should be held liable in tort to compensate B for the loss that she has suffered. If it would be contrary to the public interest to make A liable to compensate B, then it is obvious that A should *not* be held liable in tort to pay such compensation to B. If it would be in the public interest to make A compensate B, then it is equally obvious that A *should* be held liable in tort to compensate B.

So on the modern view of tort law, the courts *must* take into account considerations of public policy in determining whether A should be held liable in tort to compensate B for some loss that he has caused her to suffer. Some academics who are hostile to the modern view of tort law would like to argue that this is *wholly* wrong: considerations of public policy should not be taken into account *at all* by the courts in determining whether A should be held liable in tort to compensate B. Now – we *agree* that the mere fact that it would be in the public interest to make A compensate B is not enough to justify making A liable in tort to compensate B. If B's rights have not been violated in the situation we are considering, then A cannot be held liable *in tort* to compensate B for the loss that she has suffered. However, we cannot accept that considerations of public policy should have no role at all to play in how tort law cases are decided:

1 *Determining whether someone's rights have been violated.* If B wants to argue that A violated her rights in acting in some way, it seems to us that one has to take into account considerations of public policy in determining whether B had a right that A not act in the way he did. For example, suppose that B argues: 'A said something offensive to me and that upset me a great deal. I have an ongoing right that A not do anything that might offend

---

[16] See, in particular, Beever 2007; and, to some extent, Stevens 2007.

me, so A violated my rights in acting as he did.' In determining whether B has such a right against A,[17] it seems to us obvious that one has to take into account the impact on freedom of speech that recognising the existence of such a right would have, and that the adverse effect that recognising a 'right not to be offended' would have on freedom of speech is one of the most obvious reasons why no such right is recognised in English law.

2 *Granting a remedy in a case where a wrong has been committed.* Let's assume that A has violated B's rights and B has suffered some kind of loss as a result. B is allowed to sue A in tort for compensation for the loss that she has suffered. As we will explain in more detail in Chapter 3, it seems to us that the reason why the law allows B to sue A for compensation in this case is because it is in the public interest that wrongs should be remedied. In the words of Lord Bingham, 'the rule of *public policy* that has first claim on the loyalty of the law [is] that wrongs should be remedied.'[18]

3 *Denying a remedy in a case where a wrong has been committed.* Suppose that it is admitted that A violated B's rights in acting as he did. Let's assume, for example, that A hit B for no good reason. In this sort of case, there is a strong presumption that B should have some sort of remedy against A for his conduct. But it seems to us obvious that if it would be contrary to the public interest to allow B to sue A in this case, then no remedy should be granted to B. The Latin sentiment, 'Let justice be done, though the heavens fall'[19] is *not* one that appeals to us. As we will see – most obviously in Chapter 26 ('Limits on the Right to Sue') – English law frequently denies remedies to the victims of wrongs on the ground that it would be contrary to the public interest to allow such a remedy to be granted.

4 *Adding extra remedies onto the basic structure of tort law.* The basic rule that underlies tort law goes as follows: if A violates B's rights and B suffers loss as a result, then B will normally be entitled to sue A for compensation for that loss. However, as we will see, the law adds lots of extra rules to that basic rule, such as:

(i) If A violates B's rights and B dies as a result, and B's dependants suffer a consequent loss of support, B's dependants will normally be allowed to sue A for compensation for that loss of support.

---

[17] See, generally, Duff & Marshall 2006.

[18] *D* v *East Berkshire Community NHS Trust* [2005] 2 AC 373, at [24]–[25] (emphasis added).

[19] '*Fiat justitia, ruatcoelum*' (the statement is usually attributed to Julius Caesar's father-in-law, Lucius Calpurnius Piso Caesoninus).

(ii) If A was acting in the course of his employment by C when he violated B's rights, then B will normally be entitled not only to sue A for compensation for the loss she suffered as a result of A's wrong; she will also be entitled to sue C for such compensation.

(iii) If A violates B's rights in such an outrageous manner that he deserves to be punished for his conduct, then B may be entitled to sue A not just for damages to compensate her for the loss she has suffered as a result of A's wrong, but for extra damages designed to bring A's total liability up to a level sufficient to punish him adequately for what he has done.

As we will see when we look at these rules in more detail, it seems obvious that the law gives effect to all these extra rules because it is in the public interest to do so.

So we would reject the extremist position that considerations of public policy should not be taken into account at all in deciding tort law cases. The courts frequently take such considerations into account, and we see nothing wrong with their doing so.

APPENDIX C

Century Insurance v Northern Ireland Road Transport Board [1942] A.C. 509

[HOUSE OF LORDS.]

CENTURY INSURANCE COMPANY, LIMITED . . . . } APPELLANTS ; H. L. (N. I.)*

AND

NORTHERN IRELAND ROAD TRANS- PORT BOARD . . . . } RESPONDENTS.

1942
Jan. 19, 22,
23;
Mar. 4.

Master and servant—Transference of employment—Agreement by transport undertaking with petroleum company—Delivery of petrol in vehicles of undertaking—Obligation of employees of undertaking to obey orders of company.

Negligence—Scope of employment—Employee delivering petrol from tanker to storage tank—Smoking—Lighted match thrown on floor.

Under a contract with a petroleum company for the carriage and delivery of their petrol in its lorries, a transport undertaking agreed (*a*) to keep the petrol while in transit insured against fire and spillage ; (*b*) to dress its employees engaged in the delivery in such uniforms as the company might direct ; and (*c*) that its employees engaged in the delivery were to accept the orders of the company " regarding such delivery, the payment of accounts " and all matters incidental thereto," provided that this should not be taken as implying that its employees were the employees of the company. While one of the lorries belonging to the undertaking, in respect of which a policy had been issued by an insurance company against liability to third parties arising from damage to property caused by its use by the undertaking, was being used to deliver petrol at a garage in accordance with the agreement, the driver, while transferring petrol from the lorry to an underground tank, struck a match to light a cigarette and threw it on the floor, causing a conflagration and an explosion. Claims in respect of consequent damage having been made against the undertaking, the insurance company contended that they did not fall within the scope of the policy :—

Held, that (1.) the contract did not contemplate any transference of servants as contrasted with transference of service, and the driver at the time of the accident was acting as the servant of the undertaking ; (2.) the careless act of the driver was done in the course of his employment so that the undertaking was responsible for the consequences, and, accordingly, entitled to be indemnified under the policy.

Jefferson v. *Derbyshire Farmers, Ld.* [1921] 2 K. B. 281 followed.

Williams v. *Jones* (1865) 3 H. & C. 602 considered. Judgments of dissenting minority (Blackburn and Mellor JJ.) preferred.

Decision of the Court of Appeal in Northern Ireland [1941] N. I. 77 affirmed.

Present : VISCOUNT SIMON L.C., LORD WRIGHT, LORD ROMER and LORD PORTER.

H. L. (N. I.)

‣ 1942

CENTURY
INSURANCE
Co.
v.
NORTHERN
IRELAND
ROAD
TRANSPORT
BOARD.

APPEAL from the Court of Appeal in Northern Ireland.

The facts were stated by VISCOUNT SIMON L.C. as follows. The respondents were insured by the appellant company under s. II. of a policy of insurance against liability to third parties arising from damage to property caused by the use by them of a petrol tanker belonging to the respondents. On August 2, 1937, this tanker, which was being driven by their employee, one Davison, had taken on board a consignment of three hundred gallons of petrol at the Larne depot of Holmes, Mullin & Dunn, Ld., for delivery into the storage tank of one Catherwood, a garage proprietor, of Belfast. Davison drove the tanker to Belfast, backed it into Catherwood's garage, inserted the nozzle of the delivery hosepipe into the manhole of Catherwood's tank and turned on the stopcock at the side of the tanker. While the petrol was flowing from the tanker into the tank, Davison lighted a cigarette and threw away the lighted match. The match ignited some material on the floor of the garage and a fire was caused forthwith where the nozzle of the delivery hose was discharging into the tank. Catherwood seized a fire extinguisher and started to play it on the fire which appeared at the manhole, at the same time shouting to Davison to turn off the stopcock. Davison did not do so, or attempt to do so, but started up the tanker and drove it out of the garage until the fore wheels had about reached the water channel in the street. Davison then stopped the tanker and jumped to the ground. The fire, although extinguished at the manhole by Catherwood, pursued the trailing hose and the escaping petrol, and Davison had barely reached the ground when a very violent explosion occurred. The explosion destroyed the tanker, the motor car of Catherwood which was parked in the street, and also damaged several houses which were the property of other parties. The claims in respect of the motor and houses were settled for 1001l. 16s. 7d., which was paid by the appellants without prejudice to their ultimate rights, but they contended that they were not liable. One of the grounds on which the appellants resisted the claim of the respondents under the policy was that, in view of the terms of an agreement of October 11, 1934, between the respondents' predecessors, the Irish Road Transport Co., Ld., whose undertaking they acquired on April 30, 1937, and Messrs. Holmes, Mullin & Dunn, Ld., the liability for the damage did not rest on the respondents. By cl. 1 of this agreement the respondents, when requested to do so by Holmes, Mullin & Dunn, Ld.,

were bound to deliver petroleum spirit which Holmes,
Mullin & Dunn, Ld., had for disposal to any destination
within Northern Ireland.   The delivery was to be by
tank lorries at an agreed scale of freights. The lorries
were to be loaded at the installation of Holmes, Mullin &
Dunn, Ld., at Larne, and the respondents were to keep
sufficient tank lorries at Larne to transport all the spirit
which might be given to them for delivery. The respondents
were to keep the spirit, while in transit, insured against fire
and spillage (cl. 5) and were to dress all their employees
engaged in such delivery in such uniforms as Holmes, Mullin
& Dunn, Ld., might direct (cl. 6). The respondents undertook to effect all necessary insurances under the Workmen's
Compensation Acts (cl. 11) and to be accountable to Holmes,
Mullin & Dunn, Ld. for the product entrusted to them
for delivery (cl. 12). The clause of the agreement mainly
relied on by the appellants as establishing that, at the time
of the accident, Davison was the servant, not of the
respondents, but of Holmes, Mullin & Dunn, Ld., was cl. 9,
which provided that all the employees of the respondents
engaged in or about such delivery should accept and obey the
orders of Holmes, Mullin & Dunn, Ld., " regarding such
"delivery, the payments of accounts and all matters incidental
"thereto," and that the respondents should dismiss any
employee "disregarding or failing to obey such orders." There
followed the proviso that nothing contained in the clause
should be taken as implying that such employees were in any
way the employees of Holmes, Mullin & Dunn, Ld. The
dispute whether the appellants were liable under the policy was
referred to the arbitration of Mr. Lowry K.C., who stated his
award in the form of a special case. The relevant questions
formulated in the special case were : (1.) Was Davison at
the time of the accident acting as the servant of the
respondents or of Holmes, Mullin & Dunn, Ld. ? (2.) Was
the admittedly careless act of Davison in lighting a cigarette
and throwing the match on the floor of the garage an act done
in the course of his employment as such servant, for the consequences of which his master was responsible ? The arbitrator,
subject to the special case, answered the first question by
saying that at the time of the accident Davison was acting
as the servant of the respondents and the second question in
the affirmative. Brown J., before whom the special case came,
was of a different opinion as regards the first question, and

H. L. (N. I.) held that Davison was at the relevant moment the servant of

1942 Holmes, Mullin & Dunn, Ld. He agreed with the arbitrator

CENTURY as to the answer to the second question. The Court of

INSURANCE Appeal in Northern Ireland (Andrews L.C.J., Babington and
Co.
v. Murphy L.JJ.) unanimously reversed Brown J. on the first

NORTHERN question and affirmed the answers arrived at by the

IRELAND arbitrator (1). The appellants appealed to the House of
ROAD
TRANSPORT Lords.
BOARD.

Macaskie K.C. and *Patton* for the appellants. The respondents, and, consequently, the appellants, were not liable to
meet the claims for the damage caused by the fire and explosion
since, on the true construction of the contract, and in particular
giving effect to cl. 9, Davison was the servant of Holmes,
Mullin & Dunn, Ld., in respect of the operation then being
performed. Effect must be given to every part of the contract
and it is not permissible to strike out or nullify any clause :
In re Strand Music Hall Co., Ld. (2). Under the contract the
tanker and driver were lent to the company by the respondents
for a consideration. The right to control them in respect of
the relevant operation was vested in the company. Such
control may exist side by side with the general control exercised
in other respects by the general master over his servant, and
in this way there may be a dual control. [They referred to
Quarman v. *Burnett* (3) ; *Sadler* v. *Henlock* (4) ; *Donovan* v.
Laing, Wharton, and Down Construction Syndicate, Ld. (5) ;
Waldock v. *Winfield* (6) ; *M'Cartan* v. *Belfast Harbour Commissioners* (7) ; *Bain* v. *Central Vermont Ry. Co.* (8) ; *G. W.
Leggott & Son* v. *C. H. Normanton & Son* (9).] The appellants
rely in particular on cls. 6, 9 and 11 of the contract. Further,
the careless act of Davison was not an act done in the course of
his employment so as to make his employers liable. He was
negligent at the time of his employment but not in the course
of it : see Salmon on Torts, 9th ed., p. 104. This was merely
a case of smoking negligently ; not one of working negligently.
They relied on *Williams* v. *Jones* (10) and contended that
Jefferson v. *Derbyshire Farmers, Ld.* (11), was distinguishable on
the facts.

(1) [1941] N. I. 77.   (7) [1911] 2 Ir. R. 143.
(2) (1865) 35 Beav. 153.   (8) [1921] 2 A. C. 412.
(3) (1840) 6 M. & W. 499.   (9) (1928) 98 L. J. (K. B.) 145.
(4) (1855) 4 E. & B. 570.   (10) (1865) 3 H. & C. 602.
(5) [1893] 1 Q. B. 629.   (11) [1921] 2 K. B. 281.
(6) [1901] 2 K. B. 596.

Whitaker K.C. (of the English Bar and K.C. of the Irish Bar), *Fox K.C.* and *L. E. Curran* (both of the Irish Bar) for the respondents were not called on to argue.

The House took time for consideration.

1942. Mar. 4. Viscount Simon L.C. My Lords, in this appeal I should be well content to adopt the unanimous judgments delivered in the Court of Appeal in Northern Ireland, which appear to me to provide a conclusive answer to the argument for the appellants.

As to the first question formulated in the special case, no one disputes the proposition that a man may be in the general employment of X. and yet at the relevant moment, as the result of arrangements made between X. and a third party, may be the servant of the third party so as to make the third party and not X. responsible for his negligence, and I agree that the test to be applied is the test formulated by Bowen L.J. in *Donovan* v. *Laing, Wharton, and Down Construction Syndicate, Ld.* (1), namely, "in whose employment the man was at the "time when the acts complained of were done, in this sense, that "by the employer is meant the person who has a right at the "moment to control the doing of the act." If it were true that the effect of the written agreement under which the Board's petrol tanker was to carry and deliver Holmes, Mullin & Dunn, Ld.'s petroleum spirit to its destination was to lend the vehicle and its driver to Holmes, Mullin & Dunn, Ld., it might well be that while making delivery at the garage Davison was not acting as the servant of the respondents but as the servant of Holmes, Mullin & Dunn, Ld. Bowen L.J., in *Moore* v. *Palmer* (2), emphasized that "the great test was "this, whether the servant was transferred, or only the use and "benefit of his work," but, as Andrews C.J. observes (3): the provisions of the agreement point irresistibly to the conclusion that the agreement was one of carriage and delivery to be performed by the predecessors of the respondents with their own servants. It was not a contract for the hiring out of lorries and men, or of lending them to Holmes, Mullin & Dunn, Ld., to enable them to effect delivery. Clause 9 of the agreement does not, in my opinion, run counter to this view. The provision that the transport company's employees

H. L. (N. I.)

1942

Century
Insurance
Co.
v.
Northern
Ireland
Road
Transport
Board.

(1) [1893] 1 Q. B. 629, 633, 634.   (3) [1941] N. I. 77, 84.
(2) (1886) 2 T. L. R. 781, 782.

A. C. 1942.   3   2 N

H. L. (N. I.)
1942
CENTURY
INSURANCE
CO.
v.
NORTHERN
IRELAND
ROAD
TRANSPORT
BOARD.

Viscount Simon
L.C.

shall accept and obey the orders of Holmes, Mullin & Dunn, Ld. regarding delivery means that they shall carry out delivery orders, not that at some moment of the transit and delivery (Mr. Macaskie prefers to fix the moment no later than the time when they take on their load of spirit at Larne) they became servants of Holmes, Mullin & Dunn, Ld. In truth, the position of the respondents under the contract is not that of people who lend vehicles and drivers for the hirers to direct, but of independent contractors who undertake by the use of their own vehicles and by the activities of their own servants to produce the results, i.e., the deliveries, as ordered by Holmes, Mullin & Dunn, Ld. The decision of the Court of Appeal, overruling Brown J. on this matter, cannot be successfully impeached.

On the second question, every judge who has had to consider the matter in Northern Ireland agrees with the learned arbitrator in holding that Davison's careless act which caused the conflagration and explosion was an act done in the course of his employment. Admittedly, he was serving his master when he put the nozzle into the tank and turned on the tap. Admittedly, he would be serving his master when he turned off the tap and withdrew the nozzle from the tank. In the interval, spirit was flowing from the tanker to the tank, and this was the very delivery which the respondents were required under their contract to effect. Davison's duty was to watch over the delivery of the spirit into the tank, to see that it did not overflow, and to turn off the tap when the proper quantity had passed from the tanker. In circumstances like these, "they "also serve who only stand and wait." He was presumably close to the apparatus, and his negligence in starting smoking and in throwing away a lighted match at that moment is plainly negligence in the discharge of the duties on which he was employed by the respondents. This conclusion is reached on principle and on the evidence, and does not depend on finding a decided case which closely resembles the present facts, but the decision of the English Court of Appeal twenty years ago in *Jefferson* v. *Derbyshire Farmers, Ld.* (1), provides a very close parallel. As for the majority decision, nearly sixty years before that, of the Exchequer Chamber in *Williams* v. *Jones* (2) it may be possible to draw distinctions, as the court in *Jefferson's* case (1) sought to do, but this House is free to review the earlier decision, and for my part I prefer the view

(1) [1921] 2 K. B. 281.   (2) 3 H. & C. 602.

H. L. (N. I.)

1942

CENTURY
INSURANCE
CO.
v.
NORTHERN
IRELAND
ROAD
TRANSPORT
BOARD.

expressed in that case by the minority, which consisted of Blackburn and Mellor JJ. The second question must also be answered adversely to the appellants. I move that the appeal be dismissed with costs.

I am authorized by my noble and learned friend Lord Romer, who is not able to be present, to say that he concurs in this opinion.

LORD WRIGHT. My Lords, my noble and learned friend the Lord Chancellor has fully stated the facts. I agree with his reasoning and conclusions, and I may add with the judgments of the Lord Chief Justice and the lords justices. I should be content simply to express my concurrence with the Lord Chief Justice's convincing judgment. I add a few words merely on the two questions of law.

First comes the question in whose employment Davison was. This problem and its decision have produced a good many reported cases in the books. In *M'Cartan* v. *Belfast Harbour Commissioners* (1), this House emphatically stated that it is a question of fact how the maxim respondeat superior is to be applied in any particular case of this character. The problem is to determine who is the " superior " in the particular instance. Lord Dunedin said categorically that the facts of one case can never rule another case and are only useful so far as similarity of facts (for identity, the word so often used, is really a convenient misnomer) are a help and guide to decision, but, all the same, it has been sought to find some general idea, or perhaps mere catchword, which may serve as a clue to solve the problem, and for this purpose the idea or the word " control " has been introduced. Thus Lord Dunedin in *Bain* v. *Central Vermont Ry. Co.* (2), quotes the following language of Bowen L.J. in *Donovan* v. *Laing, Wharton, and Down Construction Syndicate, Ld.* (3) : " We have "only to consider in whose employment the man was at the "time when the acts complained of were done, in this sense, "that by the employer is meant the person who has a right "at the moment to control the doing of the act." If that were a complete statement of what Bowen L.J. said, I should be driven to question whether it was not too vague and indeterminate to afford any useful guidance, but Bowen L.J. did not stop there. Indeed, Lord Dunedin merely gives the

(1) [1911] 2 Ir. R. 143.   (3) [1893] 1 Q. B. 629, 633.
(2) [1921] 2 A. C. 412, 416.

3   2 N 2

H. L. (N. I.)

1942

CENTURY
INSURANCE
CO.
v.
NORTHERN
IRELAND
ROAD
TRANSPORT
BOARD.

Lord Wright.

quotation as the first sentence of what Bowen L.J. said. The Lord Chief Justice in the present case quotes the remainder of the passage, and this indicates that the word " control " needs explanation and gives some notion of what is necessary before one man's servant becomes pro hac vice the servant of another man. It seems to be assumed in all these cases, no doubt rightly, that the man acquiesces in the temporary change of master, though that may have consequences to him in regard to wages, workmen's compensation, common employment and the like. Bowen L.J. completes his statement thus (1) : " There are two ways in which a contractor "may employ his men and his machines. He may contract "to do the work, and, the end being prescribed, the means of "arriving at it may be left to him. Or he may contract in a "different manner, and, not doing the work himself, may place "his servants and plant under the control of another—that "is, he may lend them—and in that case he does not retain "control over the work." It was held on the facts of that case that the latter description applied.

In his judgment in *Moore* v. *Palmer* (2) Bowen L.J. stated a more concise criterion that " The great test was this, whether "the servant was transferred or only the use and benefit of "his work ? " Control is not here taken as the test. There are many transactions and relationships in which a person's servant is controlled by another person in the sense that he is required to obey the latter's directions. Such was the case of *Quarman* v. *Burnett* (3), the authority of which has never been questioned. The defendants there were sued for the negligent driving of a coachman employed by a jobmaster who had contracted with the defendants, who were two ladies, to send horses and a driver for their coach. It is clear that the ladies were intended to direct the times when and the places to and from which they took their drives. That was certainly a measure of control, but what, it was held, was transferred was the use and benefit of the coachman's work. The coachman did not become the servant of the defendants. Instances of this sort are common. In *M'Cartan's* case (4) the use and benefit of the harbour company's crane and its driver were transferred. The driver of necessity had to obey the directions as to lowering and hoisting given by those conducting the operation, but it was held that there was no

(1) [1893] 1 Q. B. 629, 633, 634.   (3) 6 M. & W. 499.
(2) 2 T. L. R. 781, 782.   (4) [1911] 2 Ir. R. 143.

transfer of employment. Another illustration is afforded by *Cameron* v. *Nystrom* (1). The question there was whether stevedores could plead the defence of common employment against a servant of the shipowner whose vessel they were discharging. The plaintiff had been injured by the negligence of one of the shipowner's servants. It was held that there was no common employment because the negligent employee had not become the shipowner's servant. No doubt, he had in many respects to obey the directions of the shipowners. Lord Herschell L.C., however, thus summed up the position (2): "There was no express agreement with regard to the extent "to which the master and mate should have control over "them [sc. the stevedore's servants]. That control is only to "be implied from the circumstances in which they were "employed. The relation of stevedore to shipowner is a well- "known relation, involving no doubt the right of the master of "the vessel to control the order in which the cargo should be "discharged, and various other incidents of the discharge, but "in no way putting the servants of the stevedore so completely "under the control and at the disposition of the master as to "make them the servants of the shipowner, who neither pays "them, nor selects them, nor could discharge them, nor stands "in any other relation to them than this, that they are the "servants of a contractor employed on behalf of the ship to "do a particular work." Lord Herschell there emphasizes that it is the extent of control which is material to be considered, but he also stresses the other elements which make up the relationship of master and servant and which have to be considered before it can be held that there has been a transfer of the man's service from his general employer to the other who is said to be his temporary employer.

It is, I think, clear that the presumption is all against there being such a transfer. Most cases can be explained on the basis of there being an understanding that the man is to obey the directions of the person with whom the employer has a contract, so far as is necessary or convenient for the purpose of carrying out the contract. Where that is the position, the man who receives directions from the other person does not receive them as a servant of that person, but receives them as servant of his employer. Where the contract is a running contract, for the rendering of certain services over a period of time, the places where, and the times at which, the services

H. L. (N. I.)

1942

CENTURY
INSURANCE
Co.
v.
NORTHERN
IRELAND
ROAD
TRANSPORT
BOARD.

Lord Wright.

(1) [1893] A. C. 308.   (2) Ibid. 312.

H. L. (N. I.) are to be performed, being left to the discretion (subject to any
1942 contractual limitations) of the other contracting party, there
CENTURY must be someone who is to receive the directions as to perform-
INSURANCE ance from the other party and they are given to the employer,
CO. whether he receives them personally or by a clerk or by the
v. servant who is actually sent to do the work. That I think is
NORTHERN the position here. The contract is of a character very
IRELAND common between the owner of lorries or other vehicles and
ROAD one who wants to hire them for the conveyance of his goods.
TRANSPORT
BOARD.

Lord Wright. In principle the facts here are indistinguishable from those in
Quarman v. *Burnett* (1). Davison was subject to the control
of Holmes, Mullin & Dunn, Ld., only so far as was necessary
to enable the respondents to carry out their contract. In
doing so he remained the respondents' servant. They paid
him and alone could dismiss him. Even in acting on the
directions of Holmes, Mullin & Dunn, Ld., he was bound to
have regard to paramount directions given by the respondents
and was to safeguard their paramount interests. This appears
from the course of business followed, and is confirmed by the
agreement dated October 11, 1934, made between Holmes,
Mullin & Dunn, Ld., and the respondents' predecessors in
title in whose shoes it is admitted that the respondents stand.
It is a contract which was intended to remain in force and has
remained in force over a period of years, and provided for the
carriage of petrol or like products to any destination within
Northern Ireland at the request of Holmes, Mullin & Dunn,
Ld. Clause 9 provides that the employees of the respondents
or their predecessors engaged in the delivery should accept
the orders of Holmes, Mullin & Dunn, Ld., " regarding such
"delivery, the payment of accounts and all matters incidental
"thereto." These are just the matters in respect of which,
for the convenient performance of the contract, the lorrymen
employed would naturally be required to obey the wishes of
those for whom the petrol was being carried. I do not find
anything in the rest of the agreement to lead to any other
conclusion. It is not, however, necessary to make any nice
examination of its terms. A question of this sort must be
decided on the broad effect of the contract. I do not attach
any decisive effect to the proviso to cl. 9 that nothing in the
agreement is to be construed to mean that the respondents'
employees are to be taken as employees of Holmes, Mullin &
Dunn, Ld., because it could not bind third parties. I think,

(1) 6 M. & W. 499.

on the whole, that the agreement goes to support the view that the parties did not contemplate that what the agreement stipulated should involve any transference of servants, as contrasted with transference of service.

Each case of this character must be decided on its particular facts. I, therefore, do not think it necessary to refer to any other of the cases which have been cited. In the great majority the conclusion has been against the servants being transferred from the general employer. Nor do I consider the cases where a man has been held to have become the servant of someone who was not otherwise his employer by voluntarily doing work for him.

On the other question, namely, whether Davison's negligence was in the course of his employment, all the decisions below have been against the appellants. I agree with them and need add little. The act of a workman in lighting his pipe or cigarette is an act done for his own comfort and convenience and, at least generally speaking, not for his employer's benefit, but that last condition is no longer essential to fix liability on the employer : *Lloyd* v. *Grace, Smith & Co.* (1). Nor is such an act prima facie negligent. It is in itself both innocent and harmless. The negligence is to be found by considering the time when and the circumstances in which the match is struck and thrown down. The duty of the workman to his employer is so to conduct himself in doing his work as not negligently to cause damage either to the employer himself or his property or to third persons or their property, and thus to impose the same liability on the employer as if he had been doing the work himself and committed the negligent act. This may seem too obvious as a matter of common sense to require either argument or authority. I think what plausibility the contrary argument might seem to possess results from treating the act of lighting the cigarette in abstraction from the circumstances as a separate act. This was the line taken by the majority judgment in *Williams* v. *Jones* (2), but Mellor and Blackburn JJ. dissented, rightly as I think. I agree also with the decision of the Court of Appeal in *Jefferson* v. *Derbyshire Farmers, Ld.* (3), which is in substance on the facts indistinguishable from the present case. In my judgment the appeal should be dismissed.

H. L. (N. I.)

1942

CENTURY
INSURANCE
Co.
v.
NORTHERN
IRELAND
ROAD
TRANSPORT
BOARD.

Lord Wright.

(1) [1912] A. C. 716.   (3) [1921] 2 K. B. 281.
(2) 3 H. & C. 602.

H. L. (N. I.)

1942

CENTURY
INSURANCE
Co.
v.
NORTHERN
IRELAND
ROAD
TRANSPORT
BOARD.

LORD PORTER. My Lords, I agree with the speeches just delivered by the noble and learned lords who have preceded me, and would dismiss the appeal.

Appeal dismissed.

Solicitors for appellants : *Berrymans, for George L. Maclaine & Co., Belfast.*

Solicitors for respondents : *Blyth, Dutton, Hartley & Blyth, for J. C. W. Rea & Son, Belfast.*

[HOUSE OF LORDS.]

H. L. (N. I.)* BENSON . . . . APPELLANT ;

1942   AND

Jan. 13, 14 ;
Feb. 9 ;
Mar. 4.
NORTHERN IRELAND ROAD TRANS-
PORT BOARD . . . . } RESPONDENTS.

Criminal law—Appeal—Dismissal of summons—Order for payment of costs by complainants—No appeal—Summary Jurisdiction and Criminal Justice Act (Northern Ireland), 1935 (25 & 26 Geo. 5, c. 13), s. 24, sub-s. 1—Road and Railway Transport Act (Northern Ireland), 1935 (25 & 26 Geo. 5, c. 15), s. 15, sub-s. 1.

By s. 24, sub-s. 1, of the Summary Jurisdiction and Criminal Justices Act (Northern Ireland), 1935, "an appeal shall lie to a "court of quarter sessions against an order of a court of summary "jurisdiction, in cases of a civil nature by either party whether "he is the complainant or defendant, and in other cases by any "party against whom an order is made for payment of any penal "or other sum, or for any term of imprisonment, or for the estreating "of any recognizance to a greater amount than twenty shillings."

A court of summary jurisdiction in Northern Ireland having dismissed a summons under s. 15, sub-s. 1, of the Road and Railway Transport Act (Northern Ireland), 1935, for contravention of which a fine of 100*l.* might be imposed, and ordered the complainants to pay a sum in respect of costs, the complainants appealed to quarter sessions, which dismissed the appeal. On a case stated, the Court of Appeal in Northern Ireland held that an offence had been committed and that the decision of the court of summary jurisdiction should be reversed. On appeal by the defendant to the House of Lords :—

Held, that the order for payment of costs was not " an order

Present : VISCOUNT SIMON L.C., LORD ATKIN, LORD WRIGHT, and LORD PORTER.

APPENDIX D

'Reasons for Studying Law'
– a speech delivered at Dr Challoner's High School, on January 19, 2012

My talk is entitled 'Reasons for Studying Law'. I'm told that most of you have already decided what you are going to study at university, and I'm assuming that most of you haven't opted to do a law degree. But that's okay because the reasons to study law that I am going to focus on apply to all of you, whatever you are going to do at university. In this talk I'm going to look at the personal qualities that people who study law tend to develop, and argue that all of us have reason to want to be someone who has these qualities. The qualities I am going to focus on are: *good judgment, humility,* and *hopefulness.* I'm going to argue that studying law is a good way of acquiring these qualities, but I definitely wouldn't say that it's the only way, or that you can't develop these qualities if you do some other subject at university.

● Judgment

Let's start with good judgment. I want to begin to explain what good judgment involves, by looking at the two most famous lines from William Butler Yeats' prophetic poem, 'The Second Coming', which was written in 1919:

> The best lack all conviction, while the worst
>
> Are full of passionate intensity

Someone who is endowed with good judgment avoids these polar extremes – they are able to chart a middle course between being someone who lacks all conviction, and being someone who is full of passionate intensity. To see why this is, let's look at 'passionate intensity' first.

Someone who is 'full of passionate intensity' lacks good judgment because they have rushed to judgment. They can only see one side of a case, and demonise those who oppose them as 'morons' or 'idiots' or 'mad' because they literally cannot understand what might lead someone to adopt a different position from them. We see this tendency – and people who are 'full of passionate intensity' – very markedly in American politics at the moment, where there is no possibility of any dialogue between people on the right and on the left of American politics because they cannot understand where the people on the other side are coming from. We also see it in the current clashes over the future of the environment where both sides of the argument regularly demonise each other, as liars or scientific illiterates, depending on which side you are on.

Studying law helps you to avoid rushing to judgment in this kind of way. It is a fundamental part of a law student's training to learn to see what can be said on both sides of a question or issue. Law students spend a lot of time looking at problem questions, where it is genuinely uncertain what the law says, and are encouraged to develop the ability to see, and explain, what can be said on both sides of the issue. And it's a standard tactic, in dealing with the student who thinks it's obvious that a particular defendant is liable or is guilty, to say to him or her, 'So – what would you say if you were the defendant's lawyer?' By asking this, we're trying to open the student's mind and get them to see what arguments might be made on the side of the defendant.

Let's now turn to the other extreme identified by Yeats in his poem – that of lacking 'all conviction'. Someone who 'lacks all conviction' lacks good judgment because they refuse to judge at all. They refuse to reach a conclusion as to what is good and what is bad, or what is right and what is wrong. Instead, when someone argues that something is good or that acting in a particular way is wrong, they say things like: 'Well, that's your opinion – and I respect it, but we should also respect people who think differently.' If what I am saying right now sounds familiar, it's because the refusal to judge is very, very common among teenagers, who think of themselves as being 'tolerant' or 'open-minded' because they refuse to judge, and disdain as 'judgmental' people who do take a stand on what's good and bad, right and wrong. And this has been the case with teenagers for a very long time.

For example, Allan Bloom's book *The Closing of the American Mind,* which was published 25 years ago, starts with the observation that 'there is one thing a professor can be certain of: almost every student entering university believes, or says he believes, that truth is relative'. Note that that comes from a book entitled *The Closing of the American Mind,* not *The Opening of the American Mind* – because someone who refuses to judge, who lacks all conviction, closes their mind down to the possibility that some things are true, and that we are better off knowing those things than not knowing those things. They refuse to acknowledge that, even if there are things that can be said on both sides of a question, the question will ultimately have a right answer, and we will do better knowing what the answer to that question is than we will if we leave it open.

Studying law helps you avoid the peril of becoming – or continuing to be – someone who 'lacks all conviction'. While you have to be aware, as a law student, of what can be said on both sides of a particular issue, you also have to decide who has the better case. In this way, law students are no different from judges who – after they have heard arguments from barristers on both sides of a case – have to decide the case. They cannot say, 'I dunno' or 'You both make very good points and I respect all of them.' They have to come down on one side or the other. And in order to determine what is the right side to come down on, you have to develop good judgment – you need to be able to see which side of an argument is better, either by spotting a logical flaw in one side's argument, or by accurately weighing the two sides' arguments against each other and seeing who comes out the stronger.

For example, let's take the debate on whether assisted dying should be legal. It used to be the case that it was a criminal offence to kill yourself. This was very cruel: anyone who tried to kill themselves and failed would have their misery compounded by the prospect that they would be sent to prison for attempted suicide, as an attempt to commit a crime amounts to crime in itself. So s. 1 of the Suicide Act 1961 abolished, and I quote, 'the rule of law that it is a crime to commit suicide'. Now, before 1961, it was also a crime to help someone to commit suicide, as helping someone to commit a crime amounts to a crime in itself. This rule was retained by s. 2 of the Suicide Act 1961, which provides that 'A person who aids, abets, counsels or procures the suicide of another' will commit an offence. It is this provision that is now the focus of public debate.

Trying as best we can to see both sides of the argument, those who would like to see s. 2 changed argue that in a case where someone is in such unendurable pain that they don't want to go on living, there is nothing wrong with helping them to die. And in the case where the person in pain is someone you love, it is very cruel for the law to hold over you the prospect that if you help them to die because you cannot stand to see them suffering any more, you can end up spending up to 14 years in prison.

Those who support the retention of s. 2 make a 'slippery slope' argument that if we retreat from the position that assisting someone to kill themselves is always unlawful, the law on assisted dying will over time become more and more lax and we will end up in a society where people are helped to kill themselves in situations where no one would currently argue that assisted suicide should be lawful – for example, in a case where someone is depressed, and has decided that they don't want to go on living.

In order to see which side of this argument is stronger, we need first to look at the arguments on each side to see if they suffer from any logical flaws.

For example, looking first at the side that wants to reform s. 2, is it ever true that helping someone to die is the only way of stopping them suffering unendurable pain? Are there really some forms of pain that cannot be managed or made tolerable through palliative drugs?

Turning to those who oppose any reform of s. 2, is it true that reform of s. 2 will inevitably cause us to slide down a slippery slope towards helping people to die whenever the thought that they can't go on enters their head? Or can we build safeguards into the law to ensure that that doesn't happen, and be confident that those safeguards will be effective and respected? On the second argument made by those who oppose the legalisation of assisted dying, it might be the case that if s. 2 were reformed, people in unendurable pain wouldn't need to call on those closest to them to help them to die – instead, they would have ready access to professionals who would help them. So the possibility that reforming s. 2 would end up poisoning people's relationships with loved ones who are in unendurable pain may be pretty remote.

I don't take a view on any of these issues – I merely mention them to show the sort of process of thinking that you have to go through in order to exercise good judgment on an issue like assisted suicide, and the sort of thinking process that tends to become second nature for people who have studied law. But let's assume that both sides of the argument on assisted dying survive this process of logical scrutiny. In other words, let's assume that sometimes pain does become unendurable, even with the assistance of drugs. And let's assume that there is a danger that if the law were to allow people to help others to kill themselves, the law would end up being abused or misused, no matter how many safeguards we put in.

Given these assumptions, which side of the argument should we favour? In order to reach a conclusion, we have to weigh up the arguments on both sides and see which side comes out stronger. On the one hand, we have an argument that pain is bad, and we should do what we can to stop people suffering pain. On the other, we have an argument that if we weaken the law on assisted suicide, people will end up dying unnecessarily. What is more important to avoid – people's pain, or unnecessary deaths? Put that way, I think it's obvious what the answer is. Pain is a bad thing, but having someone's life brought unnecessarily to an end is worse. Requiring people to live with unendurable pain is a price worth paying if it is the price we have to pay to ensure that people are not killed unnecessarily. So if relaxing the law on assisted suicide might result in unnecessary deaths, through the law being abused and misused, then the law on assisted suicide should not be relaxed.

A Commission on Assisted Dying, headed by Lord Falconer, the former Lord Chancellor, is optimistic that the law on assisted suicide can be relaxed without any dangers. That Commission – whose report was released a couple of weeks ago – thinks that we can put sufficient safeguards in place to ensure that reforming s. 2 will not result in people being helped to die unnecessarily. They argue that someone should only be helped to die if they have a terminal illness and have less than a year to live, if two independent doctors have agreed on that diagnosis, that the patient wanting help to die is acting completely voluntarily and in full knowledge of the care that would be available to them if they carried on living, and that they are not making the decision under the influence of a mental illness. The Commission thinks that, with these safeguards in place, we can be sure that only people who really need help to die will be allowed to be given that help.

I am not so sure. The next quality I am going to talk about – humility – teaches us that the 'best laid plans of mice and men' often go astray, and we shouldn't be so confident that schemes that seem to work so well on paper will not prove hopelessly counter-productive when we try to make them work in real life.

● Humility

So let's talk about humility. We like to think well of ourselves – to think that we are rational, intelligent people, the sort of people who are capable of making good decisions, using the good judgment that studying things like law helps us develop. But anyone who studies law will be able to tell you that we aren't all we crack ourselves up to be, and we suffer from deep flaws that put us in constant danger of achieving the opposite of what we are trying to achieve.

One of the most important flaws we suffer from is a tendency to rationalise our behaviour so that we identify acting in our self-interest with doing the right thing, even when acting in our self-interest is absolutely the wrong thing to do. For example, every year I earn quite a bit of money from teaching in Hong Kong. The UK government doesn't know I earn this money and so it would be quite easy for me to evade paying tax on it by not declaring it on my tax return. As it happens, I do confess and pay up, but if I did try to evade paying the tax due on my Hong Kong earnings you can bet I wouldn't just think, 'Okay, I'm going to rip off the Inland Revenue this year.' I'd dress up my behaviour so that I made it look to myself like it was the right thing to do. I'd think to myself, 'Why should I pay the government any tax on my Hong Kong earnings? They're only going to waste it. If I just kept the money for myself, I'd do so much more good with it than the government ever could. In fact, now I come to think about it, it's actually my moral duty *not* to pay any tax on my Hong Kong earnings.' And I'd end up doing the wrong thing but I'd do it with a completely clean conscience, thinking that I was doing absolutely the right thing.

So we have a tendency to fool ourselves about what's the right thing to do. This tendency is extremely important and dangerous because it may be the primary reason why people end up doing bad things. The Greek philosopher Socrates is reported by his follower Plato to have said on more than one occasion that 'no one does wrong willingly'. I believe that to be true – on most occasions where people do something bad, they don't recognise that they are doing something bad. They have fooled themselves into thinking that they are doing the right thing. And they have fooled themselves into thinking that because what they're doing happens to be in their self-interest.

Lawyers have for a very long time been aware of this tendency we have to self-deception and have developed specific rules to guard against it. For example, suppose I give you £10,000 to invest for me. As you would expect, the law imposes a duty on you to act carefully in investing my money – so you wouldn't be allowed to bet my money on a horse, or put it on red at a casino. But in order to ensure that you do act carefully in investing my money, the law imposes an additional duty on you – it requires you not to benefit from the way you invest my money. So you can't, for example, invest my money in a company that you own – and this is so even if you think your company is the most wonderful company in the world, and the absolute best thing to do with my money would be to invest it in this wonderful company of yours.

In imposing this additional duty on you not to make a profit for yourself from the way you invest my money, the law turns you into what is called a *fiduciary*. A fiduciary is supposed to act completely selflessly in looking after someone's interests. Now – the reason why the law makes you into a fiduciary is to guard against the human capacity for self-deception. If you were allowed to benefit from the way you invested my money, then it would be all too easy for you to fool yourself into thinking that the best thing for me would be for you to invest my money in a company that you just happen to own. So in order to stop you fooling yourself into thinking that this is a good idea when it may actually be a terrible idea, the law simply says that you can't benefit from the way you decide to invest my money.

The courts thought that it was so important to guard against the possibility that your self-interest might lead you into deceiving yourself into thinking that you were investing my money wisely, when in fact you were taking unjustified risks with it, that in 1874, in a case called *Parker* v *McKenna*, James LJ said that the 'safety of mankind' required that people not be allowed to profit from how they invested other people's money. Until very recently, this may have seemed like a bit of Victorian exaggeration. But in 2008 we discovered that – no, actually, this wasn't an exaggeration at all.

In 2008, we discovered that American banks had been lending people money to buy houses when they shouldn't have been. The purchasers simply weren't creditworthy and when interest rates went up they weren't able to afford to keep up the repayments on their loan. That was a problem. But the problem was compounded thousands of times over when, from 2005 onwards, American banks started issuing credit default swaps on these loans.

The credit default swap worked like this. *In return for a yearly fee* – and that's so important, I'll repeat it: *in return for a yearly fee* – the bank that issued the swap promised the holder of the swap that if a particular house purchase loan was not repaid, the bank would pay the holder of the swap the value of the loan. Now – the holder of the swap did not need to have any connection with the owner of the house, or the bank that lent him the money to buy it. All she had to do was buy the credit default swap and if the owner of the house defaulted on his house purchase loan, she would be paid the value of that loan.

So suppose someone in a low-paying job that he might get fired from at any time was given a $200,000 loan to buy a house. He soon gets fired from his job, and can't afford to repay the loan. So the bank that lent him the money is $200,000 out of pocket, less how much they can recover by selling the house. But what if 100 people have each taken out a credit default swap with Goldman Sachs in relation to that $200,000 loan? Under the terms of the swaps those 100 people will each be entitled to have Goldman Sachs pay them $200,000 – that is, $20 million in all. So instead of one bank being out $200,000 when the loan is not repaid – which is bad enough – the existence of the credit default swaps on the loan mean that the banking system is out $20 million when the loan is not repaid.

And that's basically what happened in 2008. A huge number of house owners in the United States defaulted on the loans that they had been given to help them buy their houses, and the existence of credit default swaps on those loans meant that the total loss to the American banks from those defaults was multiplied thousands of times over. The losses came to $1 trillion, and we are still living in the shadow of the effect of government attempts to staunch those losses with public money in order to stop a general failure of the banking system.

The sale of credit default swaps on loans to house buyers with poor credit histories was one of the most reckless acts in human history. So why did it happen? The reason is that there was money in it for the traders issuing the credit default swaps. Their employers, the banks, got a regularly yearly income from the people who bought the swaps, and – most crucially – some of the money the banks' traders made for their banks by issuing credit default swaps came back to the traders in the form of bonuses and performance-related pay. So the traders issuing credit default swaps made a profit for themselves from issuing the swaps and as a result had every reason to fool themselves into thinking that, actually, issuing these swaps was a really good idea: that they were tapping into new source of income for their banks at very little risk.

Studying law teaches us humility about ourselves in other ways. Attempts to plan or order our society through legislation often misfire as a result of our legislators' all-too-human inability to foresee all the consequences of their actions. For example, at the moment the law says that you are allowed to use reasonable force to defend yourself or others from harm, or to arrest people who have committed – or are reasonably suspected of having committed – a crime. If you use unreasonable force on someone, that will normally amount to a crime, and you can also be liable to be sued for compensation by the person on whom you used unreasonable force.

But the law is very vague on what amounts to 'unreasonable force'. What amounts to reasonable force depends on all the circumstances. In a case where someone else is threatening to harm you, how much force you are allowed to use against them to eliminate that threat will depend on how they are threatening to harm you, how imminent and realistic their threat is, and whether there is anything else you could do to avoid that threat. This is all very vague. As a result, when someone breaks into your house, it's not at all clear whether you would be allowed, for example, to attack them with a baseball bat to drive them off, or incapacitate them. A court could quite easily end up saying that using a baseball bat on an intruder amounted to 'unreasonable force', with the result that you will acquire a criminal record, and be liable to be sued for compensation by the burglar for the injuries sustained by him as a result of your hitting him.

Section 329 of the Criminal Justice Act 2003 was intended to provide some reassurance for householders who had attacked and injured a burglar on their premises. The intention behind s. 329 was that it should operate to prevent the burglar suing the householder for compensation for his injuries unless the householder had used 'grossly disproportionate' force against the burglar. So even if you ended up using unreasonable force against a burglar, you would be safe from being sued by him – so long as your actions weren't 'grossly disproportionate' then s. 329 would prevent him suing you for compensation. Well, that was the intention, anyway.

But s. 329 was expressed in such general terms that it has had a quite different effect from what was intended. This is what s. 329 actually says. It says that (1) if you use force against someone because you honestly think they are committing or have committed a criminal offence, and (2) you honestly think you need to use force against them to protect yourself or your property or to stop them committing a criminal offence, then you can't be sued for compensation unless you used 'grossly disproportionate' force.

So far as anyone knows, this provision has never been used by a householder to stop a burglar suing him for compensation for injuries the burglar suffered as a result of being attacked by the householder. Instead, a quite different section of society has leapt on s. 329 as a defence to being sued for compensation. And that is the police. The police have been very keen on using s. 329 to stop people suing them for compensation when they have used excessive force in arresting a criminal suspect, and have injured him as a result. They use s. 329 to argue that they cannot be sued for compensation unless the force they used was 'grossly disproportionate'.

For example, in the recent case of *Adorian* v *Commissioner of the Police of the Metropolis* (2009), Anthony Adorian got into argument with his daughter, which culminated in her walking out on him and his throwing some of her clothes out of the window of their shared flat. She called the police. The police turned up, Adorian got into an argument with them, and they arrested him for disorderly behaviour. In the course of the arrest, he suffered a hip fracture of the type normally only associated with being hit by a car or falling from a significant height. He sued the police for compensation. The claim was ultimately dismissed on the basis that even if the police had used unreasonable force in arresting Adorian, they had not used 'grossly disproportionate' force and so s. 329 applied.

It's fair to say that the court that decided *Adorian* was appalled to have to reach this conclusion. As Sedley LJ observed in the Court of Appeal:

> 'One cannot fail to notice that this section has nothing on the face of it to do with policing. In what one can call the Tony Martin situation – a sudden encounter with a crime – it gives the individual a defence of honest, even if unreasonable, belief in the need for his or her act; and it forfeits the defence only if the act was grossly disproportionate. There is nothing on the face of the section which manifests an intention to afford the police a novel protection from claims by offenders for objectively unreasonable or unnecessarily violent arrests.

> 'The section nevertheless inexorably covers police officers as well as civilians. Indeed, so far as counsel have been able to tell us, since it was brought into force in January 2004 it is only police defendants who have invoked it. The consequences should not go unnoticed. In place of the principle painstakingly established in the course of two centuries and more, and fundamental to the civil rights enjoyed by the people of this country – that an arrest must be objectively justified and that no more force may be used in effecting it than is reasonably necessary – the section gives immunity from civil suits to constables who make arrests on entirely unreasonable grounds, so long as they are not acting in bad faith, and accords them impunity for using all but grossly disproportionate force in so doing.'

I'm sure that no one who was involved in turning s. 329 into law dreamt that it would have the effect of limiting the public's right to sue the police when the police injure someone, using unreasonable force, but that is what has happened. We could blame the government and their legal advisers for failing to see that this would be the effect of s. 329. But the wiser response is to observe that this sort of thing is inevitable – legislators are not omniscient, any more than the rest of us are, and cannot be expected to anticipate every possible situation in which their legislation might apply.

English law's solution to this problem of lack of omniscience is actually its greatest contribution to the world. Instead of seeking to make law through legislation – laying down general rules that people are expected to abide by – up until the twentieth century, the dominant method for making law in England was what is known as the *common law method*: that is, deciding what the law says on a case-by-case basis. This method of making law allowed the English courts a lot of leeway to experiment with the law.

In a particular case, one judge might suggest that the law said *x*. In later cases, other judges would have a look at this suggestion and ignore it, modify it, apply it, or expand on it. And then other judges in further cases would see what they made of that development, and adjust it accordingly. In this way, the common law – the law as developed in the courts – emerged out of a process of trial and error, where only rules and doctrines that generally satisfied the judges as being reasonable would survive to become part of the established common law. In this way, the problem of lack of omniscience was avoided. If new situations came up that had not been anticipated before, the rules and doctrines of the common law could be adjusted to take account of them, and a new but necessarily temporary understanding of what those rules and doctrines were would come into existence.

As I say, up until the twentieth century, this was *the* way in which law was developed in England. It made it an absolute nightmare to say with any certainty *what* the law said on a particular question – for that, you would have to look at all the previous cases that had some bearing on that question, and make educated guesses as to what the courts would say on that question given those previous decisions. But this method of law-making was the humble tribute that English lawyers paid to their own fallibility and inability to predict the future – they adopted a method of law-making that was flexible enough to make their incapacity irrelevant. And this recognition that law-makers could not completely anticipate the future, and the consequent desire for lots of flexibility in administering the law, had a huge political effect. It may be the most important reason why the UK managed to get through the nineteenth and twentieth centuries without any kind of revolution, unlike virtually every country on the Continent. The preference that English lawyers had for changing the law through a cautious, step-by-step process made English society as a whole resistant to, and suspicious of, revolutionaries who claimed that, with one 'big leap forward', society could be transformed into a utopian ideal.

● Hope

I'll finish with the final quality that studying law helps us to encourage – and that is hopefulness. We have already seen some ways in which studying law gives us reason to be hopeful. Studying law teaches us that it is possible to have good judgment, and that even if our natural human failings might prevent us exercising that judgment wisely, there are ways in which we can get round those failings.

But there are bigger reasons why studying law gives us reasons to be hopeful. The most fundamental reason is that the very existence of law is based on a hopeful idea – that if we work together and help each other, we can all be far better off than we could ever be if we simply did whatever was in our self-interest at any given time.

I'm not sure if any of you have heard of the Prisoner's Dilemma. The basic Prisoner's Dilemma situation is this. You and I have committed a bank robbery. We've been arrested for committing the robbery, but the evidence against us is weak. We are held in separate cells and are not allowed to communicate with each other. If neither of us confesses, we'll walk free – the police won't be able to pin anything on us. To give each of us an incentive to inform on the other, the prosecutor tells each of us that if one of us confesses and the other doesn't, then the one who confessed will only get 5 years in jail; the one who didn't confess will get 15 years. If both of us confess, then we'll both get 10 years in jail.

If each of us does what is in our self-interest, then each of us will confess. I'll think – well, if I confess, the worst that can happen is that I do 10 years in jail, and I might end up only serving 5 years. That's a better option than not confessing, which could result in my serving 15 years in jail. And you'll think the same way. So we will both end up confessing, and we will both get 10 years in jail.

But look at what would have happened if each of us had refused to act on the maxim 'Look after Number One' and had instead acted on the maxim 'Look after your neighbour'. If we had done that, then neither of us would have confessed. Sitting alone in my cell, and thinking about the prosecutor's offer, I would have realised that not confessing would be the best thing I could do for you. If I didn't confess and you did, you'd only do five years in jail. And if we both didn't confess, you wouldn't do any time at all. That would have been a much, much better option for you than if I did confess, and you'd have ended up – depending on whether you did or didn't confess – either serving 10 years or 15 years in jail. And you would have thought the same way as me, and decided that the best thing to do for me would be not to confess. So neither of us would have confessed, and we both would have been free men.

So the Prisoner's Dilemma provides us with an example of a situation where we would both be far better off if we refused to act in our self-interest, and instead acted altruistically, in someone else's interests. Law gets its justification and inspiration from the idea that a society without law is one vast Prisoner's Dilemma situation. If everyone in society just acts in their own self-interest, we will be far worse off than we could be if, on occasion, we didn't act in our self-interest but did what was best for someone else. The job of the law-maker is to determine what those occasions are, and to make sure that on those occasions we don't act in our self-interest but instead look out for other people's interests.

The existence of a society that exists under the rule of law, a society where even the law-makers agree to be subject to the rules that they have laid down for others to follow, tells us two very hopeful things. First, that people are capable of wising up and realising that just selfishly pursuing their own interests is a mutually destructive strategy resulting in a society where life is, in the words of the philosopher Thomas Hobbes, 'nasty, brutish and short'. Second, that people are capable of coming together and working together to construct a better society than they could ever dream of living in if they all blindly pursued their immediate self-interest.

It may be – thanks in part to the economic events I've mentioned in this talk – that we are heading, as a society, for some very difficult and hard times. If that is to be the case, we will desperately need the qualities that studying law helps you to develop: the good judgment to know what is the right thing to do; the humility to understand our limitations as human beings and to seek ways of working around them instead of denying them; and finally, and most importantly, the hope that better times will come again if we work together and look out for each other and don't always selfishly seek just to look after ourselves.

END NOTES

● Letter 1 What Is Law?

Law as a conversation. This section is heavily influenced by Scott Shapiro's 'planning theory of law' as set out in his book *Legality* (Harvard University Press, 2010), according to which law can be seen as a plan for achieving social goals. If in the text I have avoided the language of 'plans', that's because we tend to see plans as final, whereas law is much more open-ended and ever-changing. The idea of law as a conversation is intended to convey that idea. Socrates' mysterious definition in the pseudo-Platonic dialogue *Minos* that 'Law wishes to be the discovery of what is' (315a) actually fits very well with the idea of law being advanced here. If we see law as a conversation targeted at determining what sort of society we should live in, then law is animated by a desire to discover something objective – what sort of society we *should* live in. The dialogue *Minos* is notable for its rejection of the positivist identification of law with a set of laid-down or socially accepted rules. I referred to the dialogue as pseudo-Platonic as most Plato scholars think that the dialogue is not good enough to have come from Plato. However, Leo Strauss argues that it is by Plato, and was intended as a preface to Plato's *Laws*: Strauss, 'On the *Minos*' in T. Pangle (ed.), *Roots of Political Philosophy* (Cornell University Press, 1987). For some recent discussions of *Minos,* see V. Bradley Lewis, 'Plato's *Minos*: the political and philosophical context of the problem of natural right' (2006) 60 *Review of Metaphysics* 17 and T. Lindberg, 'The oldest law: rediscovering the *Minos*' (2007) 138 *Telos* 43.

The fact that a previous generation of law-makers may have taken a particular position on what sort of society we should live in does not mean that future generations cannot take a different position, thereby bringing about a change in the law. This process of change is well described in Lord Devlin's book

The Judge (Oxford University Press, 1979), 1 (also Devlin, 'The judge as law-maker' (1976) 39 *Modern Law Review* 1, 1):

> . . . law is the gatekeeper of the status quo. There is always a host of new ideas galloping around the outskirts of a society's thought. All of them seek admission but each must first win its spurs; the law at first resists, but will submit to a conqueror and become his servant. In a changing society (and free societies that are composed of two or more generations are always changing because it is their nature to do so) the law acts as a valve. New policies must gather strength before they can force an entry; when they are admitted and absorbed into the consensus, the legal system should expand to hold them, as also it should contract to squeeze out old policies which have lost the consensus they once obtained.

You and I and a whole bunch of other people . . . I've borrowed here from the first line of G.A. Cohen's *Why Not Socialism?* (Princeton University Press, 2009), 3: 'You and I and a whole bunch of other people go on a camping trip.'

Entick v *Carrington*. The quoted section is taken from the version of Camden LCJ's judgment that appears in 19 Howell's State Trials 1029 (1765). The actual law report of Camden LCJ's judgment (at (1765) 2 Wils KB 275, 95 ER 807) is somewhat different:

> our law holds the property of every man so sacred, that no man can set his foot upon his neighbour's close without his leave; if he does he is a tres-passer, though he does no damage at all; if he will tread upon his neighbour's ground, he must justify it by law . . . we can safely say there is no law in this country to justify the defendants in what they have done; if there was, it would destroy all the comforts of society; for papers are often the dearest property a man can have.

The version of the judgment that appeared in Howell's State Trials was claimed by the editor of Howell's to be based on Camden's own notes of the judgment; as opposed to the version of the judgment in the Law Report, which was writ-ten down by a Law Reporter called Serjeant Wilson while the judgment was being delivered.

Parliament listened to the House of Lords' views. The mechanisms that now exist for fostering dialogue between legislators and judges over what sort of society we should live in are well treated in Po Jen Yap's 'Defending dialogue' [2012] *Public Law* 527 – another piece of legal writing that has had a big influ-ence on my thinking in writing this chapter.

There were plenty of alternative visions. The classic work on the most popular of these alternative visions (those of Plato and Marx) is still Karl Popper, *The Open Society and Its Enemies* (Routledge Classics, 2011). Also F.A. Hayek, *The Road to Serfdom* (Routledge Classics, 2001).

And it may be that things will be very different in future. Francis Fukuyama's thesis in *The End of History and the Last Man* (Penguin, 1993) is that – barring a disaster – things won't be so very different in the future as the sort of society we currently live in is the sort of society we should live in because no other form of society could be conceivably better. The financial crisis that began in 2008 might have prompted us to re-think the basic structure of our society but as John Lanchester points out in his excellent article, 'Marx at 193', *London Review of Books,* April 2012, 'all we've seen are suggestions for ameliorative tweaking of the existing system to make it a little less risky'. If Fukuyama is right, then the future of law-making in our society will simply involve refining and defining the details of a basic structure that is effectively unalterable.

● Letter 2 Four Reasons for Studying Law

Lord Hailsham. See *R* v *Howe* [1987] AC 417, 432.

Rhetoric. For a very good book on this relatively neglected subject, see Sam Leith, *You Talkin' To Me? Rhetoric from Aristotle to Obama* (Profile Books, 2011).

Lon Fuller and Rex. See L. Fuller, *The Morality of Law* (Yale University Press, 1964), 33–36.

Both Pound's "Portrait [d'une Femme]" and Eliot's ["Portrait of a Lady"] . . . M. McLuhan, 'Pound, Eliot and the rhetoric of *The Waste Land*' (1979) 10 *New Literary History* 557. For other examples, see the website for *Philosophy and Literature*'s Bad Writing Contest, which ran for four years from 1995 to 1998: http://denisdutton.com/bad_writing.htm

A search warrant has to be specifically justified . . . J.A. Weir, 'Police power to seize suspicious goods' (1968) 26 *CLJ* 193.

Can it be said on occasion . . . Hackney, 'The politics of the Chancery' [1981] *Current Legal Problems* 113.

Blaise Pascal. See his *Lettres Provinciales* (1657), no. 16.

The Gettysburg Address. Delivered by President Abraham Lincoln on November 19, 1863 at the dedication of the Soldiers' National Cemetery at Gettysburg, where four and a half months before the soldiers of the Union Army scored a decisive but bloody victory (roughly 50,000 Americans were killed in three days of fighting) over the rebel Confederate forces. This is regarded as the definitive text of Lincoln's address:

> Four score and seven years ago our fathers brought forth on this continent, a new nation, conceived in Liberty, and dedicated to the proposition that all men are created equal.

> Now we are engaged in a great civil war, testing whether that nation, or any nation so conceived and so dedicated, can long endure. We are met on a great battle-field of that war. We have come to dedicate a portion of that field, as a final resting place for those who here gave their lives that that nation might live. It is altogether fitting and proper that we should do this.

> But, in a larger sense, we can not dedicate – we can not consecrate – we can not hallow – this ground. The brave men, living and dead, who struggled here, have consecrated it, far above our poor power to add or detract. The world will little note, nor long remember what we say here, but it can never forget what they did here. It is for us the living, rather, to be dedicated here to the unfinished work which they who fought here have thus far so nobly advanced. It is rather for us to be here dedicated to the great task remaining before us – that from these honored dead we take increased devotion to that cause for which they gave the last full measure of devotion – that we here highly resolve that these dead shall not have died in vain – that this nation, under God, shall have a new birth of freedom – and that government of the people, by the people, for the people, shall not perish from the earth.

Dr Martin Luther King Jr. 'The arc of the moral universe is long but bends towards justice' features in his 1967 speeches 'Why I am opposed to the war in Vietnam' (delivered at Ebenezer Baptist Church in Atlanta, Georgia on April 30, 1967) and 'Where do we go from here?' (to the Southern Christian Leadership Conference on August 16, 1967). The phrase comes from Theodore Parker's sermon 'Of justice and conscience', published in his *Ten Sermons of Religion* (1810).

Lord Mansfield. The concept of the common law working itself pure comes from the case of *Omychund* v *Barker* (1744) 1 Atk 21, 26 ER 15. Before becoming Lord Mansfield, Sir William Murray was Solicitor-General and argued in *Omychund* that evidence given by Indian witnesses in an Indian court should be admissible even though the testimony was not preceded by the witnesses swearing an oath on the Bible. The relevant portion of his argument went as follows:

> Here is a . . . court erected in *Calcutta,* by the authority of the crown of *England,* where *Indians* are sworn according to the most solemn part of their own religion. All occasions do not arise at once; now a particular species of *Indians* appears; hereafter another species of *Indians* may arise; a statute very seldom can take in all cases, therefore the common law, *that works itself pure* by rules drawn from the fountain of justice, is for this reason superior to an act of parliament.

(All emphases in the original.) 'Superior' here meant superior in the sense of being better able to adapt to changing circumstances.

More organic and incremental approaches to changing society. For such an approach to questions of justice see Amartya Sen's *The Idea of Justice* (Penguin, 2010), eschewing attempts to produce abstract definitions of what a just society would look like, and instead focusing on whether a particular change in society would make society more just than it was before. The classic work on this approach to ordering society is Edmund Burke's *Reflections on the Revolution in France* (1790). See, for example, his statement:

> The science of constructing a commonwealth, or renovating it, or reforming it, is, like every other experimental science, not to be taught *a priori* . . . it is with infinite caution that any man ought to venture upon pulling down an edifice which has answered in any tolerable degree for ages the common purposes of society, or on building it up again, without having models and patterns of approved utility before his eyes.

(Page 152 in the Penguin Classics edition (1986), edited by Conor Cruise O'Brien).

Thomas Hobbes. In Hobbes' *Leviathan,* Hobbes describes the natural state of mankind (i.e. the state of mankind in a world without legal systems) as involving a 'warre of every man against every man'. In such a state, he explains:

> there is no place for Industry; because the fruit thereof is uncertain; and consequently no Culture of the Earth; no Navigation, nor use of the commodities that may be imported by Sea; no commodious Building; no Instruments of moving, and removing such things as require much force; no Knowledge of the face of the Earth; no account of Time; no Arts; no Letters; no Society; and which is worst of all, continuall feare, and danger of violent death; And the life of man, solitary, poore, nasty, brutish, and short.

A serving police officer. See the *Independent,* 25 January 2013 ('Blowing the whistle: the inside story of how targets make policing worse').

Roberto Mangabeira Unger. See *The Critical Legal Studies Movement* (Harvard University Press, 1983), 119. His quote was originally about legal academics.

● Letter 3 Why Not Just Do a Conversion Course?

Lord Sumption. See *Counsel,* July 2012, 16.

UK's long industrial decline. See Corelli Barnett's *Pride and Fall* sequence of books: *The Collapse of British Power* (1972), *The Audit of War* (1986), *The Lost Victory* (1995), and *The Verdict of Peace* (2001).

● Letter 4 But Is Law the Right Subject for Me?

Blaise Pascal. See his *Pensées* (trans. A.J. Krailsheimer), no. 136.

Marshmallow experiment. See, generally, http://en.wikipedia.org/wiki/Marshmallow_experiment

Making lists. On the importance of making checklists, see Atul Gawande, *The Checklist Manifesto: How To Get Things Right* (Profile Books, 2011).

Isaiah Berlin. See his *The Hedgehog and The Fox: An Essay on Tolstoy's View of History* (1953).

Recent research in the field of hedonic psychology. For applications of this research to law, see: J. Bronsteen, C.J. Buccafusco and J.S. Masur, 'Retribution and the experience of punishment'; and C. Essert, 'Tort law and happiness'. Both articles are available on the Social Sciences Research Network website: www.ssrn.com.

Writers whose crystal clear prose should encourage you to think clearly and logically yourself. Peter Birks: *Unjust Enrichment,* 2nd edn (Oxford University Press, 2005). H.L.A. Hart: *The Concept of Law,* 3rd edn (Oxford University Press, 2012). Philip K. Howard: *The Collapse of the Common Good: How America's Lawsuit Culture Undermines Our Freedom* (Fawcett Books, 2002); *Life Without Lawyers: Liberating Americans from Too Much Law* (W.W. Norton, 2009); *The Death of Common Sense: How Law is Suffocating America* (Random House, 2011). Tony Weir: *An Introduction to Tort Law,* 2nd edn (Oxford University Press, 2006). Daniel Kahneman: *Thinking,*

Fast and Slow (Penguin, 2012). Peter Kreeft: *Making Choices: Practical Wisdom for Everyday Moral Decisions* (Servant Books, 1990); *Philosophy 101 by Socrates: An Introduction to Philosophy* (Ignatius Press, 2002). C.S. Lewis: *Mere Christianity* (1952); *The Abolition of Man* (1943). Peter Singer: *Practical Ethics*, 3rd edn (Cambridge University Press, 2011). David Stove: *What's Wrong with Benevolence: Happiness, Private Property and the Limits of Enlightenment* (Encounter Books, 2011); *Against the Idols of the Age* (Transaction Publishers, 2011). Nick Cohen: *You Can't Read this Book: Censorship in an Age of Freedom* (Fourth Estate, 2012). Theodore Dalrymple: *Not With a Bang but a Whimper: The Politics and Culture of Decline* (Ivan R. Dee, 2010); *In Praise of Prejudice: The Necessity of Preconceived Ideas* (Encounter Books, 2007). Nick Davies: *Flat Earth News* (Vintage, 2009). Ben Goldacre: *Bad Science* (Harper Perennial, 2009); *Bad Pharma* (Fourth Estate, 2012). Clive James: *Cultural Amnesia* (Picador, 2012). Bernard Levin: *Enthusiasms* (Coronet Books, 1986).

● Letter 5 Arguing Effectively (1): Logical Arguments

In writing this chapter, I was heavily influenced by Peter Kreeft's excellent *Socratic Logic* (St Augustine's Press, 2004).

● Letter 6 Arguing Effectively (2): Speculative Arguments

Occam's Razor. Named after William of Ockham, who was a friar who lived in England in the fourteenth century and was interested in logic.

Peter Birks. See his *Unjust Enrichment* (Clarendon Law Series: 1st edn, 2003; 2nd edn 2005).

● Letter 10 Some Traps to Avoid

Allan Bloom. See his *The Closing of the American Mind* (Simon & Schuster, 1987), 25.

We know the statement 'all truth is relative' cannot be absolutely true. Similarly, if a Cretan told you 'All Cretans lie, all the time', you would automatically know that that could not be true. If his statement were true, then he would be telling the truth, in which case it wouldn't be true to say that all Cretans lie all the time.

Roger Scruton. See his *Modern Philosophy* (Pimlico, 2004), 6. For a slightly different attack on the idea that 'all truth is relative' – and the desire to be open-minded – see G. K. Chesterton, *Heretics* (1905), Chapter 20:

> The human brain is a machine for coming to conclusions; if it cannot come to conclusions it is rusty. When we hear of a man too clever to believe, we are hearing of something having almost the character of a contradiction in terms. It is like hearing of a nail that was too good to hold down a carpet; or a bolt that was too strong to keep a door shut . . . Man can be defined as an animal that makes dogmas. As he piles doctrine on doctrine and conclusion on conclusion in the formation of some tremendous scheme of philosophy and religion, he is . . . becoming more and more human. When he drops one doctrine after another in a refined scepticism, when he declines to tie himself to a system, when he says that he has outgrown definitions, when he says that he disbelieves in finality, when, in his own imagination, he sits as God, holding no form of creed but contemplating all, then he is by that very process sinking slowly backwards into the vagueness of the vagrant animals and the unconsciousness of the grass. Trees have no dogmas. Turnips are singularly broad-minded.

The Brothers Karamazov. Translation © Richard Pevear and Larissa Volokhonsky 1990.

Ronald Dworkin. See R. Dworkin, 'Rights as trumps' in Jeremy Waldron (ed), *Theories of Rights* (Oxford University Press, 1984).

● Letter 11 Some Advice Before You Start Your Studies

Robert Nozick. Philosophical Explanations (Oxford University Press, 1981), 4–5.

● Letter 12 The Challenges Ahead

Donald Rumsfeld. Press conference, February 12, 2002.

Peter Birks. See his *An Introduction to the Law of Restitution* (Oxford University Press 1989), p. 22.

● Letter 13 A Mini-Dictionary of English Law

Condemnation of Terrorism (United Nations Measures) Order 2006. See *Her Majesty's Treasury* v *Ahmed* [2010] UKSC 5, [2010] 2 AC 534.

Legislation. See further John Gardner, 'Some types of law' in Douglas Edlin (ed.), *Common Law Theory* (Cambridge University Press, 2008).

A provision in an Act of Parliament will not be given effect to by the courts if it is inconsistent with European Union law. See *Macarthys Ltd* v *Smith* [1979] 3 All ER 325, 329; *R* v *Secretary of State for Transport, ex p Factortame Ltd* [1990] 2 AC 85; and *Thoburn* v *Sunderland City Council* [2003] QB 151.

Parliament is free – within as yet unspecified limits – to pass legislation that will have the effect of changing the definition of what counts as an Act of Parliament. See *Regina (Jackson)* v *Attorney General* [2006] 1 AC 262.

Rule of law. For the first view of the rule of law, see Lon Fuller, *The Morality of Law* (New Haven, 1969), Chapter 2; also Joseph Raz, 'The rule of law and its virtue' (1977) 93 *Law Quarterly Review* 195 (reprinted in Raz, *The Authority of Law* (Clarendon Press, 1979), Chapter 11). For the second and third views of the rule of law see Friedrich Hayek, *The Constitution of Liberty* (Chicago, 1960).

Montesquieu. See his *The Spirit of the Laws,* Book XI, Chapter 6 ('On the constitution of England'):

> When the legislative and executive powers are united in the same person, or in the same body of magistrates, there can be no liberty; because apprehensions may arise, lest the same monarch or senate should enact tyrannical laws, to execute them in a tyrannical manner.
>
> Again, there is no liberty, if the judiciary power be not separated from the legislative and the executive. Were it joined with the legislative, the life and liberty of the subject would be exposed to arbitrary control; for the judge would then be the legislator. Were it joined with the executive power, the judge might behave with violence and oppression.
>
> There would be an end of everything, were the same man or the same body, whether of the nobles or of the people, to exercise those three powers, that of enacting laws, that of executing the public resolutions, and of trying the causes of individuals.

● Letter 16 Reading Cases

Arthur Schopenhauer. See his *Counsels and Maxims* (1851), Volume 2, §296a: 'Buying books would be a good thing if one could also buy the time to read them in: but as a rule the purchase of books is mistaken for the appropriation of their contents.'

● Letter 17 A Brief History of Law Reporting

Stilk v *Myrick*. See P. Luther, 'Campbell, Espinasse and the sailors: text and context in the common law' (1999) 19 *Legal Studies* 526.

● Letter 19 Reading Articles

Advice to Peter Birks. See his *Unjust Enrichment,* 2nd edn (Oxford University Press, 2005), xi.

● Letter 24 Writing Essays

Interfoto case. See *Interfoto Picture Library* v *Stiletto Visual Programmes* [1989] QB 433, CA.

Bruce McFarlane. Letter to Michael Wheeler-Booth, 18 September 1956. See G. Harriss (ed), *Bruce McFarlane's Letters to Friends 1940–1966* (Magdalen College, Oxford, 1997).

● Letter 27 Discussing Problem Questions

IRAC method. A particularly good exposition of the IRAC method of answering legal problem questions can be found in B. Friedman and J.C.P. Goldberg, *Open Book: Succeeding on Exams from the First Day of Law School* (Wolters Kluwer, 2011).

● Letter 30 Last Advice Before the Exams

Thomas Dixon. See his *How To Get A First* (Routledge, 2004), 145–146.

INDEX